WORLD INEQUALITY REPORT **2018**

DATE DUE

WORLD INEQUALITY REPORT **2018**

Facundo Alvaredo
Lucas Chancel
Thomas Piketty
Emmanuel Saez
Gabriel Zucman

THE BELKNAP PRESS OF HARVARD UNIVERSITY PRESS

Cambridge, Massachusetts

London, England

2018

Library of Congress Cataloging-in-Publication Data

Names: Alvaredo, Facundo, editor. | Chancel, Lucas, editor. | Piketty,
    Thomas, 1971- editor. | Saez, Emmanuel, editor. | Zucman, Gabriel, editor.
Title: World inequality report 2018 / edited by Facundo Alvaredo, Lucas
    Chancel, Thomas Piketty, Emmanuel Saez, and Gabriel Zucman.
Description: Cambridge, Massachusetts : The Belknap Press of Harvard
    University Press, 2018. | Includes bibliographical references and index.
Identifiers: LCCN 2018005084 | ISBN 9780674984554 (alk. paper)
Subjects: LCSH: Income distribution--Cross-cultural studies. |
    Equality—Economic aspects—Cross-cultural studies. | Economic
    history—21st century.
Classification: LCC HC79.I5 .W685 2018 | DDC 339.209/0512--dc23 LC record available at https://lccn.loc
    .gov/2018005084

In memory of

Tony Atkinson (1944–2017)

Codirector of the World Top Incomes Database (2011–2015)
and of WID.world (2015–2017)

CONTENTS

ACKNOWLEDGMENTS

Written and coordinated by:
Facundo Alvaredo
Lucas Chancel
Thomas Piketty
Emmanuel Saez
Gabriel Zucman

General coordinator:
Lucas Chancel

Report research team:
Thomas Blanchet
Richard Clarke
Leo Czajka
Luis Estévez-Bauluz
Amory Gethin
Wouter Leenders

This report emphasizes recent research articles written by:
Facundo Alvaredo
Lydia Assouad
Anthony B. Atkinson
Charlotte Bartels
Thomas Blanchet
Lucas Chancel
Luis Estévez-Bauluz
Juliette Fournier
Bertrand Garbinti
Jonathan Goupille-Lebret
Clara Martinez-Toledano
Salvatore Morelli
Marc Morgan
Delphine Nougayrède
Filip Novokmet
Thomas Piketty
Emmanuel Saez
Li Yang
Gabriel Zucman

WID.world fellows:
The report ultimately relies on the data collection, production and harmonization work carried out by more than a hundred WID.world fellows located over five continents and contributing to the World Wealth and Income Database (visit www.wid.world/team for more information). Analyses presented in the report reflect the views of the report's editors and not necessarily those of WID.world fellows.

WORLD INEQUALITY REPORT **2018**

Highlights for 2018

I. What is the aim of the *World Inequality Report 2018*?

The *World Inequality Report 2018* relies on a cutting-edge methodology to measure income and wealth inequality in a systematic and transparent manner. By developing this report, the World Inequality Lab seeks to fill a democratic gap and to equip various actors of society with the necessary facts to engage in informed public debates on inequality.

- The objective of the *World Inequality Report 2018* is to contribute to a more informed global democratic debate on economic inequality by bringing the latest and most complete data to the public discussion.
- Economic inequality is widespread and to some extent inevitable. It is our belief, however, that if rising inequality is not properly monitored and addressed, it can lead to various sorts of political, economic, and social catastrophes.
- Our objective is not to bring everyone into agreement regarding inequality; this will never happen, for the simple reason that no single scientific truth exists about the ideal level of inequality, let alone the most socially desirable mix of policies and institutions to achieve this level. Ultimately, it is up to public deliberation and political institutions and their processes to make these difficult decisions. But this deliberative process requires more rigorous and transparent information on income and wealth.
- To equip citizens to make such decisions, we also seek to relate macroeconomic phenomenon—such as nationalization and privatization policies, capital accumulation, and the evolution of public debt—to microeconomic trends in inequality focused on individuals' earnings and government transfers, personal wealth, and debt.

- Reconciling macro and microeconomic inequality data is not a straightforward exercise given that many countries do not publicly release, or may not even produce, detailed and consistent income and wealth inequality statistics. Standard measures of inequality often rely on household surveys, which routinely underestimate the income and wealth of individuals at the top of the social ladder.
- To overcome current limitations, we rely on a groundbreaking methodology which combines in a systematic and transparent manner all data sources at our disposal: national income and wealth accounts (including, when possible, offshore wealth estimates); household income and wealth surveys; fiscal data coming from taxes on income; inheritance and wealth data (when they exist); and wealth rankings.
- The series presented in this report rely on the collective efforts of more than a hundred researchers, covering all continents, who contribute to the WID.world database. All the data are available online on wir2018.wid.world and are fully reproducible, allowing anyone to perform their own analysis and make up their own mind about inequality.

II. What are our new findings on global income inequality?

We show that income inequality has increased in nearly all world regions in recent decades, but at different speeds. The fact that inequality levels are so different among countries, even when countries share similar levels of development, highlights the important roles that national policies and institutions play in shaping inequality.

Income inequality varies greatly across world regions. It is lowest in Europe and highest in the Middle East.
- Inequality within world regions varies greatly. In 2016, the share of total national income accounted for by just that nation's top 10% earners (top 10% income share) was 37% in Europe, 41% in China, 46% in Russia, 47% in US-Canada, and around 55% in sub-Saharan Africa, Brazil, and India. In the Middle East, the world's most unequal region according to our estimates, the top 10% capture 61% of national income (Figure H.1).

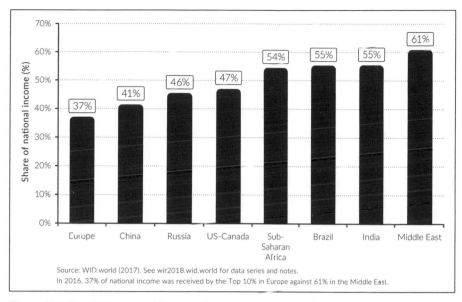

Source: WID.world (2017). See wir2018.wid.world for data series and notes.
In 2016, 37% of national income was received by the Top 10% in Europe against 61% in the Middle East.

Figure H.1 Top 10% national income share across the world, 2016

In recent decades, income inequality has increased in nearly all countries,
but at different speeds, suggesting that institutions and policies matter in
shaping inequality.

- Since 1980, income inequality has increased rapidly in North America, China, India, and Russia. Inequality has grown moderately in
  Europe (Figure H.2a). From a broad historical perspective, this
  increase in inequality marks the end of a postwar egalitarian regime
  which took different forms in these regions.

- There are exceptions to the general pattern. In the Middle East,
  sub-Saharan Africa, and Brazil, income inequality has remained
  relatively stable, at extremely high levels (Figure H.2b). Having
  never gone through the postwar egalitarian regime, these regions
  set the world "inequality frontier."

- The diversity of trends observed across countries since 1980 shows
  that income inequality dynamics are shaped by a variety of national,
  institutional, and political contexts.

- This is illustrated by the different trajectories followed by the former
  communist or highly regulated countries, China, India, and Russia
  (Figure H.2a and b). The rise in inequality was particularly abrupt
  in Russia, moderate in China, and relatively gradual in India, reflecting different types of deregulation and opening-up policies pursued
  over the past decades in these countries.

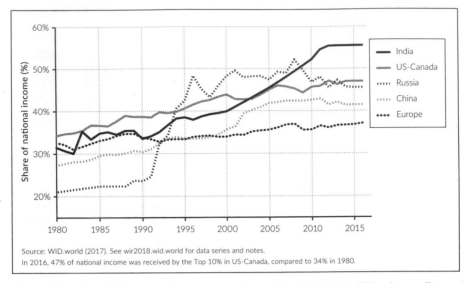

Source: WID.world (2017). See wir2018.wid.world for data series and notes.
In 2016, 47% of national income was received by the Top 10% in US-Canada, compared to 34% in 1980.

Figure H.2a Top 10% income shares across the world, 1980–2016: Rising inequality almost everywhere, but at different speeds

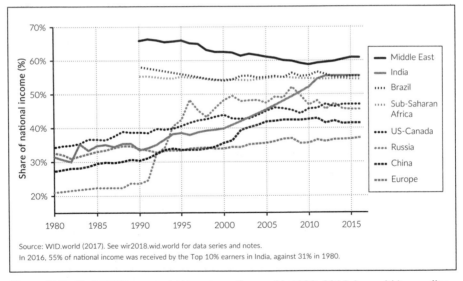

Source: WID.world (2017). See wir2018.wid.world for data series and notes.
In 2016, 55% of national income was received by the Top 10% earners in India, against 31% in 1980.

Figure H.2b Top 10% income shares across the world, 1980–2016: Is world inequality moving towards the high-inequality frontier?

- The divergence in inequality levels has been particularly extreme between Western Europe and the United States, which had similar levels of inequality in 1980 but today are in radically different situations. While the top 1% income share was close to 10% in both regions in 1980, it rose only slightly to 12% in 2016 in Western Europe while it shot up to 20% in the United States. Meanwhile, in the United States,

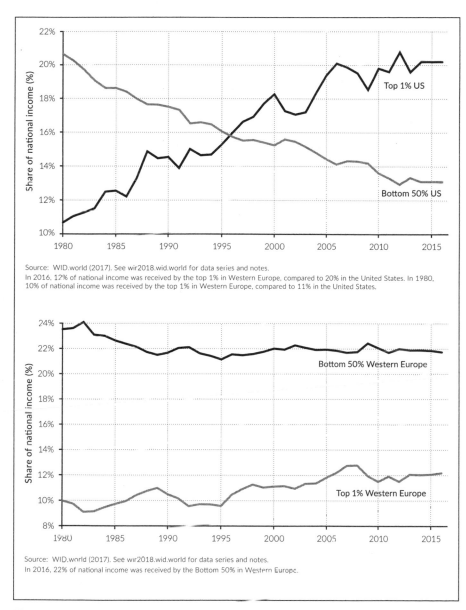

Source: WID.world (2017). See wir2018.wid.world for data series and notes.
In 2016, 12% of national income was received by the top 1% in Western Europe, compared to 20% in the United States. In 1980, 10% of national income was received by the top 1% in Western Europe, compared to 11% in the United States.

Source: WID.world (2017). See wir2018.wid.world for data series and notes.
In 2016, 22% of national income was received by the Bottom 50% in Western Europe.

Figure H.3 Top 1% vs. Bottom 50% national income shares in the US and Western Europe, 1980–2016: Diverging income inequality trajectories

the bottom 50% income share decreased from more than 20% in 1980 to 13% in 2016 (Figure H.3).

- The income-inequality trajectory observed in the United States is largely due to massive educational inequalities, combined with a tax system that grew less progressive despite a surge in top labor compensation since the 1980s, and in top capital incomes in the

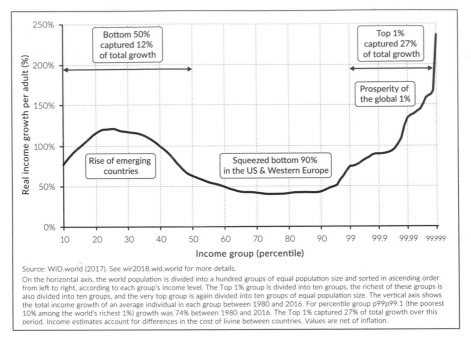

Figure H.4 The elephant curve of global inequality and growth, 1980–2016

2000s. Continental Europe meanwhile saw a lesser decline in its tax progressivity, while wage inequality was also moderated by educational and wage-setting policies that were relatively more favorable to low- and middle-income groups. In both regions, income inequality between men and women has declined but remains particularly strong at the top of the distribution.

How has inequality evolved in recent decades among global citizens? We provide the first estimates of how the growth in global income since 1980 has been distributed across the totality of the world population. The global top 1% earners has captured twice as much of that growth as the 50% poorest individuals. The bottom 50% has nevertheless enjoyed important growth rates. The global middle class (which contains all of the poorest 90% income groups in the EU and the United States) has been squeezed.

At the global level, inequality has risen sharply since 1980, despite strong growth in China.

- The poorest half of the global population has seen its income grow significantly thanks to high growth in Asia (particularly in China

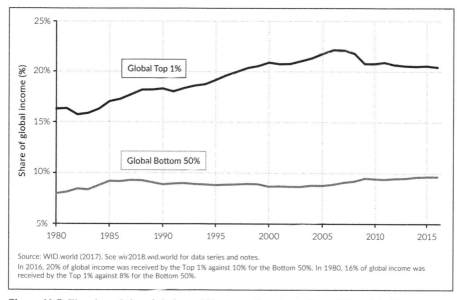

Source: WID.world (2017). See wir2018.wid.world for data series and notes.
In 2016, 20% of global income was received by the Top 1% against 10% for the Bottom 50%. In 1980, 16% of global income was received by the Top 1% against 8% for the Bottom 50%.

Figure H.5 The rise of the global top 1% versus the stagnation of the global bottom 50%, 1980–2016

and India). However, because of high and rising inequality within countries, the top 1% richest individuals in the world captured twice as much growth as the bottom 50% individuals since 1980 (Figure H.4). Income growth has been sluggish or even zero for individuals with incomes between the global bottom 50% and top 1% groups. This includes all North American and European lower- and middle-income groups.

- The rise of global inequality has not been steady. While the global top 1% income share increased from 16% in 1980 to 22% in 2000, it declined slightly thereafter to 20%. The income share of the global bottom 50% has oscillated around 9% since 1980 (Figure H.5). The trend break after 2000 is due to a reduction in between-country average income inequality, as within-country inequality has continued to increase.

III. Why does the evolution of private and public capital ownership matter for inequality?

Economic inequality is largely driven by the unequal ownership of capital, which can be either privately or public owned. We show that since 1980, very large transfers of public to private wealth occurred in nearly all countries, whether

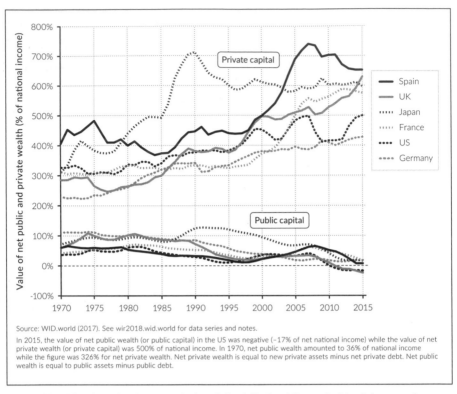

Source: WID.world (2017). See wir2018.wid.world for data series and notes.

In 2015, the value of net public wealth (or public capital) in the US was negative (–17% of net national income) while the value of net private wealth (or private capital) was 500% of national income. In 1970, net public wealth amounted to 36% of national income while the figure was 326% for net private wealth. Net private wealth is equal to new private assets minus net private debt. Net public wealth is equal to public assets minus public debt.

Figure H.6 The rise of private capital and the fall of public capital in rich countries, 1970–2016

rich or emerging. While national wealth has substantially increased, public wealth is now negative or close to zero in rich countries. Arguably this limits the ability of governments to tackle inequality; certainly, it has important implications for wealth inequality among individuals.

Over the past decades, countries have become richer but governments have become poor.

- The ratio of net private wealth to net national income gives insight into the total value of wealth commanded by individuals in a country, as compared to the public wealth held by governments. The sum of private and public wealth is equal to national wealth. The balance between private and public wealth is a crucial determinant of the level of inequality.
- There has been a general rise in net private wealth in recent decades, from 200–350% of national income in most rich countries in 1970 to 400–700% today. This was largely unaffected by the 2008 financial

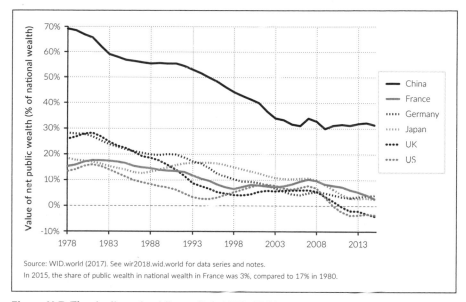

Source: WID.world (2017). See wir2018.wid.world for data series and notes.
In 2015, the share of public wealth in national wealth in France was 3%, compared to 17% in 1980.

Figure H.7 The decline of public capital, 1970–2016

crisis, or by the asset price bubbles seen in some countries such as Japan and Spain (Figure H.6). In China and Russia there have been unusually large increases in private wealth; following their transitions from communist- to capitalist-oriented economies, they saw it quadruple and triple, respectively. Private wealth–income ratios in these countries are approaching levels observed in France, the UK, and the United States.

- Conversely, net public wealth (that is, public assets minus public debts) has declined in nearly all countries since the 1980s. In China and Russia, public wealth declined from 60–70% of national wealth to 20–30%. Net public wealth has even become negative in recent years in the United States and the UK, and is only slightly positive in Japan, Germany, and France (Figure H.7). This arguably limits government ability to regulate the economy, redistribute income, and mitigate rising inequality. The only exceptions to the general decline in public property are oil-rich countries with large sovereign wealth funds, such as Norway.

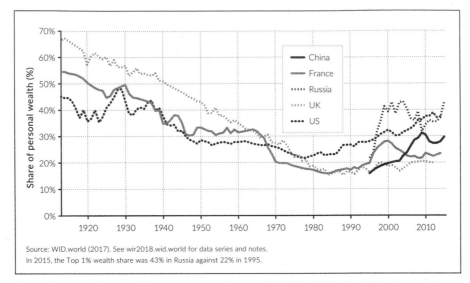

Source: WID.world (2017). See wir2018.wid.world for data series and notes.
In 2015, the Top 1% wealth share was 43% in Russia against 22% in 1995.

Figure H.8 **Top 1% wealth shares across the world, 1913–2015: the fall and rise of personal wealth inequality**

IV. What are our new findings on global wealth inequality?

The combination of large privatizations and increasing income inequality within countries has fueled the rise of wealth inequality among individuals. In Russia and the United States, the rise in wealth inequality has been extreme, whereas in Europe it has been more moderate. Wealth inequality has not yet returned to its extremely high early-twentieth-century level in rich countries.

Wealth inequality among individuals has increased at different speeds across countries since 1980.

- Increasing income inequality and the large transfers of public to private wealth occurring over the past forty years have yielded rising wealth inequality among individuals. Wealth inequality has not, however, yet reached its early-twentieth-century levels in Europe or in the United States.
- The rise in wealth inequality has nonetheless been very large in the United States, where the top 1% wealth share rose from 22% in 1980 to 39% in 2014. Most of that increase in inequality was due to the rise of the top 0.1% wealth owners. The increase in top-wealth shares in France and the UK was more moderate over the past forty years, in part due to the dampening effect of the rising housing wealth of the middle class, and a lower level of income inequality than the United States' (Figure H.8).

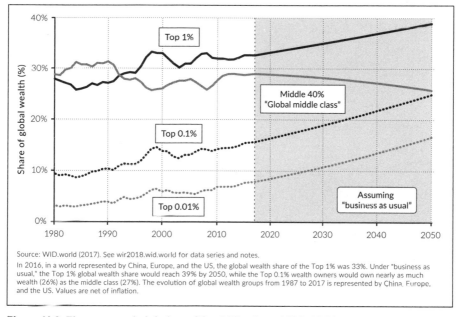

Source: WID.world (2017). See wir2018.wid.world for data series and notes.

In 2016, in a world represented by China, Europe, and the US, the global wealth share of the Top 1% was 33%. Under "business as usual," the Top 1% global wealth share would reach 39% by 2050, while the Top 0.1% wealth owners would own nearly as much wealth (26%) as the middle class (27%). The evolution of global wealth groups from 1987 to 2017 is represented by China, Europe, and the US. Values are net of inflation.

Figure H.9 The squeezed global wealth middle class, 1980–2050

- Large rises in top-wealth shares have also been experienced in China and Russia following their transitions from communism to more capitalist economies. The top 1% wealth share doubled in both China and Russia between 1995 and 2015, from 15% to 30% and from 22% to 43%, respectively.

V. What is the future of global inequality and how should it be tackled?

We project income and wealth inequality up to 2050 under different scenarios. In a future in which "business as usual" continues, global inequality will further increase. Alternatively, if in the coming decades all countries follow the moderate inequality trajectory of Europe over the past decades, global income inequality can be reduced—in which case there can also be substantial progress in eradicating global poverty.

The global wealth middle class will be squeezed under "business as usual."
- Rising wealth inequality within countries has helped to spur increases in global wealth inequality. If we assume the world trend to be captured by the combined experience of China, Europe, and the United States, the wealth share of the world's top 1% wealthiest people increased from 28% to 33%, while the share commanded

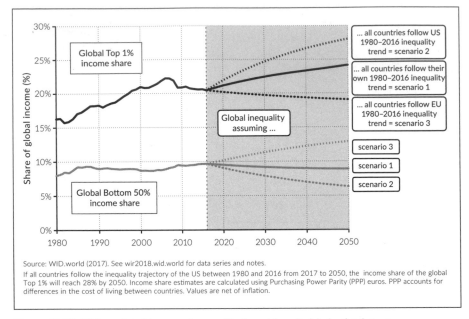

Figure H.10 Rising global income inequality is not inevitable in the future

by the bottom 75% oscillated around 10% between 1980 and 2016.
- The continuation of past wealth-inequality trends will see the wealth
  share of the top 0.1% global wealth owners (in a world represented
  by China, the EU, and the United States) catch up with the share of
  the global wealth middle class by 2050 (Figure H.9).

**Global income inequality will also increase under a "business as usual"
scenario, even with optimistic growth assumptions in emerging countries.
This is not inevitable, however.**
- Global income inequality will also increase if countries prolong the
  income inequality path they have been on since 1980—even with
  relatively high income growth predictions in Africa, Latin America,
  and Asia in the coming three decades. Global income inequality
  will increase even more if all countries follow the high-inequality
  trajectory followed by the United States between 1980 and 2016.
  However, global inequality will decrease moderately if all countries
  follow the inequality trajectory followed by the EU between 1980
  and today (Figure H.10).
- Within-country inequality dynamics have a tremendous impact on
  the eradication of global poverty. Depending on which inequality
  trajectory is followed by countries, the incomes of the bottom half

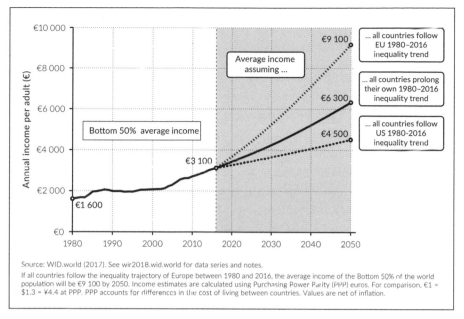

Source: WID.world (2017). See wir2018.wid.world for data series and notes.

If all countries follow the inequality trajectory of Europe between 1980 and 2016, the average income of the Bottom 50% of the world population will be €9 100 by 2050. Income estimates are calculated using Purchasing Power Parity (PPP) euros. For comparison, €1 = $1.3 = ¥4.4 at PPP. PPP accounts for differences in the cost of living between countries. Values are net of inflation.

Figure H.11 Inequality has substantial impacts on global poverty

of the world population may vary by factor of two by 2050 (Figure H.11), ranging from €4 500 to € 9100 per year, per adult.

Tackling global income and wealth inequality requires important shifts in national and global tax policies. Educational policies, corporate governance, and wage-setting policies need to be reassessed in many countries. Data transparency is also key.

Tax progressivity is a proven tool to combat rising income and wealth inequality at the top.
- Research has demonstrated that tax progressivity is an effective tool to combat inequality. Progressive tax rates do not only reduce post-tax inequality, they also diminish pre-tax inequality by giving top earners less incentive to capture higher shares of growth via aggressive bargaining for pay rises and wealth accumulation. Tax progressivity was sharply reduced in rich and some emerging countries from the 1970s to the mid-2000s. Since the global financial crisis of 2008, the downward trend has leveled off and even reversed in certain countries, but future evolutions remain uncertain and will depend on democratic deliberations. It is also worth noting that inheritance taxes are nonexistent or near zero in high-inequality

emerging countries, leaving space for important tax reforms in
these countries.

**A global financial register recording the ownership of financial assets would
deal severe blows to tax evasion, money laundering, and rising inequality.**

- Although the tax system is a crucial tool for tackling inequality, it
also faces potential obstacles. Tax evasion ranks high among these,
as recently illustrated by the Paradise Papers revelations. The wealth
held in tax havens has increased considerably since the 1970s and
currently represents more than 10% of global GDP. The rise of tax
havens makes it difficult to properly measure and tax wealth and
capital income in a globalized world. While land and real-estate
registries have existed for centuries, they miss a large fraction of
the wealth held by households today, as wealth increasingly takes
the form of financial securities. Several technical options exist for
creating a global financial register, which could be used by national
tax authorities to effectively combat fraud.

**More equal access to education and well-paying jobs is key to addressing the
stagnating or sluggish income growth rates of the poorest half of the
population.**

- Recent research shows that there can be an enormous gap between
the public discourse about equal opportunity and the reality of
unequal access to education. In the United States, for instance, out
of a hundred children whose parents are among the bottom 10% of
income earners, only twenty to thirty go to college. However, that
figure reaches ninety when parents are within the top 10% earners.
On the positive side, research shows that elite colleges who improve
openness to students from poor backgrounds need not compromise
their outcomes to do so. In both rich and emerging countries, it
might be necessary to set transparent and verifiable objectives—
while also changing financing and admission systems—to enable
equal access to education.
- Democratic access to education can achieve much, but without
mechanisms to ensure that people at the bottom of the distribution
have access to well-paying jobs, education will not prove sufficient
to tackle inequality. Better representation of workers in corporate
governance bodies and healthy minimum-wage rates are important
tools to achieve this.

Governments need to invest in the future to address current income and wealth inequality levels, and to prevent further increases in them.

- Public investments are needed in education, health, and environmental protection both to tackle existing inequality and to prevent further increases. This is particularly difficult, however, given that governments in rich countries have become poor and largely indebted. Reducing public debt is by no means an easy task, but several options to accomplish it exist—including wealth taxation, debt relief, and inflation—and have been used throughout history when governments were highly indebted, to empower younger generations.

Introduction

The objective of the *World Inequality Report 2018* is to contribute to a more informed public discussion on inequality by bringing the latest and most complete data to all sides in this global, democratic debate.

Economic inequality is widespread and to some extent inevitable. It is our belief, however, that where rising inequality is not properly addressed, it leads to all manner of political and social catastrophes. Avoiding these begins with careful monitoring.

In all societies, human beings care deeply about inequality. Changes in inequality levels have concrete consequences for people's living conditions, and they challenge our most basic and cherished notions of justice and fairness. Are different social groups getting all they deserve? Is the economic system treating different categories of labor-income earners and property owners in a balanced and equitable manner, both locally and globally? Across the world, people hold strong and often contradictory views on what constitutes acceptable and unacceptable inequality.

Again, to some extent, this will always be so. Our objective is not to bring everyone into agreement about inequality: this will never happen, for the simple reason that no single, scientific truth exists regarding the ideal level of inequality, let alone the ideal social policies and institutions to achieve and maintain it. Ultimately, it is up to public deliberation and political institutions and processes to make these difficult decisions.

Still, without aspiring to make everyone agree on the ideal level of inequality, we can hope and believe it is possible to agree about a number of inequality facts. The immediate objective of this report is to bring together new data series from the World Wealth and Income Database (WID.world) to document a number of newly discovered trends in global inequality.

WID.world is a cumulative and collaborative research process that originated in the early 2000s, and now includes over one hundred researchers covering more than seventy countries on all continents. WID.world provides open access to the most extensive available database on the historical evolution of the world distribution of income and wealth, both within and between countries.

In the context of the present report, we are able to present novel findings along three major lines. First, thanks to newly available data sources, we provide better coverage of emerging countries and of the world as a whole. Until recently, studies of inequality have tended to focus on the developed countries of Europe, North America, and Japan, largely due to better data access. Beginning with the *World Inequality Report 2018*, we are able to present findings on inequality dynamics in emerging and developing countries, including China, India, Brazil, South Africa, Russia, and the Middle East. We show that inequality has increased in most world regions in recent decades, but at different speeds, suggesting that different policies and institutions can make a substantial difference. Such geographic coverage now allows us to track income growth rates of global income groups and analyze inequality among world citizens.

Second, we cover the entire distribution of incomes, from the bottom to the top, in a consistent manner. Until recently, most available long-run series on inequality focused on top-income shares. In this report, we present new findings on how the shares going to the lowest groups of populations have evolved. We show that bottom-income shares have declined significantly in many countries. In particular, we document a dramatic collapse of the bottom 50% income share in the United States since 1980 but not in other advanced economies, again suggesting that policies play a key role.

Third, our new series allow us to analyze the distribution of wealth and the structure of property in terms of how these have evolved. Most available series on inequality have focused on income rather than wealth. We are able in the *World Inequality Report 2018* to present new findings on the changing structure of public versus private wealth and the concentration of personal wealth. We show that net public wealth (assets minus debt) is close to zero or even negative in many developed countries, which stands in contrast to the situation observed in some emerging countries (most notably China).

These are important analytical advances, yet we are very much aware that we still face heavy limitations in our ability to measure the evolution of income and wealth inequality. Our objective in WID.world and in the *World Inequality Report* is not to claim that we have perfect data series, but rather to make explicit what we know and what we do not know. We attempt to combine and reconcile in a systematic manner the different data sources at our disposal: national income and wealth accounts; household income and wealth surveys; fiscal data coming from taxes on income, inheritance, and wealth (when they exist); and wealth rankings.

None of these data sources and their associated methodologies is sufficient in itself. In particular, we stress that our ability to measure the distribution of wealth is limited, and that the different data sources at our disposal are not always fully consistent with one another. But we believe that by combining these data sources in ways that are reasonable and explicitly described we can contribute to a better informed public debate. The methods and assumptions underlying our series are transparently presented in research papers available online. We make all raw data sources and computer codes easily accessible so that our work can be reproduced and extended by others.

Part of our aim is to put pressure on governments and international organizations to release more raw data on income and wealth. In our view, the lack of transparency regarding inequality of income and wealth seriously undermines the possibilities for peaceful democratic discussion in today's globalized economy. In particular, it is critical that governments provide public access to reliable and detailed tax statistics, which in turn requires that they operate properly functioning reporting systems for income, inheritance, and wealth. Short of this, it is very difficult to have an informed debate about the evolution of inequality and what should be done about it.

Our most important reason for providing all the necessary details about data sources and concepts is to enable interested citizens to make up their own minds about these important and difficult issues. Economic issues do not belong to economists, statisticians, government officials, or business leaders. They belong to everyone, and it is our chief objective to contribute to the power of the many.

PART I

THE WID.WORLD PROJECT

1

The Measurement of Economic Inequality

This report is based on economic data available on WID.world, the most extensive database on the historical evolution of the world distribution of income and wealth, both within and between countries.

- WID.world is a cumulative and collaborative research process that originated in the early 2000s, and now includes over one hundred researchers covering more than seventy countries on all continents.
- Official inequality measures mostly rely on self-reported survey data, which frequently underestimate top income levels and usually are inconsistent with macroeconomic growth figures.
- Consequently, people often have a difficult time relating the GDP growth figures they hear about in the media to the individual income and wealth trajectories they see around them. This can lead to a lack of trust in economic statistics and get in the way of healthy public debates on inequality.
- WID.world attempts to correct for this problem by combining available sources (national accounts, fiscal and wealth data, surveys), spanning time periods as long as two hundred years for some countries, in a consistent and systematic manner.
- Our goal is to present inequality statistics that are consistent with macroeconomic statistics such as GDP and that can be easily understood and used by the public, to help ground the democratic debate in facts.
- We use modern digital tools to make these data available freely online on WID.world. Our data series are fully transparent and reproducible; our computer codes, assumptions, and detailed research papers are available online so that all interested persons can access and use them.

How to measure income and wealth inequality?

Economic inequality is a complex phenomenon that can be measured in various ways using different indicators and data sources. Choices among these indicators are not neutral and may have substantial impacts on findings. This is not only a matter of academic debate among statisticians. Anyone hoping to design appropriate policies should have a clear understanding of current and past inequality dynamics. We thus briefly discuss below key concepts which are central to understanding the rest of this report.

Whatever the source of data and the metric used to monitor economic inequality, its measurement starts from the same basic input: a distribution. For any income or wealth group, a distribution shows the number of individuals in this group and their shares of the group's total income or wealth. As such, a distribution is a relatively complex set of information, which is not straightforward to summarize. Inequality indices attempt to describe such complex data sets in a synthetic way.

Official inequality reports and statisticians often use synthetic measures of inequality such as the Gini index. Technically speaking, the Gini corresponds to the average distance between the income or wealth of all the pairs of individuals. To make it comparable between countries and over time, it is appropriately normalized so that complete equality corresponds to 0, and complete inequality (one person owning everything) corresponds to 1. The Gini index is often presented as a convenient, synthetic tool that allows comparisons of inequality across time and space.

However, this kind of index is technical both in its calculation and in the mathematical knowledge required of the reader to interpret it. According to the World Bank, for example, the Gini index for consumption inequality in Vietnam in 2014 was equal to 0.38. Is this large or small? A Gini of 0.38 implies that the distance separating Vietnam from perfect inequality (which is 1 on the index) is 0.62. Is this an acceptable distance from perfect inequality? It is not easy for citizens, journalists, and policymakers to make sense of such a metric.

Additionally, the strength of the Gini index—that it combines information on all individuals in a society—is also its main weakness. Because it summarizes a distribution in a single index, a given value for the Gini coefficient can result from distributions that are actually radically different. For example, a country may experience both a Gini-reducing decrease in poverty and a rise in the share of income going to the top 10%, which increases the Gini. If these effects offset each other, the overall Gini can remain constant, creating the impression that the distribution of income is not changing—while in fact the middle class is being squeezed out.

Because of its underlying mathematical properties, the Gini index also tends to downplay shifts happening at the top end and at the bottom of the distribution, precisely where the most evolution has taken place over the last decades. Finally, the raw data used to compute Gini indexes are often of relatively low quality, especially at the top of the distribution: top income and wealth levels are often implausibly low. The use of synthetic indexes can sometimes be a way to sweep such data issues under the rug.

Rather than use a single index, we believe it is preferable to use several metrics of inequality and to be transparent about which specific groups of the population are driving the evolution of inequality. This is the choice we make throughout this report. Distributions can be broken down into concrete social groups representing fixed fractions of the population—for example, the bottom 10% of the population, the next 10%, and so on, all the way up to the top 10% and the top 1%. For each group, it is then possible to measure the average income in that group, and the minimum income required to be part of it. For instance, in the United States in 2016, an adult needs to earn more than $124 000 per year (€95 000) to break into the top 10% group. On average, the top 10% earners make $317 000 per year (€242 000). By stark contrast, the bottom 50% earners make $16 000 per year (€13 000) on average. Arguably, anyone in the United States can relate to such measures and compare these values to their own income.

Another powerful way to measure inequality is to focus on the share of national income captured by each group. In the United States, for example, the top 10% captures 47% of national income in 2016. That is, the average income in the top 10% is 4.7 times larger than the average income in the economy as a whole; this group earns 4.7 times more than it would in a perfectly equal society. The bottom 90%, by contrast, captures 53% of national income, so individuals in the bottom 90% on average earn 59% of the average income per adult (that is, 0.53 divided by 0.90). There is no moral judgment associated with this statement: the shares of the various groups may or may not be justified. What matters here is that this metric is both accurate and meaningful.

The analysis should not stop with the top 10%, but also describe the shares and income levels of other income groups, such as the bottom 50% or the 40% who fall between the bottom 50% and the top 10% and who are often referred to as the "middle class." One may also want to refine the focus on the top of the distribution, looking at the top 1%, for instance, as recent research has shown that inequality within the top 10% is large and growing. It may then also be relevant to further decompose the top 1% into even smaller groups such as tenths of percentiles. This process can be continued, dividing the top 0.1% into tenths of tenth percentiles, and the top 0.01% into tenths of tenths of tenth percentiles. Overall, this approach allows for a more detailed but still straightforward description of the level and evolution of inequality relative to what can be achieved by using synthetic indexes.

Where to look for global inequality data

Understandable inequality indices are necessary but not sufficient to enable sound debates on inequality. Ultimately what matter are reliable and trusted economic data sources. Producing reliable inequality statistics takes time, however, and providing such estimates for several countries and over long periods is not possible without the participation of many researchers—researchers with country-specific knowledge, access to data sources, and adequate understanding of the political, economic, and cultural specificities of each country. This may help explain why, thus far, the production of inequality statistics has been decentralized across different research groups, often using different concepts and estimation techniques.

Several world inequality databases exist today. These inequality databases include for instance the World Bank's PovcalNet, the Luxembourg Income Study (LIS), the Socio-Economic Database for Latin America and the Caribbean (SEDLAC), and the OECD Income Distribution Database (IDD). There are also various sources that combine the aforementioned databases to increase their coverage, the most important being the World Panel Income Distribution (LM-WPID) and the Standardized World Income Inequality Database (SWIID). Lastly, the United Nations compiles the World Income Inequality Database (WIID), which consists of a nearly exhaustive census of all primary databases and individual research initiatives, with detailed information about the concepts used.

These databases have proved useful to researchers, policymakers, journalists, and the general public focusing on the evolution of inequality over the past decades. However, these sources also rely almost exclusively on a specific information source—namely, household surveys—which have important limitations when it comes to measuring inequality. Household surveys consist mostly of face-to-face or virtual interviews with individuals who are asked questions about their incomes, wealth, and other socio-economic aspects of their lives. Surveys are particularly valuable because they gather information about not only income or assets, but also social and demographic dimensions. They thus allow for a better understanding of the determinants of income and wealth inequality, and help place income and wealth inequality in broader contexts—such as racial, spatial, educational, or gender inequality.

The main problem with household surveys, however, is that they usually rely entirely on self-reported information about income and wealth. As a consequence, they misrepresent top income and wealth levels, and therefore overall inequality. This can also contribute to major inconsistencies between macroeconomic growth (as recorded by GDP statistics) and household income growth (as recorded by surveys for the bottom and middle parts of the distribution), thereby leading to a lack of trust in economic statistics. (Box 1.1)

Box 1.1 What type of economic inequality do we measure in the *World Inequality Report*?

This report attempts to present an integrated and consistent approach to gauging both income and wealth inequality. As its title indicates, the key ambition and novelty of the World Inequality Database (WID.world), upon which this report is built, is indeed to put equal emphasis on wealth and income, and to relate the two aspects of economic inequality as closely as possible.

There are several reasons for this. First, in order to properly analyze income inequality, it is critical to decompose total income into two categories of income flows: income from labor and income from capital. The latter category has played an important role in the rise of inequality in recent decades—and an even bigger role if we look at the evolution of the distribution of income in the very long run.

Next, one of our key goals is to relate macroeconomic issues—such as capital accumulation, the aggregate structure of property, privatization or nationalization policies, and the evolution of public debt—to the microeconomic study of inequality. Far too often, the study of the "capital" side of the economy (that is, focused on capital, investment, debt, and so forth) is separated from the study of the "household" side (that is, looking at wages, transfers, poverty, inequality, and other issues).

We should make clear, however, that a lot of progress needs to be made before we can present a fully integrated approach. The present report should be viewed as one step in this direction. For example, in Part IV of the report, we are able to fully analyze the joint evolution of inequality of income and wealth for a number of countries (in particular, the United States and France). Doing so requires careful measurement not only of the inequality of pre-tax and post-tax income, but also of the distribution of saving rates across the different deciles of the distribution of pre-tax income.

This kind of analysis will gradually be extended to more and more countries, as more data become available. The combination of series on the distribution of pre-tax and post-tax income, savings, and wealth will also allow us to relate in a systematic manner the inequality of income, wealth, and consumption (that is, income minus savings).

In our view, however, it would be a mistake to overemphasize the consumption perspective, as the literature on inequality and poverty has sometimes done. Consumption is obviously a very important indicator of wealth, particularly at the bottom of the distribution. The problem is that the household surveys routinely used to study consumption inequality tend to underestimate the consumption, income, and wealth levels reached by the top of the distribution. Also, the notion of consumption is not always well defined for top income groups, which typically save very large proportions of their income. They choose to do so partly in order to consume more in later years, but more generally in order to consume the prestige, security, and economic power conferred by wealth ownership. In order to develop a consistent and global perspective on economic inequality—that is, a perspective that views economic actors not only as consumers and workers but also as owners and investors—it is critical, in our view, to put equal emphasis on income and wealth.

Our various concepts of income and wealth—in particular, pre-tax national income, post-tax national income, and personal wealth—are defined using international guidelines in national income and wealth accounts (SNA 2008). The exact technical definitions are available online in the DINA Guidelines (Distributional National Accounts).[1]

---

1   See F. Alvaredo, A. B. Atkinson, L. Chancel, T. Piketty, E. Saez, and G. Zucman, "Distributional National Accounts (DINA) Guidelines: Concepts and Methods Used in WID.world," WID.world Working Paper no. 2016/2, December 2016, http://wid.world/document/dinaguidelines-v1/.

Fiscal data capture inequality dynamics that survey data cannot

Survey estimates of inequality rely on self-reported information collected from nationally representative groups of the population. The first problem with any such survey is its limited sample size. Given the small number of extremely rich individuals, the likelihood that they will be included in surveys is typically very small. Some surveys attempt to address this issue by oversampling the rich—select more rich individuals to be surveyed—but this is typically insufficient to obtain reliable information on the wealthy, because non-response rates are high among the rich. Furthermore, because very large self-reported incomes in surveys are sometimes due to reporting errors, surveys often use top codes (or corrections) to clean up extreme values. Therefore, surveys generally severely underestimate the income and wealth levels at the very top of the distribution, precisely where some of the largest changes have occurred over the past decades.

The best way to overcome this limitation is to combine different types of data sources, and in particular to use administrative tax data together with survey data. Initially compiled for tax collection purposes, tax data are also valuable for researchers. As compared to surveys, they give a more complete and reliable picture of the distribution of income and wealth among the wealthy.

To illustrate the differences in inequality estimates between survey and fiscal data, consider the following examples. According to official survey data, the top 1% of Chinese earners captured 6.5% of national income in 2015. However, new estimates produced as part of the WID.world project show that correcting surveys with newly released tax data on high-income earners is enough to increase the income share of the top 1% from 6.5% to close to 11.5% of national income.[1] In Brazil, survey data indicate that the income received by the richest 10% is just over 40% of total income in 2015, but when surveys are combined with fiscal data and national accounts, we find that this group receives, in fact, more than 55% of national income (Figure 1.1). As can be seen from these two examples, the extent to which surveys underestimate top shares can vary from one country to another—and also from one percentile to another—but it is always likely to be substantial. Comparisons between countries are likely to be unreliable if made based on survey data without adjusting for the top by including fiscal and national accounts data.

Poor coverage of the wealthy in household surveys can also impede accurate comparisons across time. For example, according to Brazilian survey data, inequality in the country decreased between 2001 and 2015—but income tax data show that, in fact, inequality remained stubbornly high over this period. Similar results can be found in China, where the income share of the top 10% increased by fifteen percentage points from 1978 to 2015, while, according to

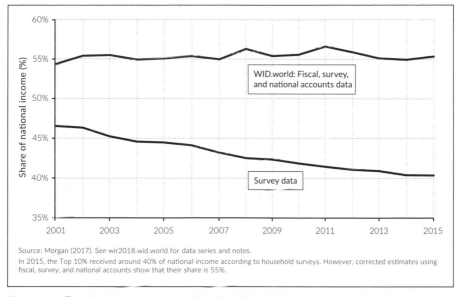

Source: Morgan (2017). See wir2018.wid.world for data series and notes.
In 2015, the Top 10% received around 40% of national income according to household surveys. However, corrected estimates using fiscal, survey, and national accounts show that their share is 55%.

Figure 1.1 Top 10% income share in Brazil, 2001–2015: survey vs. national accounts (WID.world) series

official survey estimates, the increase was only by nine percentage points. In India, the absence of top earners in survey data could explain up to 30% of the gap between the very low macroeconomic growth of consumption seen in survey data, and the much faster growth rate seen in national account data.[2]

Administrative tax data are not free from measurement issues at the top. They also tend to underestimate top income and wealth levels, due to tax evasion. For this reason, our inequality estimates should be viewed in most cases as lower-bound estimates—but at least these are more plausible lower bounds than survey-based measures. In all countries, including in countries with potentially widespread evasion, we find that top income levels reported in tax data are substantially larger than in surveys. The reason for this is simple: noncompliant taxpayers face at least some potential sanctions if they underreport their incomes to tax authorities, whereas no such sanctions exist for underreporting income in a survey. Furthermore, tax authorities increasingly collect data from third parties (such as employers and banks), which increases tax compliance.

Another advantage of tax data over surveys is coverage of longer time periods. Administrative tax data are usually available on a yearly basis starting with the beginning of the twentieth century for the income tax, and as far back as the early nineteenth century for the inheritance tax in some countries. In contrast, nationally representative surveys are rarely carried out annually, and were not generally carried out at all before the 1970s–1980s. Using them, it would be impossible to study long-run evolutions—a serious limitation given that some of the most important transformations in inequality span long periods of time. Having data covering many decades helps disentangle long-term trends reflecting major macroeconomic transformations from short-term variations due to episodic shocks or measurement issues.

The renewed focus on income inequality and the World Top Incomes Database

During the past fifteen years, there has been renewed interest in understanding the long-run evolution of income inequality. Many studies have constructed top income share series for a large number of countries.[3] These studies have generated large volumes of data, intended as a research resource for further analysis as well as a source to inform the public debate on inequality trends. To a large extent, this literature followed the pioneering work of Simon Kuznets, extending his income share measurement to more countries and years.[4]

In January 2011, The World Top Incomes Database (WTID) was created to provide convenient and free access to these series. Thanks to the contribution of over a hundred researchers, the WTID expanded to include series on income inequality for more than thirty countries, spanning most of the twentieth and early twenty-first centuries. These series had a large impact on the global inequality debate because they made it possible to compare the income shares of top groups (for example, the top 1%) over long periods of time, revealing new facts and refocusing the discussion on the rise in inequality seen in recent decades.

Although the top income share series available in the WTID all had a common methodological underpinning and goal—using tax data to document the long-run evolution of income concentration—the units of observation, the income concepts, and the statistical methods used were never made fully homogeneous over time and across countries. Attention was restricted for the most part, moreover, to the top decile rather than to the entire distribution, and these series were mostly about income, not wealth. All this pointed to the need for a methodological reexamination and clarification.

In December 2015, the WTID was subsumed into the WID, the World Inequality Database (WID.world). The change in name reflects the extended scope and ambition of the project. The new database aims at measuring not only income but also wealth inequality, and it aims at capturing the dynamics of income and wealth across the entire distribution and not only at the top. The database also plans to progressively develop historical inequality series on dimensions such as gender or pollution.

WID.world's key novelty: distributing national accounts in a consistent way

The key novelty of the WID.world project is to produce Distributional National Accounts (DINA) relying on a consistent and systematic combination of fiscal, survey, wealth, and national accounts data sources.[5] The complete DINA methodological guidelines (Alvaredo et al., 2016), as well as all computer codes and detailed data series and research papers, are available online on WID.world. Here we summarize only some of the main methodological points.

As explained above, administrative data on income and wealth tend to be more reliable sources of information than surveys. Unfortunately, they provide information on only a subset of the population—namely, the part filing tax returns. This issue is particularly important in emerging countries. In India, for example, income taxpayers represent only slightly more than 6% of the adult population; thus, survey data are the only available sources of information to measure inequality in the bottom 94% of the distribution. We must critically and cautiously rely on survey data sources in combination with fiscal and wealth sources and national accounts to estimate the distribution of national income or wealth.

Another limitation of tax data is that they are subject to changes in fiscal concepts over time and across countries. Typically, depending on whether income components (such as labor income, dividends, and capital income) are subject to tax, they may or may not appear in the tax data from which distributional statistics can be computed. These differences can make international and historical comparisons difficult.

To some extent, these harmonization issues can be overcome by using national account data—and in particular, the concepts of national income and national wealth—as a benchmark. Our choice of these concepts for the analysis of inequality does not mean that we consider them perfectly satisfactory. Quite the contrary, our view is that national accounts statistics are insufficient and need to be greatly improved.

In our view, however, the best way to improve on the national accounts is to confront them with other sources and to attempt to distribute national income and wealth across percentiles. The key advantage of national accounts is that they follow internationally standardized definitions for measuring the economic activity of nations. As such, they allow for a more consistent comparison over time and across countries than fiscal data. National accounts definitions, in particular, do not depend upon local variations in tax legislation or other parts of the legal system.

One of the most widely used aggregate of the national accounts is gross domestic product (GDP). But GDP statistics do not provide any information about the extent to which the different social groups benefit (or not) from growth.[6] In addition, GDP is not a satisfactory measure of the total income of a country, because a country with extensive capital depreciation or large income flowing abroad can have a large GDP but much less income to distribute to its residents.

The concept of national income (NI) is a better benchmark indicator to compare countries and to analyze the distribution of income and growth. National income is equal to GDP minus capital depreciation plus net foreign income. It reflects a nation's income more closely than GDP does. The WID.world database combines macroeconomic data from different sources in order to produce national income series for about two hundred countries. These national income estimates are consistent with those of international organizations, with one important improvement: our series address the issue that some income is missing from published national accounts. In the official data, foreign income paid is higher than foreign income received at the global level—because some of the income received in tax havens is nowhere recorded. We allocate this global missing income drawing on methods first developed by Zucman (2013).[7]

Total fiscal income (as measured by tax data) is always less than national income (as measured in the national accounts). Part of the difference is due to tax-exempt income flows such as imputed rent (the rental value of owner-occupied housing) and undistributed profits (the profits of corporations not distributed to individuals but ultimately benefiting owners of corporations). When data are available and sufficiently precise, we attribute the fraction of national income missing from fiscal data to the income groups who benefit from these sources of income. This operation can have significant implications for the distribution of income. For example, once we add undistributed profits to fiscal income, the share of income earned by the top 1% in China increases from 11.5% to 14% in 2015. A number of recent research papers have attempted to construct inequality statistics accounting for tax-exempt income, both in developed and emerging countries, including the United States, China, France, Brazil, and Russia.

Data limitations currently make such adjustments impossible, however, in a number of countries, which implies that inequality estimates for these countries tend to be downwardly biased. In such cases, we simply use our national income series to scale up fiscal incomes proportionally so that they add up to national income.[8] This transformation does not affect the distribution of income, but allows us to compare the evolution of income levels over time and across countries more meaningfully. For example, our data show that the average pre-tax national income per adult within the top 1% is similar in India and China in 2013 (€131 000 versus €157 000, respectively) but much higher in Brazil (€436 000) and in the United States (€990 000).

Taking wealth inequality into account

One reason for the growing interest in wealth inequality is the recognition that the increase in income inequality in recent years is partly a result of rising capital incomes (in addition to changes in wages and earned income). These capital incomes include interest, dividends, retained earnings of corporations, and rents. While most of the population earns little capital income, this form of income accounts for a significant proportion of income at the top of the income distribution.

Another reason for the renewed interest in wealth is that aggregate wealth itself is rising faster than income—so the ratio of national wealth to national income is rising fast in many countries (as was first shown by Piketty and Zucman, 2014). One consequence is that inherited wealth—which declined for much of the twentieth century—is taking on renewed significance in a number of countries. There is also extensive evidence (in billionaire rankings, for example) that top global wealth-holders have accumulated wealth at a much faster rate than the average person and have therefore benefited from a substantial increase in their share of global wealth.

Because most countries do not tax wealth directly, producing reliable estimates of wealth inequality requires combining different data sources, such as billionaire rankings and also income tax data and inheritance tax data—as in the pioneer-

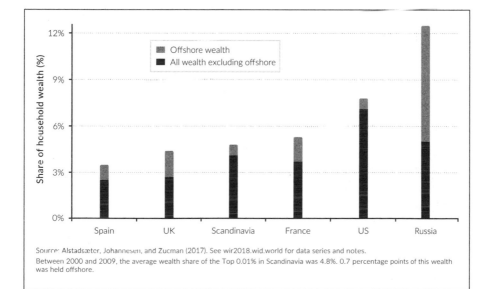

Source: Alstadsæter, Johannesen, and Zucman (2017). See wir2018.wid.world for data series and notes.
Between 2000 and 2009, the average wealth share of the Top 0.01% in Scandinavia was 4.8%. 0.7 percentage points of this wealth was held offshore.

Figure 1.2 Top 0.01% wealth share and its composition in emerging and rich countries, 2000–2009

ing work of A. B. Atkinson and A. Harrison (1978).[9] The globalization of wealth management since the 1980s raises additional new challenges, as a growing amount of world wealth is held in offshore financial centers. Work led by Gabriel Zucman shows that accounting for these offshore assets has large implications for the measurement of wealth at the very top end of the distribution (Figure 1.2).[10] More generally, it is becoming critical to measure the inequality of income and wealth from a global perspective, and not simply at the country level, as we discuss below.

From national to regional and global distributions of income and wealth

One central objective of the WID.world project is to produce global income and wealth distributions. This amounts to ranking individuals from the poorest to the richest at the global level, ignoring national boundaries. We also provide estimates of income and wealth inequality for broad regions, such as Europe and the Middle East.

One might wonder whether it makes sense to produce global inequality estimates, given that most policies (including policies to tackle inequality) are voted and implemented at the national level. In our view, it is complementary to study inequality dynamics at the national, regional, and global levels. First, although there exists no global government, there are attempts to foster global cooperation to tackle issues such as tax havens and environmental inequalities. Next, growing economic interdependence implies that one needs to look at global inequality dynamics to fully understand the underlying economic forces shaping national inequality. Finally, political perceptions about inequality might be determined by one's position not only within a given country but also by comparison to others at the regional and global levels.

Since the 1980s the world has evolved towards more economic, financial, and cultural integration. Even if globalization may be called into question today—as recent elections in the UK and the United States have proved—the world remains an interconnected environment where capital, goods, services, and ideas are highly mobile and their circulation is facilitated by innovations in information technology. To some extent, there is already a global community, and in this global environment it is logical for citizens to compare themselves to one another.

Individuals in one country may feel deeply concerned, from an ethical perspective, by the situations of those at the bottom of the global distribution.[11] They may also be concerned about their own positions in the global or regional distributions of income and wealth. The stagnating or sluggish income growth of lower- and middle-income groups in rich countries, considered in a context of high growth in emerging countries and at the top of the global income pyramid, may have contributed to anti-establishment votes over recent years. National citizens may already be thinking across borders.

Global inequality data are also necessary to analyze the distributional consequences of globalization. Is growth at the global top disproportionately high? Or is the share of total growth captured by the global top 1% small compared to the growth that has accrued to the bottom 50%? The first step toward answering these fundamental questions is to collect and produce global inequality statistics that cover all groups of the population, up to the very top.

As will be described in Chapter 2, we move toward this goal carefully, aggregating only regions and countries for which we have consistent data series. We present results for the global distribution of income, but data limitations do not allow us yet to analyze the global distribution of wealth. (Our "global" wealth estimates take into account only the United States, Europe, and China.) Producing truly global wealth distribution series will be a major goal of future editions of the *World Inequality Report*. Eventually, we also seek to deepen our understanding of the interplay between global economic inequality and other forms of global inequality, such as environmental injustice.[12] Such inequality metrics can help environmental and economic policy making—for example, when it comes to allocating efforts to tackle climate change across individuals, countries, and regions.

WID.world and the *World Inequality Report*: open access, transparency, and replicability at its core

In January 2017, we released the first version of the WID.world website with the objective of reaching a wide audience of researchers and the general public with a user-friendly interface. Thanks to the work of over a hundred researchers located on five continents, the WID.world website now gathers income inequality data for more than 70 countries, wealth inequality and public and private wealth data for more than 30 countries, and national income and GDP data for more than 180 countries. Thus WID.world provides access to the most extensive available database on the historical evolution of income and wealth inequality, both between and within countries. As part of our attempts to democratize access to inequality data, we have also made WID.world available in four languages—Chinese (Mandarin), English, French, and Spanish—and thus to three billion people in their own language (Figure 1.3).

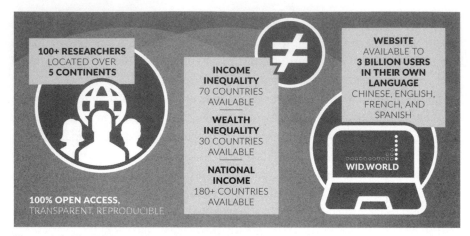

Figure 1.3 The WID.world project in 2018

Open access, transparency, and reproducibility are the core values of the WID
.world project. The website was designed to allow anyone, expert or nonexpert,
to access and make sense of historical global inequality data. All WID.world
series, moreover, are accompanied with a methodological paper providing extensive descriptions of the method and concepts used.

Raw data and the computer codes used to generate inequality estimates are
also updated on the website. This level of transparency is another key innovation
in the landscape of economic data providers. It allows any interested researcher
to refine our estimates, make different assumptions if they wish, and help develop
new ideas for how inequality can be better measured and how these data can be
used for the benefit of society. Our website comes along with a set of tools to
analyze economic inequality.

The *World Inequality Report 2018* is part of this initiative to democratize access
to inequality statistics. All the series discussed and presented in the report are
also available online and can be entirely reproduced. We should note, however,
that this report contains analyses carried out specifically for the report, and
hence, the report may not necessarily represent the views of all WID.world fellows.
The *World Inequality Report* is a product of the World Inequality Lab, which
relies on research completed as part of the WID.world project and novel research
on global inequality dynamics.

PART II

TRENDS IN GLOBAL INCOME INEQUALITY

2

Global Income Inequality Dynamics

The information in this chapter draws on "The Elephant Curve of Global Inequality and Growth," by Facundo Alvaredo, Lucas Chancel, Thomas Piketty, Emmanuel Saez, and Gabriel Zucman, 2017. WID.world Working Paper Series (No. 2017/20), forthcoming in American Economic Association P&P.

- Data series on global inequality are scarce and caution is required in interpreting them. However, by combining consistent and comparable data, as we have done in this *World Inequality Report*, we can provide striking insights.
- Since 1980, income inequality has increased rapidly in North America and Asia, grown moderately in Europe, and stabilized at an extremely high level in the Middle East, sub-Saharan Africa, and Brazil.
- The poorest half of the global population has seen its income grow significantly thanks to high growth in Asia. But the top 0.1% has captured as much growth as the bottom half of the world adult population since 1980.
- Income growth has been sluggish or even nil for individuals between the global bottom 50% and top 1%. This includes North American and European lower- and middle-income groups.
- The rise of global inequality has not been steady. While the global top 1% income share increased from 16% in 1980 to 22% in 2000, it declined slightly thereafter to 20%. The trend break after 2000 is due to a reduction in between-country average income inequality, as within-country inequality has continued to increase.
- When measured using market exchange rates, the top 10% share reaches 60% today, instead of 53% when using purchasing power parity (PPP) exchange rates.
- Global income growth dynamics are driven by strong forces of convergence between countries and divergence within countries.

Standard economic trade models fail to explain these dynamics properly—in particular, the rise of inequality at the very top and within emerging countries. Global dynamics are shaped by a variety of national institutional and political contexts, described and discussed in the following chapters of this report.

Managing data limitations to construct a global distribution of income

The dynamics of global inequality have attracted growing attention in recent years.[1] However, we still know relatively little about how the distribution of global income and wealth is evolving. Available studies have largely relied on household surveys, a useful source of information, but one that does not accurately track the evolution of inequality at the top of the distribution. New methodological and empirical work carried out in the context of WID.world allows a better understanding of global income dynamics.

We stress at the outset that the production of global inequality dynamics is in its infancy and will still require much more work. It is critical that national statistical and tax institutions release income and wealth inequality data in many countries where data are not available currently—in particular, in developing and emerging countries. Researchers also need to thoroughly harmonize and analyze these data to produce consistent, comparable estimates. The World Inequality Lab and the WID.world research consortium intend to continue contributing to these tasks in the coming years.

Even if there are uncertainties involved, it is already possible to produce meaningful global income inequality estimates. The WID.world database contains internationally comparable income inequality estimates covering the entire population, from the lowest to the highest income earners, for many countries: the United States, China, India, Russia, Brazil, the Middle East, and the major European countries (such as France, Germany, and the United Kingdom). A great deal can already be inferred by comparing inequality trends in these regions. Using simple assumptions, we have estimated the evolution of incomes in the rest of the world so as to distribute 100% of global income every year since 1980 (Box 2.1). This exercise should be seen as a first step towards the construction of a fully consistent global distribution of income. We plan to present updated and extended versions of these estimates in the future editions of the *World Inequality Report* and on WID.world, as we gradually manage to access more data sources, particularly in Africa, Latin America, and Asia.

The exploration of global inequality dynamics presented here starts in 1980,

Box 2.1 How did we construct global income inequality measures?

Global estimates in the *World Inequality Report* are based on a combination of sources used at the national level (including tax receipts, household surveys, and national accounts as discussed in Part 1). Consistent estimates of national income inequality are now available for the US, Western Europe (and in particular France, Germany, the United Kingdom) as well as China, India, Brazil, Russia, and the Middle East. These regions represent approximately two thirds of the world adult population and three quarters of global income.

In this chapter on global income inequality, we have ultimately distributed the totality of global income to the totality of the world population. To achieve this, we had to distribute the quarter of global income to the third of the global population for which there are currently no consistent income inequality data available. Some crucial information we have, however, is total national income in each country. This information is essential, as it already determines a large part of global income inequality among individuals.

How, then, to distribute national income to individuals in countries without inequality data? We tested different ways and found that these had very moderate impacts on the distribution of global income, given the limited share of income and population concerned by these assumptions. In the end, we assumed that countries with missing inequality information had similar levels of inequality as other countries in their region. For example, we know the average income

level in Malaysia, but not (yet) how national income is distributed to all individuals in this country. We then assumed that the distribution of income in Malaysia was the same, and followed the same trends, as in the region formed by China and India. This is indeed an oversimplification, but to some extent this is an acceptable method as alternative assumptions have a limited impact on our general conclusions.

Sub-Saharan Africa is a particular case: we did not have any country with consistent income inequality data over the past decades (whereas in Asia we have consistent estimates for China and India, in Latin America, we have estimates for Brazil, etc.). For Sub-Saharan Africa, we thus relied on household surveys available from the World Bank (these estimates cover 70% of Sub-Saharan Africa's population and yet a higher proportion of the region's income). These surveys were matched with fiscal data available from WID.world so as to provide a better representation of inequality at the top of the social pyramid (see Part 1).

Doing so then allowed us to produce a global distribution of income. The methodology we followed[1] is available on wir2018.wid.world, as well as all the computer codes we used, so as to allow anyone to make alternative assumptions or contribute to extend this work. In future editions of the *World Inequality Report*, we will progressively expand the geographical coverage of our data.

1   See L. Chancel and A. Gethin, "Building a global income distribution brick by brick," WID.world Technical Note, 2017/5 as well as L. Chancel and L. Czajka. "Estimating the regional distribution of income in Sub-Saharan Africa." WID.world Technical Note, 2017/6.

for two main reasons. First, 1980 corresponds to a turning point in inequality and redistributive policies in many countries. The early 1980s mark the start of a rising trend in inequality and major policy changes, both in the West (with the elections of Ronald Reagan and Margaret Thatcher, in particular) and in emerging economies (with deregulation policies in China and India). Second, 1980 is the date from which data become available for a large enough number of countries to allow a sound analysis of global dynamics.

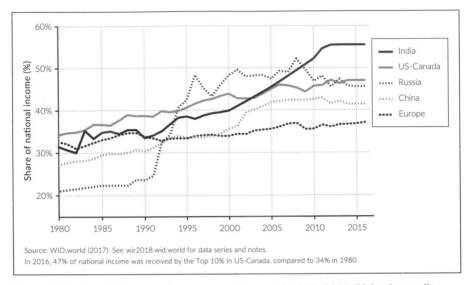

Source: WID.world (2017). See wir2018.wid.world for data series and notes.
In 2016, 47% of national income was received by the Top 10% in US-Canada, compared to 34% in 1980.

Figure 2.1a Top 10% income shares across the world, 1980–2016: Rising inequality almost everywhere, but at different speeds

We start by presenting our basic findings regarding the evolution of income inequality within the main world regions. Three main findings emerge.

First, we observe rising inequality in most of the world's regions, but with very different magnitudes. More specifically, we display in Figure 2.1a the evolution of the top 10% income share in Europe (Western and Eastern Europe combined, excluding Ukraine, Belorussia, and Russia), North America (defined as the United States and Canada), China, India, and Russia. The top 10% share has increased in all five of these large world regions since 1980. The top 10% share was around 30–35% in Europe, North America, China, and India in 1980, and only about 20–25% in Russia. If we put these 1980 inequality levels into broader and longer perspective, we find that they were in place since approximately the Second World War, and that these are relatively low inequality levels by historical standards (Piketty, 2014). In effect, despite their many differences, all these world regions went through a relatively egalitarian phase between 1950 and 1980. For simplicity, and for the time being, this relatively low inequality regime can be described as the "post-war egalitarian regime," with obvious important variations between social-democratic, New Deal, socialist, and communist variants to which we will return.

Top 10% income shares then increased in all these regions between 1980 and 2016, but with large variations in magnitude. In Europe, the rise was moderate, with the top 10% share increasing to about 35–40% by 2016. However, in North America, China, India, and even more so in Russia (where the change in policy

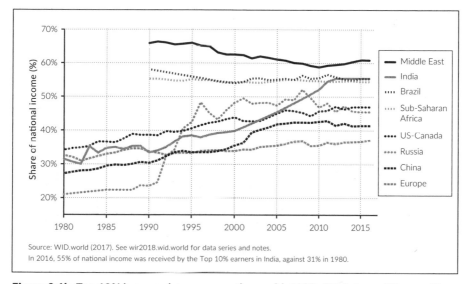

Source: WID.world (2017). See wir2018.wid.world for data series and notes.
In 2016, 55% of national income was received by the Top 10% earners in India, against 31% in 1980.

Figure 2.1b Top 10% income shares across the world, 1980–2016: Is world inequality moving toward the high-inequality frontier?

regime was particularly dramatic), the rise was much more pronounced. In all these regions, the top 10% share rose to about 45–50% of total income in 2016. The fact that the magnitude of rising inequality differs substantially across regions suggests that policies and institutions matter: rising inequality cannot be viewed as a mechanical, deterministic consequence of globalization.

Next, there are exceptions to this general pattern. That is, there are regions—in particular, the Middle East, Brazil (and to some extent Latin America as a whole), and South Africa (and to some extent sub-Saharan Africa as a whole)—where income inequality has remained relatively stable at extremely high levels in recent decades. Unfortunately, data availability is more limited for these three regions, which explains why the series start in 1990, and why we are not able to properly cover all countries in these regions (Figure 2.1b).

In spite of their many differences, the striking commonality in these three regions is the extreme and persistent level of inequality. The top 10% receives about 55% of total income in Brazil and sub-Saharan Africa, and in the Middle East, the top 10% income share is typically over 60% (Figure 2.1c). In effect, for various historical reasons, these three regions never went through the post-war egalitarian regime and have always been at the world's high-inequality frontier.

The third striking finding is that the variations in top-income shares over time and across countries are very large in magnitude, and have a major impact on the income shares and levels of the bottom 50% of the population. It is worth

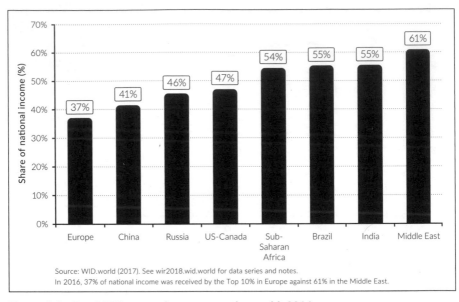

Source: WID.world (2017). See wir2018.wid.world for data series and notes.
In 2016, 37% of national income was received by the Top 10% in Europe against 61% in the Middle East.

Figure 2.1c Top 10% income shares across the world, 2016

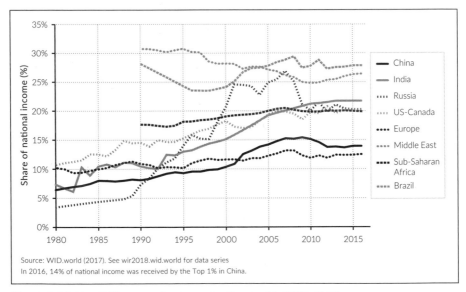

Source: WID.world (2017). See wir2018.wid.world for data series
In 2016, 14% of national income was received by the Top 1% in China.

Figure 2.1d Top 1% income shares across the world, 1980–2016

keeping in mind the following orders of magnitude: top 10% income shares vary
from 20–25% to 60–65% of total income (see Figures 2.1a and 2.1b). If we focus
upon very top incomes, we find that top 1% income shares vary from about 5%
to 30% (Figure 2.1d), just like the share of income going to the bottom 50% of
the population (Figure 2.1e).

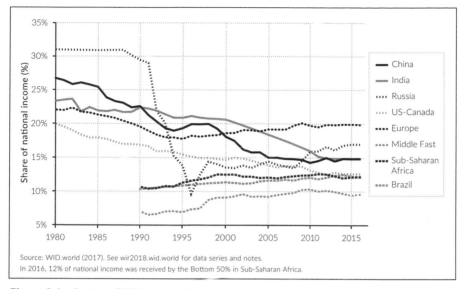

Source: WID.world (2017). See wir2018.wid.world for data series and notes.
In 2016, 12% of national income was received by the Bottom 50% in Sub-Saharan Africa.

Figure 2.1e Bottom 50% income shares across the world, 1980–2016

In other words, the same aggregate income level can give rise to widely different income levels for the bottom and top groups depending on the distribution of income prevailing in the specific country and time period under consideration. In brief, the distribution matters quite a bit.

What have been the growth trajectories of different income groups in these regions since 1980? Table 2.1 presents income growth rates in China, Europe, India, Russia, and North America for key groups of the distribution. The full population grew at very different rates in the five regions. Real per-adult, national income growth reached an impressive 831% in China and 223% in India. In Europe, Russia, and North America, income growth was lower than 100% (40%, 34%, and 74%, respectively). Behind these heterogeneous average growth trajectories, the different regions all share a common, striking characteristic.

In all these countries, income growth is systematically higher for upper income groups. In China, the bottom 50% earners grew at less than 420% while the top 0.001% grew at more than 3 750%. The gap between the bottom 50% and the top 0.001% is even more important in India (less than 110% versus more than 3 000%). In Russia, the top of the distribution had extreme growth rates; this reflects the shift from a regime in which top incomes were constrained by the communist system towards a market economy with few regulations constraining top incomes. In this global picture, in line with Figure 2.1, Europe stands as the region with the lowest growth gap between the bottom 50% and the full population, and with the lowest growth gap between the bottom 50% and top 0.001%.

Table 2.1 Global income growth and inequality, 1980–2016

Income group	\multicolumn{6}{c}{Total cumulative real growth per adult}
Income group	China	Europe	India	Russia	US-Canada	World
Full Population	831%	40%	223%	34%	63%	60%
Bottom 50%	417%	26%	107%	-26%	5%	94%
Middle 40%	785%	34%	112%	5%	44%	43%
Top 10%	1316%	58%	469%	190%	123%	70%
Top 1%	1920%	72%	857%	686%	206%	101%
Top 0.1%	2421%	76%	1295%	2562%	320%	133%
Top 0.01%	3112%	87%	2078%	8239%	452%	185%
Top 0.001%	3752%	120%	3083%	25269%	629%	235%

Source: WID.world (2017). See wir2018.wid.world for data series and notes.
From 1980 to 2016, the average income of the Bottom 50% in China grew 417%. Income estimates are calculated using 2016 Purchasing Power Parity (PPP) euros. PPP accounts for differences in the cost of living between countries. Values are net of inflation.

The right-hand column of Table 2.1 presents income growth rates of different groups at the level of the entire world. These growth rates are obtained once all the individuals of the different regions are pooled together to reconstruct global income groups. Incomes across countries are compared using purchasing power parity (PPP) so that a given income can in principle buy the same bundle of goods and services in all countries. Average global growth is relatively low (60%) compared to emerging countries' growth rates. Interestingly enough, at the world level, growth rates do not rise monotonically with income groups' positions in the distribution. Instead, we observe high growth at the bottom 50% (94%), low growth in the middle 40% (43%), and high growth at the top 1% (more than 100%)—and especially at the top 0.001% (close to 235%).

To better understand the significance of these unequal rates of growth, it is useful to focus on the share of total growth captured by each group over the entire period. Table 2.2 presents the share of growth per adult captured by each group. Focusing on both metrics is important because the top 1% global income group could have enjoyed a substantial growth rate of more than 100% over the past four decades (meaningful at the individual level), but still represent only a little share of total growth. The top 1% captured 35% of total growth in the US-Canada, and an astonishing 69% in Russia.

At the global level, the top 1% captured 27% of total growth—that is, twice as much as the share of growth captured by the bottom 50%. The top 0.1% captured

Table 2.2 Share of global growth captured by income groups, 1980–2016

Income group	China	Europe	India	Russia	US-Canada	World
Full Population	100%	100%	100%	100%	100%	100%
Bottom 50%	13%	14%	11%	-24%	2%	12%
Middle 40%	43%	38%	23%	7%	32%	31%
Top 10%	43%	48%	66%	117%	67%	57%
Top 1%	15%	18%	28%	69%	35%	27%
Top 0.1%	7%	7%	12%	41%	18%	13%
Top 0.01%	4%	3%	5%	20%	9%	7%
Top 0.001%	2%	1%	3%	10%	4%	4%

Source: WID.world (2017). See wir2018.wid.world for data series and notes.

From 1980 to 2016, the Middle 40% in Europe captured 38% of total income growth in the region. Income estimates are calculated using 2016 Purchasing Power Parity (PPP) euros. PPP accounts for differences in the cost of living between countries. Values are net of inflation.

about as much growth as the bottom half of the world population. Therefore, the income growth captured by very top global earners since 1980 was very large, even if demographically they are a very small group.

Building a global inequality distribution brick by brick

A powerful way to visualize the evolution of global income inequality dynamics is to plot the total growth rate of each income group (Box 2.2). This provides a more precise representation of growth dynamics than Table 2.1. To properly understand the role played by each region in global inequality dynamics, we follow a step-by-step approach to construct this global growth curve by adding one region after another and discussing each step of the exercise.

We start with the distribution of growth in a region regrouping Europe and North America (Figure 2.2). These two regions have a total of 880 million individuals in 2016 (520 million in Europe and 360 million in North America) and represent most of the population of high-income countries. In Euro-America, cumulative per-adult income growth over the 1980–2016 period was +28%, which is relatively low as compared to the global average (+66%). While the bottom 10% income group saw their income decrease over the period, all individuals between percentile 20 and percentile 80 had a growth rate close to the average growth rate. At the very top of the distribution, incomes grew very rapidly; individuals

Box 2.2 Interpreting inequality graphs in this report

Total growth curves (or "growth incidence curves") shed light on the income growth rate of each income group in a given country or at the world level. The popularization of such graphs is largely due to their use by Christoph Lakner and Branko Milanovic. In this report we are able to provide novel insights on global income dynamics thanks to the new inequality series constructed in WID.world (as detailed in Part 1). In particular, we are able to decompose the top 1% of the global distribution into smaller groups and observe their relative importance in total growth. If anything, our general conclusion is that the "elephant curve" is even more marked than what was initially pointed out by Lakner and Milanovic.

How to interpret these graphs? The horizontal axis sorts global income groups in ascending order from the poorest (left-hand side) to the richest (right-hand side). The first ninety-nine brackets correspond to each of the bottom ninety-nine percentiles of the global population. Each bracket represents 1% of the global population and occupies the same length on the graph. The global top 1% group is not represented on the same scale as the bottom 99%. We split it into twenty-eight smaller groups in the following way. The group is first split into ten groups of equal size (representing each 0.1% of the population). The richest of these groups is then itself split into ten groups of equal size (each representing 0.01% of the global population). The richest of these groups is again split into ten groups of equal size. The richest group represented on the horizontal axis (group 99.999) thus corresponds to the top 0.001% richest individuals in the world. This represents 49 000 individuals in 2016.

Each of these twenty-eight groups comprising the top 1% earners occupies the same space as percentiles of the bottom 99%. This is a simple way to represent clearly the importance of these groups in total income

growth. The global top 1% group captured 27% of total growth from 1980 to 2016—that is, about a quarter of total growth. On the horizontal axis, this group occupies about a quarter of the scale.

There are other ways to scale percentiles on the horizontal axis. Appendices A2.1 and A2.2 show two variants. In the first, each group occupies a space that is proportional to its population size; in effect, the 28 groups decomposing the top 1% are squeezed together. In the other, each group is given a segment that is proportional to its share of total growth captured. In this case, it is the groups at the bottom of the global distribution that are squeezed. Our benchmark representation is a combination of these two variants.

The vertical axis presents the total real pre-tax income growth rate for each of the 127 groups defined above. Real income means that incomes are corrected for inflation. "Pre-tax" refers to incomes before taxes and transfers (but after the operation of the pension system). Note that the values are presented as total growth rates over the period rather than as annualized growth rates, which are perhaps somewhat more common in economic debates. Over long time spans such as the 1980–2016 period analyzed here, it is generally more meaningful to discuss total growth rates than to discuss average annual growth rates. Because of the multiplicative power of growth rates, small differences in annualized growth rates lead to large differences in total growth rates over long time spans. To illustrate this, let us take two income groups whose incomes grow at 4% and 5% over thirty-five years, respectively. The first group does not grow as fast as the second one, but the difference may seem limited. In fact, over thirty-five years, the total income growth is 295% in the first case and 452% in the second, which indeed represents a substantial difference in terms of purchasing power and standards of living.

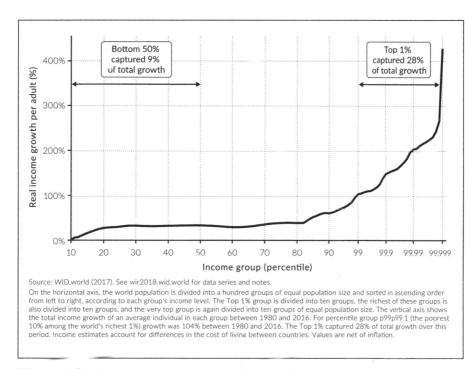

Source: WID.world (2017). See wir2018.wid.world for data series and notes.

On the horizontal axis, the world population is divided into a hundred groups of equal population size and sorted in ascending order from left to right, according to each group's income level. The Top 1% group is divided into ten groups, the richest of these groups is also divided into ten groups, and the very top group is again divided into ten groups of equal population size. The vertical axis shows the total income growth of an average individual in each group between 1980 and 2016. For percentile group p99p99.1 (the poorest 10% among the world's richest 1%) growth was 104% between 1980 and 2016. The Top 1% captured 28% of total growth over this period. Income estimates account for differences in the cost of living between countries. Values are net of inflation.

Figure 2.2 Total income growth by percentile in US-Canada and Western Europe, 1980–2016

in the top 1% group saw their incomes rise by more than 100% over the time period and those in the top 0.01% and above grew at more than 200%.

How did this translate into shares of growth captured by different groups? The top 1% of earners captured 28% of total growth—that is, as much growth as the bottom 81% of the population. The bottom 50% earners captured 9% of growth, which is less than the top 0.1%, which captured 14% of total growth over the 1980–2016 period. These values, however, hide large differences in the inequality trajectories followed by Europe and North America. In the former, the top 1% captured as much growth as the bottom 51% of the population, whereas in the latter, the top 1% captured as much growth as the bottom 88% of the population. (See Chapter 4 for more details.)

The next step is to add the population of India and China to the distribution of Euro-America. The global region now considered represents 3.5 billion individuals in total (including 1.4 billion individuals from China and 1.3 billion from India). Adding India and China remarkably modifies the shape of the global growth curve (Figure 2.3).

The first half of the distribution is now marked by a "rising tide" as total income growth rates increase substantially from the bottom of the distribution

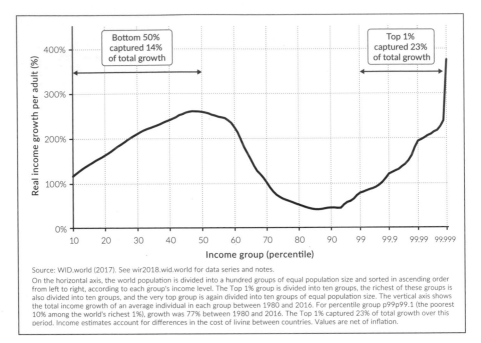

Figure 2.3 Total income growth by percentile in China, India, US-Canada, and Western Europe, 1980–2016

to the middle. The bottom half of the population records growth rates which go as high as 260%, largely above the global average income growth of 146%. This is due to the fact that Chinese and Indians, who make up the bulk of the bottom half of this global distribution, enjoyed much higher growth rates than their European and North American counterparts. In addition, growth was also very unequally distributed in India and China, as revealed by Table 2.1.

Between percentiles 70 and 99 (individuals above the poorest 70% of the population but below the richest 1%), income growth was substantially lower than the global average, reaching only 40–50%. This corresponds to the lower- and middle-income groups in rich countries which grew at a very low rate. The extreme case of these is the bottom half of the population in the United States, which grew at only 3% over the period considered. (See Chapter 5.)

Earlier versions of this graph have been termed "the elephant curve," as the shape of the curve resembles the silhouette of the animal. These new findings confirm and amplify earlier results.[2] In particular they make it possible to measure much more reliably the share of income growth captured at the top of the global income distribution—a figure which couldn't be properly measured before.

At the top of the global distribution, incomes grew extremely rapidly—around 200% for the top 0.01% and above 360% for the top 0.001%. Not only were these growth rates important from the perspective of individuals, they also matter a lot in terms of global growth. The top 1% captured 23% of total growth over the period—that is, as much as the bottom 61% of the population. Such figures help make sense of the very high growth rates enjoyed by Indians and Chinese sitting at the bottom of the distribution. Whereas growth rates were substantial among the global bottom 50%, this group captured only 14% of total growth, just slightly more than the global top 0.1%—which captured 12% of total growth. Such a small share of total growth captured by the bottom half of the population is partly due to the fact that when individuals are very poor, their incomes can double or triple but still remain relatively small—so that the total increase in their incomes does not necessarily add up at the global level. But this is not the only explanation. Incomes at the very top must also be extraordinarily high to dwarf the growth captured by the bottom half of the world population.

The next step of the exercise consists of adding the populations and incomes of Russia (140 million), Brazil (210 million), and the Middle East (410 million) to the analysis. These additional groups bring the total population now considered to more than 4.3 billion individuals—that is, close to 60% of the world total population and two thirds of the world adult population. The global growth curve presented in Appendix Figure A2 is similar to the previous one except that the "body of the elephant" is now shorter. This can be explained by the fact that Russia, the Middle East, and Brazil are three regions which recorded low growth rates over the period considered. Adding the population of the three regions also slightly shifts the "body of the elephant" to the left, since a large share of the population of the countries incorporated in the analysis is neither very poor nor very rich from a global point of view and thus falls in the middle of the distribution. In this synthetic global region, the top 1% earners captured 26% of total growth over the 1980–2016 period—that is, as much as the bottom 65% of the population. The bottom 50% captured 15% of total growth, more than the top 0.1%, which captured 12% of growth.

The final step consists of including all remaining global regions— namely, Africa (close to 1 billion individuals), the rest of Asia (another billion individuals), and the rest of Latin America (close to half a billion). In order to reconstruct income inequality dynamics in these regions, we take into account between-country inequality, for which information is available, and assume that within countries, growth is distributed in the same way as neighboring countries for which we have specific information (see Box 2.1). This allows us to distribute the totality of global income growth over the period considered to the global population.

When all countries are taken into account, the shape of the curve is again transformed (Figure 2.4). Now, average global income growth rates are further

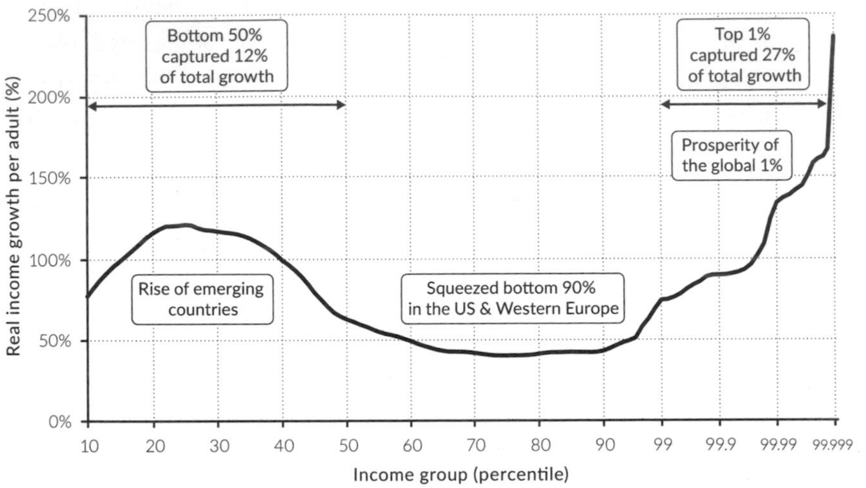

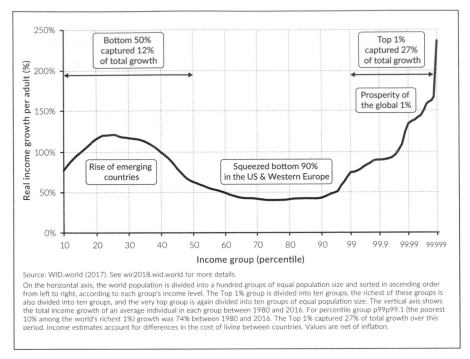

Source: WID.world (2017). See wir2018.wid.world for more details.
On the horizontal axis, the world population is divided into a hundred groups of equal population size and sorted in ascending order from left to right, according to each group's income level. The Top 1% group is divided into ten groups, the richest of these groups is also divided into ten groups, and the very top group is again divided into ten groups of equal population size. The vertical axis shows the total income growth of an average individual in each group between 1980 and 2016. For percentile group p99p99.1 (the poorest 10% among the world's richest 1%) growth was 74% between 1980 and 2016. The Top 1% captured 27% of total growth over this period. Income estimates account for differences in the cost of living between countries. Values are net of inflation.

Figure 2.4 Total income growth by percentile across all world regions, 1980–2016

reduced because Africa and Latin America had relatively low growth over the period considered. This contributes to increasing global inequality as compared to the two cases presented above. The findings are the same as those presented in the right-hand column of Table 2.2: the top 1% income earners captured 27% of total growth over the 1980–2016 period, as much as the bottom 70% of the population. The top 0.1% captured 13% of total growth, about as much as the bottom 50%.

The geography of global income inequality was transformed over the past decades

What is the share of African, Asians, Americans, and Europeans in each global income groups and how has this evolved over time? Figures 2.5 and 2.6 answer these questions by showing the geographical composition of each income group in 1990 and in 2016. Between 1980 and 1990, the geographic repartition of global incomes evolved only slightly, and our data allow for more precise geographic repartition in 1990, so it is preferable to focus on this year. In a similar way to how Figures 2.2 through 2.4 decomposed the data, Figures 2.5 and 2.6 decompose

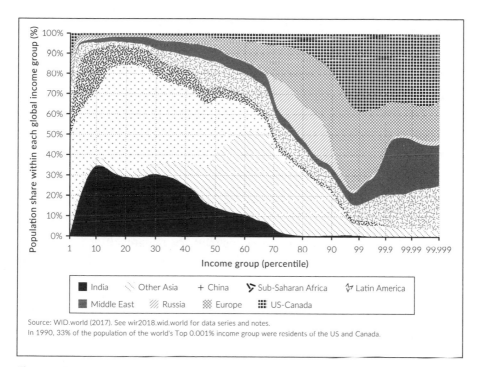

Source: WID.world (2017). See wir2018.wid.world for data series and notes.
In 1990, 33% of the population of the world's Top 0.001% income group were residents of the US and Canada.

Figure 2.5 Geographic breakdown of global income groups in 1990

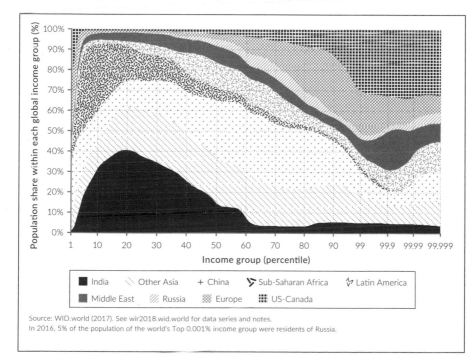

Source: WID.world (2017). See wir2018.wid.world for data series and notes.
In 2016, 5% of the population of the world's Top 0.001% income group were residents of Russia.

Figure 2.6 Geographic breakdown of global income groups in 2016

the top 1% into 28 groups (see Box 2.1). To be clear, all groups above percentile 99 are the decomposition of the richest 1% of the global population.

In 1990, Asians were almost not represented within top global income groups. Indeed, the bulk of the population of India and China are found in the bottom half of the income distribution. At the other end of the global income ladder, US-Canada is the largest contributor to global top-income earners. Europe is largely represented in the upper half of the global distribution, but less so among the very top groups. The Middle East and Latin American elites are dispropor-tionately represented among the very top global groups, as they both make up about 20% each of the population of the top 0.001% earners. It should be noted that this overrepresentation only holds within the top 1% global earners: in the next richest 1% group (percentile group p98p99), their share falls to 9% and 4%, respectively. This indeed reflects the extreme level of inequality of these regions, as discussed in Chapters 11 and 12. Interestingly, Russia is concentrated between percentile 70 and percentile 90, and Russians did not make it into the very top groups. In 1990, the Soviet system compressed income distribution in Russia.

In 2016, the situation is notably different. The most striking evolution is perhaps the spread of Chinese income earners, which are now located through-out the entire global distribution. India remains largely represented at the bottom with only very few Indians among the top global earners.

The position of Russian earners was also stretched throughout from the poor-est to the richest income groups. This illustrates the impact of the end of communism on the spread of Russian incomes. Africans, who were present throughout the first half of the distribution, are now even more concentrated in the bottom quarter, due to relatively low growth as compared to Asian countries. At the top of the distribution, while the shares of both North America and Europe decreased (leaving room for their Asian counterparts), the share of Europeans was reduced much more. This is because most large European countries followed a more equitable growth trajectory over the past decades than the United States and other countries, as will be discussed in Chapter 4.

Since 2000, the picture is more nuanced but within-country inequality is on the rise

How did global inequality evolve between 1980 and 2016? Figure 2.7 answers this question by presenting the share of world income held by the global top 1% and the global bottom 50%, measured at purchasing power parity. The global top 1% income share rose from about 16% of global income in 1980 to more than 22% in

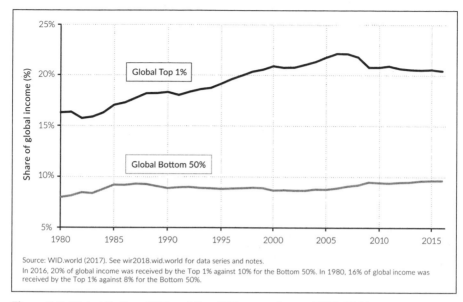

Source: WID.world (2017). See wir2018.wid.world for data series and notes.
In 2016, 20% of global income was received by the Top 1% against 10% for the Bottom 50%. In 1980, 16% of global income was received by the Top 1% against 8% for the Bottom 50%.

Figure 2.7 Global Bottom 50% and Top 1% income shares, 1980–2016

2007 at the eve of the global financial crisis. It was then slightly reduced to 20.4% in 2016, but this slight decrease hardly brought back the level of global inequality to its 1980 level. The income share of the bottom half of the world population oscillated around 9% with a very slight increase between 1985 and 2016.

The first insight of this graph is the extreme level of global inequality sustained throughout the entire period with a top 1% income group capturing two times the total income captured by the bottom 50% of the population—implying a factor 100 difference in average per-adult income levels. Second, it is apparent that high growth in emerging countries since 2000, in particular in China, or the global financial crisis of 2008 was not sufficient to stop the rise in global income inequality.

When global inequality is decomposed into a between- and within-country inequality component, it is apparent that within-country inequality continued to rise since 2000 whereas between-country inequality rose up to 2000 and decreased afterwards. Figure 2.8 presents the evolution of the global 10% income share, which reached close to 50% of global income in 1980, rose to 55% in 2000–2007, and decreased to slightly more than 52% in 2016. Two alternative scenarios for the evolution of the global top 10% share are presented. The first one assumes that all countries had exactly the same average income (that is, that there was no between-country inequality), but that income was as unequal within these countries as was actually observed. In this case, the top 10% share would have risen from 35% in 1980 to nearly 50% today. In the second scenario, it is

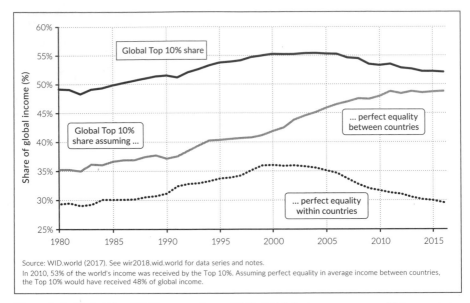

Source: WID.world (2017). See wir2018.wid.world for data series and notes.
In 2010, 53% of the world's income was received by the Top 10%. Assuming perfect equality in average income between countries, the Top 10% would have received 48% of global income.

Figure 2.8 Global Top 10% income share, 1980–2016: between versus within country inequality

assumed that between-country inequality evolved as observed but it is also assumed that everybody within countries had exactly the same income level (no within-country inequality). In this case, the global top 10% income share would have risen from nearly 30% in 1980 to more than 35% in 2000 before decreasing back to 30%.

Measured at market exchange rate, global inequality is even higher

Prices can be converted from one currency to another using either market exchange rates or purchasing power parities (as we did above). Market Exchange Rates are the prices at which people are willing to buy and sell currencies, so at first glance they should reflect people's relative purchasing power. This makes them a natural conversion factor between currencies. The problem is that Market Exchange Rates reflect only the relative purchasing power of money in terms of tradable goods. But non-tradable goods (typically services) are in fact cheaper relative to tradable ones in emerging economies (given the so-called Balassa-Samuelson effect). Therefore, Market Exchange Rates will underestimate the standard of living in the poorer countries. In addition, Market Exchange Rates can vary for all sorts of other reasons—sometimes purely financial and/or political—in a fairly chaotic manner. Purchasing Power Parity is an alternative conversion factor

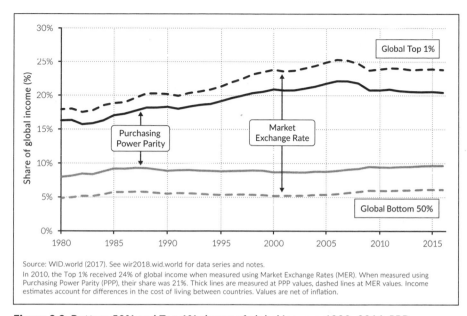

Source: WID.world (2017). See wir2018.wid.world for data series and notes.
In 2010, the Top 1% received 24% of global income when measured using Market Exchange Rates (MER). When measured using Purchasing Power Parity (PPP), their share was 21%. Thick lines are measured at PPP values, dashed lines at MER values. Income estimates account for differences in the cost of living between countries. Values are net of inflation.

Figure 2.9 Bottom 50% and Top 1% shares of global income, 1980–2016: PPP versus market exchange rates

that addresses these problems (based on observed prices in the various countries). The level of global income inequality is therefore substantially higher when measured using Market Exchange Rates than it is with Purchasing Power Parity. It increases the global top 1% share in 2016 from 20% to 24% and reduces the bottom 50% share from nearly 10% to 6% (Figure 2.9).

Purchasing Power Parity definitely gives a more accurate picture of global inequality from the point of view of individuals who do not travel across the world and who essentially spend their incomes in their own countries. Market Exchange Rates are perhaps better to inform about inequality in a world where individuals can easily spend their incomes where they want, which is the case for top global earners and tourists, and increasingly the case for anyone connected to the internet. It is also the case for migrant workers wishing to send remittances back to their home countries. Both Purchasing Power Parity and Market Exchange Rates are valid measures to track global income inequality, depending on the object of study or which countries are compared to one another.

In this report, we generally use Purchasing Power Parity for international comparisons, but at times, Market Exchange Rates are also used to illustrate other meaningful aspects of international inequality.

Carefully looking at countries' diverse growth trajectories and policy changes is necessary to understand drivers of national and global inequality

The past forty years were marked by a steep rise of global inequality, and growth in emerging countries was not high enough to counterbalance it. Whether future growth in emerging countries might invert the trend or not is a key question, which will be addressed in Part V of this report. Before turning to that question, one should understand better the drivers of the trends observed since 1980.

Given that this period was marked by increasing trade integration between countries, it might seem reasonable to seek explanations in economic trade models. The standard economic models of international trade, however, fail to account for dynamics of inequality observed over the past four decades. Take Heckscher-Ohlin, the most well-known of the two-skill-groups economic trade models. According to it, trade liberalization should increase inequality in rich countries, but reduce it in low-income countries.

How does the model reach this conclusion? The underlying mechanism is fairly simple. It is built around the fact that there are more high-skilled workers (such as aeronautical engineers) in the United States than in China, and more low-skilled workers (such as textile workers) in China than in the United States. Before trade liberalization started between these two countries, aeronautical engineers were relatively scarce in China and thus enjoyed relatively high pay compared to textile workers, which were abundant. Conversely, in the United States, low-skilled earners were relatively scarce at the time, and the income differential between engineers and textile workers was limited.

When the United States and China started to trade, each country specialized in the domain for which they had the most workers, in relative terms. China thus specialized in textiles, so that textile workers were in higher demand and saw their wages increase, while aeronautical engineers came to be in lower demand and saw their wages decrease. Conversely, the United States specialized in aircraft building, so the aeronautical engineers saw their wages increase, while the textile workers saw their wages decrease. By virtue of the factor price equalization theorem, the wages of low-skilled workers in China and the United States started to converge, along with the wages of high-skilled workers.

While inequality did rise in the United States, as this model predicts, it also sharply rose in China, as well as in India and Russia, as seen in Figure 2.1a—contrary to the model's predictions. Regardless of whether the Heckscher-Ohlin is otherwise valid or not, it cannot account for the evolution of global inequality. How can we account for these empirical findings? As Table 2.1 suggests, countries followed very different growth and inequality trajectories over the past decades.

It seems necessary to carefully look at these trajectories as well as the institutional and policy shifts which may have occurred in various regions of the world over the past forty years.

Understanding the drivers of global income inequality requires a thorough analysis of the distribution of national income growth within countries. These dynamics are explored in the following chapters.

3

Trends in Income Inequality
Between Countries

Information in this chapter is based on "National Accounts Series Methodology," by Thomas Blanchet and Lucas Chancel, 2016. WID.world Working Paper Series (No. 2016/1) and on subsequent WID.world updates.

- When focusing on income inequalities between countries, it is more meaningful to compare national incomes than gross domestic product (GDP). National income takes into account depreciation of obsolete machines and other capital assets as well as flows of foreign income.

- At the global level, average per-adult national income is €1 340 per month. North Americans enjoy an income three times higher, while Europeans have an income two times higher. Average per-adult income in China is slightly lower than the global average. As a country, however, China represents a higher share of global income than North America or Europe (19%, 17%, and 17%, respectively).

- This situation sharply contrasts with that of 1980, when China represented only 3% of total global income. Over this period, strong converging forces were in play which reduced global income inequality between countries. While growth slowed in Western Europe, it skyrocketed in Asia and China in particular, following the modernization of its economy and its opening to global markets.

- However, diverging forces were also in play in other parts of the world. From 1980 to now, average incomes in sub-Saharan Africa and South America fell behind the world average.

National income is more meaningful than GDP to compare income inequalities between countries

Public debates generally focus on the growth of gross domestic product (GDP) to compare countries' economic performance. However, this measure is of only limited use in measuring national welfare. GDP measures the value of all goods and services sold in an economy, after having subtracted the costs of materials or services incurred in production processes. As such, it does not properly account for capital depreciation, or for public "bads" such as environmental degradation, rising crime, or illnesses (because these lead to expenditures that contribute to GDP). These limitations have led many statistical agencies, and a growing number of governments, to develop and use complementary indicators of economic performance and well-being.[3]

Beyond the fact that the GDP framework is not meant for the analysis of inequality within countries, it has two other important limitations when the focus is on income inequality between countries. The first one is that gross domestic product, as its name indicates, is a gross measure: it does not take into account expenses required to replace capital that has been deteriorated or that has become obsolete during the course of production of goods and services in an economy. Machines, computers, roads, and electric systems have to be repaired or replaced every year. This has been termed capital depreciation or consumption of fixed capital (CFC). Subtracting it from GDP yields the net domestic product, which is a more accurate measure of true economic output than GDP. Consumption of fixed capital actually varies over time and countries (Table 3.1). Countries that have an important stock of machines in their overall stock of capital tend to replace higher shares of overall capital. This is generally true for advanced and automatized economies—in particular, for Japan, where consumption of fixed capital is equal to 21% of its GDP (which reduces GDP by close to €8 000 per year and per adult). Consumption of fixed capital is also high in the European Union and the United States (16–17%). On the contrary, economies that possess relatively fewer machines and a higher share of agricultural land in their capital stock tend to have lower CFC values. CFC is equal to 11% of GDP in India, and 12% in Latin America. CFC variations thus modify the levels of global inequality between countries. Such variations tend to reduce global inequality, since the income dedicated to replacing obsolete machines tends to be higher in rich countries than in low-income countries. In the future, we plan to better account for the depreciation of natural capital in these estimates.

GDP figures have another important limitation when the need is to compare income inequality between countries and over time. At the global level, net

Table 3.1 The distribution of world national income and gross domestic product, 2016: Purchasing Power Parity

	Population (million)				GDP (trillion 2016 € PPP)	CFC (% of GDP)	NFI (% of GDP)	National Income (trillion 2016 € PPP)		Per adult National Income (2016 € PPP)	Equivalent per adult monthly income (2016 € PPP)
	Total		Adult								
World	7372	100%	4867	100%	92	14%	-0.5%	78	100%	16100	1340
Europe	747	10%	593	12%	19	15%	-0.6%	16	20%	27100	2260
incl. European Union	523	7%	417	9%	16	17%	-0.2%	13	17%	31400	2620
incl. Russia/ Ukraine	223	3%	176	4%	3	9%	-2.5%	3	4%	16800	1400
America	962	13%	661	14%	23	15%	-0.2%	19	25%	29500	2460
incl. United States/Canada	360	5%	263	5%	16	16%	0.9%	13	17%	50700	4230
incl. Latin America	602	8%	398	8%	7	12%	-2.5%	6	8%	15400	1280
Africa	1214	16%	592	12%	4	10%	-2.1%	4	5%	6600	550
incl. North Africa	240	3%	140	3%	2	9%	-1.7%	2	2%	11400	950
incl. Sub-Saharan Africa	974	13%	452	9%	3	11%	-2.3%	2	3%	5100	430
Asia	4410	60%	2994	62%	44	14%	-0.4%	38	49%	12700	1060
incl. China	1382	19%	1067	22%	18	14%	-0.7%	15	19%	14000	1170
incl. India	1327	18%	826	17%	7	11%	-1.2%	6	7%	7000	580
incl. Japan	126	2%	105	2%	4	21%	3.5%	3	4%	31000	2580
incl. Other	1575	21%	995	20%	16	13%	-0.7%	14	18%	14200	1180
Oceania	39	1%	27	1%	1	16%	-1.5%	1	1%	31700	2640
incl. Australia and NZ	29	0.4%	21	0.4%	1	16%	-1.5%	1	1%	38200	3180
incl. Other	10	0.1%	5	0.1%	0.03	7%	-2.4%	0.03	0%	5600	470

Source: WID.world (2017). See wir2018.wid.world for data series and notes.

In 2016, Europe represented 20% of world income measured using Purchasing Power Parity. Europe also represented 12% of the world's adult population and 10% of the world's total population. GDP: Gross Domestic Product. CFC: Consumption of Fixed Capital. NFI: Net Foreign Income. PPP: Purchasing Power Parity. All values have been converted into 2016 Purchasing Power Parity (PPP) euros at a rate of €1 = $1.3 = ¥4.4. PPP accounts for differences in the cost of living between countries. Values are net of inflation. Numbers may not add up due to rounding.

domestic product is equal to net domestic income: by definition, the market value of global production is equal to global income. At the national level, however, incomes generated by the sale of goods and services in a given country do not necessarily remain in that country. This is the case when factories are owned by foreign individuals, for instance. Taking foreign incomes into account tends to increase global inequality between countries rather than reduce it. Rich countries generally own more assets in other parts of the world than poor countries do. Table 3.1 shows that net foreign income in North America amounts to 0.9% of its GDP (which corresponds to an extra €610 or $670) received by the average North American adult from the rest of the world.[4] Meanwhile, Japan's net foreign income is equal to 3.5% of its GDP (corresponding to €1 460 per year and per adult). Net foreign income within the European Union is slightly negative when measured at PPP values (Table 3.1) and very slightly positive when measured at Market Exchange Rates values (Table 3.2). This figure in fact hides strong disparities within the European Union. France and Germany have strongly positive net foreign income (2 to 3% of their GDP), while Ireland and the United Kingdom have negative net foreign incomes (this is largely due to the financial services and foreign companies established there). On the other hand, Latin America annually pays 2.4% of its GDP to the rest of the world. Interestingly, China has a negative net foreign income. It pays close to 0.7% of its GDP to foreign countries, reflecting the fact that the return it receives on its foreign portfolio is lower than the return received by foreign investments in China.

By definition, at the global level, net foreign income should equal zero: what is paid by some countries must be received by others. However, up to now, international statistical institutions have been unable to report flows of net foreign incomes consistently. At the global level, the sum of reported net foreign incomes has not been zero. This has been termed the "missing income" problem: a share of total income vanishes from global economic statistics, implying non-zero net foreign income at the global level.

The *World Inequality Report 2018* relies on a novel methodology which takes income flows from tax havens into account. Our methodology relies on estimations of offshore wealth measured by Gabriel Zucman.[5] It should be noted that, when measured at Market Exchange Rates, net foreign income flows should sum to zero (Table 3.2), but there is no reason for this to happen when incomes are measured at Purchasing Power Parity (Table 3.1). Taking into account missing net foreign incomes does not radically change global inequality figures but can make a large difference for particular countries. This constitutes a more realistic representation of income inequality between countries than figures generally discussed.

Table 3.2 The distribution of world national income and gross domestic product, 2016: Market Exchange Rates

	Population (million)				GDP (trillion 2016€ MER)	CFC (% of GDP)	NFI (% of GDP)	National Income (trillion 2016€ MER)		Per adult National Income (2016€ MER)	Equivalent per adult monthly income (2016€ MER)
	Total		Adult								
World	7372	**100%**	4867	**100%**	68	15%	0%	58	**100%**	11800	980
Europe	747	**10%**	593	**12%**	17	16%	-0.2%	14	**24%**	23800	1980
incl. European Union	523	**7%**	417	**9%**	16	17%	0.04%	13	**23%**	31100	2590
incl. Russia/Ukraine	223	**3%**	176	**4%**	1	9%	-2.5%	1	**2%**	6500	540
America	962	**13%**	661	**14%**	23	15%	0.2%	19	**34%**	29400	2450
incl. United States/Canada	360	**5%**	263	**5%**	18	16%	0.9%	16	**27%**	59500	4960
incl. Latin America	602	**8%**	398	**8%**	4	12%	-2.4%	4	**7%**	9600	800
Africa	1214	**16%**	592	**12%**	2	10%	-2.0%	2	**3%**	2900	240
incl. North Africa	240	**3%**	140	**3%**	1	9%	-1.5%	1	**1%**	4300	360
incl. Sub-Saharan Africa	974	**13%**	452	**9%**	1	11%	-2.2%	1	**2%**	2500	210
Asia	4410	**60%**	2994	**62%**	25	15%	0.1%	21	**37%**	7100	590
incl. China	1382	**19%**	1067	**22%**	10	14%	-0.7%	9	**15%**	8300	690
incl. India	1327	**18%**	826	**17%**	2	11%	-1.2%	2	**3%**	2200	180
incl. Japan	126	**2%**	105	**2%**	4	23%	3.5%	4	**6%**	34400	2870
incl. Other	1575	**21%**	995	**20%**	8	14%	-0.5%	7	**12%**	7000	580
Oceania	39	**1%**	27	**1%**	1	18%	-1.9%	1	**2%**	38800	3230
incl. Australia and NZ	29	**0.4%**	21	**0.4%**	1	18%	-1.9%	1	**2%**	47500	3960
incl. Other	10	**0.1%**	5	**0.1%**	0.03	7%	-2.4%	0.02	**0%**	4300	360

Source: WID.world (2017). See wir2018.wid.world for data series and notes.

In 2016, Europe represented 24% of world income measured using Market Exchange Rates. Europe also represented 12% of the world's adult population and 10% of the world's total population. GDP: Gross Domestic Product. CFC: Consumption of Fixed Capital. NFI: Net Foreign Income. MER: Market Exchange Rate. All values have been converted into 2016 Market Exchange Rate euros at a rate of €1 = $1.1 = ¥7.3. Figures take into account inflation. Numbers may not add up due to rounding.

Asian growth contributed to reduce inequality between countries over the past decades

At the global level, per-adult monthly income in 2016 is €1 340 ($1 740) at Purchasing Power Parity (PPP) and €980 ($1 090) at Market Exchange Rates (MER). As discussed, PPP and MER are different ways to measure incomes and inequality across countries. Whereas MER reflects market prices, PPP aims to take price differences between countries into account.

National income is about three times higher in North America at PPP (€4230 or $5500 per adult per month) than the global average and it is two times higher in the European Union at PPP than the global average (€2620 or $3410 per adult per month). Using MER values, gaps between rich countries and the global average are reinforced: United States and Canada are five times richer than the world average whereas the EU is close to three times richer.[6] In China, per-adult income is €1 170 or $1 520 at PPP—that is, slightly lower than world average (€1 340 or $1 740). China as a whole represents 19% of today's global income. This figure is higher than North America (17%) and the European Union (17%). Measured at MER, the Chinese average is, however, equal to €690 or $760, notably lower than the world average (€980 or $1080). The Chinese share of global income is reduced to 15% versus 27% for US-Canada and 23% for the EU.

This marks a sharp contrast with the situation in 1980. Thirty-eight years ago, China represented only 3% of global income versus 20% for US-Canada and 28% for the European Union (at Purchasing Power Parity estimates: Table 3.3). Indeed, China's impressive real per-adult national income growth rate over the period (831% from 1980 to 2016, versus 114% from 1950 to 1980: Table 3.4) highly contributed to reducing between-country inequalities over the world. Another converging force lies in the reduction of income growth rates in Western Europe, as compared to the previous decades (180% per-adult growth between 1950 and 1980 versus 45% afterward). This deceleration in growth rates was due to the end of the "golden age" of growth in Western Europe but also due to the Great Recession, which led to a decade of lost growth in Europe. Indeed, per-adult income in Western Europe was in 2016 the same as ten years before, before the onset of the financial crisis.

Despite a reduction of inequality between countries, average national income inequalities remain strong among countries. Developing and emerging countries did not all grow at the same rate as China. India's average monthly per-adult income (€580 or $750) is still only 0.4 times the world average measured at PPP, while sub-Saharan Africa is only 0.3 times the world average (€430 or $560) today.

Table 3.3 The distribution of world national income and gross domestic product, 1980: Purchasing Power Parity

	Population *(million)*				GDP *(trillion € PPP 2016)*	CFC *(% of GDP)*	NFI *(% of GDP)*	National Income *(trillion 2016 € PPP)*		Per adult National Income *(2016 € PPP)*	Equivalent per adult monthly income *(2016 € PPP)*
	Total		Adult								
World	4 389	**100%**	2 400	**100%**	28	13%	-0.2%	25	**100%**	10 500	880
Europe	673	**15%**	470	**20%**	11	14%	-0.1%	9	**37%**	20 000	1 670
incl. European Union	469	**11%**	328	**14%**	8	14%	-0.2%	7	**28%**	21 600	1 800
incl. Russia/ Ukraine	204	**5%**	142	**6%**	3	17%	0.0%	2	**9%**	16 200	1 350
America	598	**14%**	343	**14%**	9	14%	-0.4%	7	**30%**	21 700	1 810
incl. United States/Canada	252	**6%**	172	**7%**	6	15%	0.9%	5	**20%**	29 600	2 470
incl. Latin America	346	**8%**	172	**7%**	3	11%	-3.0%	2	**9%**	13 800	1 150
Africa	477	**11%**	215	**9%**	1.3	10%	-1.9%	1	**5%**	5 500	460
incl. North Africa	111	**3%**	51	**2%**	0.5	10%	-2.1%	0.5	**2%**	9 200	770
incl. Sub-Saharan Africa	365	**8%**	163	**7%**	0.8	10%	-1.8%	1	**3%**	4 332	360
Asia	2 619	**60%**	1 359	**57%**	7.1	12%	0.2%	7	**27%**	5 000	420
incl. China	987	**22%**	532	**22%**	0.9	11%	0.0%	1	**3%**	1 500	130
incl. India	697	**16%**	351	**15%**	0.8	7%	0.6%	1	**3%**	2 200	180
incl. Japan	117	**3%**	81	**3%**	1.9	17%	0.0%	2	**6%**	19 900	1 660
incl. Other	817	**19%**	394	**16%**	3.4	10%	0.4%	4	**15%**	9 300	780
Oceania	22	**1%**	14	**1%**	0.4	15%	-1.6%	0.3	**1%**	21 300	1 780
incl. Australia and NZ	18	**0.4%**	12	**0.5%**	0.3	16%	-1.5%	0.3	**1%**	24 200	2 020
incl. Other	5	**0.1%**	2	**0.1%**	0.0	7%	-4.2%	0.0	**0%**	4 400	370

Source: WID.world (2017). See wir2018.wid.world for data series and notes.

In 1980, Europe represented 37% of world income measured using Purchasing Power Parity. Europe also represented 20% of the world's adult population and 15% of the world's total population. GDP: Gross Domestic Product. CFC: Consumption of Fixed Capital. NFI: Net Foreign Income. PPP: Purchasing Power Parity. All values have been converted into 2016 Purchasing Power Parity (PPP) euros at a rate of €1 = $1.3 = ¥4.4. PPP accounts for differences in the cost of living between countries. Values are net of inflation. Numbers may not add up due to rounding.

Table 3.4 Total national income growth rates by world region, 1950–2016

	National Income		National Income per capita		National Income per adult	
	1950–1980	1980–2016	1950–1980	1980–2016	1950–1980	1980–2016
World	282%	226%	116%	85%	122%	54%
Europe	256%	79%	181%	54%	165%	36%
incl. European Union	259%	94%	192%	66%	180%	45%
incl. Russia/ Ukraine	249%	31%	156%	18%	129%	4%
America	227%	163%	78%	62%	80%	36%
incl. United States/ Canada	187%	164%	89%	84%	82%	71%
incl. Latin America	365%	161%	116%	49%	117%	12%
Africa	258%	233%	72%	30%	85%	20%
incl. North Africa	394%	235%	130%	58%	148%	24%
incl. Sub-Saharan Africa	203%	232%	46%	22%	58%	10%
Asia	446%	527%	188%	230%	198%	152%
incl. China	273%	1864%	106%	1237%	114%	831%
incl. India	199%	711%	61%	299%	67%	223%
incl. Japan	740%	103%	504%	86%	372%	56%
incl. Other	518%	376%	187%	99%	203%	52%
Oceania	208%	194%	38%	69%	50%	49%
incl. Australia and NZ	199%	193%	69%	81%	71%	58%

Source: WID.world (2017). See wir2018.wid.world for data series and notes.

Between 1950 and 1980, Africa's income grew by 258%, whereas income per adult grew by only 85% during the same period. Income estimates account for differences in the cost of living between countries. Values are net of inflation.

Average North Americans earn close to ten times more than average sub-Saharan Africans.

Diverging forces were also at play in certain parts of the world, such as sub-Saharan Africa and Latin America

Huge inequalities persist among countries but, in some cases, they actually worsened. Certain low- to middle-income regions are relatively worse off today than four decades ago. Between 1980 and 2016, per-adult incomes in Africa grew more slowly (18%) than the world's average per-adult incomes (54%). This growth trend, marked by a combination of political and economic crises and wars, is not limited to the poorest region of the world. In South America, as well, incomes have grown by only 12% since 1980. As a result, these regions' average incomes fell relative to the world average, from 65% to only 40% of the world average in 1950, versus 140% to less than 100% in Latin America (Figures 3.1 and 3.2).

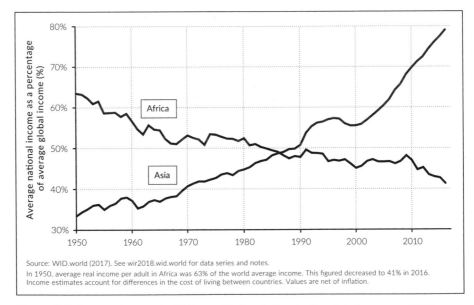

Source: WID.world (2017). See wir2018.wid.world for data series and notes.
In 1950, average real income per adult in Africa was 63% of the world average income. This figured decreased to 41% in 2016. Income estimates account for differences in the cost of living between countries. Values are net of inflation.

Figure 3.1 Average income in Africa and Asia relative to the global average, 1950–2016

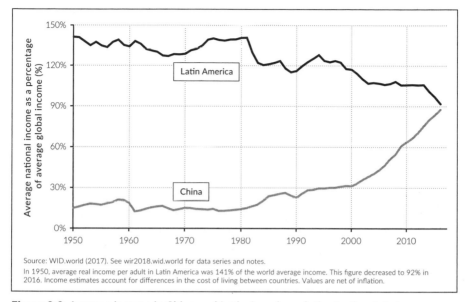

Source: WID.world (2017). See wir2018.wid.world for data series and notes.

In 1950, average real income per adult in Latin America was 141% of the world average income. This figure decreased to 92% in 2016. Income estimates account for differences in the cost of living between countries. Values are net of inflation.

Figure 3.2 Average income in China and Latin America relative to the global average, 1950–2016

4

Trends in Income Inequality
within Countries

- After a historical decline in most parts of the world from the 1920s
  to the 1970s, income inequality is on the rise in nearly all countries. The past four decades, however, display a variety of national
  pathways, highlighting the importance of political and institutional factors in shaping income dynamics.
- In the industrialized world, Anglo-Saxon countries have experienced a sharp rise in inequality since the 1980s. In the United
  States, the bottom 50% income share collapsed while the top share
  boomed. Continental European countries were more successful at
  containing rising inequality, thanks to a policy and institutional
  context more favorable to lower- and middle-income groups.
- In China, India, and Russia, three formerly communist or highly
  regulated economies, inequality surged with opening-up and
  liberalization policies. The steepest rise occurred in Russia, where
  the transition to a market economy was particularly abrupt.
- Inequality is extreme in Brazil, the Middle East, and South Africa,
  the world's most unequal regions. In these three large emerging
  markets, inequality currently reaches extreme levels: the top 10%
  earners capture 55% to 65% of national income.
- Little is known of the long-run dynamics of income inequality
  in many low-income countries. More information is essential for
  peaceful democratic debates in these countries, especially given
  that official estimates are very likely to understate existing levels
  of inequality.

After a historical decline from the 1920s to the 1970s, income inequality is on the rise in most regions of the world

Income inequality was sharply reduced in the first half of the twentieth century—more precisely, between the 1920s and the 1970s—in most countries of the world, but it has been on the rise almost everywhere since the late 1970s. In Europe and North America, the long-run decline in income inequality was due to the combination of political, social, and economic shocks already discussed. These included the destruction of human and physical capital led by the World Wars, the Great Depression, nationalization policies, and government control over the economy. After the Second World War, a new policy regime was put in place, including the development of social security systems, public education, social and labor policies, and progressive taxation. This combination of factors severely affected very high fortunes, and enabled the rise of a patrimonial middle class and a general decline in inequality in Europe—and to a lesser extent, in North America.[7]

In emerging economies, political and social shocks led to an even more radical reduction of income inequality. The abolition of private property in Russia, land redistribution, massive investments in public education, and strict government control over the economy via five-year plans effectively spread the benefits of growth from the early 1920s to the 1970s. In India, which did not undergo a communist revolution but implemented socialist policies after gaining its independence, income inequality was also severely reduced over the same period. For most of the global population, the first three-quarters of the twentieth century corresponded to a very strong compression in the distribution of national incomes. The economic elite captured a much smaller share of economic growth in the late 1970s than it did at the beginning of the century.

The trend was then reversed in most countries—even though there are notable exceptions deserving attention. Countries did not all follow the same path. Large emerging countries, as they underwent profound deregulations of their economies, saw inequalities surge as they opened up and liberalized but followed different transition strategies. In rich countries, inequality levels also varied largely according to changes in institutional and policy contexts, with sharp income inequality rises in the Anglo-Saxon world and more moderate increases in continental Europe and Japan. Certain Western European and Northern European countries almost contained the rise in income inequality.

Given the multitude of trends presented in this chapter, it would be imprudent to seek a single story line behind the rise of inequality across countries. Our findings show that national cultural, political, and policy contexts are key to understanding the dynamics of income inequality. In this chapter, we largely focus on the evolution of top-income shares, as they are now available for a very large set of countries. In the country-by-country chapters that come next, the focus will be more detailed and we will shift the attention to bottom-income groups.

Bottom-income groups were shut off from economic growth in the United States, while top incomes surged in the Anglo-Saxon world

Top 1% income shares have been steadily increasing in Anglo-Saxon countries since the early 1980s, after a historical decline throughout the first part of the twentieth century (Figure 4.1). Inequality exploded in the United States: the top percentile income share there was less than 11% in 1980, and it was slightly above 20% in 2014. Britain's top percentile share rose from less than 6% in the late 1970s to nearly 14% in the mid-2010s. Britain had the same level of top 1% income share as Ireland in the late 1970s, but is now nearly on a level with Canada, where the top share increased from less than 9% in 1980 to almost 14%. Australia and New Zealand, with levels of inequality much lower throughout the entire period (around 5% in the early 1980 and rising to less than 10%) also show a broadly similar pattern.[8] The impact of the financial crisis is visible on top-income shares, which exhibit a marked decline after 2007. Novel data suggest that top incomes have either recovered their shares or are progressively recovering them.

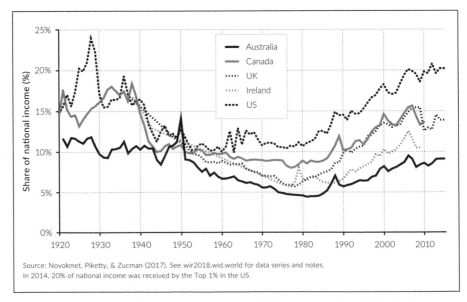

Source: Novokmet, Piketty, & Zucman (2017). See wir2018.wid.world for data series and notes.
In 2014, 20% of national income was received by the Top 1% in the US.

Figure 4.1 Top 1% national income share in Anglophone countries, 1920–2015

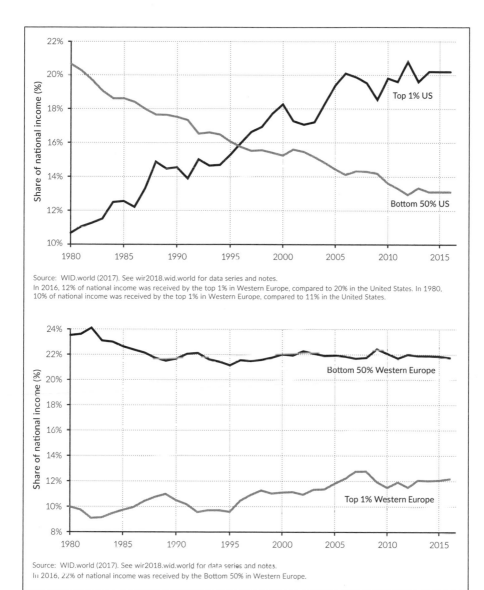

Figure 4.2a Top 1% vs. Bottom 50% national income shares in the US and Western Europe, 1980–2016

The rise in labor income inequality played an important role in the rise of inequality in Anglo-Saxon countries, and particularly in the United States before the turn of the century, as discussed in Chapter 5. This phenomenon is owing to the "rise of super managers"—that is, the rise in super wages received by CEOs of large financial and nonfinancial firms. This evolution was also accompanied by an increased polarization of income between low-wage and high-wage firms.

This contrasted with European countries, where the dynamics at the top of the distribution have been more moderate. New estimates also show that the upsurge in top incomes has mostly been a capital income phenomenon after 2000 in the United States, shedding new light on the process of unequal growth generation.

Our novel estimates also allow a better understanding of the dynamics at the bottom of the distribution—at least for certain countries. In the United States, the bottom 90% of the population benefited from a large share of growth in the three decades following the Second World War. Total per-adult pre-tax income growth for the bottom 50% and for the middle 40% was higher than 100%, while total growth for the top 10% earners was less than 80%. But since the 1980s, the bottom 50% was shut off from national income growth. While average per-adult pre-tax incomes increased by 60%, growth was close to zero for the bottom 50% of the population. The bottom 50% did benefit from a very modest post-tax income growth, thanks to redistribution, but this has been eaten up by rising health spending. Government provided little support to help low-income individuals cope with the situation.

The comparison of inequality trajectories between the United States and Western Europe is particularly striking. The two regions had similar levels of inequality in 1980 (top 1% share at 10–11% and bottom 50% share at 21–23%). However, today the situations are radically different as the relative positions of the bottom 50% and top 1% group in the United States have been inverted (see Figure 4.2a).

Inequality in enlarged Europe (with a population of 520 million) is now substantially smaller than in the United States (320 million)

We also compare in Figures 4.2b through 4.2c the evolution of income inequality between the United States, Western Europe, and enlarged Europe (that is, including Eastern Europe). Enlarged Europe includes ex-communist East European countries with lower average incomes than Western European averages, leading to higher inequality levels. However, it is striking to see that inequality levels in enlarged Europe remain much smaller than in the United States. In particular, in spite of Europe's bigger size and potential heterogeneity (520 million for enlarged Europe, 320 million for the United States), the bottom 50% income share is substantially larger in Europe: 20–22% of total income at the end of the period versus 12% in the United States.

This conclusion would likely be exacerbated if we were to compare enlarged Europe to enlarged North America (including not only Canada but also Mexico),

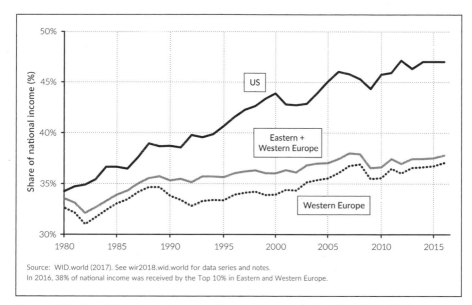

Figure 4.2b Top 10% national income share in Europe and the US, 1980–2016

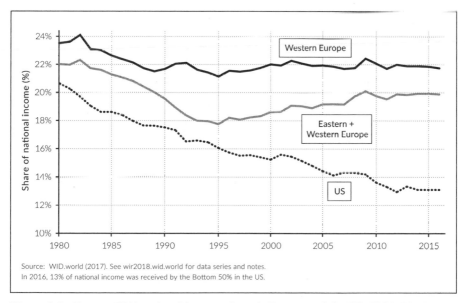

Figure 4.2c Bottom 50% national income share in Europe and the US, 1980–2016

which we plan to do in the near future as new data become available for Mexico. Another important issue for future research is to better understand which part of Europe's lower inequality level can be attributed to redistributive policies at the regional level (including EU regional development funds), as opposed to national factors (such as the relatively egalitarian legacy of Eastern European

countries and the fact that the transition from communism was not as abrupt as
in Russia).

Continental European countries were more successful in preventing the rise of incomes at the top and the stagnation of incomes at the bottom

In western continental Europe, inequality has also been on the rise since the late
1970s, though both the levels of inequality and the rise in inequality were less
striking than in the United States. The German top 1% income share rose from
slightly less than 11% in the early 1980s to 13% today, as described in Chapter 7.
In France, the top 1% pre-tax income share increased from approximately 7% in
1983 to nearly 11% in 2014, as discussed in more detail in Chapter 6. Spain displays
a different picture. The impact of the financial crisis and the bursting of the real
estate bubble in 2007–2008, which represented a substantial share of national
income, severely hampered incomes at the bottom of the distribution, but also
at the top: the top 1% income share decreased from close to 13% in 2006 to less
than 9% in 2012, and still shows no sign of recovery. (Figure 4.3)

For France, new estimates also allow us to track the dynamics of growth at the
bottom of the distribution. While growth was higher than average at the bottom
50% and middle 40% during the postwar period and up to the early 1980s, the
situation was reversed afterward. The "thirty glorious years"—as the high-growth

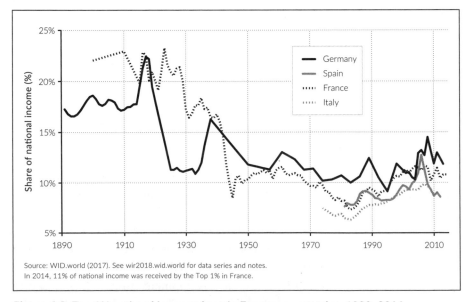

Source: WID.world (2017). See wir2018.wid.world for data series and notes.
In 2014, 11% of national income was received by the Top 1% in France.

Figure 4.3 Top 1% national income share in European countries, 1890–2014

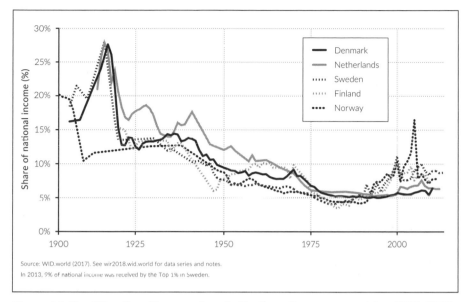

Figure 4.4 Top 1% national income share in Northern European countries, 1900–2013

1950–1980 period is commonly referred to in France—continued after the 1980s, but only for the top income earners. This increase in inequality is characterized by rises in both labor and capital income. However, the bottom half of the population was not shut off from growth after the 1980s. This part of the population enjoyed close to average income growth rates—a strikingly different picture than in the United States.

Northern European countries had among the lowest levels of income inequality in the world in the early 1980s. Growth has been more unequal in these countries after 1980 than before, yet income concentration at the top of the distribution remains limited. Top 1% income earners capture less than 10% of total income in Denmark, Finland, Norway, and Sweden. In Denmark and in the Netherlands, the rise in top percentile share has been small, from about 5% to 6% since the 1980s. As we can see, many European countries have been able to generate relatively high average income growth rates and maintain the rise in income inequality (Figure 4.4).

In Russia, China, and India, income inequality surged after the 1980s

Income concentration and wealth concentration were particularly high in tsarist Russia before the Soviet revolution of 1917 (see Chapter 9 on Russia), and in colonial India (see Chapter 10 on India). In Russia, the communist revolution

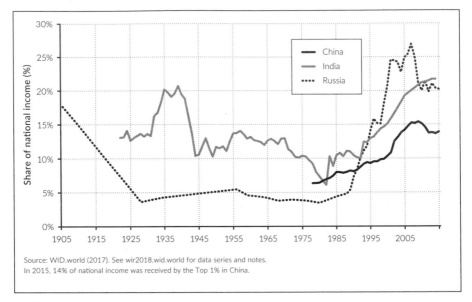

Source: WID.world (2017). See wir2018.wid.world for data series and notes.
In 2015, 14% of national income was received by the Top 1% in China.

Figure 4.5 Top 1% national income share in emerging countries, 1900–2015

led to an extreme compression of money incomes. During the entire communist period, the top 1% income share represented around 5% of national income, down to less than 4% in the seventies (Figure 4.5). It is worth stressing, however, that this extremely low level of monetary inequality is partly artificial. Soviet inequality took other, non-monetary forms, such as privileged access to particular shops and vacation centers for the political elite, and brutal political repression for large segments of the population.

In India, the top percentile income share decreased from around 20% at the end of the colonial period to 6% in the early 1980s, after four decades of socialist-inspired policies aiming at reducing the economic power of the elite, including nationalizations, government control over prices, and extreme tax rates on top incomes. The implosion of the Soviet block and "shock policies" in Russia, and deregulation and opening-up policies in India from the 1980s onwards, contributed to strong increases in top percentile income shares. The top 1% share increased to 26% in 1996 in Russia and is now at 20%. In India, the top percentile is now around 22%.

The Chinese opening-up policies established from 1978 (discussed in Chapter 8 on China), which included important privatization plans, had a lesser effect on inequality than reforms had in Russia or India. China shows a substantial rise in inequality (the top share rose from 6.5% to 14% in twenty years). However, as compared to Russia, China's transition to a liberalized, open economy was less abrupt and more gradual. Since 2006, inequality at the top has stagnated. In

China and to a lesser extent in India, the rise in inequality occurred in the context of high average income growth, enabling important growth at the bottom of the distribution.

Brazil, South Africa, and the Middle East can be characterized as "extreme inequality" regimes: they have the highest inequality levels observed

In Brazil, South Africa, and the Middle East, income has been historically highly concentrated (Figure 4.6). In Brazil, wage inequality has decreased over the past twenty years (in particular due to rising minimum wage) and there have been important and often lauded cash-transfer systems to the poor. However, due to a large concentration of business profits and capital incomes, the top 10% national income share reaches 55% in Brazil today and this value has not changed significantly for the past twenty years as is shown in Chapter 12. Together with huge regional inequalities, the legacy of racial inequality still plays an important role; Brazil was the last major country to abolish slavery, back in 1887, at a time when slavery made up a very large fraction of the population, up to about 30% of the population in certain regions.

The extreme inequality evident in South Africa can obviously be linked to the

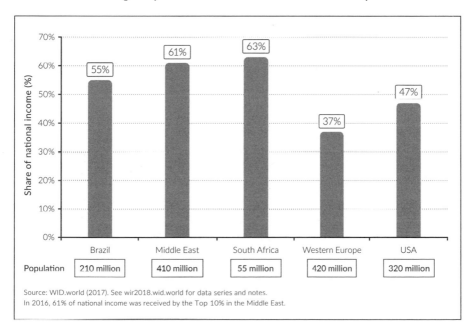

Figure 4.6 Top 10% national income share in Brazil, the Middle East, South Africa, and other countries, 2012–2016

historical legacy of the apartheid regime (only fully abolished in 1994), seen today in the country's dualistic economy and society. As discussed in Chapter 13, the top 10% is largely made up of whites. This group earns more than 60% of national income and enjoys income levels similar to those of Europeans, while the bottom 90% live with incomes comparable to those of low-income African countries. But in contrast to Brazil and the Middle East, inequality increased significantly over the past decades in South Africa. The trade and financial liberalization that occurred after the end of apartheid, coupled with the failure to redistribute land equally, can help to explain these dynamics — yet more research will be required to better track and understand recent South African income inequality dynamics.

Despite its much larger racial and ethno-cultural homogeneity, levels of inequality in the Middle East are similar to (or possibly even higher than) those in Brazil and South Africa, with a top 10% share above 60%. As discussed in Chapter 11, regional income and wealth are largely concentrated in the hands of a small group that is located in the Gulf countries and Saudi Arabia. This is yet another inequality-generating mechanism: the geography of oil property and the frontier system have led to extreme inequality in this region.

In low-income countries, inequality is likely to be higher than previously thought, but data are scarce

We still know very little about the evolution of income inequality in the rest of the developing and emerging world. The first explanation for this situation is that there is a lack of proper income-tax data, either because governments have not shared it, or because the data simply do not exist anymore, or because the data are still decentralized and not digitized.

In the absence of administrative data, most of what we know is based on survey estimates. As discussed in Part I, survey-based estimates of inequality can have a number of limitations. Surveys are often more sporadic in time, lack consistency with national accounts estimates, and miss top incomes. As demonstrated in this report, for numerous emerging countries, these weaknesses can lead to significant underestimation of inequality levels. (See Chapters 8 and 13.) In Côte d'Ivoire, novel estimates show that the income share of the top 1% is approximately 17% of the country's total income, contrary to the 12% previously estimated by surveys. WID.world work also shows that the share of income earned by the top 1% in China was at least twice as great as official estimates previously suggested. We are currently devoting great energies to accessing income tax data in other African countries, following the lead of Côte d'Ivoire, and hope to be able to report more findings in the near future. At this stage, however, we have only limited access to adequate data.

Collectively, these factors mean that we can assess the evolution of income inequality for only a few developing countries in the years before the 1980s, and over a short or interrupted time period. Given that most individuals earned below the first income-tax threshold, our analysis is also restricted to a tiny fraction of the population. Out of the nine sub-Saharan African countries for which we have historical income tax data, the income share earned by the top 1% can only be properly computed in two small countries—Mauritius and the Seychelles—and for only a few years in Zambia and Zimbabwe. For the remaining countries (Ghana, Kenya, Tanzania, Nigeria, and Uganda), the income-tax data encompass less than 1% of the estimated adult population. While this may appear surprising, it is worth remembering that in the early days of the US personal income tax (1913–1915), the proportion of taxpayers was 0.9%.

Nevertheless, some lessons can be drawn from these data. In Africa, from the mid-1940s until the early 1980s, the income share of the top 0.1% decreased in Zimbabwe, Zambia, Malawi, Kenya, Tanzania, and South Africa, following a trend similar to that of most rich countries. But compared to European levels over the same period, income inequality was much higher in these African countries, and even reached the most extreme levels. In 1950, the richest 0.1% of Zambia commanded a bit more than 10% of total national income. Income inequality was, however, seemingly lower in West African countries such as Nigeria and Ghana, where the top 0.1% averaged 2.5% of total income between 1940 and 1960. Interestingly, this pattern of geographical differences in inequality is still evident in survey data that have been collected in recent decades.

Where it is possible to break down tax data by race or nationality, historical data in African countries demonstrate that most taxpayers were non-African— mainly Europeans, followed by Arabs, then Asians. This dominance is likely to have been mitigated in recent decades, but it is still important in former settlement colonies such as South Africa. Recent research on Côte d'Ivoire for the period 1985–2014 further illustrates how the aforementioned discrepancy between survey data and administrative data can be partly due to the undersampling of non-African individuals.[9]

Available data for Latin American countries show that income inequality in the region is generally higher than the levels seen in European and Asian countries. For example, recent data collected in Latin America indicate that the total income share of the top 1% in Argentina, Colombia, and Brazil is greater than 16%. Interestingly, when only survey data have been used to estimate inequality in the region, the results suggest that income inequality has decreased significantly, while WID.world estimates for Brazil and Colombia show that they have in fact remained stubbornly high.

In conclusion, the scarcity of available data makes it challenging to develop a conclusive picture of inequality levels in lower-income countries. From the data that are available, however, inequality estimations suggest that in most cases the distribution of income is more concentrated than previously thought in low-income countries. While important efforts have been made in the past years to produce and analyze consistent inequality estimates in emerging countries (which are presented for the first time together in this report), the study of the analysis of income inequality based on sound and consistent data in low-income countries is still only in its infancy.

5

Income Inequality in the United States

Information in this chapter is based on the article "Distributional National Accounts: Methods and Estimates for the United States," by Thomas Piketty, Emmanuel Saez, and Gabriel Zucman, forthcoming in the Quarterly Journal of Economics *(2018).*

- Income inequality in the United States is among the highest of all rich countries. The share of national income earned by the top 1% of adults in 2014 (20.2%) is much larger than the share earned by the bottom 50% of the adult population (12.5%).
- Average pre-tax real national income per adult has increased 60% since 1980, but it has stagnated for the bottom 50% at around $16 500. While post-tax cash incomes of the bottom 50% have also stagnated, a large part of the modest post-tax income growth of this group has been eaten up by increased health spending.
- Income has boomed at the top. While the upsurge of top incomes was first a labor-income phenomenon in the 1980s and 1990s, it has mostly been a capital-income phenomenon since 2000.
- The combination of an increasingly less progressive tax regime and a transfer system that favors the middle class implies that, even after taxes and all transfers, bottom 50% income growth has lagged behind average income growth since 1980.
- Increased female participation in the labor market has been a counterforce to rising inequality, but the glass ceiling remains firmly in place. Men make up 85% of the top 1% of the labor income distribution.

Income inequality in the United States is among the highest of rich countries

In 2014, the distribution of US national income exhibited extremely high inequalities. The average income of an adult in the United States before accounting for taxes and transfers was $66 100, but this figure masks huge differences in the distribution of incomes. The approximately 117 million adults that make up the bottom 50% in the United States earned $16 600 on average per year, representing just one-fourth of the average US income. As illustrated by Table 5.1, their collective incomes amounted to a 13% share of pre-tax national income. The average pre-tax income of the middle 40%—the group of adults with incomes above the median and below the richest 10%, which can be loosely described as the "middle class"—was roughly similar to the national average, at $66 900, so that their income share (41%) broadly reflected their relative size in the population. The remaining income share for the top 10% was therefore 47%, with average pre-tax earnings of $311 000. This average annual income of the top 10% is almost five times the national average, and nineteen times larger than the aver-

Table 5.1 The distribution of national income in the US, 2014

Income group	Number of adults	Pre-tax national income			Post-tax national income		
		Income threshold ($)	Average income ($)	Income share	Income threshold ($)	Average income ($)	Income share
Full Population	234 400 000	–	66 100	100%	–	66 100	100%
Bottom 50%	117 200 000	–	16 600	12.5%	–	25 500	19.3%
Bottom 20%	46 880 000	–	5 500	1.7%	–	13 400	4.1%
Next 30%	70 320 000	13 100	24 000	10.9%	23 200	33 600	15.2%
Middle 40%	93 760 000	36 900	66 900	40.4%	45 000	68 800	41.6%
Top 10%	23 440 000	122 000	311 000	47.0%	113 000	259 000	39.1%
Top 1%	2 344 000	469 000	1 341 000	20.2%	392 000	1 034 000	15.7%
Top 0.1%	234 400	2 007 000	6 144 000	9.3%	1 556 000	4 505 000	6.8%
Top 0.01%	23 440	9 789 000	28 773 000	4.4%	7 035 000	20 786 000	3.1%
Top 0.001%	2 344	48 331 000	124 821 000	1.9%	35 122 000	90 826 000	1.4%

Source: Piketty, Saez, and Zucman (2018). See wir2018.wid.world for data series and notes.

In 2014, the average pre-tax income of the Top 10% was $311 000. Pre-tax national income is measured after the operation of pension and unemployment insurance systems (which cover the majority of cash transfers), but before direct income and wealth taxes. Post-tax national income is measured after all taxes, transfers, and government spending. All values have been converted to 2016 constant US dollars (accounting for inflation). For comparison, $1 = €0.8 = ¥3.3 at Market Exchange Rates, and $1 = €0.9 = ¥6.6 at Purchasing Power Parity. Numbers may not add up due to rounding.

age for the bottom 50%. Furthermore, the 1:19 ratio between the incomes of the bottom 50% and the top 10% indicates that pre-tax income inequality between the "lower class" and the "upper class" is more than twice the (1:8 ratio) difference between the average national incomes in the United States and China, using market exchange rates.

Income is very concentrated, even among the top 10%. For example, the share of national income going to the top 1%, a group of approximately 2.3 million adults who earn $1.3 million on average per annum, is over 20%—that is, 1.6 times larger than the share of the entire bottom 50%, a group fifty times more populous. The incomes of those in the top 0.1%, top 0.01%, and top 0.001% average $6 million, $29 million, and $125 million per year, respectively, before personal taxes and transfers.

As shown by Table 5.1, the distribution of national income in the United States in 2014 was generally made slightly more equitable by the country's taxes and transfer system. Taxes and transfers reduce the share of national income for the top 10% from 47% to 39%, which is split between a one percentage point rise in the post-tax income share of the middle 40% (from 40.5% to 41.6%) and a seven percentage point increase in the post-tax income share of the bottom 50% (from 12.5% to 19.4%). The trend is also of relatively large proportionate losses in income shares as one looks further up the income distribution, indicating that government taxes are slightly progressive for the United States' richest adults.

National income grew by 61% from 1980 to 2014 but the bottom 50% was shut off from it

Income inequality in the United States in 2014 was vastly different from the levels seen at the end of the Second World War. Indeed, changes in inequality since the end of that war can be split into two phases, as illustrated by Table 5.2. From 1946 to 1980, real national income growth per adult was strong—with average income per adult almost doubling—and moreover, was more than equally distributed as the incomes of the bottom 90% grew faster (102%) than those of the top 10% (79%).[10] However, in the following thirty-four-year period, from 1980 to 2014, total growth slowed from 95% to 61% and became much more skewed.

The pre-tax incomes of the bottom 50% stagnated, increasing by only $200 from $16 400 in 1980 to $16 600 in 2014, a minuscule growth of just 1% over a thirty-four-year period. The total growth of post-tax income for the bottom 50% was substantially larger, at 21% over the full period 1980–2014 (averaging 0.6% a year), but this was still only one-third of the national average. Growth for the

Table 5.2 The growth of national income since World War II in the US, 1946–2014

Income group	Pre-tax income growth		Post-tax income growth	
	1946–1980	1980–2014	1946–1980	1980–2014
Full Population	95%	61%	95%	61%
Bottom 50%	102%	1%	129%	21%
Bottom 20%	109%	-25%	179%	4%
Next 30%	101%	7%	117%	26%
Middle 40%	105%	42%	98%	49%
Top 10%	79%	121%	69%	113%
Top 1%	47%	204%	58%	194%
Top 0.1%	54%	320%	104%	298%
Top 0.01%	76%	453%	201%	423%
Top 0.001%	57%	636%	163%	616%

Source: Piketty, Saez, and Zucman (2018), available from WID.world

Between 1980 and 2014, the average pre-tax income of the Top 10% grew by 113%. Pre-tax national income is measured after the operation of pension and unemployment insurance systems (which cover the majority of cash transfers), but before direct income and wealth taxes. Post-tax national income is measured after all taxes, transfers, and government spending.

middle 40% was weak, with a pre-tax increase in income of 42% since 1980 and a post-tax rise of 49% (an average of 1.4% a year). By contrast, the average income of the top 10% doubled over this period, and for the top 1% it tripled, even on a post-tax basis. The rates of growth further increase as one moves up the income ladder, culminating in an increase of 636% for the top 0.001% between 1980 and 2014, ten times the national income growth rate for the full population.

The rise of the top 1% mirrors the fall of the bottom 50%

This stagnation of incomes of the bottom 50%, relative to the upsurge in incomes experienced by the top 1% has been perhaps the most striking development in the United States economy over the last four decades. As shown by Figure 5.1a, the groups have seen their shares of total US income reverse between 1980 and 2014. The incomes of the top 1% collectively made up 11% of national income in 1980, but now constitute above 20% of national income, while the 20% of US national income that was attributable to the bottom 50% in 1980 has fallen to just 12% today. Effectively, eight points of national income have been transferred from the bottom 50% to the top 1%. Therefore, the gains in national income share

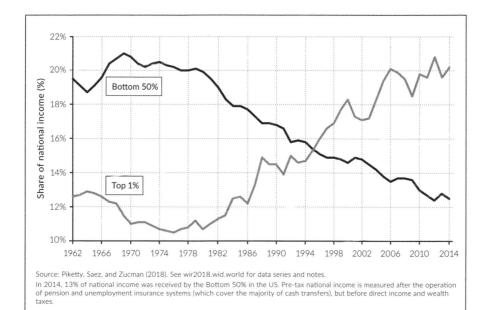

Source: Piketty, Saez, and Zucman (2018). See wir2018.wid.world for data series and notes.
In 2014, 13% of national income was received by the Bottom 50% in the US. Pre-tax national income is measured after the operation of pension and unemployment insurance systems (which cover the majority of cash transfers), but before direct income and wealth taxes.

Figure 5.1a Pre-tax income shares of the Top 1% and Bottom 50% in the US, 1962–2014

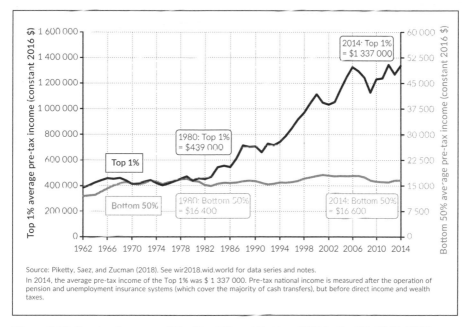

Source: Piketty, Saez, and Zucman (2018). See wir2018.wid.world for data series and notes.
In 2014, the average pre-tax income of the Top 1% was $ 1 337 000. Pre-tax national income is measured after the operation of pension and unemployment insurance systems (which cover the majority of cash transfers), but before direct income and wealth taxes.

Figure 5.1b Pre-tax incomes of the Top 1% and Bottom 50% in the US, 1962–2014

made by the top 1% have been more than large enough to compensate for the fall in income share of the bottom 50%, a group demographically fifty times larger. Figure 5.1b shows that while average pre-tax income for the bottom 50% has stagnated at around $16 500 since 1980, the top 1% has experienced 300% growth in their incomes to approximately $1 340 000 in 2014. This has increased the average earnings differential between the top 1% and the bottom 50% from twenty-seven times in 1980 to eighty-one times today.

Excluding health transfers, average post-tax income of the bottom 50% stagnated at $20 500

The stagnation of incomes among the bottom 50% was not the case throughout the postwar period, however. The pre-tax share of income owned by this chapter of the population increased in the 1960s as the wage distribution became more equal, in part as a consequence of the significant rise in the real federal minimum wage in the 1960s, and reached its historical peak in 1969. These improvements were supported by President Johnson's "war on poverty," whose social policy provided the Food Stamp Act of 1964 and the creation of the Medicaid healthcare program in 1965.

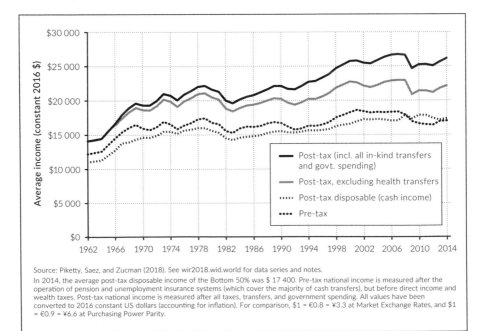

Source: Piketty, Saez, and Zucman (2018). See wir2018.wid.world for data series and notes.
In 2014, the average post-tax disposable income of the Bottom 50% was $ 17 400. Pre-tax national income is measured after the operation of pension and unemployment insurance systems (which cover the majority of cash transfers), but before direct income and wealth taxes. Post-tax national income is measured after all taxes, transfers, and government spending. All values have been converted to 2016 constant US dollars (accounting for inflation). For comparison, $1 = €0.8 = ¥3.3 at Market Exchange Rates, and $1 = €0.9 = ¥6.6 at Purchasing Power Parity.

Figure 5.2 Pre-tax and post-tax income of the Bottom 50% in the US, 1962–2014

However, the share of both pre-tax and post-tax US income accruing to the bottom 50% began to fall notably from the beginning of the 1980s, and the gap between pre-tax and post-tax incomes also diverged significantly from this point onwards. Indeed, the data indicate that virtually all of the meager growth in the real post-tax income of the bottom 50% since the 1970s has come from Medicare and Medicaid. Excluding these two health care transfers, the average post-tax income of the bottom 50% would have stagnated since the late 1970s at just below $20 500 (see Figure 5.2). The bottom half of the US adult population has therefore been effectively shut off from pre-tax economic growth for over forty years, and the increase in their post-tax income of approximately $5 000 has been almost entirely absorbed by greater healthcare spending, in part as a result of increases in the cost of healthcare provision.[11] Furthermore, it is solely through the in-kind health transfers and collective expenditures that the bottom half of the distribution sees its income rise above its pre-tax level and becomes a net beneficiary of redistribution; up until the government ran large deficits during the 2008 Great Recession, the bottom 50% paid more in taxes than it received in individualized cash transfers.

Among the bottom 50%, the pre-tax income of working-age adults is falling

The stagnation in the incomes of the bottom 50% could in principle reflect demographic changes rather than deeper evolutions in the distribution of lifetime incomes. People's incomes tend to first rise with age—as workers build human capital and acquire experience—and then fall during retirement. Population aging might therefore have pushed the bottom 50% income share down. However, this is not the case for the United States. This can be shown by examining the bottom 50% of income earners within specific age categories such as 20–45 year-olds, 45–65-year-olds, and 65+-year-olds, as in Figure 5.3.

Figure 5.3a shows that the average pre-tax income of working-age adults in the bottom 50% has collapsed since 1980, falling by 20% for adults aged 20–45 and by 8% for those between ages 45 and 65. It is only for the elderly (aged 65+) that pre-tax income has been rising, due to increases in social security benefits and private pension distributions. Figure 5.3b shows that these trends are even more pronounced on a post-tax basis. The average income of bottom 50% income earners among those aged 65+ has grown by 70% since 1980s and now exceeds the average income of bottom 50% income earners among all adults. Indeed, all the growth in the post-tax incomes of the bottom 50% is attributable to this increase in income for the elderly.[12] For the working-age population in the bottom 50%, the increase in post-tax income since 1980 has been essentially nil.

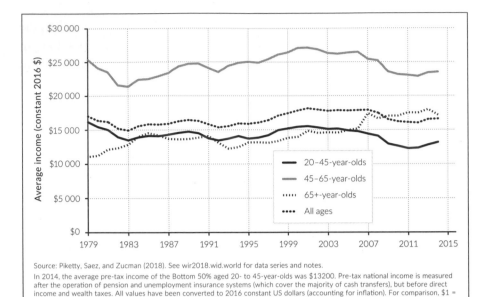

Source: Piketty, Saez, and Zucman (2018). See wir2018.wid.world for data series and notes.
In 2014, the average pre-tax income of the Bottom 50% aged 20- to 45-year-olds was $13200. Pre-tax national income is measured after the operation of pension and unemployment insurance systems (which cover the majority of cash transfers), but before direct income and wealth taxes. All values have been converted to 2016 constant US dollars (accounting for inflation). For comparison, $1 = €0.8 = ¥3.3 at Market Exchange Rates, and $1 = €0.9 = ¥6.6 at Purchasing Power Parity. Numbers may not add up due to rounding.

Figure 5.3a Pre-tax income of the Bottom 50% by age group in the US, 1979–2014

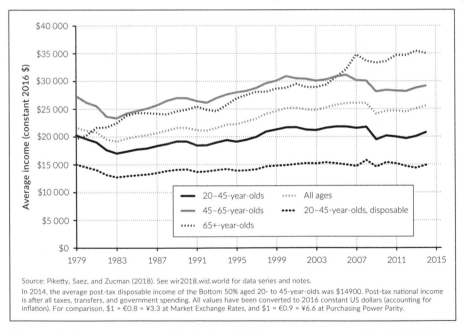

Source: Piketty, Saez, and Zucman (2018). See wir2018.wid.world for data series and notes.
In 2014, the average post-tax disposable income of the Bottom 50% aged 20- to 45-year-olds was $14900. Post-tax national income is after all taxes, transfers, and government spending. All values have been converted to 2016 constant US dollars (accounting for inflation). For comparison, $1 = €0.8 = ¥3.3 at Market Exchange Rates, and $1 = €0.9 = ¥6.6 at Purchasing Power Parity.

Figure 5.3b Post-tax income of the Bottom 50% by age group in the US, 1979–2014

Three key insights can be drawn from the evolution of bottom 50% incomes in the United States. First, as the income of all working-age groups within the bottom 50% has collapsed—including experienced workers above 45 years old— it is unlikely that the cumulative income that someone from the bottom 50% group has earned across their lifetime has grown much since the 1980s. Second, the stagnation in the incomes of the bottom 50% is not due to population aging. To the contrary, at the bottom half of the income spectrum, the elderly's incomes are the only ones rising. Third, despite the rise in means-tested benefits, government redistribution has not enhanced income growth for low- and moderate-income, working-age Americans over the last three decades. This, along with the real level of pre-tax inequality, indicates that there are clear limits to what taxes and transfers can achieve in the face of such massive changes in the pre-tax distribution of income as have occurred in the United States since 1980. This combination of factors supports the view that policy discussions should focus on how to equalize the distribution of primary assets, including human capital, financial capital, and bargaining power, rather than merely focus on ex-post redistribution.

Pre-tax income inequality has risen notably since the 1980s, slightly more than post-tax income inequality

The trends described above should also be put into their longer historical context. An analysis of data going as far back as 1917 indicates that there have been considerable changes in income inequality in the United States over the last century. As shown in Figure 5.4, the share of national income going to the top 10% has followed a U-shaped curve over the last century. On a pre-tax basis, the top 10% income share today is almost as high as it was at its peak in the late 1920s.

The shares of income attributed to top earners, after accounting for taxes and transfers, have also followed a U-shaped evolution over time, though they exhibit a less marked upward swing in recent decades than do the pre-tax figures. This difference is mainly due to the smaller size of government a century ago, and lower tax rates relative to the present day, which meant the difference between pre- and post-tax incomes was less pronounced in the early 1900s. Pre-tax and post-tax shares of income started diverging after 1933 as President Roosevelt's New Deal impacted the top 1% and policies to raise money for Second World War–related spending led to significant increases in federal income taxation of the top 10%.

Although post-tax inequality has increased significantly since 1980, it has risen at a slower rate than pre-tax inequality. As can be seen in Figure 5.4, the

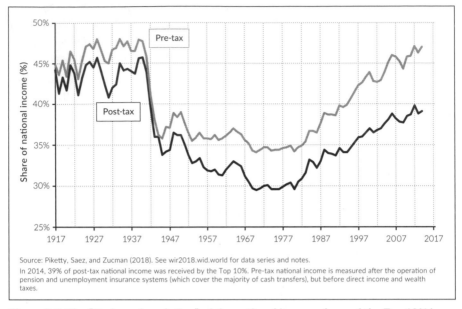

Source: Piketty, Saez, and Zucman (2018). See wir2018.wid.world for data series and notes.
In 2014, 39% of post-tax national income was received by the Top 10%. Pre-tax national income is measured after the operation of pension and unemployment insurance systems (which cover the majority of cash transfers), but before direct income and wealth taxes.

Figure 5.4 The "U-shaped evolution" of the national income share of the Top 10% in the US, 1917–2014

share of total income attributable to the top 10% rose from 30% to 40% post-tax, and from 35% to 47% pre-tax between 1980 and 2014. Significant tax increases implemented in 2013 for those with the largest incomes may have played a role in the slower growth of post-tax top-income shares relative to pre-tax income shares over the last few years. Overall, redistributive policies have prevented post-tax inequality from returning all the way to pre–New Deal levels (as discussed in more detail below). Further reducing taxes on top earners, as envisioned by the current administration and Congress, could sharply increase post-tax income inequality in coming years. (Box 5.1)

Despite fluctuations, the share of aggregate capital in total pre-tax income has remained relatively stable over the last century. Significantly larger concentrations of earnings continue to be derived from capital, rather than labor, as one moves up the income distribution. The vast majority of Americans have earned little capital income over the last century, with the bottom 90%—which includes both the middle and lower-income classes—rarely receiving more than 10% of their income from capital before the 1970s (Figure 5.5). The rise of pension funds (which now account for 36% of all household wealth) has helped to increase the share of capital in the pre-tax income of the bottom 90%, rising to approximately 16% in 2014. While lower than their highs of over 50% in the mid-60s, the top 10% income earners still derive over 40% of their incomes

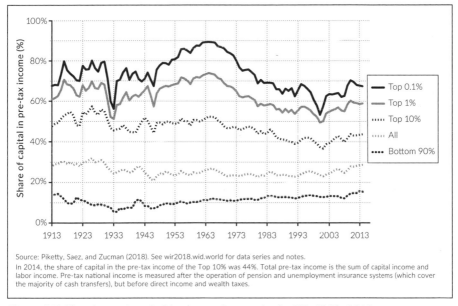

Source: Piketty, Saez, and Zucman (2018). See wir2018.wid.world for data series and notes.
In 2014, the share of capital in the pre-tax income of the Top 10% was 44%. Total pre-tax income is the sum of capital income and labor income. Pre-tax national income is measured after the operation of pension and unemployment insurance systems (which cover the majority of cash transfers), but before direct income and wealth taxes.

Figure 5.5 The share of capital in pre-tax income in the US, 1913–2014

from capital in 2014; this figure was almost 60% for the top 1%, and 70% for the top 0.1% in 2014.

Fluctuations in the share of income coming from capital have been remarkable for those with the highest incomes. Early in the twentieth century, the top 0.1% derived 70–80% of its income from capital, but this share collapsed to just over 50% during the Great Depression when corporate profits slumped, before rebounding in the 1950s and 1960s to around 90%. As described in Piketty's *Capital in the Twenty-First Century,* top executive compensation and labor incomes hit an historical low during the postwar decades.[13] They then rose very rapidly from the 1970s through the late 1990s, culminating in 2000 when the capital share of the top 0.1% reached a low point of 49%. Since the turn of the twenty-first century, however, capital has bounced back, with a surge in profits from corporate equities. The share of capital income in national income grew from 22% to 29% between 2000 and 2014, and indeed almost all of the 0.6% average yearly growth of income per adult in the United States over this period was a result of the rise in capital income; labor income per adult grew by 0.1% per year while capital income per adult grew by 2.2% per year. This rise in wealth inequality led to an increase in capital income concentration, which then reinforced wealth inequality itself as top capital incomes were saved at a high rate. Consequently, as the twenty-first century progresses, the working rich of the late

Box 5.1 Measuring pre-tax and post-tax income inequality

In this chapter, we present estimates of pre- and post-tax income inequality for the United States, which are two complementary concepts for the analysis of inequality. Comparing pre- and post-tax income inequality allows better assessment of the impact of personal taxes and in-kind transfers on the dynamics of income inequality.

In the WID.world database, pre-tax income refers to incomes measured before personal income and wealth taxes and in-kind transfers (typically health transfers) but after the operation of the pension and employment insurance systems (as well as after social security and disability transfers in the case of the United States).

In contrast, post-tax income refers to incomes measured after all taxes (in particular, after direct personal and wealth taxes) and after all government transfers (cash and in-kind).

It is important to note that pensions and unemployment insurance represent the vast majority of cash transfers in the United States and more generally in rich countries. Therefore our notion of pre-tax income inequality (which we used in previous chapters to make international comparisons) already includes most cash redistribution.

In practice, other cash transfers tend to be relatively small. For instance, in the case of the United States, pre-tax income is virtually equal to post-tax cash income for the bottom 50%, at around $16 500 in 2014—and this figure has remained more or less the same since 1980. This means that the poor contribute about as much to taxes as they benefit from them in cash transfers (other than pensions and unemployment insurance), and this has not changed in forty years.

That being said, it is critical to study post-tax inequality and not only pre-tax inequality, first because in-kind transfers (in particular, access to free education and health services) play a very important role for bottom groups, and next because post-tax incomes can be substantially smaller than pre-tax incomes at the top of the distribution (at least in countries with highly progressive tax systems).

Unfortunately, the United States is the only country for which complete pre- and post-tax income inequality estimates are available in this Report. Would focusing on post-tax income inequality in other countries modify the general conclusions of the Report?

Based on the findings of this chapter and on preliminary results for other countries, it seems likely that focusing on post-tax incomes would tend to reinforce our main conclusions.

For instance, the magnitude of in-kind education and health transfers tends to be higher in Europe than in the United States, particularly for the bottom 50%, so our conclusion about higher inequality in the US is likely to be magnified when we move from pre-tax to post-tax inequality.

Next, we know that tax progressivity was reduced, rather than increased, in most countries since the 1980s (see Chapter 5.2). Taking into account post-tax estimates therefore tends to reinforce the rise in inequality observed in pre-tax series. In France, for instance, effective tax rates are lower for the very rich than for the middle class, and new tax legislations will further decrease these rates for the richest (see Chapter 2.5).

In emerging countries, the tax and transfer systems are generally less developed and less progressive than in the United States and Europe (as discussed in Chapter 5.2, there are no estate taxes in emerging countries, while the poor pay high taxes on some basic consumption goods such as energy), so the gap between extreme inequality countries and other regions discussed in Chapter 2.1 may in fact be reinforced with post-tax estimates.

The exact magnitude of these variations remains unknown at this stage. The WID.world consortium is currently producing novel post-tax income inequality estimates for various parts of the world (in particular for Europe and Latin America), but taking into account consistently all forms of incomes, taxes, and transfers of all individuals in a given country over long time periods requires tremendous efforts. This is an exciting agenda for economic research and future editions of this Report will present new results and progress made along these lines.

twentieth century may increasingly live off their capital income, or could be in the process of being replaced by their offspring who can live off their accumulated inheritance.

Taxes have become less progressive over the last decades

The progressivity of the US tax system has declined significantly over the last few decades, as illustrated in Figure 5.6. The country's macroeconomic tax rate (that is, the share of total taxes in national income including federal, state, and local taxes) increased from 8% in 1913 to 30% in the late 1960s, and has remained at the latter level since. Effective tax rates have become more compressed, however, across the income distribution. In the 1950s, the top 1% of income earners paid 40–45% of their pre-tax income in taxes, while the bottom 50% earners paid 15–20%. The gap in 2014 was much smaller. In 2014, top earners paid approximately 30–35% of their income in taxes, while the bottom 50% of earners paid around 25%. The main factor explaining why the effective tax rates paid by the top 1% have declined over time is the fall in corporate and estate taxes; in the 1960s, the top 1% paid close to 20% of its pre-tax income in corporate and estate taxes, while by 2014, this had fallen to approximately 10%.

The 2013 tax reforms partly reversed the long-run decline in top tax rates. The surtaxes introduced by the Affordable Care Act, and the expiration of the 2001 Bush tax cuts for top earners, together increased marginal tax rates for the richest on their capital income (+9.5 percentage points) and labor income (+6.5 percentage points).[14] These increases were the largest hikes in top tax rates since the 1950s, exceeding those implemented by the Clinton administration in 1993. The effective tax rate paid by top 1% earners has risen by approximately four percentage points between 2011 (32%) and 2013 (36%), and is now back to its level of the early 1980s.[15] Still, it is worth noting that inequality was much lower in the 1980s and that the long-run declines in corporate-tax and estate-tax revenues continue to exert downward pressure on effective tax rates at the top. Compared to the period between 1940 and 1960, when the level of taxation of the top 1% was consistently above 40%, the average tax rate as a percentage of pre-tax income was more than five percentage points lower in 2014, and ten percentage points lower than before the financial crisis.

In contrast to the overall fall in tax rates for top earners since the 1940s, taxes on the bottom 50% have risen from 15% to 25% between 1940 and 2014. This has been largely due to the rise of payroll taxes paid by the bottom 50%, which have risen from below 5% in the 1960s to more than 10% in 2014. Indeed, payroll

Source: Piketty, Saez, and Zucman (2018). See wir2018.wid.world for data series and notes.

In 2014, the average tax rate on the incomes of the Top 1% was 36%. Pre-tax national income is measured after the operation of pension and unemployment insurance systems (which cover the majority of cash transfers), but before direct income and wealth taxes. Taxes include all forms of taxes at the federal, state, and local level. Tax rates are expressed as a fraction of pre-tax income.

Figure 5.6 Average tax rate by pre-tax income group in the US, 1913–2014

taxes are now much more important than any other taxes—federal or state—borne by the bottom 50%. In 2014, payroll taxes amounted to 11% of pre-tax income, significantly above the next largest items: federal and state income taxes, which made up 7% of pre-tax income, and sales taxes, at 5%.[16] Although payroll taxes finance transfers including social security and Medicare, which in part go to the bottom 50%, their increase also contributes to the stagnation of the post-tax income of working-age Americans who make up a notable proportion of the bottom 50% of the income distribution.

Transfers essentially target the middle class, leaving the bottom 50% with little support in managing the collapse in their pre-tax incomes

While taxes have steadily become less progressive since the 1960s, one major evolution in the US economy over the last fifty years has been the rise of individualized transfers, both monetary and in-kind. Public-goods spending has remained constant, at around 18% of national income, but transfers—other than social security, disability, and unemployment insurance, which are already included in calculations of pre-tax income—increased from around 2% of national income in 1960 to 11% in 2014. The two largest transfers were Medicaid and Medicare, representing 4% and 3%, respectively, of national income in 2014.

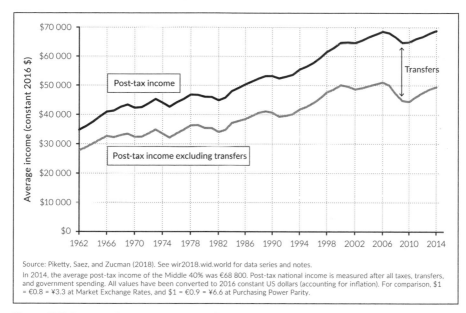

Source: Piketty, Saez, and Zucman (2018). See wir2018.wid.world for data series and notes.

In 2014, the average post-tax income of the Middle 40% was €68 800. Post-tax national income is measured after all taxes, transfers, and government spending. All values have been converted to 2016 constant US dollars (accounting for inflation). For comparison, $1 = €0.8 = ¥3.3 at Market Exchange Rates, and $1 = €0.9 = ¥6.6 at Purchasing Power Parity.

Figure 5.7 Post-tax income of the Middle 40% in the US, 1962–2014: The role of transfers

Other important transfers include refundable tax credits (0.8% of national income), veterans' benefits (0.6%), and food stamps (0.5%).

Perhaps surprisingly, individualized transfers tend to target the middle class. Despite Medicaid and other means-tested programs which go entirely to the bottom 50%, the middle 40% received larger transfers in 2014 (totaling 16% of per-adult national income) than the bottom 50% of Americans (10% of per-adult national income). With the top 10% of income earners receiving approximately 8% of per-adult national income in transfers, there is an inverted U-shaped relationship between post-tax income and transfers received (when social security benefits are included in transfers). These transfers have been key to enabling middle-class incomes to grow as, without them, average income for the middle 40% would not have grown at all between 1999 and 2014. (Figure 5.7) By contrast, transfers have not been sufficient to enable the incomes of the bottom 50% to grow significantly and counterbalance the collapse in their pre-tax income.

The reduction in the gender wage gap has been an important counterforce to rising US inequality

The reduction in the gender gap has been an important force in mitigating the rise in inequality that has largely taken place after 1980. To examine this process,

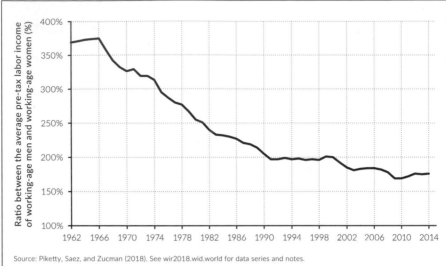

Source: Piketty, Saez, and Zucman (2018). See wir2018.wid.world for data series and notes.

In 2014, the average pre-tax labor income of men aged 20–64 years old was 1.76 times greater (76% higher) than the average pre-tax labor income of women aged 20–64 years old. Pre-tax labor income is composed of wages as well as pensions, social security, and unemployment insurance benefits, minus the corresponding contributions.

Figure 5.8 Difference in the pre-tax labor income between working-age men and women in the US, 1962–2014

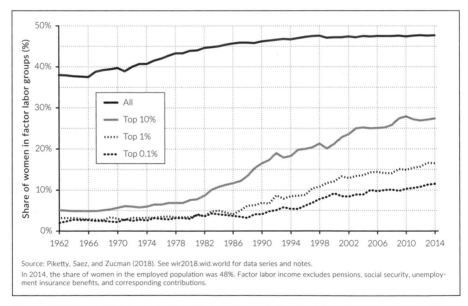

Source: Piketty, Saez, and Zucman (2018). See wir2018.wid.world for data series and notes.

In 2014, the share of women in the employed population was 48%. Factor labor income excludes pensions, social security, unemployment insurance benefits, and corresponding contributions.

Figure 5.9 Share of women in the employed population by labor income group in the US, 1962–2014

the data must be analyzed on an individual rather than on a tax-unit basis (such as a couple or a family). The overall gender gap has been almost halved over the last half-century, but it has far from disappeared. The more comprehensive way to measure the gender gap is to compute the ratio of average labor income of working-age men (aged 20–65) to average labor income of working-age women (aged 20–65), regardless of whether and how much they work. As illustrated in Figure 5.8, this income ratio has fallen from highs of 3.7:1 in the 1960s to approximately 1.75:1 in 2014.

Still, considerable gender inequalities persist, particularly at the top of the labor income distribution, as illustrated by Figure 5.9. In 2014, women accounted for close to 27% of the individuals in the top 10% of the income distribution, up 22 percentage points from 1960. Their representation, however, grows smaller at each higher step along the distribution of income. Women make up only 16% of the top 1% of labor income earners (a 13 percentage point rise from the 1960s), and only 11% of the top 0.1% (an increase of 9 percentage points). There has been only a modest increase in the share of women in top labor income groups since 1999. The glass ceiling is still far from being shattered.

6

Income Inequality in France

Information in this chapter is based on "Income Inequality in France, 1900–2014: Evidence from Distributional National Accounts (DINA)," by Bertrand Garbinti, Jonathan Goupille-Lebret, and Thomas Piketty, 2017. WID.world Working Paper Series (No. 2017/4).

- In 2014, the share of total pre-tax income received by the bottom 50% earners was 23%, while the share of the top 10% was 33%. Although income inequality in France was by no means insignificant in 2014, it sharply contrasts with the situation a century ago. In 1900, the top 10% of the income distribution received half of total French national income.
- Income inequality decreased significantly between the start of the First World War and the end of the Second World War due to the fall of top capital incomes resulting from the destruction of physical capital, the damaging impact of inflation, and the effects of nationalizations and rent-control policies.
- The struggle between labor and capital to share the fruits of growth between 1945 and 1983 characterized a turbulent period for income inequality, rising until 1968, when civil unrest pressured the government into reducing wage differentials.
- Austerity measures introduced in 1983, including the end of indexing wages to inflation, started a trend of rising inequality. Wage differentials and returns to capital increased thereafter.
- While gender pay gaps have consistently fallen since the 1970s, women made up just 30% of the top 10% of French earners in 2012, and if current trends continue, women cannot expect to make up a proportion of the top 10% equal to men until 2102.

In 2014, the top 10% French earners captured 33% of national income

In 2014, the average national income per adult in France was €33 400. This average, however, disguises significant variations among groups within the distribution. The bottom 50% earned around €15 000 on average in 2014, notably less than half the national average, and thus their share of total French income was less than a quarter (22.5%). The middle 40% had an annual average income of almost €37 500, and accordingly held a 45% share of national income, while the top 10% received approximately €109 000, more than three times the national average. These relative differences grow ever larger for the richest, with the top 1% having an 11% share in national income, and the top 0.1% and 0.01% having incomes 37 and 129 times the national average, as shown in Table 6.1.

Table 6.1 The distribution of national income in France, 2014

Income group	Number of adults	Income threshold (€)	Average income (€)	Income share
Full Population	51 722 000	–	33 400	100%
Bottom 50%	25 861 000	–	15 000	22.5%
Middle 40%	20 689 000	26 600	37 500	44.9%
Top 10%	5 172 000	56 100	109 000	32.6%
Top 1%	517 000	161 400	360 600	10.8%
Top 0.1%	51 700	544 600	1 234 400	3.7%
Top 0.01%	5 200	2 002 000	4 318 600	1.3%
Top 0.001%	500	6 976 500	13 175 100	0.4%

Source: Garbinti, Goupille-Lebret, and Piketty (2017). See wir2018.wid.world for data series and notes.

In 2014, 33% of national income was earned by the Top 10% in France. All values have been converted into 2016 Purchasing Power Parity (PPP) euros at a rate of €1 = $1.3 = ¥4.4. PPP accounts for differences in the cost of living between countries. Values are net of inflation. Numbers may not add up due to rounding.

Income inequality in France has varied significantly since the start of the twentieth century

While income inequality in France is by no means insignificant today, it has fallen notably since 1900. At the beginning of the twentieth century, the top 10% of the income distribution (which can be thought of as the "upper class") received 50% of total national income, while the middle 40% (the so-called "middle class") had around 35%. Meanwhile, the bottom 50% (the "lower class") had less than 15% of national income. The increased shares for the middle (+10 percentage points) and lower class (+8 percentage points) between 1900 and 2014 have thus come at the expense of the richest in roughly equal amounts. This reduction in inequality has taken place, however, in a haphazard and disorderly manner, undergoing numerous evolutions over the last century that are the result of a complex mix of historical events and political decisions.

To better comprehend recent developments in income inequality in France, it is first important to analyze how average income evolved from 1900 to 2014. Per-adult national income has risen approximately sevenfold over the last century in France, from around €5 500 in the year 1900. However, this growth in national income per adult was far from steady. Between 1900 and 1945, per-adult national income declined on average by −0.1% per year, but then increased at an average of 3.7% during the postwar period until 1980; dubbed *les trente glorieuses*. These "thirty glorious years" were followed by a period in which per-adult national incomes grew four times slower than previously, averaging 0.9% per annum from 1980 to 2014. This pattern was not unique to France, however. Similar trends were experienced in most European countries and Japan, and to a lesser extent in the United States and in the UK, where the shocks created by the First and Second World Wars were less damaging than in Continental Europe.

The evolution of income inequality over the last century can be broken down into three broad periods. The first of these periods was from the start of the First World War to the end of the Second World War. As visualized in Figure 6.1, the share of income of the top 10% of earners fell abruptly during the 1914–1945 period, from more than 50% of total income on the eve of the First World War to slightly above 30% of total income in 1945. This decline was mainly due to the collapse of capital income, which was hit by a number of negative shocks. Capital income generally makes up a significantly higher proportion of income for the richest 10% of the population, and particularly the top 1%, than it does for other groups. Both wars involved the destruction of capital stocks, and bankruptcies were not infrequent. They led to a collapse in gross domestic product (GDP), which lost 50% of its value between 1929 and 1945. Inflation reached record levels (the price index was multiplied by more than a hundred between 1914 and 1950), severely penalizing individuals with bond holdings and, more broadly, with fixed income assets. The control of rents during the period of inflationism led to a tenfold fall in their real value, and additionally, nationalization and the high level of taxation of certain assets in 1945 contributed to a sharp fall in capital income. The result for the top 1%—that is, those earning the most income from capital— was to see their share of national income halved in around thirty years.

The second period, between 1945 and 1983, was characterized by a struggle between labor and capital to share the fruits of growth, which reached very high

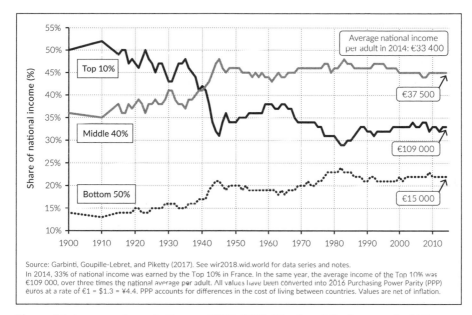

Source: Garbinti, Goupille-Lebret, and Piketty (2017). See wir2018.wid.world for data series and notes.
In 2014, 33% of national income was earned by the Top 10% in France. In the same year, the average income of the Top 10% was €109 000, over three times the national average per adult. All values have been converted into 2016 Purchasing Power Parity (PPP) euros at a rate of €1 = $1.3 = ¥4.4. PPP accounts for differences in the cost of living between countries. Values are net of inflation.

Figure 6.1 Incomes shares in France, 1900–2013: The rise of the lower and middle classes

levels (+3.3% per year on average). From 1945 to 1968, the inequality in wages that had existed before the world wars was rebuilt and the share of capital in the French economy also rose, leading to a period of rising income inequality. As illustrated by Figure 6.1, the income share of the top 10% had risen from around 30% to 38% during this twenty-three-year period, while the share of the bottom 50% fell from approximately 23% to 17%. Following the events of May 1968, however, this trajectory of rising inequality abruptly stopped.

May 1968 was a volatile period of civil unrest in France, punctuated by demonstrations, general strikes, and protester occupations of universities and factories across the country. The French government, under Charles de Gaulle's presidency, introduced a number of conciliatory policies in the following month in an attempt at appeasement, including a boost in the real minimum wage of approximately 20%. This marked the beginning of a period of steady increases in the minimum wage and of the purchasing power of the poor between 1968 and 1983. The purchasing power of those with lower wages rose substantially more than did GDP, which itself grew by a noteworthy 30%. These factors led to a compression in the distribution of wages and reduced income inequality more generally. In the early 1980s, the top 10% had their lowest share of pre-tax national income recorded, at 30%, while the middle 40% had a historic high of approximately 48%, and the bottom 50% accounted for 23%. However, the rise in unemployment that started during the mid-1970s also marked the beginning of a new period.

The third period, marked by a substantial reduction in income growth rates (1% per year on average), began in 1982–1983 when successive governments decided to end the policy of indexing wages to prices and therefore reduced the rate of wage increases for the low-paid.[17] This was initially part of an austerity program known as the *tournant de la rigueur* (austerity turn), introduced by President Mitterrand's then newly elected left-wing government. The program was an attempt to combat high inflation rates and rapid deteriorations in the budget and trade deficits between 1981 and 1983 that could have seen France leave the European Monetary System. Taxes were also increased, subsidies to state-owned enterprises were reduced, and social security and unemployment insurance payments were restrained.[18] The overall effect of these policy choices was an increase in the pay gaps between those who earned the lowest wages and others. During this period, inequality was relatively stable except at the top of the distribution. Very top incomes increased substantially.

The end of the "thirty glorious years" for the bottom 95%, but not for those at the top

One way to better understand the magnitude of the turning point that occurred in the 1980s is to look at the total growth curve by income group. That is, we can ask: What was the change in the average income of each group over the different time periods? Between 1983 and 2014, average national income per adult rose by 35% (1% per annum) in real terms in France. However, actual total growth was not the same for all income groups, as illustrated by the impressive upward slope on the right hand of the 1983–2014 growth curve in Figure 6.2. Total growth between 1983 and 2014 was 31% on average (0.9% per annum) for the bottom 50% of the distribution, 27% for next 40% (0.8% per annum), and 49% for the top 10% (1.3% per annum). Moreover, total growth remained below the economy-wide average until the ninety-ninth percentile, and then rose steeply, up to as much as 98% growth over the thirty-one-year period (2.2% per annum) for the top 0.1% and 144% for the top 0.001% (2.9% per annum).

The contrast between 1950 and 1983 and 1983 and 2014 in terms of the total growth rates of income groups is particularly stark. As Table 6.2 and Figure 6.2 show, growth rates were very high for the bottom 99% of the population during the "thirty glorious years" between 1950 and 1983, at around 200%, while growth for the top 1% was markedly lower at 109% (2.3% per annum). Growth rates were even lower at the very top, at around 80% (1.8% per annum) for the top 0.1 and 0.01%.

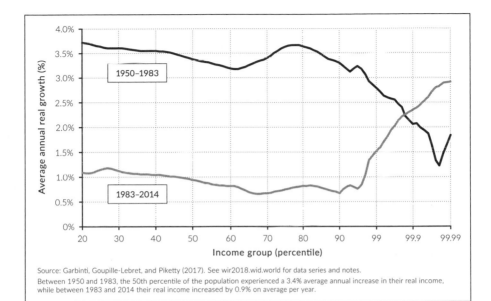

Figure 6.2 Average annual real growth by income group in France, 1950–2014

Table 6.2 Income growth and inequality in France, 1900–2014

Income group	1900–1950			1950–1983			1983–2014		
	Average annual growth rate	Total cumu-lated growth	Share of total cumu-lated growth	Average annual growth rate	Total cumu-lated growth	Share of total cumu-lated growth	Average annual growth rate	Total cumu-lated growth	Share of total cumu-lated growth
Full Popula-tion	1.0%	64%	100%	3.3%	194%	100%	1.0%	35%	100%
Bottom 50%	1.8%	144%	30%	3.7%	236%	25%	0.9%	31%	21%
Middle 40%	1.5%	108%	61%	3.4%	204%	48%	0.8%	27%	37%
Top 10%	0.2%	11%	8%	2.9%	157%	27%	1.3%	49%	42%
Top 1%	0.6%	37%	16%	3.1%	178%	21%	0.9%	33%	21%
Top 0.1%	-0.5%	-23%	-8%	2.3%	109%	6%	2.2%	98%	21%
Top 0.01%	-1.1%	-44%	-7%	1.7%	75%	1%	2.8%	133%	8%
Top 0.001%	-2.0%	-63%	-5%	1.8%	83%	0%	2.9%	144%	3%

Source: Garbinti, Goupille-Lebret, and Piketty (2017). See wir2018.wid.world for data series and notes.

Between 1900 and 1950, the share of national income growth captured by the Top 10% was 8%.

Another way to measure these diverging evolutions is to compare the shares of total economic growth going to the different income groups. Between 1950 and 1983, 25% of total growth went to the bottom 50% of the population, versus only 6% to the top 1%. Between 1983 and 2014, 21% of total growth went to the bottom 50%, as much as the share of growth which went to the top 1%.

Summing up, although the rise of inequality was less pronounced in France (and to a large extent in Europe) than in the United States, the break between the 1950–1983 period, when bottom groups enjoyed larger growth than the top, and the 1983–2014 period, when the exact opposite pattern prevailed, is very visible.

Recent growth at the top is due to higher salaries and returns on capital assets

As a result of the unequal distribution of growth, the share of income attributed to the top 1% has seen a notable increase between 1983 and 2007, rising from less than 8% of total income to over 12% over this period—that is, rising by over 50%. Between 2008 and 2013, the income share of the top 1% fluctuated between 10% and 12%, remaining significantly larger than when income inequality was at its lowest point in the early eighties (see Figure 6.1). As stated above, this trend of rising inequality among the highest earners is even more pronounced for the top 0.1% and the top 0.01% (Figure 6.3). The difference between the average national income before tax and those of top earners has almost doubled over the preceding thirty years. The top 0.1% average income increased from 21 times above average in 1983 to 37 times in 2014, while the figure increased from 71 times average to 129 times for the top 0.01%.

Why has there been a rise in top incomes over the recent period? In the case of France, top earners have experienced significant increases in their incomes from both labor and capital. Between 1983 and 2013, the labor income of the top 0.01% rose 53%, while their capital income increased by 48%. It is difficult for standard explanations based on technical change and the changing supply and demand of skills to explain rising income concentration at the very top, whether around the world or in France specifically.[19] The rise of labor incomes at the top is more likely to be the result of evolutions in institutional factors governing pay-setting processes for top managerial compensation, including changes in corporate governance and the decline of unions and collective bargaining processes. Evolutions in top marginal tax rates have also likely had an impact on labor income inequality. Reduced top income tax rates can affect wage-setting at the top; as top earners expect less taxes, they may be more inclined to ask for

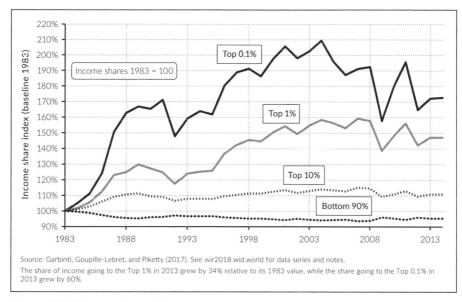

Figure 6.3 Rising top inequality in France, 1983–2013

Increases in wages.[20] Top income tax rates were above 60% during *les trente glorieuses* and rose to 70% in the early 1980s. They fell to about 50% in the late 2000s. Effective tax rates (total taxes paid on total income) are actually inferior for very top income groups than for the middle class.[21] Recent tax legislation supported by the current government are about to further reduce tax rates at the top, in particular due to reduction in tax rates on capital.

Increases in top labor income inequality have in certain cases been correlated with increases in top capital income inequality. Top managers, for example, have benefited first from very high labor incomes through large bonuses or stock options (some of which have been largely mediatized) and then from very high capital incomes derived from improvements in the price of the stocks that they have come to own. Top capital incomes have also been rising due to the rising share of macroeconomic capital in a context of declining labor bargaining power and privatization policies.

Gender pay gaps may be falling, but men are still paid approximately 50% more than women

While income inequality has increased since the 1980s, gender gaps have been declining since the 1970s. Still, gender gaps remain very high in France today. In the 1970s (the "age of patriarchy") men earned 3.5 to 5 times the labor income

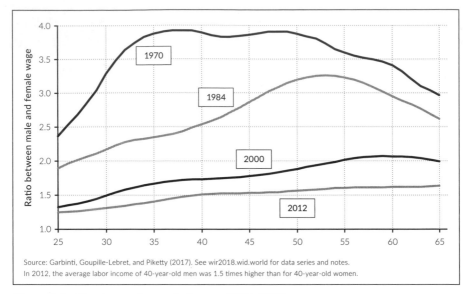

Source: Garbinti, Goupille-Lebret, and Piketty (2017). See wir2018.wid.world for data series and notes.
In 2012, the average labor income of 40-year-old men was 1.5 times higher than for 40-year-old women.

Figure 6.4a Gender gap by age in France, 1970–2012

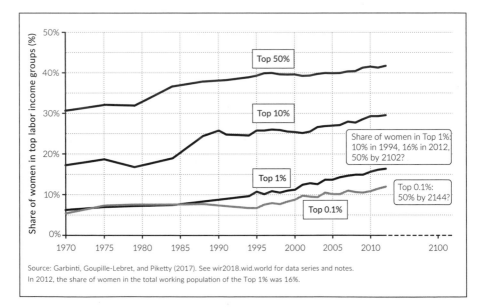

Source: Garbinti, Goupille-Lebret, and Piketty (2017). See wir2018.wid.world for data series and notes.
In 2012, the share of women in the total working population of the Top 1% was 16%.

Figure 6.4b Share of women in top labor income groups in France, 1970–2012

of women, and women's labor force participation rate was around 45%. The share of working women rose dramatically to 80% in 2012 and the women-to-men pay ratio decreased to 1:1.5 on average. There are, however, strong variations in gender income gaps over age groups. As can be seen in Figure 6.4a, in 2012, men earned 1.25 times more on average than women at the age of 25, and 1.64 times more at age 65.

Gender inequalities are also particularly high among higher paying jobs. Despite moderate improvements since 1994, women still do not have equal access to them. In 2012, the female share of the top 50% of earners was 42%, while women made up just 30% and 12% of the top 10% and top 0.1% earners, respectively. If current trends continue, women can expect to make up the same proportion as men of the top 10% and top 0.1% shares by 2102 and 2144, respectively. (Figure 6.4b)

7

Income Inequality in Germany

Information in this chapter is based on "Top incomes in Germany, 1871–2013," by Charlotte Bartels, 2017. WID.world Working Paper Series (No. 2017/18).

- In 2013, the share of total income received by the bottom half of the population was 17%, while the share of the top decile was 40%. In 1913, the share of the top 10% was also 40%. The top 1% is, however, lower today than in 1913 (18% versus 13%).
- The top 1% increased sharply between the creation of the Reich in 1871 and the establishment of the Weimar Republic in 1918. It then decreased dramatically when social policies were implemented by the Weimar Republic. The Nazi prewar period is associated with economic recovery and favorable policies for large businesses, and saw temporary surges in top incomes. The top 1% share was then reduced to 10–12% during the 1950–1990 period and has been on the rise since reunification.
- Top income earners in Germany have been business owners throughout the twentieth century and up to the present. As most German firms are family owned, with some family members more involved than others, it is difficult to judge how much of top incomes are labor incomes and which part is "pure" capital income (with limited labor input). Starting in the 1980s, however, highly qualified employees have increasingly entered top-income groups.
- In Germany, high income concentration of the industrialization period dropped as early as the 1920s and fluctuated around this level throughout the postwar period. This contrasts with other rich countries like the United States, the United Kingdom, and France, where the Second World War brought strong and lasting reductions in income concentrations at the top.

Investigating the evolution of inequality using German income tax data has a long tradition, as particularly Prussian and Saxon tax data are internationally praised for their accuracy. Simon Kuznets partly drew his famous hypothesis of rising inequality in the early phase of industrialization from Prussian income tax data. The early introduction of modern income taxation in German states at the end of the nineteenth century offers a special opportunity to compute inequality series from the industrialization phase until today.

The series presented in this chapter are based on pre-tax income data from historical German income-tax statistics collected by Charlotte Bartels. One should note, however, that the impressive length of the period covered in Germany comes with a price, in that changing territories are covered by the series. The two world wars of the twentieth century, the division of Germany after the Second World War, and its reunification in 1990 leave the researcher with income tax systems applying across time to quite differently sized territories and populations.

Long-run German income inequality dynamics can be split into five periods

The evolution of income inequality from 1871 to 2013 can be split into five periods. Figure 7.1 shows the evolution of the top 1% income share from 1871 to 2013. The first period starts with the foundation of the German Reich in 1871, which unified German states, and ends with the First World War. The top percentile was the greatest beneficiary of this industrialization period. Its income share moderately increased from 16% in 1871 to 18% in 1913 and then rose to 23% during the First World War. The sharp increase observed during that war might have been the result of extraordinarily high profits from military spending. By 1918, authorities managed to restrict those profits, which contributed to bringing the top 1% share back down to 20% of national income.

The second period includes the years of the Weimar Republic (1918–1933), which brought a variety of inequality-reducing policies, including an increase in the top marginal tax rate from 5% to 60% in Prussia, the introduction of unemployment insurance, and employment law including employment protections. Strong unions and the rise of collective bargaining contributed to an increase in wages, which resulted in lower labor income inequality. Hyperinflation eroded financial assets and greatly reduced capital incomes during this period. Additionally, industrial firms generated very low profits throughout the 1920s, if any at all, and mostly did not pay out dividends. As a consequence, the top percentile's income share decreased significantly from 20% in 1918 to 11% in 1925 and remained at the latter level until 1933.

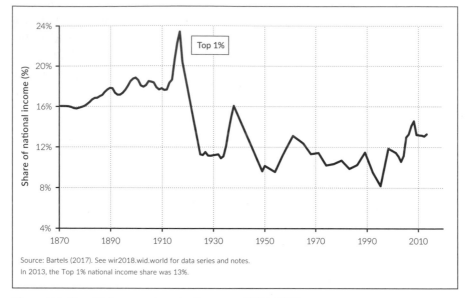

Source: Bartels (2017). See wir2018.wid.world for data series and notes.
In 2013, the Top 1% national income share was 13%.

Figure 7.1 Top 1% income share in Germany, 1871–2013

The third period starts with the Nazis' seizure of control in 1933 and ends at the eve of the Second World War in 1938. After 1938, the Statistical Office stopped publishing income tax statistics so it is impossible to know how income distribution changed during the Second World War. This prewar Nazi period is marked by an extraordinary increase in the top percentile's income share from 11% in 1934 to 17% in 1938, contrasting with the initial anti-big-business rhetoric of the Nazi Party. In contrast, to the top percentile, the P95–P99 group (the top 5% richest, minus the very top 1%) gained only moderately during this period. As in most rich countries, economic recovery after the Great Depression started in 1932 in Germany. Industrial firms saw their profits rise sharply between 1933 and 1939. Ferguson and Voth find evidence that firms with strong ties to the Nazi Party disproportionately benefited from the recovery, which probably contributed to further concentration of incomes at the top.[22] The larger firms across all sectors were more likely to form connections with the Nazi government, but this was particularly the case for the rearmament industry.

The post-war period is marked by a relatively stable but high top percentile income share

The German postwar period is characterized by a comparably high income concentration at the top, paralleled by a rather compressed wage distribution.

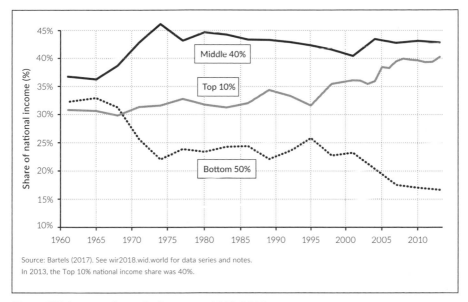

Source: Bartels (2017). See wir2018.wid.world for data series and notes.
In 2013, the Top 10% national income share was 40%.

Figure 7.2 Income shares in Germany, 1961–2013

From the mid-1950s until the 1980s, the top percentile's share oscillates between 11% and 13%. This is higher than the top percentile's share in postwar United States, United Kingdom, or France in the same period. This finding is particularly striking as the policies (especially nationalizations and rent control) after the Second World War and destructions during the Second World War are generally seen as long-lasting equalizing forces both in Germany and in other war-partic-ipating countries. The currency reform in 1948 eradicated capital incomes from financial assets for the second time in the twentieth century, while leaving busi-ness assets and real estate untouched. Savings accounts were reduced to about a tenth of their former value. As rents were heavily regulated, top incomes stemmed from business profits. On the other hand, strong labor demand and the high national income growth rates of the German *Wirtschaftswunder* coincided with powerful unions, low unemployment, and a rather compressed wage distribution. The bottom 50% then received a third of total income, as Figure 7.2 shows. It was not until the 1980s that top wage earners increasingly entered top-income groups and the wage distribution became increasingly unequal. With the oil crises and the onset of mass unemployment, the share of the bottom 50% decreased to less than a fifth of national income. The fall of the bottom half was mirrored by an increase of the middle 40%, who received slightly more than 40% of national income beginning in the 1970s.

Income inequality is rising at the top since reunification

The fifth and last period corresponds to reunified Germany. Political unification on October 3, 1990, brought the eastern states of Berlin, Brandenburg, Mecklenburg–Western Pomerania, Saxony, Saxony-Anhalt, and Thuringia into the Federal Republic of Germany. The first years after reunification were marked by exceptionally high national income growth rates for the reunified German economy. Industrial production quickly collapsed in the East and unemployment rose accordingly. Those keeping their jobs benefited from an unprecedented jump in real wages, thanks to bargaining by the East German labor unions that aimed to reach parity with West German wage levels in 1994. Taking these effects together, the top percentile's income share fell sharply, whereas the bottom 50% gained in the first years following reunification. The start of the new millennium marked another turning point; the share of the bottom half declined significantly from 22% in 2001 to 17% in 2013, a trend that went hand in hand with the growth of the low-income sector.

The top 10% income group quite steadily increased its income share over the entire postwar period. Highly qualified employees like engineers, lawyers, and doctors have benefited from high wage growth and have been increasingly present in top-income groups. However, very top incomes are still exclusive to business owners, and profits fluctuate with business cycles. The top percentile's share is volatile, as shown in Figure 7.3. It suffered large shocks in the German unifi-

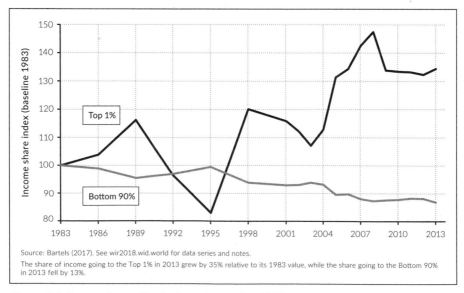

Source: Bartels (2017). See wir2018.wid.world for data series and notes.
The share of income going to the Top 1% in 2013 grew by 35% relative to its 1983 value, while the share going to the Bottom 90% in 2013 fell by 13%.

Figure 7.3 Income inequality in Germany, 1983–2013

cation crisis in the mid-1990s, the burst of the new economy bubble in the early 2000s, and the Great Recession in 2009. But despite the large drop after the Great Recession, the top percentile's income share still grew by almost 40% between 1983 and 2013, while the bottom 90% share fell by 10%. In 2013, while the average income in Germany was €36 200, the top 10% earned €146 000, the middle 40% earned €39 000, and the bottom 50% earned €12 000.

Income Inequality in China

Information in this chapter is based on "Capital Accumulation, Private Property and Rising Inequality in China, 1978–2015," by Thomas Piketty, Li Yang, and Gabriel Zucman, 2017. WID.world Working Paper Series (No. 2017/6).

- China's opening-up policies established from the late 1970s onward were followed by unprecedented rises in national income, but also significant changes to the country's distribution of income.
- While the top 10% and bottom 50% both shared 27% of national income in 1978, they diverged dramatically thereafter, with the former experiencing a substantial increase to 42% by 2015 and the latter a substantial decrease to 15%.
- The top 10% of the income distribution enjoyed total growth rates higher than the national average (approximately 1 200% versus 800%), while the bottom 50% and middle 40% experienced slower growth (400% and 700%, respectively).
- The urban-rural gap in national income has grown considerably between 1978 and 2015 due to a rise in urban incomes and population. Despite this rising gap, it is mainly inequality within regions that has spurred the growth of inequality at the national level.

Chinese average incomes grew ninefold since 1978

The Communist Party of China, then led by Deng Xiaoping, implemented a series of policies in the People's Republic of China starting in December 1978 to reform and open up the Chinese economy, as the Party sought a new economic model based on the principle of "socialism with Chinese characteristics." The transition away from the communist model of the previous decades ushered in gradual but nevertheless wide-reaching reforms, expanding geographically from special economic zones in coastal cities toward inland provincial regions, and in sectoral waves. During the first stage of reform, market principles were introduced into the agricultural sector through the de-collectivization of production. While foreign investment and entrepreneurship were permitted under state guidance, the vast majority of industry remained state-owned until the mid-1980s. The following decades saw a second stage of deeper reforms implemented. Soviet-style central planning in industry was dismantled through the privatization and contracting out of state-owned enterprises, though the state maintained its control of monopolies in some sectors, including banking and petroleum. Furthermore, liberalization of markets over this period saw the lifting of price controls and the reduction of protectionist policies and regulations, aiding the dramatic growth of the private sector. These changes were particularly evident in the country's housing market. The private housing stock rose from roughly 50% in 1978 to over 95% in 2015. For other forms of domestic capital, the public share declined, though it is still around 50%.

The subsequent impacts of these privatization and opening-up reforms have been of great interest worldwide, particularly given the significant growth the country has experienced over the last forty years and its accompanying improvements in poverty rates. Indeed, between 1978 and 2015, China moved from a poor, low-income country to the world's leading emerging economy. Despite the decline in its share of world population, China's share of world national income increased from less than 3% in 1978 to 19% in 2015, and real per-adult national income multiplied more than ninefold. Indeed, average national income per adult was about €1 400 per year in 1978 (less than 15% of global average), but exceeded €13 100 in 2015 (close to 90% of the global average).

In a recent paper, Thomas Piketty, Li Yang, and Gabriel Zucman analyze how this exceptional growth was distributed across the Chinese population (reported below), and the impact that privatization policies had on the country's capital-income ratios (see Chapter 16 of the report).[23] To form distributional national accounts, the authors combine survey data, national accounts, and recently released income tax data on high-income taxpayers. They find a significant increase in per-adult pre-tax income inequality from 1978 to 2015.[24] These results largely increase existing official inequality statistics and probably represent a lower bound to inequality, as they remain imperfect.

The shares of the top 10% and bottom 50% diverged after the opening-up reforms

As China began its privatization process (as also discussed in Chapter 17 on Chinese public and private wealth dynamics), the share of national income going to the top 10% of the population was 27%, equal to the share going to the bottom 50%. Put in another way, these groups captured the same amount of total income, but the former had a population five times smaller than the latter. The average income of the bottom 50% was thus one-fifth of the top 10%. In 1978, the income share of the middle 40% represented just over 46% of national income; their average income was only slightly higher than the national average. The past four decades show a large divergence in the shares of the bottom 50% and the top 10% income earners (Figure 8.1).

The income share of the bottom 50% in 2015 was just below 15%, a twelve-percentage-point fall since 1978. The share of the top 10% had increased to 41%. In 2015, the average income of the bottom 50% (€3 900 or ¥17 000) was approximately 13.5 times smaller than that of the richest 10% in 2015 (€54 500 or ¥238 000). The bottom 50% consequently earned roughly 3.4 times less than the average national income per adult in China of €13 100 or ¥57 000 in 2015, while the top 10% earned around four times more than the average income. The share of national income going to the middle 40% is only marginally different than in 1978 at almost 44%. The average income of this middle class (€14 400 or ¥63 000) was slightly higher than the average Chinese adult's income in 2015. (Table 8.1)

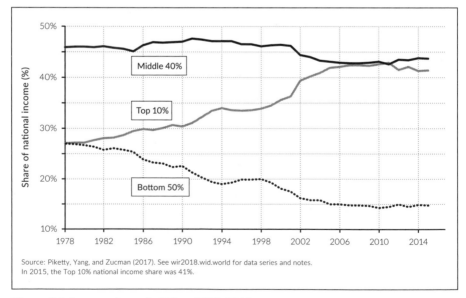

Source: Piketty, Yang, and Zucman (2017). See wir2018.wid.world for data series and notes.
In 2015, the Top 10% national income share was 41%.

Figure 8.1 Income shares in China, 1978–2015

Table 8.1 The distribution of national income in China, 2015

Income group	Number of adults	Income threshold (€)	Average income (€)	Income share
Full Population	1 063 543 000	–	13 100	100%
Bottom 50%	531 771 000	–	3 900	14.8%
Middle 40%	425 417 000	7 800	14 400	43.7%
Top 10%	106 354 000	27 000	54 500	41.4%
Top 1%	10 635 000	79 000	183 000	13.9%
Top 0.1%	1 064 000	244 000	828 000	6.3%
Top 0.01%	106 000	1 411 000	4 207 000	3.2%
Top 0.001%	11 000	6 868 000	17 925 000	1.4%

Source: Piketty, Yang, and Zucman (2017). See wir2018.wid.world for data series and notes.

In 2015, the average income of the Top 1% was €183 000 (¥800 000). All values have been converted into 2016 Purchasing Power Parity (PPP) euros at a rate of €1 = $1.3 = ¥4.4. PPP accounts for differences in the cost of living between countries. Values are net of inflation. Numbers may not add up due to rounding.

Income inequality stabilized after 2006

While the incomes of the top 10% and the bottom 50% in China began to diverge in 1978, the greatest divergence took place from 1998 to 2006. This coincided with the eight-year period that saw the Chinese government introduce a new set of policies for the privatization of state-owned enterprises, mainly in the tertiary sector. Part of the resulting effect was a reduction in the bottom 50% share of national income from 20% to 15%, and an increase in the share of the top 10% from around 34% to 43%. Income inequality apparently stabilized thereafter, with the shares of all three of the main income groups in 2015 remaining pretty much similar to their levels in 2006. This stabilization of inequality since 2006 should be regarded with caution as it could partly reflect data limitations, due in particular to the lack of national data made available on high-income taxpayers since 2011.[25] Still, this trend is considered valid by a number of researchers who speculate that a turnaround took place around 2006 as a result of two factors: new policies that reflected changing priorities toward more equitable growth; and the slowdown of structural transformations, such as a shrinking rural labor force, which caused wages to grow more rapidly than output.[26]

Comparing Piketty, Yang, and Zucman's inequality series to the survey-based estimates used by the Chinese government, two remarks are in order. First, the official survey data also show a strong rise in the national income share of the top 10% and a strong decline in the top 50% income share from 1978 to 2015. Second, both the level and the rise of inequality are larger in the aforementioned corrected series than in the official series. The top 10% income share rises 14 percentage points over the observed period (from 27% to 41% of national income)—which is 6 percentage points more than that seen in the official statistics—while the upward correction for the top 1% sees their share of total income for 2015 rise to 14%, versus 6.5% in the raw surveys. Most of the difference between these estimates and the raw surveys comes from the finer level of precision among top income earners enabled by income tax data. In 2015, for example, the raw surveys identify the income share of the top 1% to be 6.5%, but this reaches 11.5% after factoring in data from high-income taxpayers, and 14% following the inclusion of undistributed profits and other tax-exempt income.

Since 1980, Chinese top-income groups benefited from quadruple-digit growth rates

The new data series constructed by Piketty, Yang, and Zucman on the distribution of national income also allow a decomposition of national income growth

Table 8.2 Income growth and inequality in China, 1980–2015

Income group	China		US		France	
	Average annual growth rate	Total cumulated growth	Average annual growth rate	Total cumulated growth	Average annual growth rate	Total cumulated growth
Full Population	6.4%	776%	1.4%	63%	0.9%	38%
Bottom 50%	4.6%	386%	0.1%	3%	0.8%	33%
Middle 40%	6.2%	733%	1.0%	44%	0.9%	35%
Top 10%	7.7%	1232%	2.3%	124%	1.1%	46%
Top 1%	8.8%	1800%	3.3%	208%	1.6%	77%
Top 0.1%	9.5%	2271%	4.2%	325%	1.7%	81%
Top 0.01%	10.2%	2921%	5.0%	460%	1.9%	91%
Top 0.001%	10.8%	3524%	5.9%	646%	2.2%	110%

Source: Piketty, Yang, and Zucman (2017). See wir2018.wid.world for data series and notes.
Between 1980 and 2015, the average pre-tax income of the Top 10% in China grew by 1232%. Values are net of inflation.

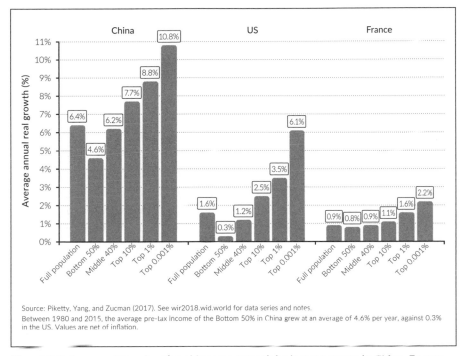

Figure 8.2 Average annual national income growth by income group in China, France, and the US, 1980–2015

by income group. This in turn enables a quantitative assessment of the extent to which various groups of the population have benefited from the enormous growth China has experienced since 1980. (See Table 8.2 and Figure 8.2)

Average national income per adult has grown close to ninefold between 1980 and 2015, corresponding to an average annual increase of 6.4% and a total growth rate of 780%. This growth has not been equally shared; the higher the income level, the higher the rate of growth over the time period considered. Growth for the bottom 50% over the period was 390%, while it was 730% for the middle 40%, and 1 230% for the top 10%. Within the top 10%, growth was also unequally shared. The top 1% experienced total income growth of 1 800%—a huge figure, but notably less than the increases of over 2 270%, 2 920%, and 3 520% for the top 0.1%, top 0.01%, and top 0.001%, respectively.

By contrast, average national income per adult rose by just 63% and 38% in the United States and France over the same period, respectively—approximately fourteen and twenty-one times less than in China. The difference in income growth across the distribution was also markedly different at the bottom of the distribution; the cumulative national income growth of the bottom 50% was 3%

for Americans, while for French citizens, it rose at 33%, i.e., less than the average. However, the same pattern, by which income growth rates rise more quickly the higher up the distribution one goes, was evident for all countries.

The urban-rural gap continues to grow, but it is within-region inequality that spurs overall growth in inequality

What role has the urban-rural gap played in the evolution of Chinese inequality? This question is important as inequality could be driven mainly by growing differences between cities and rural areas and not by inequality among individuals within areas. Policy implications are indeed dependent on which force dominates in the mix. To answer this question, it is first important to identify how the populations of urban and rural areas have changed post 1978, as this will in part determine the urban and rural shares in national income. In the urban areas of China, the adult population rose from 100 million in 1978 to almost 600 million in 2015. During this same period, the adult rural population remained roughly stable, rising from 400 million in 1978 to almost 600 million by the mid-1990s, before declining to less than 500 million in 2015. Second, the income gap between urban and rural China has always been large and it has grown over time. Urban households earned twice as much income on average as

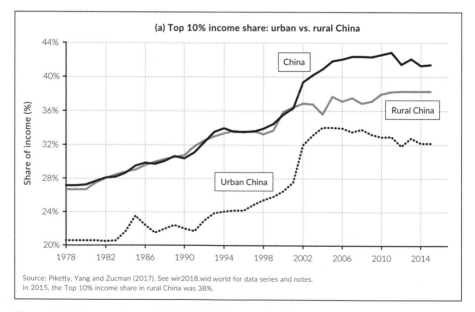

(a) Top 10% income share: urban vs. rural China

Source: Piketty, Yang and Zucman (2017). See wir2018.wid.world for data series and notes.
In 2015, the Top 10% income share in rural China was 38%.

Figure 8.3a Income share of the Top 10% in rural and urban China, 1978–2015

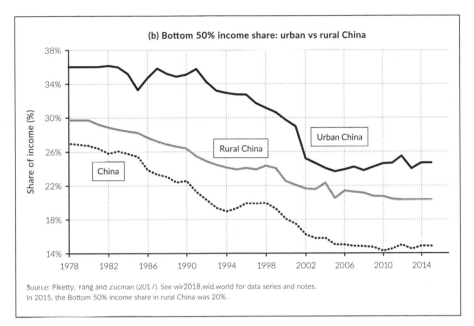

Figure 8.3b Income share of the Bottom 50% in rural and urban China, 1978–2015

rural households in 1978, but in 2015 they earned 3.5 times as much. Thus, while the urban share in the adult population has grown from 20% in 1978 to 55% in 2015, the urban share in national income has increased from 30% to 80%.

Despite the increase of inequality both in urban and rural China, the level of income inequality in China as a whole is markedly higher at the national level (where the bottom 50% captures only 15% of total income) than it is within rural China (where the figure is 20%) or urban China (25%) considered alone.[27] As evidenced in the previous sections, the trend for the top 10% largely mirrored that of the bottom 50%, but in the opposite direction, with rising income shares for the top 10%. Combining this data also demonstrates that there has always been more inequality within rural areas than within urban China, and this will remain the case if current trends continue. (Figure 8.3)

Income Inequality in Russia

Information in this chapter is based on "From Soviets to Oligarchs: Inequality and Property in Russia 1905–2016," by Filip Novokmet, Thomas Piketty, and Gabriel Zucman, 2017. WID.world Working Paper Series (No. 2017/9).

- Russia's transition from a communist to a capitalist economic model after 1989 brought about a large divergence in the income shares and growth rates of different income groups.
- The share of national income attributable to the bottom 50% has fallen from 30% in 1989 to less than 20% today, while the share of the top 1% has rocketed upward from around 25% to over 45% of national income.
- Russia's rapid and chaotic "shock therapy" of privatization, capital flight, and the rise of offshore wealth, along with high inflation and a new market environment, have contributed to the rise of top Russian incomes since 1989.
- Today's inequality levels are comparable, and somewhat higher, than those observed during the tsarist period. The Russian Revolution led to a significant redistribution of income, with the top 1% share of national income falling from 18% in 1905 to less than 4% in 1928.
- The most equitable distribution of income in Russia's recent history followed the introduction of comparatively liberal de-Stalinization policies from 1958 onward, with large investments in education and infrastructure.

Since the 1990s, Russia's convergence toward Western European levels of GDP has been far from smooth

Since the fall of the Soviet Union in 1990–1991, Russia has experienced dramatic economic and political transformations. National income and gross domestic product fell abruptly from 1992 to 1995, when inflation skyrocketed, but then started to recover during 1998 and 1999, ushering in a decade of robust growth. The world financial crisis and the fall in oil prices interrupted this process in 2008–2009 and, since then, growth has been sluggish. However, there is little doubt that average incomes are significantly higher in Russia today than they were in 1989–1990. Indeed, the gap between Russia's per-adult national income and the West European average narrowed from approximately 60–65% of the West European average in 1989–1990, to around 70–75% in mid-2010.[28] This can be seen in Figure 9.1.

While average national income per adult in Russia reached almost €23 200 in 2016, this figure hides considerable variations in its distribution. The lowest-earning 50% of the adult population—a group of almost 115 million people—earned just under €7 800 on average in 2016, close to three times less than the national average. The middle 40% also received less income than the national average, earning approximately €21 700. The richest 10% of the population earned

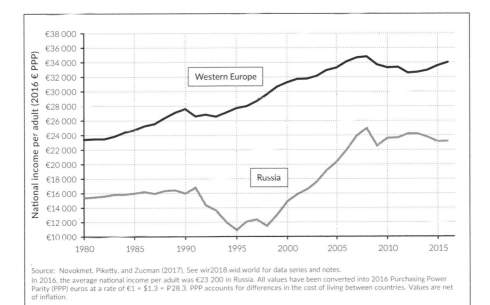

Source: Novokmet, Piketty, and Zucman (2017). See wir2018.wid.world for data series and notes.
In 2016, the average national income per adult was €23 200 in Russia. All values have been converted into 2016 Purchasing Power Parity (PPP) euros at a rate of €1 = $1.3 = ₽28.3. PPP accounts for differences in the cost of living between countries. Values are net of inflation.

Figure 9.1 Average national income per adult in Russia and Western Europe, 1980–2016

Table 9.1 The distribution of national income in Russia, 2016

Income group	Number of adults	Income threshold (€)	Average income (€)	Income share
Full Population	114 930 000	–	23 180	100%
Bottom 50%	57 465 000	–	7 880	17.0%
Middle 40%	45 972 000	14 000	21 700	37.5%
Top 10%	11 493 000	36 300	105 500	45.5%
Top 1%	1 149 300	133 000	469 000	20.2%
Top 0.1%	114 930	638 000	2 494 000	10.8%
Top 0.01%	11 493	3 716 000	12 132 000	5.2%
Top 0.001%	1 149	18 770 000	58 576 000	2.5%

Source: Novokmet, Piketty, and Zucman (2017). See wir2018.wid.world for data series and notes.

In 2016, the average pre-tax income of the Top 10% was €105 500. All values have been converted into 2016 Purchasing Power Parity (PPP) euros at a rate of €1 = $1.3 = P28.3. PPP accounts for differences in the cost of living between countries. Values are net of inflation. Numbers may not add up due to rounding.

considerably more, however, receiving over €105 500 on average in 2016. These differences in income left Russia with a very high concentration of income among the country's richest individuals. The share of national income attributable to the top 10% was 45.5% in 2016, making it considerably larger than that of the bottom 50% (17%) and the middle 40% (37.5%). The top 1% earners capture more than 20% of national income. The average income of the 1.15 million adults in the top 1% was approximately €470 000 in 2016 whereas the top 0.01% and top 0.001% had average incomes of €12.1 million and €58.6 million, respectively—over 523 times and 2527 times greater than the Russian national average. (Table 9.1.)

The best available estimates indicate that Russia's per-adult national income stagnated at around 35–40% of West European levels between 1870 and the First World War, but this ratio rose spectacularly to a high of 65% in the aftermath of Second World War as the Soviet state implemented its modernization strategy of rapid industrialization and mass investment in basic education. As depicted by Figure 9.2, Russia's relative position plateaued at around 55–65% of West European levels between 1950 and 1990—and while Russian living standards stagnated between the 1950s and 1980s, substantial improvements were experienced in Western Europe and the United States. Together with rising shortages and general frustration among the comparatively highly educated population, the relative sluggishness of living-standard improvements arguably contributed to the complex social and political processes that eventually led to the fall of the Soviet Union.[29]

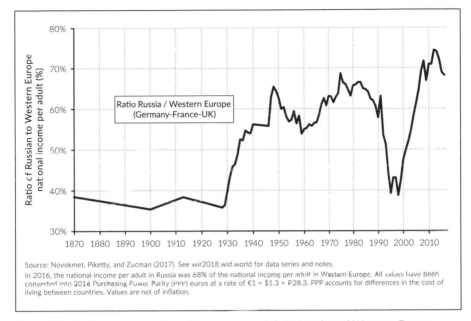

Source: Novokmet, Piketty, and Zucman (2017). See wir2018.wid.world for data series and notes.
In 2016, the national income per adult in Russia was 68% of the national income per adult in Western Europe. All values have been converted into 2016 Purchasing Power Parity (PPP) euros at a rate of €1 = $1.3 = ₽28.3. PPP accounts for differences in the cost of living between countries. Values are net of inflation.

Figure 9.2 Ratio between national income per adult in Russia and Western Europe, 1870–2016

Yet the consequences of these dramatic transformations of the distribution of income and wealth are not well documented or well understood, particularly following the fall of the Soviet Union. There is no doubt that income inequality has increased substantially since 1989–1990—at least in part because monetary inequality was unusually, and to some extent artificially, low under communism—but there has been little empirical work to measure the exact magnitude of the increase and how this compares to change in other countries. It is to these points and many others that Novokmet, Piketty, and Zucman's recent paper seeks to respond, by creating distributional national accounts for Russia that combine national accounts, survey, and wealth and fiscal data, including recently released tax data on high-income taxpayers, in essentially the way described earlier in this Report.

"Shock therapy" transition policies drastically increased the top 10% share of national income

The striking rise in income inequality after the fall of the Soviet Union was dramatic in terms of both speed and quantitative change. This period was shaped by a "shock therapy" and "big-bang" model of transition from the previously

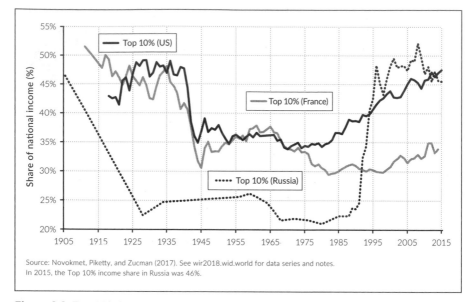

Figure 9.3 Top 10% income share in France, Russia, and the US, 1905–2015

planned, state-led economy to one that was to be led by free-market principles.[30] With this came the privatization of the significant wealth of Russia's state-owned enterprises and the liberalization of prices and capital and labor markets, among many other political and economic changes. According to benchmark estimates provided by Novokmet, Piketty, and Zucman, the income share of the top 10% rose from less than 25% in 1990–1991 to more than 45% in 1996 (see Figure 9.3), while the income share of the top 10% rose moderately from 39% to 41% in the United States, and remained at around 30–31% in France.

Privatizations were partly done through a voucher privatization strategy, whereby citizens were given books of free vouchers that represented potential shares in any state-owned company. However, voucher privatization of state-owned enterprises took place very quickly, with the ownership of over fifteen thousand firms transferred from state control between 1992 and 1994.[31] This happened, moreover, within such a chaotic monetary and political context that small groups of individuals were able to buy back large quantities of vouchers at relatively low prices, and also in some cases were able to obtain highly profitable deals with public authorities—for example, via the infamous loans-for-shares agreements.[32] Together with capital flight and the rise of offshore wealth, this process arguably led to a much higher level of wealth and income concentration in Russia than in other ex-communist countries.

The transformation of the labor market from state-led to market-led also led to an increase in income inequality through higher inequality of labor income.[33]

In communist Russia, unemployment was virtually nonexistent with only small wage differentials used to reward differential inputs and to motivate effort. This ensured generally egalitarian inequality outcomes as compared to market economies. When the transition toward free markets began, however, a significant amount of unemployment was created as workers moved from the state to the private sector. Both state and private employment fell with the closure of state and private enterprises, while the imposition of hard budgets created intensely unfavorable conditions for investment and hiring, and left very little support for those seeking unemployment benefits—all of which hit the lowest earners the hardest. Given the abundance of excess labor and greater concentration of wealth, the labor market transition and the privatization process favored owners of capital to the detriment of labor.[34]

Price liberalization also saw the consumer price index multiply by nearly five thousand between 1990 and 1996. Inflation was particularly high in 1992 and 1993 (when it hit 1 500% and 900%, respectively) after official price liberalization occurred on January 1, 1992. While these episodes of hyperinflation affected the whole of the Russian economy—national income per adult fell from approximately €17 000 in 1991 to €11 000 in 1995—it was the poorest who were hit the hardest. A large part of the bottom 50% of the income distribution was made up of pensioners and low-wage workers whose nominal incomes were not fully indexed to price inflation, and this resulted in massive redistribution and impoverishment for millions of Russian households, particularly among the retired population. The share of national income accruing to the bottom 50% collapsed, dropping from about 30% of total income in 1990–1991 to less than 10% in 1996.

Concurrent with the rapid collapse in the share of incomes for the poorest 50% of the population, a more gradual and continuous process of rising top 1% income shares can be observed. The income share of the top 1% grew from less than 6% in 1989 to approximately 26% in 1996. This was a huge turnaround in just over seven years; note that the income share of the bottom 50% was five times greater than that of the top 1% in 1989, but by 1996, it was almost two times smaller. Meanwhile, the middle 40% appear to have been relatively unaffected by the initial transition reforms; their share of national income saw only a muted fall over the same period, from approximately 46% to 43%.

Following the 1996 reelection of President Boris Yeltsin, income shares began to stabilize for Russia's poorest 50% of the population. The income share of the bottom 50% rose over five percentage points between 1996 and 1998 as low-end pensions and wages benefited from a gradual recovery process between 1996 and 2015. They never fully returned, however, to their 1990–1991 relative income share. The top 10% share fell from around 48% to 43% between 1996 and 1998,

Table 9.2 Income growth and inequality in Russia, 1989–2016

Income group	Average annual real growth rate	Total cumulated real growth	Share in total macro growth
Full Population	1.3%	41%	100%
Bottom 50%	-0.8%	-20%	-15%
Middle 40%	0.5%	15%	16%
Top 10%	3.8%	171%	99%
Top 1%	6.4%	429%	56%
Top 0.1%	9.5%	1054%	34%
Top 0.01%	12.2%	2134%	17%
Top 0.001%	14.9%	4122%	8%

Source: Novokmet, Piketty, and Zucman (2017). See wir2018.wid.world for data series and notes.

Between 1989 and 2016, the income of the Top 1% grew at an average rate of 6.4% per year.

before averaging around 47% until 2015. This latter period saw consistent rises in the income share of the top 10% in the United States, and by 2015, income concentration was higher than in Russia. The top 10% income share also rose in France, but very steadily to a more modest 34% by 2015.

This twelve-year period also saw strong macroeconomic growth, with Russia's per-adult national income more than doubling from around €12 000 in 1996 to approximately €25 000 in 2008.[35] However, it was the top 10% who were to be the main beneficiaries of this growth, as their share of national income rose from 43% to 53% across the ten years leading up to 2008. This upward trend for the top 10% was the opposite of that experienced by the middle 40%, whose share of national income fell from almost 40% in 1998 to 35% in 2008. The world financial crisis and precipitous drop in oil prices interrupted Russian national income growth in 2008–2009, and economic activity remained sluggish after that—only to fall again in 2014–2015, partly due to the international sanctions that followed the Russian military intervention in Ukraine. Average per-adult national income fell by over €2 000 in 2008–2009 before recovering rather lethargically to just over €24 000 in 2013, and then falling back down to €23 000 in 2015–2016. The richest part of the population experienced the largest fall in their share of national income as a result of the crisis, as the top 10% income share lost six percentage points in the two years leading up to 2010. It later settled to just over 45% in 2014–2015. The bottom 50% and middle 40% experienced four-percentage-point rises in their respective shares of national income, to approximately 18% and 39%, respectively.

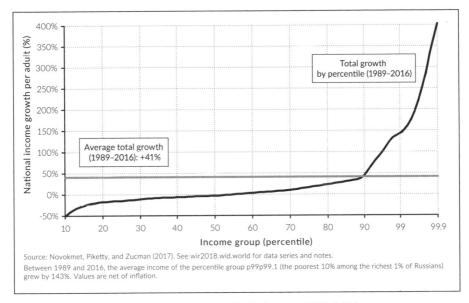

Source: Novokmet, Piketty, and Zucman (2017). See wir2018.wid.world for data series and notes.
Between 1989 and 2016, the average income of the percentile group p99p99.1 (the poorest 10% among the richest 1% of Russians) grew by 143%. Values are net of inflation.

Figure 9.4 Total income growth by percentile in Russia, 1989–2016

Considering the period 1989–2016 together, average per-adult national income in Russia increased by 41%—that is, by approximately 1.3% per year. However, as a result of the dynamics described above, the different income groups have enjoyed widely different growth experiences. On average, the bottom earners benefited from very small or negative growth over the twenty-seven-year period (–0.8% per year and –20% over the entire period for the bottom 50%), due principally to the inflation-induced loss of incomes before 1996. The middle 40% had positive but very modest average growth of just 0.5% per year, and thus their incomes grew by 15% over the period. The experience of the top 10%, meanwhile, has been vastly different. Indeed, as Table 9.2 shows, the growth in income these groups saw only increases as one looks further up the income distribution. The average per-adult incomes of the top 10% grew by 3.8% per year between 1989 and 2016, providing the 11.5 million top earners with a cumulative income growth of 171%. Moreover, it is almost solely this top 10% that has benefited from Russia's macroeconomic growth over the period. Their share in the country's growth has been 99%, as opposed to only 1% for the bottom 90%, made up of almost 103.5 million adults.

Figure 9.4 shows the annual and total growth rates over the period for different groups of the population. Interestingly, these figures show the same upward-sloping pattern as those constructed by The European Bank for Reconstruction and Development (EBRD).[36] They do, however, differ on two points. First, they show an even stronger tilt toward the top incomes due to a more precise estimation of top Russian incomes.[37] Second, there are meaningful differences in the income concepts employed.[38] The latter difference has a notable impact on the rate of total real growth over the 1989–2016 period; the EBRD find this to be 70% rather than the 41% presented above. Such a difference is far from marginal. Consistent with the concepts used in this report and throughout WID.world, Novokmet et al. use national income rather than solely self-reported survey data. In doing so, they recognize the significant challenges of comparing real incomes for the Soviet and post-Soviet periods in a satisfactory manner. For example, if the researchers were to evaluate the welfare costs of shortages and queuing in 1989–1990, then it is possible that their aggregate growth figure might increase from 41% to 70%, or perhaps even more.

Long-run Russian inequality follows a U-shaped pattern

The changes in the distribution of income that took place in the post-communism period of 1989–2016 look very different from those that took place after 1905. In the tsarist Russia of 1905, the share of national income attributable to the top 10% was approximately 47%, while the bottom 50% share was about 17%, and the middle 40% share was 36%. Following the Russian Revolution of 1917, which dismantled the tsarist autocracy and paved the way for the creation of the Union of Soviet Socialist Republics (USSR) in 1922, these shares changed dramatically. By 1929, the top 10% earned just 22% of national income, twenty-five percentage points down from twenty-four years earlier. The loss in the share of national income of the top 10% was subsumed by an approximate thirteen-percentage-point rise in the share of the bottom 50% and middle 40% to almost 30% and 48% of national income, respectively, as seen in Figure 9.5. The top 1% income share, meanwhile, was somewhat below 20% in 1905 and dropped to as little as 4–5% during the Soviet period. The vast majority of growth up until 1956 (the start of the so-called de-Stalinization policies) was therefore shared by the bottom 90%, with mass investment in publication and the introduction of the five-year plans—plans that brought about the accumulation of capital resources through the buildup of heavy industry, the collectivization of agriculture, and the restricted manufacturing of consumer goods, all under state control.[39]

The death of Joseph Stalin in 1953 and the introduction thereafter of comparatively liberal policies known as de-Stalinization policies, which included the end of mass forced labor in Gulags, saw further changes to income shares that favored those earning lower incomes. The bottom 50% experienced gains in their

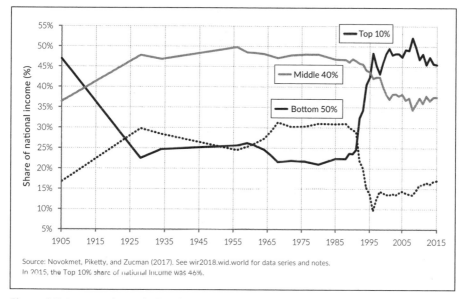

Figure 9.5 Income shares in Russia, 1905–2015

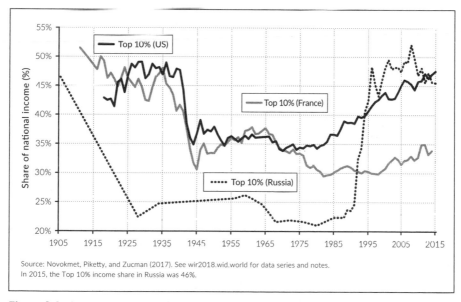

Figure 9.6 Average annual real growth by percentile in Russia, 1905–2016

share of national income from 24% in 1956 to 32% in 1968, while the share of
the top 10% fell from 26% to 22% over the same period. Shares of national income
then remained fairly constant for these groupings and for the middle 40% until
1989, and growth was thus relatively balanced between them, as illustrated by
Figure 9.6 and Table 9.3.

Table 9.3	Average annual real growth rates			
Income group	1905–2016	1905–1956	1956–1989	1989–2016
Full Population	1.9%	1.9%	2.5%	1.3%
Bottom 50%	1.9%	2.6%	3.2%	-0.8%
Middle 40%	2.0%	2.5%	2.3%	0.5%
Top 10%	1.9%	0.8%	2.3%	3.8%
Top 1%	2.0%	-0.3%	2.5%	6.4%
Top 0.1%	2.3%	-1.2%	2.7%	9.5%
Top 0.01%	2.5%	-2.1%	3.0%	12.2%
Top 0.001%	2.7%	-3.0%	3.3%	14.9%

Source: Novokmet, Piketty and Zucman (2017). See wir2018.wid.world for data series and notes.

Between 1989 and 2016, the income of the Top 1% grew at an average rate of 6.4% per year.

These figures reiterate the stark difference between living under the communist system and living after its end, in terms of the variance in average annual real growth rates experienced by income groups. Throughout 1905–1956 and 1956–1989, the bottom 50% and middle 40% saw their average annual real incomes increase by at least as much as those of the top 10%, and at considerably higher rates from 1905 to 1956. In this earlier period, growth notably favored both the bottom 50% and middle 40% (with 2.6% and 2.5% annual growth rates, respectively) over the top 10% (0.8%). From 1956 to 1989, the bottom 50% experienced an annual growth rate that was higher than in the preceding periods, but the difference with top groups was remarkably reduced. The top 1% grew at 2.3%—as much as the middle 40%. Interestingly, annual growth rates were increasingly negative within the top 1% income brackets between 1905 and 1956, but were then increasingly positive within these groups from 1956 to 1989. The real contrast, however, is in the post-1989 period, when the divergence in annual growth rates rose to 15.7 percentage points between the top 0.001% (14.9%) and the bottom 50% earners (−0.8%). Such a divergence in growth rates at different ends of the distribution has not been witnessed throughout the twentieth century, even during the socialization of the Russian economy.

More detailed data are required for more precise conclusions to be drawn

As already mentioned, there are a number of limitations in the data sources employed by Novokmet, Piketty, and Zucman, which suggests that while broad orders of magnitude can be considered reliable, small variations in inequality should not be viewed as precisely true. Indeed, their estimates suggest that inequality levels in tsarist and post-Soviet Russia are roughly comparable. But the lack of detailed income tax data—and the general lack of financial transparency—make their estimates for the recent period relatively imprecise, perhaps most importantly because their estimate for 1905 is at least as imprecise.[40] Thus, it seems safer to conclude only that inequality levels in tsarist Russia were very high and are comparable with the possibly even greater levels seen in post-Soviet Russia.

It is also worth stressing that the measures of monetary inequality depicted in Figure 9.1 and Figure 9.5 neglect non-monetary dimensions of inequality, which may bias comparisons of inequality over time and across societies. For example, inequalities in personal status and basic rights, including mobility rights, were pervasive in tsarist Russia, and persisted long after the official abolition of serfdom in 1861. Summarizing such inequalities with a single monetary indicator is clearly an oversimplification of a complex set of power relations and social domination. The same general remark applies to the Soviet period, when monetary inequality was reduced to very low levels under communism. However, the then relatively small difference between the incomes of the top 10% and bottom 50% did not prevent the Soviet elite from having access to superior goods, services, and opportunities. This could take different forms, including access to special shops and vacation facilities, which allowed the Soviet top 1% to enjoy living standards that in some cases might have been substantially higher than their annual incomes of four to five times the national average would have suggested. These factors should be kept in mind when making historical and international comparisons—in Russia or elsewhere.

10

Income Inequality in India

Information in this chapter is based on the working paper "Indian Income Inequality, 1922–2014: From British Raj to Billionaire Raj?," by Lucas Chancel and Thomas Piketty, 2017. WID.world Working Paper Series (No. 2017/11).

- Income inequality in India has reached historically high levels. In 2014, the share of national income accruing to India's top 1% of earners was 22%, while the share of the top 10% was around 56%.
- Inequality has risen substantially from the 1980s onwards, following profound transformations in the economy that centered on the implementation of deregulation and opening-up reforms.
- Since the beginning of deregulation policies in the 1980s, the top 0.1% earners have captured more growth than all of those in the bottom 50% combined. The middle 40% have also seen relatively little growth in their incomes.
- This rising inequality trend is in contrast to the thirty years that followed the country's independence in 1947, when income inequality was widely reduced and the incomes of the bottom 50% grew at a faster rate than the national average.
- The temporary end to the publication of tax statistics between 2000 and 2010 highlights the need for more transparency on income and wealth statistics that track the long-run evolution of inequality. This would allow for a more informed democratic debate on inequality and inclusive growth in India.

India entered the digital age without inequality data

India introduced an individual income tax with the Income Tax Act of 1922, under the British colonial administration. From that date up to the turn of the twentieth century, the Indian Income Tax Department produced income tax tabulations, making it possible to track the long-run evolution of top incomes in a systematic manner. Given the profound evolutions in India's economy since the country's independence, this provides a rich data resource for researchers to access.[41] Research has shown that the incomes of the richest—the "top incomes"—declined significantly from the mid-1950s to the mid-1980, but this trend was reversed thereafter, when pro-business, market deregulation policies were implemented.

Little has been known, however, about the distributional impacts of economic policies in India after 2000, when real income growth was substantially higher than in previous decades. This is largely because the Indian Income Tax Department stopped publishing income tax statistics in 2000, but also because self-reported survey data often do not provide adequate information concerning the top of the distribution. In 2016, the Income Tax Department released tax tabulations for recent years, making it possible to track the evolution of income inequality during the high average income growth years post-2000.

Inequality rose from the mid-1980s after profound transformations of the economy

Over the past four decades, the Indian economy has undergone profound evolutions. In the late seventies, India was recognized as a highly regulated, centralized economy with socialist planning. But from the 1980s onward, a large set of liberalization and deregulation reforms were implemented. Liberalization and trade openness became recurrent themes among Indian policymakers, epitomized by the Seventh Plan (1985–1990) led by Prime Minister Rajiv Gandhi (1984–1989). That plan promoted the relaxation of market regulation, with increased external borrowing and increased imports. These free-market policy themes were then further embedded in the conditions attached to the International Monetary Fund's assistance to India in its balance of payment crisis in the early 1990s, which pushed further structural reforms for deregulation and liberalization. This period also saw the tax system undergo gradual transformation, with top marginal income tax rates falling from as high as 97.5% in the 1970s to 50% in the mid-1980s.

The structural changes to the economy, along with changes in tax regulation, appear to have had significant impact on income inequality in India since the 1980s. In 1983, the share of national income accruing to top earners was the

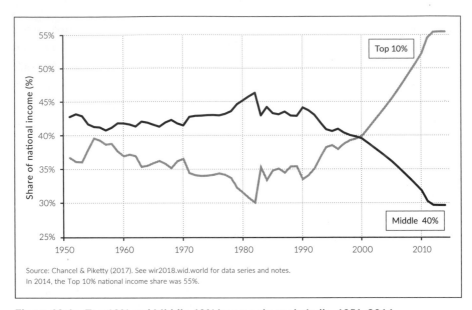

Figure 10.1a Top 10% and Middle 40% income shares in India, 1951–2014

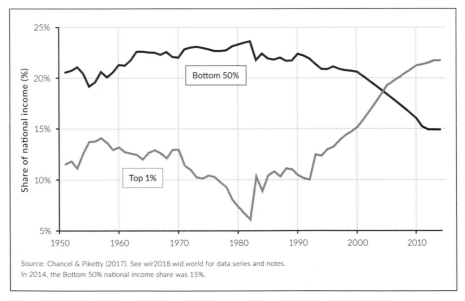

Figure 10.1b Top 1% and Bottom 50% income shares in India, 1951–2014

lowest since tax records started in 1922: the top 1% captured approximately 6% of national income, the top 10% earned 30% of national income, the bottom 50% earned approximately 24% of national income and the middle 40% just over 46% (Figure 10.1a and b). But by 1990, these shares had changed notably with the share of the top 10% growing approximately 4 percentage points to 34% from

1983, while the shares of the middle 40% and bottom 50% both fell by 2 percentage points to around 44% and 22%, respectively.

What came to be known as the first set of economic reforms were implemented from 1991 to 2000 and in practice were the continuation of the mid-1980s policy shift. These reforms placed the promotion of the private sector at the heart of economic policies, via denationalizations, disinvestment of the public sector and deregulation (de-reservation and de-licensing of public companies and industries)[42], weighing the economy substantially in favor of capital above labor. These reforms were implemented both by the Congress government and its Conservative successors. As illustrated by Figure 10.1, these reforms were concomitant with a dramatic rise in Indian income inequality by 2000. The top 10% had increased its share of national income to 40%, roughly the same as that attributable to the middle 40%, while the share of the bottom 50% had fallen to around 20%.

These pro-market reforms were prolonged after 2000, under the 10th and subsequent five-year plans. The plans ended government fixation of petrol, sugar, and fertilizer prices and led to further privatizations, in the agricultural sector in particular. Inequality trends continued on an upward trajectory throughout the 2000s and by 2014 the richest 10% of the adult population shared around 56% of the national income. This left the middle 40% with 32% of total income and the bottom 50%, with around half of that, at just over 16%.

Indian inequality was driven by the rise in very top incomes

Inequality within the top 10% group was also high. The higher up the Indian income distribution one looks, the faster the rise in their share of the national income has been since the early 1980s. As depicted by Figure 10.2, the income share of India's top 1% rose from approximately 6% in 1982–1983 to above 10% a decade after, then to 15% by 2000, and further still to around 23% by 2014. The latest data thus show that during the first decade after the millennium, the share of national income attributable to the top 1% grew to be larger than that pertaining to the bottom 50%. By 2014, the national income share of the bottom 50%—a group of approximately 390 million adults—was just two-thirds of the share of the top 1%, who totaled 7.8 million. An even stronger increase in the share of national income was experienced by the top 0.1% and top 0.01%, whose shares grew fivefold and tenfold, respectively, from 2% and 0.5% to almost 10% and 5%, between 1983 and 2014. Income growth rates at the very top were extreme, as shown by Table 10.1.

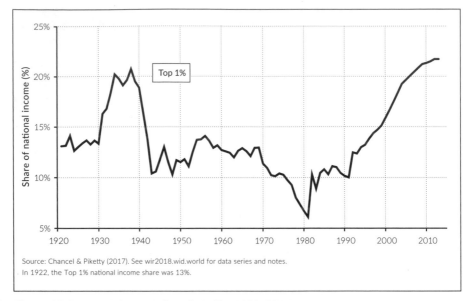

Figure 10.2 Top 1% income share in India, 1922–2014

Table 10.1 Total income growth by percentile in China, France, India, and the US, 1980–2014

Income group	India	China	France	US
Full Population	187%	659%	35%	61%
Bottom 50%	89%	312%	25%	1%
Middle 40%	93%	615%	32%	42%
Top 10%	394%	1074%	47%	121%
Top 1%	750%	1534%	88%	204%
Top 0.1%	1138%	1825%	161%	320%
Top 0.01%	1834%	2210%	223%	453%
Top 0.001%	2726%	2546%	261%	636%

Source: Chancel & Piketty (2017). See wir2018.wid.world for data series and notes.
Between 1980 and 2014, the average income of the Top 10% grew by 394% in India. Values are net of inflation.

These evolutions are consistent with the dynamics of Indian wealth inequality, which exhibit a strong increase in the top 10% wealth share in the recent period, in particular after 2002.[43] Highly unequal income growth at the top mechanically drives wealth inequality across the population, which in return fuels income concentration.

The recent surge in inequality mirrors inequality declines from the 1940s to the 1980s

After independence, Jawaharlal Nehru implemented a set of socialist policies, with strict government control over the economy, with an explicit goal to limit the power of the elite. The policies implemented by himself and his followers, including his daughter Indira Gandhi, up to the late 1970s, included nationalizations, strong market regulation, and high tax progressivity. Nationalizations involved the railways and air transport in the early-1950s, oil in the mid-1970s and banking throughout the entire period, to cite but a few. Along with the transfer of private to public wealth and their implicit reduction in capital incomes, nationalizations brought government pay-scale setting with them that compressed wage distributions. In the private sector, incomes were constrained by extremely high tax rates: between 1965 and 1973, top marginal income tax rates rose from 27% to almost 98%. These changes may have discouraged rent-seeking behavior at the top of the distribution, which can be seen as an efficient strategy in the presence of excessive bargaining power and rent-seeking activity. The impact on income inequality was substantial, as the top 1% income share decreased from 21% before the second World War to approximately 10–12% in the 1950s and 1960s and fell further to 6% in the early 1980s.

Revisiting "Shining India's" income growth rates

How do these vast institutional and policy changes translate in terms of income growth rates for different groups of the population? As Figure 10.3 illustrates, the average growth of real incomes has varied notably between the different groups in the income distribution since the 1950s. The annual real incomes of the bottom 50% grew at a faster rate than the countrywide average during the 1960s and 1970s when socialist central planning dominated the Indian economy, and at a notably higher pace than the growth experienced by those in the top 10% and top 1% of earners. However, this dynamic changed dramatically during the 1980s and has remained as such ever since. The 1980s saw a much higher average income growth rates than in the previous decades, but growth was only marginally higher for the bottom 90% of the population. High growth was in fact concentrated among the top 10%. This situation was prolonged throughout the 1980–2000s. During the 2000s, the annual real income growth of the top 1% was close to 8.5%, followed by the top 10% at around 7% and the bottom 50% at less than 2.5%. India's countrywide average was 4.5% over the decade.

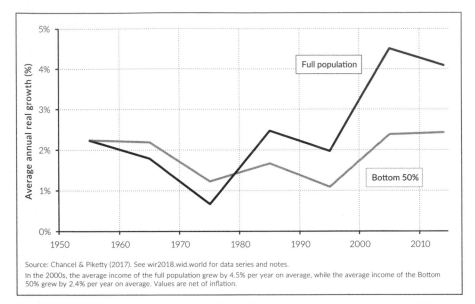

Source: Chancel & Piketty (2017). See wir2018.wid.world for data series and notes.
In the 2000s, the average income of the full population grew by 4.5% per year on average, while the average income of the Bottom 50% grew by 2.4% per year on average. Values are net of inflation.

Figure 10.3a Income growth in India, 1951–2014: Full population vs. Bottom 50%

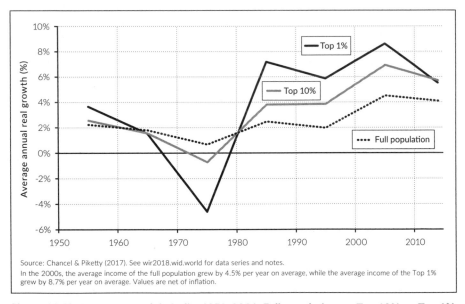

Source: Chancel & Piketty (2017). See wir2018.wid.world for data series and notes.
In the 2000s, the average income of the full population grew by 4.5% per year on average, while the average income of the Top 1% grew by 8.7% per year on average. Values are net of inflation.

Figure 10.3b Income growth in India, 1951–2014: Full population vs. Top 10% vs. Top 1%

Table 10.2 shows the growth rate and the percentage of growth captured by different income groups in India between 1951 and 1980. During this period, the higher the group in the distribution of income, the lower the growth rate they experienced. Real per-adult incomes of the bottom 50% and middle 40% groups grew substantially faster than average income, increasing by 87% and 74%, respec-

Table 10.2 Income growth and inequality in India, 1951–1980

Income group	Total real per-adult income growth	Share of growth captured by income group
Full Population	65%	100%
Bottom 50%	87%	28%
Middle 40%	74%	49%
Top 10%	42%	24%
Top 1%	5%	1%
Top 0.1%	-26%	-2%
Top 0.01%	-42%	-1%
Top 0.001%	-45%	-0.4%

Source: Chancel & Piketty (2017). See wir2018.wid.world for data series and notes.

Between 1951 and 1980, the average income of the Top 1% grew by 5%. The Top 1% captured 1% of total growth over this period. Values are net of inflation.

tively, compared to the 65% growth of average income per adult. Furthermore, the top 0.1%, top 0.01% and top 0.001% income groups experienced a significant reduction in their real incomes, falling –26%, –42% and –45%, respectively, over the 30-year period. The bottom 50% group captured 28% of total growth between 1951 and 1980, while the middle 40% captured almost half of total growth.

It is particularly interesting to compare the pre-1980 with the post-1980 growth rates. From 1980 to 2014, the bottom 50% and middle 40% grew at 89% and 93%, respectively. Whereas average income growth is substantially higher after 1980, there is very little difference in growth rates for the bottom 50% and middle 40%. Since 1980, it is also striking that the top 0.1% earners captured more of the total growth than the bottom 50% (12% versus 11% of total growth). The top 0.1% of earners represented less than 800 000 individuals in 2014; this is equivalent to a population smaller to Delhi's IT suburb, Gurgaon. It is a sharp contrast with the 389 million individuals that made up the bottom half of the adult population in 2014. At the opposite end of the distribution, the top 1% of Indian earners captured as much growth as the bottom 84%.

Table 10.3 illustrates the income levels and income thresholds for different groups and their corresponding adult population in 2014. The bottom 50% earned significantly less than the average income per adult, receiving less than one-third of the nationwide mean income before tax, while the average income of the middle 40% was around four-fifths the national average. Those in the top 10% earned five times the national average, and when one examines further up the income

Table 10.3 The distribution of national income in India, 2014

Income group	Number of adults	Income threshold (€)	Average income (€)	Comparison to average income (ratio)	Income share
Full Population	794 306 000	–	6 200	1	100%
Bottom 50%	397 153 000	–	1 900	0.3	15.3%
Middle 40%	317 722 000	3 100	4 700	0.8	30.5%
Top 10%	79 431 000	9 200	33 600	5	54.2%
Top 1%	7 943 000	57 600	134 600	22	21.7%
Top 0.1%	794 000	202 000	533 700	86	8.6%
Top 0.01%	79 400	800 100	2 377 000	384	3.8%
Top 0.001%	7 900	3 301 900	11 589 000	1871	1.9%

Source: Chancel & Piketty (2017). See wir2018.wid.world for data series and notes.

In 2014, the average income of the Top 10% was €33 600 (₹779 000). All values have been converted into 2016 Purchasing Power Parity (PPP) euros at a rate of €1 = $1.3 = ₹23. PPP accounts for differences in the cost of living between countries. Values are net of inflation. Numbers may not add up due to rounding.

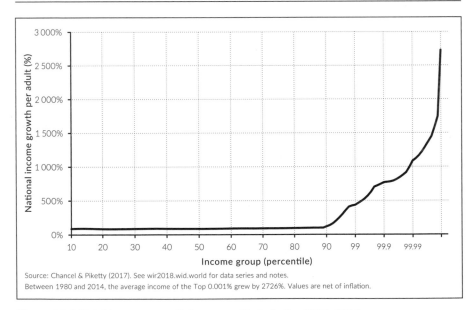

Source: Chancel & Piketty (2017). See wir2018.wid.world for data series and notes.
Between 1980 and 2014, the average income of the Top 0.001% grew by 2726%. Values are net of inflation.

Figure 10.4 Total income growth by percentile in India, 1980–2014

distribution, the same exponential trend as seen in the growth statistics is evident. The top 1% of earners, for example, received around €134 600 (₹3.12 million) per year on average, while the top 0.1% receive approximately €533 700 (₹12.4 million), 22 and 86 times the average income for Indian adults, respectively. For the top 0.001%, this ratio is 1871. (Figure 10.4)

11

Income Inequality in the Middle East

Information in this chapter is based on "Measuring Inequality in the Middle East, 1990–2016: The World's Most Unequal Region?" by Facundo Alvaredo, Lydia Assouad, and Thomas Piketty, 2017. WID.world Working Paper Series (No. 2017/16).

- The Middle East appears to be the most unequal region in the world, with the share of income accruing to the top 10 and 1% exceeding 60% and 25% of total regional income in 2016. The levels of inequality remained extreme over the 1990–2016 period, with the top 10% income share varying between 60% and 66% and a bottom 50% share consistently below 10%. These inequality levels are comparable to or higher than those observed in Brazil and South Africa.
- This high level of income concentration is due to both enormous inequality between countries, particularly between oil-rich and population-rich countries, and is also the result of very large inequality within countries.
- Inequality between countries is largely due to the geography of oil ownership and the transformation of oil revenues into permanent financial endowments. As a result, the income of the oil-rich Gulf countries made up 42% of the total regional income in 2016 despite only representing a small share of the total population (15% in 2016). The gap in per-adult national income between Gulf countries and the other countries is therefore extremely large.
- These new results also show that inequalities within countries are much larger than previously estimated. However, given the lack of data available, these estimations are likely to be substantially underestimated. The problem is particularly acute in the Gulf countries, for which the low official inequality statistics contradict important aspects of their political economy, namely, the growing population share of low-paid foreign workers.

The Arab Spring's demands for greater social justice have led researchers to reexamine inequality in the Middle East

Following the Arab Spring movement, there has been renewed interest in inequality measurement in Middle East countries, as calls for greater social justice were among the leading demands of these popular movements. However, existing studies have argued that income inequalities within these countries do not seem to be particularly high by international standards, suggesting that the source of dissatisfaction might lie elsewhere. This somewhat surprising fact, coined "the Enigma of Inequality"[44] or the "Arab Inequality Puzzle,"[45] has led to a growth in the literature on inequality in the region.

Among the literature seeking to address this surprising finding is a recent paper by Facundo Alvaredo, Lydia Assouad, and Thomas Piketty. They argue that previous results, based on household survey data only, highly underestimate inequality and they offer novel estimates using the only fiscal data available in the region that have been recently released.

Inequality in the Middle East is among the highest of any region worldwide

Income inequality in the Middle East remains extremely high over the 1990–2016 period: the top 10% income share fluctuated at around 60–66% of total income, while the share of the bottom 50% and middle 40% varied between 8% and 10% and 27% and 30% of total income, respectively. Regional income has largely been concentrated among the top 1% of the adult population, which receives 27% of total income, that is three times more than the bottom 50%, and approximately the same as the middle 40% of the population. Inequality in the Middle East is therefore among the highest of any region worldwide. (Figure 11.1)

Comparing the Middle East performance in terms of inequality with other countries in the world is legitimate and informative—at least as much as the usual inequality comparisons between nation-states. The total population of the region (about 410 million in 2016) is comparable to Western Europe (420 million) and the United States (320 million), and is characterized by a relatively large degree of cultural, linguistic, and religious homogeneity. The authors find that the share of total income going to the top 10% income earners in the Middle East, is significantly greater than in the largest rich countries in Western Europe (36%) and the United States (47%) but also than in Brazil (55%), a country that is often described as one of the most unequal in the world. The only country for which higher inequality estimates can be currently found is South Africa, whose top 10% received approximately 65% of national income in 2012. (Figure 11.2)

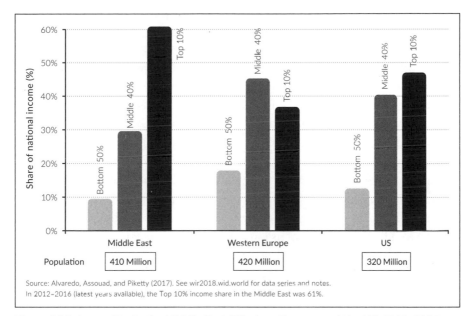

Figure 11.1 Inequality in the Middle East, Western Europe, and the US, 2012–2016

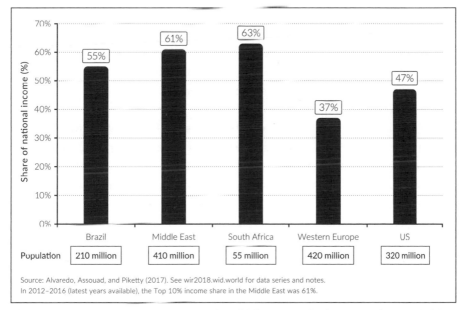

Figure 11.2 Top 10% income shares in the Middle East and other countries, 2012–2016

While these results contradict the aforementioned studies, they are robust to different estimation techniques. When the income distribution is computed using Purchasing Power Parity figures, which reflect the difference in the living standards of each country, inequality levels decline but not by a significant amount. Changing the geographical definition of the Middle East also has a relatively limited impact on inequality: by excluding Turkey from the analysis, a country whose average income is between those of the poorest countries—Egypt, Iraq, Syria, Yemen, etc.—and the oil-rich Gulf countries, inequalities unsurprisingly increase, but only by a small margin.

The origins of inequality are, however, distinctive among these different groups of countries. In the case of the Middle East, they are largely due to the geography of oil ownership and the transformation of oil revenues into permanent financial endowments, as we shall see below. In contrast, in Brazil the legacy of racial inequality continues to play an important role together with huge regional inequalities (see Chapter 12). Extreme inequality in South Africa is intimately related to the legacy of the apartheid system (see chapter 13). It is striking to see that the Middle East, in spite of its much larger racial and ethno-cultural homogeneity, has reached inequality levels that are comparable to, and even higher than, those observed in South Africa or Brazil.

Extreme inequality in the Middle East is driven by enormous and persistent between-country inequality

The 1990–2016 period has been a period of rapid population growth in the Middle East: total population rose by about 70%, from less than 240 million in 1990 to almost 410 million in 2016. The rise in average income has been much more modest, however. Using Purchasing Power Parity estimates (expressed in 2016 euros), per-adult national income rose from about €20 000 in 1990 to €23 000 in 2016, that is, by about 15%. Using Market Exchange Rates, per-adult national income rose from less than €9 000 in 1990 to about €10 000 in 2016 (Figure 11.3). In Western Europe—a relatively low growth region by world standards—per-adult growth was 22%.

Should Middle East inequality be measured at Purchasing Power Parity (PPP) or at Market Exchange Rates (MER)? Both the PPP and the MER viewpoints express valuable and complementary aspects of international inequality patterns. The PPP viewpoint should of course be preferred if we are interested in the living standards of the inhabitants living, working, and spending their incomes in the various countries (which is the case of most inhabitants). However, the MER viewpoint is more relevant and meaningful if we are interested in external economic relations: e.g., the ability of tourists and visitors from Europe or from Gulf countries to purchase goods and services when they travel to other countries; or the ability of migrants or prospective migrants from Egypt or Syria to send part of their euro wages back home. Here Market Exchange Rates matter a lot,

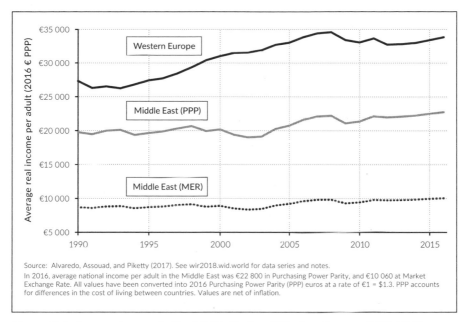

Figure 11.3 Average income in the Middle East and Western Europe, 1990–2016

and may also have an important impact on perceptions of inequality. This is why MER are used as benchmark measures of inequality in the Middle East.

It is critical to stress that enormous and persistent between-country inequality exists behind the Middle East average. In order to summarize the changing population and income structure of the Middle East, it is useful to decompose the region into five blocs: Turkey; Iran; Egypt; Iraq-Syria (including other Arab, non–Gulf countries: Jordan, Lebanon, Palestine, Yemen); and Gulf countries (including Saudi Arabia, Oman, Bahrain, UAE, Qatar, and Kuwait) (Table 11.1).

The first four blocs all represent approximately 20–25% of total population of the Middle East, whereas Gulf countries represent 15% of the population. In contrast, Gulf countries represent almost half of the total income of the region in Market Exchange Rates. This reveals the large gap in per-adult national income between Gulf countries and other countries in the region. These marked differences help us understand why, despite being novel, regional Middle East inequality estimates are not entirely unexpected.

The evolution of income inequality in the Middle East has been driven by the dynamics of between-country inequality. In 1990, Gulf countries' share in the Middle East population was 10%, and their income share was between 44% (PPP) and 48% (MER). The narrowing of per-adult income inequality between Gulf countries and the other four country blocs identified above reduced regional

Table 11.1 Population and income in the Middle East, 2016

	Population (million)	Adult Population (million)	Adult Population (% of ME total)	National Income (Billion 2016 € PPP)	% ME Total Income (PPP)	National Income (Billion 2016 € MER)	% ME Total Income (MER)
Turkey	80	53	21%	1073	19%	548	22%
Iran	80	56	22%	896	16%	330	13%
Egypt	93	54	22%	800	14%	234	9%
Iraq-Syria-Other (non-Gulf)	102	52	21%	570	10%	243	10%
Gulf Countries	54	37	15%	2394	42%	1179	47%
Total Middle East	409	252	100%	5733	100%	2534	100%

Source: Alvaredo, Assouad, and Piketty (2017). See wir2018.wid.world for data series and notes.

In 2016, Gulf countries earned €2,400 billion in Purchasing Power Parity. All values have been converted into 2016 Purchasing Power Parity (PPP) euros at a rate of €1 = $1.3, and into 2016 Market Exchange Rate (MER) euros at a rate of €1 = $1.1. PPP accounts for differences in the cost of living between countries. Values are net of inflation. Numbers may not add up due to rounding.

inequality over the 1990–2016 period. However, the income gap between these two groupings remains enormous.

The fall in the income gap between Gulf countries and the rest of the Middle East reflects a number of complex and contradictory forces. It was partly due to the evolution of oil prices and output levels in Gulf countries, as well as to the relative fast output growth in non–Gulf countries, including Turkey, but the very large rise of migrant workers also played a significant role, leading to an artificial reduction of national income per adult in Gulf countries. The massive inflow of foreign workers, especially in the construction sector and domestic services sector, quite simply led to a stronger increase in the population denominator than in the income numerator of Gulf countries. This massive rise of migrant workers saw the shares of foreigners in Gulf countries increase from less than 50% in 1990 to almost 60% in 2016.

From this viewpoint, it is also useful to distinguish between two groups of Gulf countries. The first of these groups is made up of Saudi Arabia, Oman, and Bahrain, where nationals still make a small majority of the population, with the foreign population share remaining relatively stable at around 40–45% of the total adult population between 1990 and 2016. The second group is that of the United Arab Emirates (UAE), Kuwait, and Qatar, where the nationals have made up a smaller and smaller minority of the resident population, given that the foreign share rose from 80% to 90% of the total population. This second group made up about one-quarter of the total population of Gulf countries in 1990, but this rose to about one-third by 2016.

Within-country inequality is likely to be high in Middle East countries

Income tax data are unfortunately extremely limited in the Middle East and therefore prevent a detailed and precise analysis of within-country inequality. It is unfortunate that the only country for which data are currently available is Lebanon, as household surveys in the Middle East appear to underestimate top incomes at least as much as in the rest of the world (and possibly more). The Lebanese data confirm the general finding that top income levels reported in tax data are much higher than in household surveys: top 1% incomes are typically two to three times higher, with large variations across income levels and over years.

The lack of good data is particularly acute in the case of the Gulf countries, where the low official Gini coefficient might indeed hide important aspects of their political economy—namely, the growing share of the non-national population, a large majority of which is composed of low-paid workers, living in difficult conditions. The substantial growth of migrant workers in Gulf countries gives incentives to nationals within Gulf countries to defend their numerous privileges, beginning by restraining naturalization given that national citizens typically do not pay income tax, benefit from significant social spending, including free health-care and education, receive subsidies for electricity and fuel, and often receive other benefits such as land grants. Furthermore, some citizens also have expectations that the state provides them with a job and housing, an idea enshrined in some Gulf country constitutions.[46] (Figure 11.4)

But perhaps the most striking manifestation of the difference between the local and foreign populations is the restrictions imposed on the migrant population through the "sponsorship system," or the "kafala system," as it is known in Arabic.[47] This system requires all unskilled laborers to have an in-country sponsor, usually their employer, who is responsible for their visa and legal status.[48] As a report by the Chatham House think tank describes, this system can lead to the creation of an extremely polarized social structure with two groups which are not legally, socially, and economically equals.[49] As far as is known, little

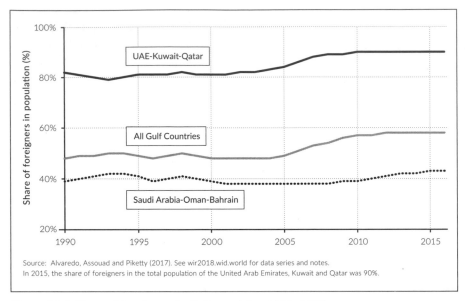

Source: Alvaredo, AssoUad and Piketty (2017). See wir2018.wid.world for data series and notes.
In 2015, the share of foreigners in the total population of the United Arab Emirates, Kuwait and Qatar was 90%.

Figure 11.4 **Share of foreigners in Gulf countries, 1990–2015**

research has been conducted to study the two populations to measure income inequality within Gulf societies given the aforementioned data limitations, and therefore our quantitative understanding of these issues is still somewhat limited. Alvaredo, Assouad, and Piketty are the first researchers to distinguish system- atically between the two populations (and lead to a large upward revisions of inequality estimate in the survey distribution). Unfortunately, there are still important limitations to the empirical understanding of these issues.

Better data on income inequality are crucially needed in the Middle East

Accessing better quality and larger volumes of country-level inequality data for the whole of the 1990–2016 period in Middle East countries might lead to differ- ent conclusions than those presented in this Report. In particular, a rise of with- in-country inequality could possibly counterbalance the reduction of between-country inequality between Gulf countries. Rising within-country inequality trends are found in a large number of very different countries across the world, e.g., in the United States, Europe, India, China, South Africa, Russia, with varying magnitudes as described in other chapters of this report. It is also possible that Middle East countries—along with Brazil—belong to a different category, that is, countries where inequality has always been very large historically and thus has not risen in recent decades. However, given the data sources currently available, it is not possible to draw precise conclusions on this phenomenon with a satisfactory degree of precision.

All in all, it is very difficult to have an informed public debate about inequality trends—and also about a large number of substantial policy issues such as taxation and public spending—without proper access to such data. While the lack of transparency on income and wealth is an important issue in many, if not most, areas of the world, it appears to be particularly extreme in the Middle East, and arguably raises a problem of democratic accountability in itself, independent from the levels of inequality observed.

12

Income Inequality in Brazil

Information in this chapter is based on "Extreme and Persistent Inequality: New Evidence for Brazil Combining National Accounts, Survey and Fiscal Data," by Marc Morgan, 2017. WID.world Working Paper Series (No. 2017/12).

- Novel and more precise inequality data show that the level of inequality is much higher in Brazil than previously estimated.
- Previous inequality estimates suggested that policies targeting inequality over the past decades had been successful in significantly reducing it, but recent evidence suggests that national income inequality has remained relatively persistent at high levels over the past 15 years. At the time, the fall in labor income inequality, even if more moderate than previously thought, is confirmed by the new estimates.
- The distribution of income in Brazil has remained stable and extremely unequal over the last 15 years, with the top 10% receiving over 55% of total income in 2015, while the share of the bottom 50% was just above 12% and the middle 40%, approximately 32%. While inequality within the bottom 90% fell, driven by compression of labor incomes, concentration at the top of the distribution grew over the period, reflecting the increasing concentration of capital income.
- Since the global financial crisis in 2008, the share of total growth in income captured by the top 10% of earners has been the same than in the years of strong growth leading up to the crisis.
- The bottom 50% captured a very limited share of total growth between 2001 and 2015. So far, cash transfers had only a limited impact on the reduction of national income inequality.

Brazil's inequality is higher than previously estimated and relatively stable over the past two decades

Brazil has consistently been ranked among the most unequal countries in the world since data became widely available in the 1980s. However, from the mid-1990s, household surveys began to show that inequality was falling, due to a combination of strong labor market performance, declines in the skill wage premium due to educational expansion, systematic increases in the minimum wage (indexed to social benefits), and the growing coverage of social assistance programs.[50] This household data provided evidence that government policies had been effective in reducing inequality. Indeed, this apparent decline in Brazilian income inequality drew significant attention worldwide, as examples of large economies that could reduce inequality while growing solidly are relatively rare.[51]

However, as described earlier in this report, household surveys only tell part of the story. Recent releases of income tax data by the federal tax office have painted a different picture, showing that inequality in Brazil was higher than previously thought.[52] Marc Morgan has generated a series of distributional national accounts for Brazil, which combine annual and household survey data with detailed information on income tax declarations and national accounts. By ensuring the consistency of the surveys and tax declarations with macroeconomic totals, he is able to provide the most representative income inequality statistics to date that show a sharp upward revision of the official estimates of inequality in Brazil. The novel data also suggests that, if contrary to other emerging countries such as Russia, India, or China, pre-tax inequality has remained relatively stable in Brazil since the turn of the new century, it has not declined as much as many commentators have argued.

Total income inequality has remained at very high levels in Brazil despite the fall in labor income inequality

The findings highlight the large extent of income concentration in Brazil. The richest 10% of Brazilian adults—around 14 million people—received over half (55%) of all national income in 2015, while the bottom half of the population, a group five times larger, earned between four and five times less, at just 12%. The middle 40% of the distribution receives just less than one-third of total income (32%), a figure which is low by international standards. This clearly reveals that inequality in Brazil is principally affected by the extreme concentration at the top of the distribution. This concentration becomes less extreme when we look at the labor income distribution. The top 10% highest earners received 44% of all national labor income in 2015, with the middle 40% taking home almost 40% and the bottom 50% in this distribution receiving about 15%. (Figure 12.1)

Since 2000, total income inequality has remained relatively stable. Small gains were made by the bottom 50%, who increased their share of national income from 11% to 12% from 2001 to 2015, while the top 10% income share evolved from 54% to just over 55% over the period. Both of these gains were at the expense of a continuous squeeze on the middle 40%, whose

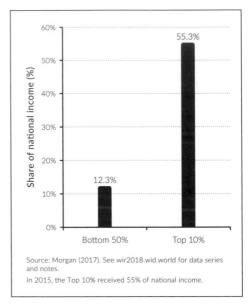

Source: Morgan (2017). See wir2018.wid.world for data series and notes.

In 2015, the Top 10% received 55% of national income.

Figure 12.1 Bottom 50% and Top 10% income shares in Brazil, 2015

share of national income fell from 34% to just above 32%. The stability in the total income inequality should not mask the registered decline in the inequality of labor incomes. The bottom 50% of earners made greater gains in this distribution, increasing their share from 12% to 15% from 2001 to 2015, while the top 10% labor income share fell from 47% to 44%. The middle 40% share increased from 37% to almost 40%, which confirms the overall compression in the labor income distribution and conveys the importance of capital income in the total income distribution. This is even more apparent the higher up in the hierarchy the comparison is made. For instance, while the top 1% of labor earners received 14% of national labor income in 2015, the same group in the national total income distribution received double this share (28%).

These extreme levels of inequality manifested themselves in large differences between the average incomes of the aforementioned groups, as represented by Table 12.1. In 2015, the average income of an adult living in Brazil was around €13 900 (R$37 100), but for those among the bottom 50% of earners, the average income was less than €3 400 (R$9 200, around a quarter of the national average). Moving up the income distribution, the average annual income of adults in the middle 40% was approximately €11 300 (R$30 500), meaning that a significant percentage of 90% of Brazil's adult population earned less than the national average, which highlights the extent of income skewness in Brazil and the lack of a broad "middle class." Consequently, the average income of the top 10% was over five times greater

Table 12.1 The distribution of national income in Brazil, 2015

Income group	Number of adults	Income threshold (€)	Average income (€)	Income share
Full Population	142 521 000	–	13 900	100%
Bottom 50%	71 260 000	–	3 400	12.3%
Middle 40%	57 008 000	6 600	11 300	32.4%
Top 10%	14 252 000	22 500	76 900	55.3%
Top 1%	1 425 000	111 400	387 000	27.8%
Top 0.1%	142 500	572 500	2 003 500	14.4%
Top 0.01%	14 300	2 970 000	10 397 600	7.5%
Top 0.001%	1 430	15 400 000	53 986 200	3.9%

Source: Morgan (2017). See wir2018.wid.world for data series and notes.

In 2015, the average income of the Top 10% was €76 900. All values have been converted into 2016 Purchasing Power Parity (PPP) euros at a rate of €1 = $1.3 = R$2.7. PPP accounts for differences in the cost of living between countries. Values are net of inflation. Numbers may not add up due to rounding.

Table 12.2 Survey income and national income series in Brazil, 2015: Comparing income shares

Income group	Survey income series (survey data)	WID.world series (survey + tax + national accounts data)
Bottom 50%	16.0%	12.3%
Middle 40%	43.6%	32.4%
Top 10%	40.4%	55.3%
Top 1%	10.7%	27.8%
Top 0.1%	2.2%	14.4%
Top 0.01%	0.4%	7.5%
Top 0.001%	0.1%	3.9%
Total (% national income)	57.1%	100%

Source: Morgan (2017). See wir2018.wid.world for data series and notes.

In 2015, the share of survey income attributable to the Top 10% was 40%, while the share of national income attributable to the Top 10% was 55%.

than the national average at €76 900 (R$207 600). The magnitudes increase substantially as one moves toward the upper echelons of the income distribution, with the average income of the richest 1% being around €387 000 (R$1 044 900).

Table 12.2 presents refined shares at the top of the income distribution for 2015, to show more precisely how national income is shared across the adult

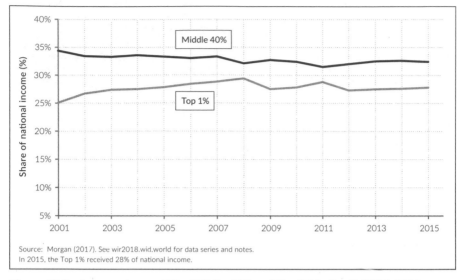

Figure 12.2a Income shares of the Middle 40% and Top 1% in Brazil, 2001–2015

population and also compares how inequality estimates differ between the DINA series and survey data. Using only the survey data, the top 1% (about 1.4 million adults) received 10.7% of national income in 2015. However, when income from fiscal data and undistributed income from national accounts is included, the share of this top 1% increases dramatically, to 28%. The large share of national income captured by the top 1% therefore seems to be gradually reducing the share of the middle 40% over time.

Higher up the distribution, the trend is similar, with the elites capturing a disproportionate share of Brazilian income. Figure 12.2 compares the income share of the bottom 50% (70 million adults), with that of the top 0.1% (140 000 adults) over the fifteen-year time period. Having started at similar levels of national income in 2001—around 11% each—the two groups quickly experienced diverging fortunes, with the top 0.1% share growing to just under 15% of national income by 2004 and the share of the bottom 50% remaining virtually unchanged. By 2015 the gap between the groups' respective shares had grown to 4 percentage points, such that the collective incomes of the top 0.1% were significantly larger than those of the bottom 50% despite the top 0.1% being 500 times smaller in population size.

Morgan in the same work also compares the raw estimates from the surveys with his benchmark national income series (combining national accounts, surveys, and fiscal data). There are clear, large discrepancies in the level and change in inequality that grow increasing larger the higher up the distribution one looks. These discrepancies thus highlight why relying exclusively on surveys and ignoring undistributed income in national accounts flowing to corporations

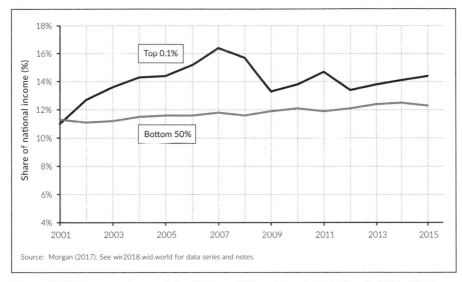

Source: Morgan (2017). See wir2018.wid.world for data series and notes.

Figure 12.2b Income shares of the Bottom 50% and Top 0.1% in Brazil, 2001–2015

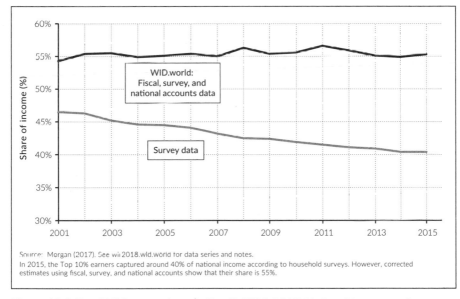

Source: Morgan (2017). See wir2018.wid.world for data series and notes.
In 2015, the Top 10% earners captured around 40% of national income according to household surveys. However, corrected estimates using fiscal, survey, and national accounts show that their share is 55%.

Figure 12.3 Top 10% income share in Brazil, 2001–2015: National income series vs. survey income series

can distort understanding of how income inequality has developed in Brazil. For example, household surveys indicate that income inequality fell between 2001 and 2015, with the top 10% share of national income falling from 47% to just above 40% and the bottom 50% share rising from just over 12% to 16%. These are in stark contrast with the trends and levels presented above, with a top 10%

share oscillating around 55% (Figure 12.3). The general trend is therefore one of an increase in the concentration of national income shares at the top of the income distribution, small increases at the bottom, and an ever-smaller share for the middle.

Brazilian income inequality rises as the richest experience higher growth in incomes

Distributional National Accounts also enable us to examine how growth at the macroeconomic level in Brazil has affected the income shares of the country's population. Between 2001 and 2015, cumulative real growth of national income per adult in Brazil totaled 18%. (Table 12.3) The question that arises from this evolution is how the income growth of different groups of the income distribution compares to these numbers. The real growth of average incomes in the bottom 50% was strong, increasing approximately by 29% over the fifteen-year period. This was comparatively higher than the growth in incomes of the middle 40% (12%) and the top 10% (21%). However, growth was strongest among the top percentiles. The income of the top 1% grew by almost double the national average, at 31%, while the incomes of the top 0.1% grew at almost 55%, three times the national average. Growth was strongest at the very summit of the distribution, with the incomes of the top 0.01% and the 0.001% growing by 85% and 122%, respectively.

Despite the growth of incomes in the bottom half of the income distribution, the top of the distribution captured a disproportionately large part of the total income growth between 2001 and 2015. For example, the top 10% captured 61% of total growth, while the top 1% captured 43%. Even with the strongest growth performance over the period of three major income groupings, the low average incomes of the bottom 50% meant that the fraction of total growth they were able to capture was relatively small, at 18%. Subsequently, the change in the bottom 50% share of total national income was also small. The figures relating to the middle 40% help to reinforce the importance of the size of incomes in analyzing how group shares in national income have changed: despite their total cumulative growth rate being smaller than the bottom 50%, the fraction of total growth captured by the middle 40% was higher than that of the poorest half of the population, at 22%.

Table 12.3 also subdivides the incidence of growth by two roughly equal periods, relating to the time before the global financial crisis, and the time during and after it. During the first period (2001–2007), all groups experienced strong

Table 12.3 Income growth and inequality in Brazil, 2001–2015

Income group	2001–2015		2001–2007		2007–2015	
	Total cumulated growth	Fraction of total growth captured	Total cumulated growth	Fraction of total growth captured	Total cumulated growth	Fraction of total growth captured
Full Population	56.1%	100%	26.9%	100%	23.0%	100%
Bottom 50%	71.5%	16.1%	32.5%	15.3%	29.4%	16.9%
Middle 40%	44.2%	26.1%	22.3%	27.4%	17.9%	24.9%
Top 10%	59.7%	57.8%	28.5%	57.4%	24.3%	58.2%
Top 1%	68.8%	32.2%	37.0%	36.0%	23.2%	28.6%
Top 0.1%	65.4%	15.0%	34.9%	16.7%	22.7%	13.5%
Top 0.01%	57.5%	6.6%	38.2%	9.1%	13.9%	4.2%
Top 0.001%	50.2%	2.9%	48.0%	5.7%	1.5%	0.2%

Source: Morgan (2017). See wir2018.wid.world for data series and notes.

Between 2001 and 2015, the Top 10% captured 57% of total growth.

increases in their average incomes as the economy grew solidly, with only the middle 40% growing at a slower pace than the national average. Nevertheless, the overwhelming gains went to the top decile, with the top 1% capturing over 65% of total growth. Growth in the years between 2007 and 2015 was slightly weaker, with average incomes expanding by 7% as compared to 10% in the previous period, but growth was equally concentrated in the top decile after the financial crisis. The impact of the crisis was notably felt by the highest groups, as the average incomes of groups above the top 0.1% had not yet recovered to their 2007 levels by 2015.

Income Inequality in South Africa

Information in this chapter is based on "Colonial rule, apartheid and natural resources: Top incomes in South Africa, 1903–2007," by Facundo Alvaredo and Anthony B. Atkinson (Centre for Economic Policy Research Discussion Paper, 2010, No. 8155), as well as on WID.world updates.

- South Africa stands out as one of the most unequal countries in the world. In 2014, the top 10% received 2/3 of national income, while the top 1% received 20% of national income.
- During the twentieth century, the top 1% income share was halved between 1914 and 1993, falling from 20% to 10%. Even if these numbers must be qualified, as they are surrounded by a number of uncertainties, the trajectory is similar to that of other former dominions of the British Empire, and is partly explained by the country's economic and political instability during the 1970s and 1980s.
- During the early 1970s the previously constant racial shares of income started to change in favor of the blacks, at the expense of the whites, in a context of declining per capita incomes. But while interracial inequality fell throughout the eighties and nineties, inequality within race groups increased.
- Rising black per capita incomes over the past three decades have narrowed the interracial income gap, although increasing inequality within the black and Asian/Indian population seems to have prevented any decline in total inequality.
- Since the end of apartheid in 1994, top-income shares have increased considerably. In spite of several reforms targeting the poorest and fighting the segregationist heritage, race is still a key determinant of differences in income levels, educational attainment, job opportunities, and wealth.

South Africa's dual economy is among the most unequal in the world

South Africa is one of the most unequal countries in the world. In 2014, the top
10% of earners captured two-thirds of total income. This contrasts with other
high-income inequality countries such as Brazil, the United States, and India
where the top 10% is closer to 50–55% of national income. However, unlike other
highly unequal countries, the divide between the top 1% and the following 9%
in South Africa is much less pronounced than the gap between the top 10% and
the bottom 90%. Otherwise said, in terms of top income shares, South Africa
ranks with the most unequal Anglo-Saxon countries, but, at the same time, there
is less concentration within the upper income groups, mostly composed by the
white population. The average income among the top 1% was about four times
greater than that of the following 9% in 2014 (for comparative purposes, the top
1% in the United States earn seven times more than the following 9%), while
average income among the top 10% was more than seventeen times greater than
the average income of the bottom 90% (it is eight times more in the United States).
It is then only logical that the income share of the top 1% is high, capturing 20%
of national income, though this is not the largest share in the world.

The South African "dual economy" can be further illustrated by comparing
South African income levels to that of European countries. In 2014, the average
national income per adult among the richest 10% was €94 600, at Purchasing
Power Parity, that is, comparable to the average for the same group in France,

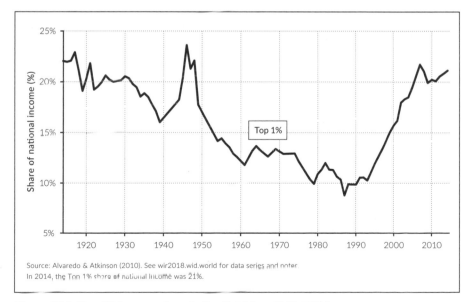

Source: Alvaredo & Atkinson (2010). See wir2018.wid.world for data series and notes.
In 2014, the Top 1% share of national income was 21%.

Figure 13.1 Top 1% income share in South Africa, 1914–2014

Spain, or Italy. But average national income of the bottom 90% in South Africa is close to the average national income of the bottom 16% in France. In light of these statistics, the recently debated emergence of a so-called middle class is still very elusive. Rather, two societies seem to coexist in South Africa, one enjoying living standards close to the rich or upper middle class in advanced economies, the other left behind. (Figure 13.1)

Inequality has decreased from the unification of South Africa to the end of apartheid

South Africa is an exception in terms of data availability in comparison with other African countries. The period for which fiscal data are available starts in 1903 for the Cape Colony, seven years before the Union of South Africa was established as a dominion of the British Empire, and ends in 2014, with some years sporadically missing, and noticeably an eight-year interruption following the end of apartheid in 1994. As is often the case with historical tax data series, only a very small share of the total adult population was eligible to pay tax in the first half of the twentieth century. Therefore, the fiscal data from which we can estimate top-income shares allow us to track the top 1% income share since 1913, but only cover the top 10% of the population from 1963 (with a long interruption between 1971 and 2008).

With important short run variations, the evolution of income concentration over the 1913–1993 period seems to follow a very clear long-term trend. The income share of the richest 1% was more than halved between 1913 and 1993, falling from 22% to approximately 10%. Not only did the income share attributable to the top 1% decrease, but inequality within this upper group was also reduced. Indeed, the share of the top 0.5% fell more quickly than the share of the next 0.5% (from percentile 99 to percentile 99.5). Consequently, while the top 0.5% represented about 75% of the top 1% in 1914, by the end of the 1980s, their representative proportion fell to 60%.

Despite the extreme social implications of the first segregationist measures that were implemented in the early 1910s, these policies did not lead to large increases in income concentration among the top 1%. This was also a time in which South Africa progressively developed its industrial and manufacturing sector, enjoying notable accelerations in the 1930s that were to the benefit of the large majority of the population. Aside from a brief fall during the Great Depression, average real income per adult then increased steadily. Following a trend similar to other former Dominions of the British Empire (Australia, Canada, and New Zealand), inequality decreased significantly in South Africa from 1914 to the beginning of the the Second World War, despite some short-run variations in the late 1910s: the income share of the top 1% fell from 22% to 16%.

During the Second World War, the national average continued to follow its previous trend, but the average real income of the richest 1% took off. As a consequence of the demand shock during the war, the agricultural export prices boomed, the manufacturing sector more than doubled its output between 1939 and 1945, and profits for the foundry and engineering industries increased by more than 400%.[53] However, the wage differential between skilled/white and unskilled/black workers remained extremely large. As C. H. Feinstein described, "black workers [were] denied any share of the growing income in the new economy they were creating."[54] The fact that the peak in the income share of the top 1%—as high as 23% in 1946—was concomitant with the war effort thus seems essentially due to a brief enrichment of the upper class.

In contrast, income growth in the 1950s was more inclusive, as average real income per adult increased by 29% between 1949 and 1961, while the average real income of the top 1% slightly decreased. By 1961 the income share of the top 1% had fallen to around 14%. In the 1960s, both averages grew approximately at the same rate such that inequality remained relatively constant. Following 60 years of successive increases, national average income was almost four times

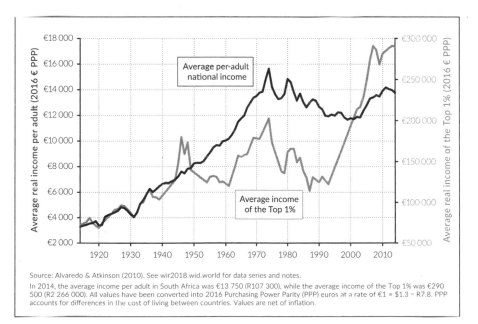

Source: Alvaredo & Atkinson (2010). See wir2018.wid.world for data series and notes.

In 2014, the average income per adult in South Africa was €13 750 (R107 300), while the average income of the Top 1% was €290 500 (R2 266 000). All values have been converted into 2016 Purchasing Power Parity (PPP) euros at a rate of €1 = $1.3 – R7.8. PPP accounts for differences in the cost of living between countries. Values are net of inflation.

Figure 13.2 Average income per adult and average income of the Top 1% in South Africa, 1914–2014

greater by the early 1970s than in 1913. Inequality resumed its downward sloping trend from 1973, but this also marked a period of overall income growth stagnation in South Africa until 1990 that culminated in a three-year recession.

For the first time in the previous 90 years, gold output started falling. Richer seams were exhausted and extraction costs increased rapidly. The industry that was once the engine of the economy started to weaken. Increases in oil prices and other commodities accelerated inflation dramatically, averaging about 14% per year between 1975 and 1992. In the 1980s, international sanctions and boycotts were placed on South African trade as a response to the apartheid regime, adding further pressure to that created by domestic protests and revolts, and contributed to the destabilization of the regime in place. White dominance was challenged on both economic and political grounds, to which the ruling government progressively made concessions, recognizing trade unions and the right to bargain for wages and conditions; this could partly explain why the average real income per adult of the top 1% decreased faster than the national average. (Figure 13.2)

The progressive policies implemented after the apartheid were not sufficient to counter a profoundly unequal socio-economic structure

There are no fiscal data to estimate top-income shares for the eight years that followed 1993. However, joining up the data points to the next available figure in 2002 suggests that income inequality has increased sharply between the end of apartheid and the present, even if the magnitude of the increase must be viewed with caution, as the estimates in these two periods may not be totally comparable. The income share of the top 1% increased by 11 percentage points from 1993 to 2014. Part of the increase from 1993 to 2002 should come from changes in the tax code. In particular, before 2002, capital gains were totally excluded, which is very likely to downward-bias the share of top-income groups. Also, tax collection capabilities seem to have increased substantially in the last years. That being said, using household survey data for the years 1993, 2000, and 2008 demonstrates that inequality increased significantly during the period for which we have no fiscal data.[55]

At first, it might seem puzzling that the abolishment of a segregationist regime was followed by an aggravation of economic inequality. The establishment of a multi-racial democracy, with a new constitution and a president of the same ethnic origin as the majority of the population, did not automatically transform the inherited socio-economic structure of a profoundly unequal country. Interracial inequality did fall throughout the eighties and nineties, but inequality within race groups increased: rising black per capita incomes over the past three decades have narrowed the black-white income gap, although increasing inequality within the black and Asian/Indian population seems to have prevented any decline in aggregate inequality. In explaining these changes scholars agree that the labor market played a dominant role, as a rise in the number of blacks employed in skilled jobs (including civil service and other high-paying government positions) combined with increasing mean wages for this group of workers.

Since 1994, several redistributive social policies have been implemented and/ or extended, among which important unconditional cash transfers targeting the most exposed groups (children, disabled, and the elderly). At the same time, top marginal tax rates on personal income were kept relatively high and recently increased to 45%. However, in spite of these redistributive policy efforts, surveys consistently show that top-income groups are still overwhelmingly white. Other studies further demonstrate that such dualism is itself salient along other key dimensions such as unemployment and education. Furthermore wealth, and in particular land, is still very unequally distributed. In 1913, the South African parliament passed the Natives Land Act which restricted land ownership for Africans to a specified area, amounting to only 8% of the country's total land area, and by the early 1990s, less than 70 000 white farmers owned about 85% of agriculture land.[56] Some land reforms have been implemented, but with seemingly poor results,[57] and it is likely that the situation has not improved much since, although precise data about the recent distribution of land still need to be collected.

Given this socio-economic structure, the interruption of the international boycotts in 1993 might have more directly favored a minority of highly skilled and/or richer individuals who were able to benefit from the international markets, which therefore contributed to increase inequality. This hypothesis would also explain the fact that income inequality in South Africa did not increase in the 1980s, while boycotts were put in place, contrary to other former Dominions (New Zealand, Canada, and Australia), despite the country having so far followed a similar trend. Furthermore, the implementation of the Growth, Employment and Redistribution (GEAR) program in 1996, which consisted of removing trade barriers, liberalizing capital flows, and reducing fiscal deficit, might also have contributed, at least in the short run, to enrich the most well off while exposing the most vulnerable, in part by increasing returns to capital over labor and to skilled workers over unskilled workers.

The rapid growth experienced from the early 2000s until the mid-2010s was essentially driven by the rise in commodity prices and was not accompanied with

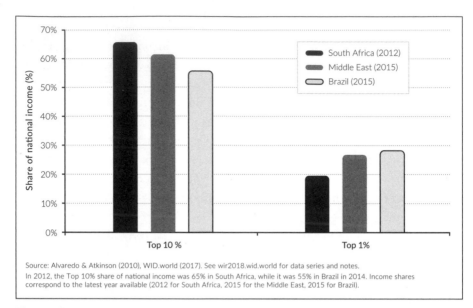

Source: Alvaredo & Atkinson (2010), WID.world (2017). See wir2018.wid.world for data series and notes.
In 2012, the Top 10% share of national income was 65% in South Africa, while it was 55% in Brazil in 2014. Income shares correspond to the latest year available (2012 for South Africa, 2015 for the Middle East, 2015 for Brazil).

Figure 13.3 South Africa: the world's highest top 10% income share, but not the highest top 1% share

significant job creation as the government hoped it would. The income share of the top 1% grew from just less than 18% in 2002 to over 21% in 2007, then decreased by about 1.5 percentage points and increased again in 2012–2013 as prices reached a second peak. The fact that these variations closely mirror the fluctuation in commodity prices suggests that a minority benefiting from resource rents could have granted themselves a more than proportional share of growth.

Last, it should be stressed that the top 1% only represents a small part of the broader top 10% elite, which is mostly white. While the share of income held by the top 1% is relatively low as compared to other high inequality regions such as Brazil or the Middle East, the income share of the top 10% group is extreme in South Africa (Figure 13.3). The historical trajectory of the top 10% group may be different from that of the top 1%—potentially with less ups and downs throughout the twentieth century. Unfortunately at this stage, historical data on the top 10% group do not go as far back in time as for the top 1% group.

PART III

PUBLIC VERSUS PRIVATE CAPITAL DYNAMICS

14

Wealth-Income Ratios across the World

- Analyzing the composition of an economy's national wealth, between assets that are privately and publicly owned, is a prelude to understanding the dynamics of wealth inequality among individuals. New data have allowed us to better comprehend the evolution of countries' wealth-income ratios and can help answer crucial policy questions.
- A general rise in the ratio between net private wealth and national income has been observed in nearly all countries in recent decades. It is striking to see that this long-run finding has largely been unaffected by the 2008 financial crisis, or by asset price bubbles in countries such as Japan and Spain.
- There have been unusually large increases in the ratios for China and Russia, which have quadrupled and tripled, respectively, following their transition from a communist- to a capitalist-oriented economy. Private wealth-income ratios in these countries are approaching levels observed in France, the UK, and the United States.
- Public wealth has declined in most countries since the 1980s. Net public wealth (public assets minus public debts) has even become negative in recent years in the United States and the UK, and is only slightly positive in Japan, Germany, and France. This arguably limits government ability to regulate the economy, redistribute income, and mitigate rising inequality.
- In China, public property largely declined but remains at a high level today: net public wealth has stabilized at about 30% of national wealth since 2008 (as compared to 15–25% in the West during the mixed-economy 1950–1980 period).
- The only exceptions to the general decline in public property seen in the data are oil-rich countries with large public sovereign funds, such as Norway.

- The structural rise of private wealth-income ratios in recent decades is due to a combination of factors including high saving rates and growth slowdowns (volume factors), the increase of real estate and stock prices (relative asset price factors), and the transfer of public wealth to private wealth (institutional factors), described in the next chapters.

New data have allowed us to better understand the relationship between wealth and inequality

Understanding how the level and structure of national wealth have evolved in the long run is one of the most fundamental economic questions. National income is a "flow" concept: it is defined as the sum of all income flows produced and distributed in a given country during a given year; it can also be broken down between the remuneration of labor and capital. National wealth, on the other hand, is a "stock" concept: it is defined as the sum of all assets—in particular housing, business, and financial assets, net of debt—that were accumulated in the past. The relationship between national wealth and national income can inform us about a number of key economic, social, and political evolutions, including the relative importance of capital in an economy and the structure of ownership.

Before we look at distribution of private wealth (that is, what share of private wealth is owned by the bottom 50% of the population, the top 10%, and so on), it is critical to better understand the evolution of total private wealth, and how it compares to public wealth and to total national wealth—which by definition is equal to the sum of private and public wealth. It is also important to keep in mind that the very notions of private property and public property can have very different meanings depending on the country or the period considered. For instance, private property in land or housing can take very different forms, depending on the extent of tenant rights, the length of their tenures, the ability of landlords to change their rents or expel them unilaterally, and so forth. In a similar way, corporate property may not have the same meaning when workers' representatives hold substantial voting rights in corporate boards (such as in Nordic countries or Germany) as in countries where shareholders control all voting rights.

Also, public property in China today is a different reality from public property in this country forty years earlier, or in the context of Norway's public sovereign fund today, and so on. Understanding the details of the legal, political, and governance system is important to understanding the interplay between property structure and power relations between social groups. The study of private and public wealth cannot be limited to the analysis of trends and levels; it must be grounded in a deeper understanding of the countries' institutions and how these affect political and social inequality, as well.

Studying the evolution of national wealth-national income ratios can also help improve our knowledge on the structure of wealth, savings, and investment and thus can be used to study fundamental macroeconomic questions. These questions include: What are the long-run dynamics and prospects regarding the evolution of public debt? And what are the patterns of net foreign asset positions? In order to properly analyze these issues, it is critical to look at the entire national balance sheet—that is, the overall structure of who owns what. Public debt or foreign assets are not owned by the planet Mars; by definition, they belong to private or public property owners. Monitoring the evolution of capital accumulation and the composition of private assets, for example, can also help identify potential signs of instability in an economy. Indeed, in the cases of Japan and Spain, wealth-income ratios reached historical highs in 1990 and 2008, respectively, as both countries experienced asset market bubbles.

Until recently it was difficult to fully get to grips with such dynamics because of a lack of data. Thomas Piketty and Gabriel Zucman have recently presented harmonized annual series of wealth-income ratios for the eight largest rich economies in the world from 1700 onward. These series have also been discussed in *Capital in the Twenty-First Century* and in the ensuing debates on the return to a patrimonial society.

Their work has been extended by other researchers. The WID.world database now contains data on more than twenty countries, which we discuss in this report. In particular, we currently have series on the structure of private and public wealth in a number of emerging and ex-communist economies, which are able to provide new insights on crucial public policy issues.

We should stress, however, that this is an area where we still need to make a lot of progress. In particular, we still know far too little about the structure of public, private, and foreign ownerships in many areas of the developing and emerging world, particularly in Africa, Latin America, and Asia.

Private wealth-income ratios have risen remarkably since the 1970s

In 1970, private wealth-national income ratios ranged from around 200–350% in most developed countries (Figure 14.1 and Figure 14.2). The past four decades saw a sharp rise in these ratios in all countries. By 2007, the year in which the global

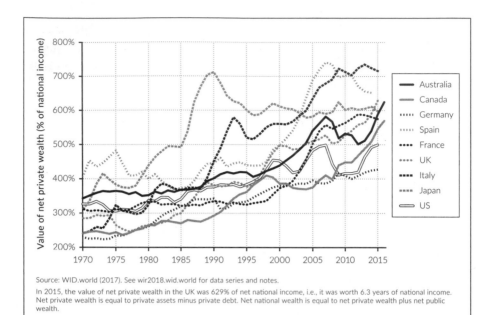

Source: WID.world (2017). See wir2018.wid.world for data series and notes.

In 2015, the value of net private wealth in the UK was 629% of net national income, i.e., it was worth 6.3 years of national income. Net private wealth is equal to private assets minus private debt. Net national wealth is equal to net private wealth plus net public wealth.

Figure 14.1 Net private wealth to net national income ratio in rich countries, 1970–2016

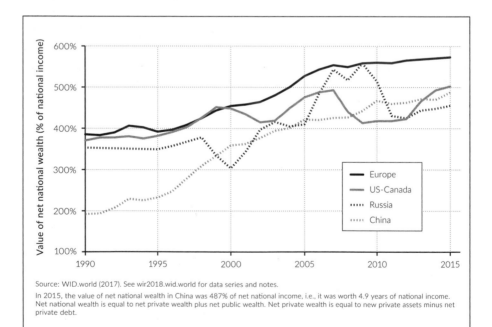

Source: WID.world (2017). See wir2018.wid.world for data series and notes.

In 2015, the value of net national wealth in China was 487% of net national income, i.e., it was worth 4.9 years of national income. Net national wealth is equal to net private wealth plus net public wealth. Net private wealth is equal to new private assets minus net private debt.

Figure 14.2 Net national wealth to net national income ratio in emerging and rich countries, 1990–2015

financial crisis began, private wealth-national income ratios in the countries observed averaged 550%, peaking at 800% in the extreme case of Spain. Despite the fall in these ratios in some of the countries following the financial crisis and the decline in housing prices, the multi-decade trend seems to have been largely unaltered. By 2016, the market value aggregate private wealth—measured in years of national income—is typically twice as large in 2016 as in 1970.

There have, however, been interesting cross-country variations in magnitudes and levels. Within Europe, country trajectories have been roughly similar as net private wealth rose from 250–400% of net national income in 1970 to 450–750% by 2016. Italy showed the most spectacular rise in its private wealth-to-income ratio, which approximately tripled from 250% in 1970 to over 700% in 2015, followed by the UK where the private wealth-national income ratio more than doubled, from approximately 300% to 650%, over the same forty-five years. France (from approximately 300% to more than 550%) followed a similar trajectory, though at a slightly lower order of magnitude, while this trend was also followed by Germany (from approximately 250% to 450%) and Spain (from about 400% to 650%) over the same period.

Outside Europe, Australia and Canada demonstrated comparable evolutions in their private wealth-national income ratios to France, Italy, and the UK. Canada's private wealth more than doubled between 1970 and 2016, from around 250% of net national income to more than 550%, while Australia's rise was still significant but less striking, increasing from slightly less than 350% to over 550% of national income. In the United States, private wealth—relative to national income—rose by a half over the same time period, from less than 350% of national income to around 500%.

In Japan, the private wealth-income ratio also almost doubled over the time period (300% to almost 600%) and, like Spain, experienced enormous fluctuations as a result of its asset price bubble in the years leading up to 1990. In Japan, real estate and stock market prices rose dramatically from around 1986 as overly optimistic expectations regarding future economic fundamentals increased the value of the country's capital assets and sent its private wealth-national income ratio soaring to as much as 700% by 1990. But soon after the Nikkei stock market index had plummeted and the price of assets followed suit, leading to what was dubbed the "lost decade" and a 150-percentage-point fall in the wealth-income ratio by 2000. However, despite further falls, the wealth-income ratio remained one of the highest among the rich countries. As explained in detail in Chapter 24, Spain has followed a similar trend since the bursting of the country's asset price bubble, with its wealth-to-income ratio falling by around 150 percentage points from its peak in 2007 to approximately 650% in 2014.

Thanks to recent research that has been completed on some of the world's largest emerging economies, it is now also possible to compare how these countries' wealth-income ratios have evolved. This is particularly interesting given the changes in political and economic regimes experienced in the emerging world over the period considered. As depicted in Figure 14.2, China and Russia both experienced large rises in their private wealth-income ratios after their transitions away from communism. While to some extent these increases are to be expected (as a large proportion of public wealth is transferred to the private sector), the scale of change experienced is particularly striking in China. The comparison with the trajectories observed in developed countries is also of particular interest (about which more will be said below).

At the time of the "opening-up" policy reforms in 1978, private wealth in China amounted to just over 110% of national income, but by 2015, this figure had reached 490%, following almost unrelenting rises. Russia's transition began twelve years later in 1990, but the change since has been no less spectacular. Over this shorter period of time, Russia's private wealth-income ratio more than tripled from around 120% to 370%. It is interesting to compare these changes with those in Europe and North America, described above, as China's ratio is only just below that of the United States, and Russia is not a long way behind, either. Furthermore, the speed and scale of the change in these emerging economies far surpasses that seen in rich countries. By way of comparison, the only time the UK or the United States experienced a similar magnitude of change in wealth-income ratios followed their huge falls at the beginning of the twentieth century.

Rising national wealth-to-income ratios in recent decades come exclusively from the rise of private wealth

From Figure 14.3 it quickly becomes clear that the recent upward trend in national wealth-to-income ratios has exclusively been the result of private wealth accumulation. Indeed, in the UK and the United States, national wealth consists entirely of private wealth, as net public wealth has become negative (that is, public assets are now below public debt). France, Japan, and Germany have also experienced a significant decline in public wealth, which is now worth just about 10–20% of national income according to official estimates—that is, a very tiny fraction of total national wealth. The domination of private wealth in national wealth represents a marked change from the situation which prevailed in the 1970s, when net public wealth was typically between 50% and 100% of national income in most developed countries (and over 100% in Germany). Today, with

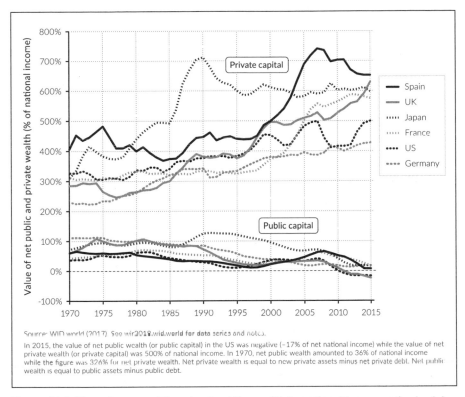

Source: WID.world (2017). See wir2018.wid.world for data series and notes.

In 2015, the value of net public wealth (or public capital) in the US was negative (−17% of net national income) while the value of net private wealth (or private capital) was 500% of national income. In 1970, net public wealth amounted to 36% of national income while the figure was 326% for net private wealth. Net private wealth is equal to new private assets minus net private debt. Net public wealth is equal to public assets minus public debt.

Figure 14.3 Net private wealth and net public wealth to national income ratios in rich countries, 1970–2015

either small or negative net public wealth, the governments of developed countries are arguably limited in their ability to intervene in the economy, redistribute income, and mitigate rising inequality. (More on this will be said below.)

In practice, the decline in net public wealth in recent decades is mostly due to the rise of public debt, while the ratios of public assets to national income have remained relatively stable in most countries (Figures 14.4a and 14.4b). The relative stability of public assets—relative to national income—can be viewed as the consequence of two conflicting effects: on the one hand, a significant fraction of public assets were privatized (particularly shares in public or semi-public companies, which used to be relatively important in a number of developed countries between the 1950s and the 1970s); on the other hand, the market value of the remaining public assets—typically public buildings hosting administrations, schools, universities, hospitals, and other public services—has increased over this time period.

China and Russia provide two contrasting examples of how private-wealth-to-national-income ratios have evolved, relative to the aforementioned countries,

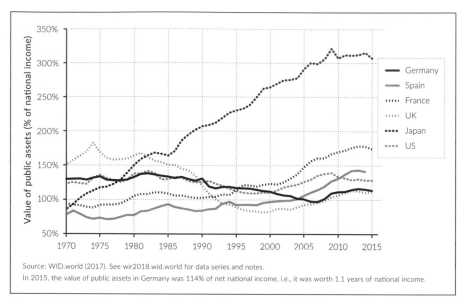

Figure 14.4a Public assets to net national income ratio in rich countries, 1970–2015

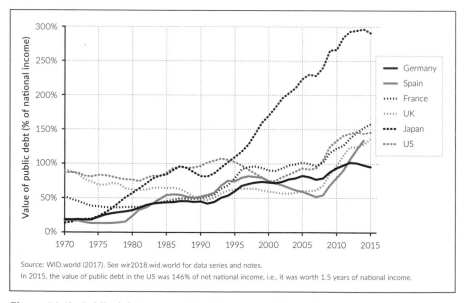

Figure 14.4b Public debt to net national income ratio in rich countries, 1970–2015

for which the privatization strategies chosen by the two countries play an integral role. (This is further analyzed in Chapters 15 through 17.) The gradual process of privatization of public wealth in China led to a slight over-fall in the value of public wealth as a proportion of national income, from just over 250% of national income in 1978 to approximately 230% in 2015, in a context of rapidly rising asset

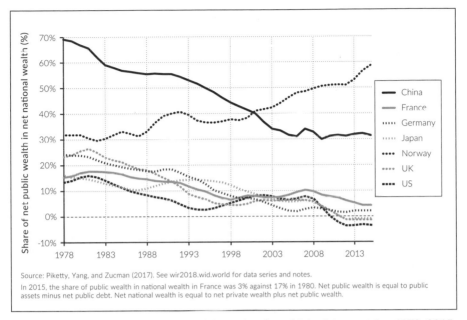

Source: Piketty, Yang, and Zucman (2017). See wir2018.wid.world for data series and notes.

In 2015, the share of public wealth in national wealth in France was 3% against 17% in 1980. Net public wealth is equal to public assets minus net public debt. Net national wealth is equal to net private wealth plus net public wealth.

Figure 14.5 The share of public wealth in national wealth in rich countries, 1978–2015

prices. In Russia, the voucher privatization strategy chosen aimed to transfer public assets into the private sector as quickly as possible, and subsequently had the effect of reducing the net public wealth to national income ratio enormously, from over 230% of national income in 1990 to around 90% in 2015.

The dominance of private wealth over public wealth within countries is further highlighted by their relative shares in national wealth. As depicted by Figure 14.5, all observed countries (with the exception of Norway) have seen a decline in the value of public property relative to private property. In the late 1970s, the share of net public wealth in net national wealth was positive and substantial in all developed countries: it was as large as 25% in countries including Germany and Britain, and 15% in Japan, France, and the United States. By 2016, the share of public wealth has become negative in Britain and the United States, and is only marginally positive in Japan, Germany, and France. In China, the share of public wealth was as large as 70% in 1978, and seems to have stabilized around 30% since 2008—a level that is somewhat larger (but not incomparable) to that observed in Western countries during the mixed-economy period of the 1950s–1970s.

Norway, along with some other resource-rich countries, is unique in this sense, using its large sovereign investment fund to invest in projects that can increase the wealth of the state. Following oil and gas discoveries in 1969, the Norwegian government established a Global Pension Fund in the 1990s to invest a proportion of the revenue earned from these nonrenewable energy sources and ensure that the benefits from North Sea oil production accrued not just to the current generation, but also to future generations. This is seen as an important instrument of economic policy in Norway to support government saving, finance public expenditure, and wealth accumulation. As a result, the share of public wealth within total national wealth rose from around 30% in 1978 to almost 60% by 2015 as the value of public wealth rose to roughly 300% of national income (considerably greater than in China's in relative terms).

There are two interesting comparisons to be made here that illustrate the importance of political institutions and ideologies in determining national wealth-to-income ratios. To summarize, it's not only a question of oil—it depends on what the government decides to do with public wealth and with the economy. The first comparison is with Russia. Despite accumulating similar trade surpluses in relative terms to Norway—equal to around 200% of national income—according to official statistics, Russia has been unable to accumulate large foreign assets, and a significant proportion of these surpluses are estimated to be held in offshore assets and thus cannot be taxed or used for government expenditure (unlike in Norway). The second comparison is with the UK, given that it also was able to benefit from North Sea oil. In his book *Inequality, What Can Be Done?*, Anthony Atkinson poses a thoughtful question. "It is an interesting piece of conjectural history," he writes, "to ask what would have happened if the UK had created such a fund in 1968 and had spent only the real return" in a similar way to Norway. Atkinson goes on to show that the accumulated fund for the UK would have been very considerable at some £350 billion, or about 60% of the Norwegian fund. As the UK is a larger country, the fund would have represented a smaller percentage of national income, but nevertheless, the fiscal cushion would have enabled the UK's net worth to be positive rather than negative today.

Recent evolutions in wealth-income ratios are likely the result of economic policy decisions and country-specific contexts

The following chapters provide a more detailed analysis of why wealth-income ratios developed as described above in developed countries since the 1970s (Chapter 15), and in China and Russia since their respective transitions away from communist-dominated economic and political models (Chapter 16).

In summary, the structural rise of private wealth-income ratios in recent decades has been due to a combination of factors. High saving rates and growth slowdowns (volume factors) were responsible for approximately 60% of the increase in national wealth-income ratios in the rich countries observed, while rises in real estate and stock prices (relative asset price factors) represented the remaining 40%. The transfer of public wealth to private wealth (institutional factors) is critical to understanding the evolution of private wealth-income ratios in China and Russia, but also in developed countries that underwent large privatization exercises (generally in the mid-1980s), though on a much smaller scale.

Since the financial crisis, trends in wealth-income ratios have varied between countries, underlining the importance of institutional and country-specific contexts. Wealth-income ratios dipped in all of the observed countries following the crisis, suggesting short-term capital losses were experienced as a result of falling asset prices, as evidenced by lower house prices and stock market indices across countries from 2008. The size, speed, and timing of the fall and subsequent recovery in ratios—which occurred to some extent in all but two countries for which data are available (Japan and Spain)—vary significantly, again highlighting how individual country circumstances can substantially affect the wealth-income ratio. For example, the fall in ratios in Spain (down 150%) and the United States (down 140%) are likely to have been larger than in other countries due to overinflated prices for stocks and property assets that helped to create the emergence of these bubbles in the first place (see Chapter 23 in particular).

15

The Evolution of Aggregate Wealth-Income in Developed Countries

- National savings and economic growth and asset prices are key to understanding how national wealth has evolved in the long run. National savings and growth account for about 60% of the rise in national wealth in rich countries, while asset prices account for the remaining 40%.
- The rise in housing largely drove domestic capital accumulation since the late 1970s, with significant variations across countries.
- External wealth has played an important role in the general evolution of wealth-income ratios.
- Today's private wealth-national income ratios in rich countries appear to be returning to the high values observed in the late 19th century, which were as high as 600–700%

National savings, economic growth, and asset prices are key to understanding how national wealth-income ratios have evolved in the long run

In order to properly analyze the evolution of national wealth-national income ratios and the structure of property, we need to combine a large number of complex explanatory factors and processes.

First, for a given level of national wealth, the division between private and public wealth is largely a consequence of government policies. If the government in Russia or China decides to privatize public assets—typically below market prices—then the share of private wealth will mechanically increase. More generally, if a government decides to run fiscal surpluses in order to accumulate public assets (and/or nationalize private assets, sometimes below or sometimes above market prices, depending on the historical and ideological context), then other things being equal, the share of public wealth will rise. If a government runs fiscal deficits and finances its deficits by issuing public debt or privatizing public assets, then the share of public wealth will decline.

In the case of developed countries, the combination of public policies (fiscal deficits, privatization of public assets, and expansion of public debt) followed since the 1970s led to a reduction of the share of public wealth from around 20% of national wealth in the 1970s (between 15% and 25%, depending on the specific country) to about 0% (or slightly negative levels) by 2016 (see Figure 14.5). If different fiscal and regulation policies had been followed, and if the public share in national wealth had remained at the same level as in the 1970s, then by definition the level of private wealth would be about 20% lower in 2016 than what it actually was (other things equal, that is, for a given level of national wealth). In that sense, the decline in public wealth explains a very large fraction of the overall rise in private wealth–national income ratios.

The other issue is to understand the evolution of national wealth–national income ratios. Here one needs to consider the interplay between the level of national savings (the sum of public and private saving), the level of economic growth (itself determined by population and productivity growth), and the evolution of relative asset prices. More precisely, following the work by Piketty and Zucman (2014), one can decompose the evolution of national wealth-national income ratios into two components: volume effects and price effects.

Volume effects are largely determined by the evolution of national savings: the higher the level of national savings, the larger the accumulation of national assets and hence national wealth. They also depend on the level of growth: for given savings, a lower population and/or productivity growth will tend to raise the ratio of national wealth to national income (simply because national income is lower). In sum, countries with high savings and low growth (for example, because of demographic stagnation, as in Japan and large parts of Europe) naturally tend to accumulate high national wealth–national income ratios.

Price effects are determined by the evolution of asset prices—in particular, housing and equity prices—relative to consumer prices. This in turn depends on a number of institutional and policy factors—for example, the gradual lift of rent control contributed to the large increase in housing prices over the period—as well as on the patterns of saving and investment strategies. For example, if the aging households in Japan or Europe choose to invest a large proportion of their savings in domestic assets including real estate (and do not, or cannot, diversify their portfolio internationally as much as would have been possible) then it is perhaps not too surprising that high upward pressure is generated on housing prices.

By combining systematic data series on the patterns of saving, investment, and economic growth in developed countries since 1970, one can show that both volume and price effects have played a significant role. For example, looking at the eight largest developed economies, one finds that about 60% of national wealth accumulation between 1970 and 2010 can be attributed on average to volume effects, versus about 40% to price effects. It is worth noting, however, that there are very large cross-country variations. For instance, volume effects explain 72% of the accumulation of national wealth in the United States between 1970 and 2010, while residual capital gains explain 28%. Similar to the United States, new savings also appear to explain around 70–80% of national wealth accumulation in Japan, France, and Canada between 1970 and 2010, while residual capital gains accounted for the remaining 20–30%. Capital gains were larger, however, in Australia, Italy, and the UK, where they accounted for more than 40–60% of the increase in wealth. In the UK, more than half of the country's growth in wealth (58%) over the period was attributable to improvements in asset prices. On the contrary, asset prices were reduced over the period in Germany so savings accounted for all the rise in in national wealth—while capital gains actually moderated this rise.

Our new extended series confirm these general findings. In particular, following the 2008 financial crisis, we observe very different patterns of asset price adjustments. For example, housing prices fell substantially in the United States and Spain (more on this below), and much more moderately in the UK and France. The general conclusion, however, is that the decline in asset prices observed in some countries in recent years is relatively small as compared to the long-run rise in relative asset prices observed since 1970.

What explains these important long-run capital gains in most countries identified in the data? To some extent, the capital gains made in the housing and stock markets since the 1970s–1980s can be understood as the outcome of a long-run asset price recovery. Asset prices fell substantially during the 1910–1950 period mainly due to low savings rates and negative valuation effects (including losses on foreign portfolios) and have been rising regularly ever since 1950. There might, however, have been some overshooting in the recovery process, particularly in housing prices. This could be explained by the kind of home portfolio bias described above.

Germany was the one interesting exception to the general pattern of positive capital gains. Given the country's relatively large saving flows, one would expect to observe a higher national wealth-income ratio than the 430% recorded in 2015. According to estimates that include research and development expenditure in saving flows, "missing wealth" in Germany is of the order of 50–100% of national income, suggesting that German statisticians may have either overestimated saving and investment flows, or underestimated the current stock of private wealth, or both. However, another possibility is that Germany had not experienced a long-run asset price recovery of the same magnitude as other countries because of the importance the German legal system places on the rights to control private assets by stakeholders other than private property owners. Rent controls, for example, may have prevented the market value of real estate from increasing as much as in other countries. Similarly, voting rights granted to employee representatives on corporate boards may reduce the market value of corporations. Germans may also not have the same preferences for expensive capital goods, especially housing, than the British, French, and Italians, perhaps the result of historical and cultural reasons that mean they favor living in a more polycentric country rather than one with a large centralized capital city.

Last, it is worth noting that when an average of wealth accumulation is computed for European countries as a whole, capital gains and losses become less important as a factor in understanding gains in wealth-income ratios. Europe overall experienced lower residual capital gains than in France, Italy, and the UK due to the impact of Germany. Had regional balance sheets for the United States been available, it is possible that decomposing wealth accumulations would reveal that regional asset price variations within the United States would not be too different from those found in Europe. Therefore, it is possible that substantial relative asset price movements can become permanent within relatively small national or regional economic units, but these effects tend to correct themselves at a larger scale.

The rise in housing wealth largely drove domestic capital accumulation

The accumulation of housing wealth has played a large role in the total accumulation of domestic capital, but with significant variations between countries. In France, Italy, and the UK, the rise in domestic capital-national income ratios is almost entirely due to the rise of housing (Table 15.1). In Japan, housing represents less than half of the total rise of domestic capital—and an even smaller proportion of the total rise of national wealth, given the large accumulation of net foreign assets.

In most countries, other domestic capital goods have also contributed to the rise of national wealth, in particular because their market value has tended to increase. In particular, we can look at Tobin's Q ratios—a definition of the gap between the market and the book value of corporations. These were much below

Table 15.1 Domestic capital accumulation in rich countries, 1970–2015: Housing vs. other domestic capital

	1970 domestic capital / national income ratio		2015 domestic capital / national income ratio		1970–2015 rise in domestic capital / national income ratio	
	incl. Housing	incl. Other domestic capital	incl. Housing	incl. Other domestic capital	incl. Housing	incl. Other domestic capital
US	357%		518%		161%	
	132%	225%	179%	339%	48%	113%
Japan	378%		532%		154%	
	150%	228%	214%	318%	64%	90%
Germany	326%		393%		67%	
	160%	166%	268%	125%	108%	-41%
France	343%		576%		233%	
	122%	221%	412%	164%	290%	-57%
UK	339%		624%		376%	
	99%	240%	334%	290%	290%	50%
Italy	238%		612%		374%	
	108%	130%	439%	173%	331%	43%
Canada	304%		520%		237%	
	126%	178%	302%	218%	190%	47%
Australia	429%		715%		286%	
	184%	245%	410%	305%	227%	59%

Source: Piketty & Zucman (2014) and Estevez-Bauluz (2017). See wir2018.wid.world for data series and notes.

In 2015, the value of domestic capital in Italy was 612% of net national income, i.e., it was worth 6.1 years of national income. Domestic capital is the market-value of national wealth minus net foreign assets.

1 in the 1970s, meaning that the market value of wealth assets (that is, their price on the stock market) was considerably below their book value (that is, the value of assets based on the company's balance sheet account; their assets minus liabilities) and were closer to 1 (and at times above 1) in the 1990s–2000s. But there are again interesting cross-country variations. Tobin's Q was very low in Germany, remaining well below 1 (and typically around 0.5), contrary to values in the UK and the United States. One interpretation is the "stakeholder effect" described briefly above. Shareholders of German companies do not have full control of

company assets—they share their voting rights with workers' representatives and sometimes regional governments—which might push a company's stock market value below its book value. However, another possibility is that some of the variations in Tobin's Q reflect data limitations. Quite puzzlingly, indeed, in most countries Tobin's Q appears to be structurally below 1, although intangible capital is imperfectly accounted for, which in principle should push values above 1. Part of the explanation may be that the book value of corporations tend to be overestimated in national accounts.

External wealth has played an important role in the general evolution of wealth-income ratios

The above analysis of how wealth has been accumulated in rich countries does not differentiate whether wealth was accumulated domestically or abroad. National wealth can be viewed as the sum of domestic wealth and net foreign wealth—that is, foreign assets (assets owned by domestic residents in other countries) minus its gross foreign liabilities (domestic assets owned by residents from other countries). Reviewing the data on national and net foreign wealth for the 1970–2016 period indicates that net foreign wealth—whether positive or negative—has been a relatively small part of national wealth in rich countries throughout the 1970–2016 period (Figure 15.1).

Despite net foreign assets representing a relatively small fraction of national wealth, external wealth has played an important role in the general evolution of wealth-income ratios. First, Japan and Germany accumulated sizable positive net foreign positions in the 1990s and 2000s, as these export-oriented economies generated large trade surpluses, and by 2015, the countries owned the equivalent of about 50% and 70% of national income in net foreign assets, respectively. Although Japan's and Germany's net foreign positions are still substantially smaller than the positions reached by France and the UK before the First World War, they have nonetheless grown to be substantial. As a result, the rise in net foreign assets represents more than a quarter of the total rise of the national wealth-national income ratios in the two countries. By contrast, most of the other rich nations exhibit net foreign positions which are negative—typically between –10% and –30% of national income—and which have generally declined over the period. One caveat to these official net foreign asset positions is that they do not include the sizable assets held by a number of developed country residents in tax havens. In all likelihood, including these assets would turn the rich world's total net foreign asset position from negative to positive, and this improvement would

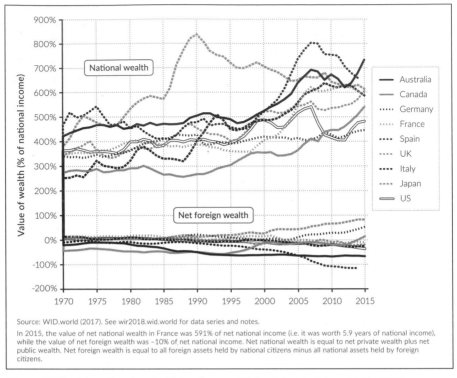

Source: WID.world (2017). See wir2018.wid.world for data series and notes.

In 2015, the value of net national wealth in France was 591% of net national income (i.e. it was worth 5.9 years of national income), while the value of net foreign wealth was –10% of net national income. Net national wealth is equal to net private wealth plus net public wealth. Net foreign wealth is equal to all foreign assets held by national citizens minus all national assets held by foreign citizens.

Figure 15.1 Net national and net foreign wealth in rich countries, 1970–2015

probably be particularly large for Continental Europe where 15% of the region's GDP is estimated to be held in offshore tax havens. Chapter 17 and Chapter 23 also provide estimations of offshore wealth in Russia and Spain, respectively.

Second, there has been a huge rise in the total amount of foreign assets owned by countries since the 1970s, such that a significant share of each rich country's domestic capital is now owned by other countries. The rise in cross-border positions is significant everywhere, being spectacularly large in Europe, and a bit less so in the larger economies of Japan and the United States. One implication is that capital gains and losses on foreign portfolios can be large and volatile over time and across countries, and indeed foreign portfolios have generated large capital gains in the United States (but also in Australia and the UK) and significant capital losses in some other countries (Japan, Germany, France). Strikingly, in Germany, virtually all capital losses at the national level can be attributed to foreign assets. In the United States, net capital gains on cross-border portfolios represent one-third of total capital gains at the national level, and the equivalent of the total rise in the US national wealth-national income ratio since 1970.

Returning to the Gilded Age?

It is almost impossible to properly understand the rise of wealth-income ratios in developed countries in recent decades without putting the recent period into a longer historical perspective. As outlined above, a significant part of the rise of wealth-income ratio since 1970 is due to capital gains: about 40% on average, with large differences between countries. But the key question is: Were these capital gains due to a structural, long-run rise in the relative price of assets (caused, for example, by uneven technical progress), or was this a recovery effect that could have compensated for capital losses observed during earlier parts of the twentieth century?

Analyzing the evolution of wealth-income ratios over a further one hundred years reveals that capital gains experienced since 1970 were due to recovery effects. Because of historical data limitations, this long-term analysis is restricted to four countries—namely, France, Germany, the UK, and the United States. However, these countries indicate two clear patterns. For the three European countries, similar U-shaped patterns are evident, such that today's private wealth-national income ratios appear to be returning to the high values observed over the period 1870–1910, which were as high as 600–700%.

In addition, European public wealth-national income ratios have followed an inverted U-curve over the past century. However, the magnitude of the pattern of public wealth accumulation is very limited compared to the U-shaped evolution of private wealth, meaning that European national wealth-income ratios are strongly U-shaped, too (Figure 15.2). It can also be observed that at around the start of the twentieth century, European countries held a very large positive net foreign asset position, averaging around 100% of national income. Interestingly, the net foreign position of Europe has again turned (slightly) positive in 2000–2010, when the national wealth-income ratio again exceeded that of the United States.

Starting from this set of descriptive facts, and using the best historical estimates of saving and growth rates, it is also possible to estimate the relative contribution of savings and capital gains since 1870. This exercise shows that total accumulation of national wealth over this 140-year-long period appears to be well accounted for by saving flows. But in order to fully reconcile differences in private wealth-income ratios, small residual capital gains are required for France, the UK, and the United States, and a small residual capital loss for Germany. In all cases, however, saving flows account for the bulk of wealth accumulation: capital gains seem to wash out in the long run.

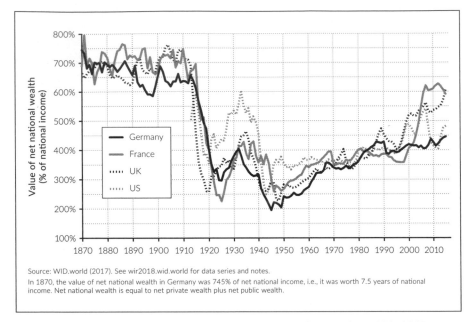

Source: WID.world (2017). See wir2018.wid.world for data series and notes.
In 1870, the value of net national wealth in Germany was 745% of net national income, i.e., it was worth 7.5 years of national income. Net national wealth is equal to net private wealth plus net public wealth.

Figure 15.2 Long-run trends in the national wealth of rich countries, 1870–2015

Dividing the analysis by sub-periods, it becomes clear that in every European country a strong U-shaped relative capital price effect was experienced. In the UK, for example, negative rates of real capital losses near –2% per year were experienced between 1910 and 1950, followed by real gains of approximately +1% per year between 1950 and 1980 and around 2.5% between 1980 and 2010. France also exhibits similar patterns, and collectively the data for these two countries seem to illustrate a slight overshooting in the recovery process so that the total relative asset price effect over the 1910–2010 period appears to be somewhat positive. In Germany, by contrast, the recovery seems like it is yet to emerge, as the total relative asset price effect averaged close to –1% between 1910 and 2010.

This sub-period analysis allows for the huge decline in wealth-income ratios that occurred in Europe between 1910 and 1950 to be decomposed. In the UK, war destructions played a negligible role, accounting for an estimated 4% of the total decline in the wealth-income ratio. Instead, low national savings during this period accounted for 46% of the fall in the wealth-income ratio and negative valuation effects (including losses on foreign portfolios) for the remaining 50%. These negative valuation effects were in part due to the numerous anti-capital policies that were then put into place after the First World War—before which, capital markets largely ran unfettered. These policies were gradually lifted from the 1980s on, contributing to an asset price recovery.

In France and Germany, cumulated physical war destructions account for about one-quarter of the fall in wealth-income ratios. Low national saving and real capital losses each explain about half of the remaining three-quarters. Interestingly, the private wealth-national income ratio declined less in the UK than in France and Germany between 1910 and 1950, but the reverse holds for the national wealth-income ratio, due to the large quantity of public debt held by the UK around 1950. The US case is again fairly different from that of Europe, however, as the fall in the country's wealth-income ratio during the 1910–1950 period was more modest, and so was the recovery since 1950. Regarding capital gains, every sub-period in the United States shows small but positive relative price effects. The capital gain effect grew larger in the recent decades and was largely derived from United States' growing foreign portfolio, as it seems too large to be accounted for by underestimated saving and investment flows.

These results show that over a few years and even a few decades, valuation effects and war destructions are of paramount importance in determining wealth-to-income ratios. But in the main rich economies, today's wealth levels are reasonably well explained by saving and income growth rates across the period since 1870.

These findings have a number of implications for the future and for policy making. First, the low wealth-income ratios of the mid-twentieth century were due to very special circumstances. The World Wars and anti-capital policies destroyed a large fraction of the world capital stock and reduced the market value of private wealth, which is unlikely to happen again with free markets. By contrast, the determinants of the wealth-income ratio—saving and growth rates—will in all likelihood matter a great deal in the foreseeable future. As long as countries keep saving sizable amounts (due to a mixture of bequest, life cycle, and precautionary reasons), countries with low growth rates are bound to have high wealth-income ratios. For the time being, this effect is stronger in Europe and Japan, but to the extent that growth will ultimately slow everywhere, wealth-income ratios may well ultimately rise across the whole world.

The return of high wealth-income ratios is certainly not bad in itself, but it raises new issues about capital taxation and regulation. Because wealth is always very concentrated (due in particular to the cumulative and multiplicative processes governing wealth inequality dynamics—see Part IV for more detail on this), high wealth-income ratios imply that the inequality of wealth, and potentially the inequality of inherited wealth, is likely to play a bigger role for the overall structure of inequality in the twenty-first century than it did in the postwar period. This evolution might reinforce the need for progressive capital and inheritance taxation. If international tax competition prevents this policy change from happening, one cannot exclude the development of a new wave of anti-globalization and anti-capital policies.

Furthermore, because saving and growth rates are largely determined by different forces, wealth-income ratios can vary a great deal between countries. This fact has important implications for financial regulation. With perfect capital markets, large variations in wealth-income ratios potentially imply large net foreign asset positions, which can create political tensions between countries. With imperfect capital markets and home portfolios bias, structurally high wealth-income ratios can contribute to domestic asset price bubbles such as those seen in Japan and Spain. Housing and financial bubbles are potentially more devastating when the total stock of wealth amounts to six to eight years of national income rather than only two to three years. The fact that the Japanese and Spanish bubbles are easily identifiable in the dataset also suggests that monitoring wealth-income ratios may help designing appropriate financial and monetary policy. In Japan and Spain, most observers had noticed that asset price indexes were rising fast, but in the absence of well-defined reference points, it is always difficult for policy makers to determine when such evolutions have gone too far and whether they should act. Wealth-income ratios and wealth accumulation decompositions can provide useful, if imperfect, reference points here.

Comparing the Experiences of Former Communist States

Information in this chapter is based on two sources. The first is "From Soviets to Oligarchs: Inequality and Property in Russia 1905–2016," by Filip Novokmet, Thomas Piketty, and Gabriel Zucman, 2017. WID.world Working Paper Series (No. 2017/9). The second is "Capital Accumulation, Private Property and Rising Inequality in China, 1978–2015," by Thomas Piketty, Li Yang, and Gabriel Zucman, 2017. WID.world Working Paper Series (No. 2017/6).

- The evolution of public and private wealth in China and Russia since their transitions away from communism can be viewed as extreme cases of the general rise of private wealth relative to national income in rich countries since the 1970s–1980s.
- Their experiences are largely explained by institutional differences, particularly their respective privatization strategies for public assets. Privatization occurred at a much faster rate, in a more chaotic manner and at a larger extent in Russia than in China due to its "shock therapy" liberalization policies and voucher privatization schemes for state-owned enterprises.
- Despite being at roughly equal levels in 1980, private wealth reached approximately 500% of national income in China by 2015—roughly equal to levels seen in the US and just below those of France and the UK (550–600%), while this figure was notably smaller for Russia, on the order of 350–400%.
- Public wealth remained at around 200–250% in China between 1980 and 2015, but decreased tremendously from 300% to less than 100% in Russia, again reflecting differences in the countries' privatization strategies.
- Differences in savings and investment incentives saw a significant proportion of Russian wealth leave the country to be held

in offshore assets, while the overwhelming majority of Chinese wealth stayed within the country's boundaries to be invested in domestic assets.

Privatization strategies were key in determining wealth accumulation differences between China and Russia

The transition away from communism in both China and Russia had profound effects on aggregate wealth in both countries. However, there were also considerable differences between the two countries, which are first evident in the evolution of their respective private wealth–national income ratios. As examined in detail in Chapter 15, the general rise of private wealth relative to national income in rich countries since the 1970s–1980s can be attributed to a combination of factors including the combination of growth slowdowns and relatively high saving rates and general rises in asset prices. The case of Russia together with that of China and other ex-communist countries can be viewed as an extreme case of this general evolution, but the liberalization and public asset privatization strategies chosen by the two countries also had crucial impacts on the development of these countries' wealth to national income ratios.

In Russia as in China, private wealth was very limited back in 1980, at slightly more than 100% of national income in both countries. But by 2015, private wealth reached approximately 500% of national income in China, roughly equal to levels seen in the US, and rapidly approaching the levels observed in countries such as France and the UK (550–600%). Private wealth in Russia has also increased enormously relative to national income, but the ratio was comparatively only of the order of 350–400% in 2015—that is, at a markedly lower level than in China and in Western countries as illustrated by Figure 16.1. This gap would have been larger if estimates of offshore wealth were not included in Russia's private wealth (more to come on this in Chapter 18). This is an important source of wealth to include in estimates for Russia as it represents approximately 70% of national income, while the global average offshore wealth is estimated to be in the region of 10% of national income.

The rise of national wealth in Russia has been almost exclusively driven by increases in private wealth, which have themselves come at the expense of public wealth. National wealth increased only weakly relative to national income during the last quarter of a century, rising from 400% in 1990 to 450% by 2015, with public wealth falling from around 300% of national income to below 90%. In contrast, China's public wealth remained relatively constant from 1978 to 2015,

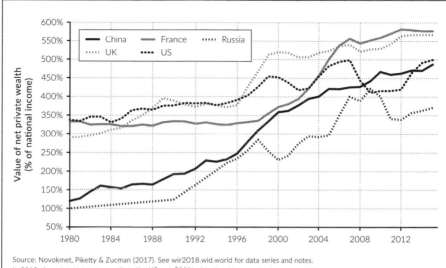

Source: Novokmet, Piketty & Zucman (2017). See wir2018.wid.world for data series and notes.
In 2015, the value of private wealth in the US was 500% of national income, i.e., it was worth 5 years of national income. Net private wealth is equal to net private assets minus net private debt.

Figure 16.1 Net private wealth to net national income ratios in China, Russia, and rich countries, 1980–2015: The rise of private wealth

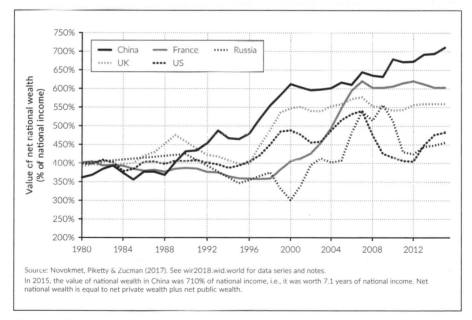

Source: Novokmet, Piketty & Zucman (2017). See wir2018.wid.world for data series and notes.
In 2015, the value of national wealth in China was 710% of national income, i.e., it was worth 7.1 years of national income. Net national wealth is equal to net private wealth plus net public wealth.

Figure 16.2 Net national wealth to net national income ratios in China, Russia, and rich countries, 1980–2015: National wealth accumulation

staying above 230% of national income. Given the large rise in private wealth described above, national wealth has thus doubled from around 350% to 700% of national income over the period (Figure 16.2). Interestingly, national wealth fell notably following the end of communism in Russia, dropping from around 425% of national income in 1990 to 300% in 2000. This was largely due to the speed at which the so-called shock therapy and voucher privatization strategy was implemented to transfer public wealth to the private sector (particularly that of state-owned enterprises). However, while public wealth-income ratios in China fluctuated during the first decade that followed the "reform and opening up" policies of 1978, they have risen almost constantly since. The speed of privatization of both state-owned enterprises and housing stock was much slower in China than in Russia, allowing for a more gradual and consistent transfer of wealth from the public to the private sector. The larger variations seen in Russian wealth as compared to Chinese wealth that occurred between 1998 and 2002, and between 2006 and 2010, can in large part be explained by the stock market fluctuations experienced in Russia during these periods of time.

Understanding the differences in wealth accumulation between China and Russia

The widely divergent patterns of national wealth accumulation observed in Russia and China can be accounted for by a number of factors. First, saving rates (net of depreciation) have been markedly higher in China, typically as large as 30–35%, as compared to 15–20% at most in Russia. If a country saves more, it is natural that it will accumulate more wealth. Second, these Chinese savings were used for the most part to finance domestic investment and hence domestic capital accumulation in China. In contrast, a very large fraction—typically about half— of Russia's national savings were used to finance foreign investment, via very large trade surpluses and current account surpluses, rather than domestic investment. This is not necessarily disadvantageous in itself, but these large flows of foreign savings resulted in little wealth accumulation as a result of the general mismanagement of the surpluses, including bad portfolio investment, capital flight, and offshore leakages.

Again, the gap between Russia and China would be even larger if offshore wealth were not included in Russian national wealth calculations. Its inclusion is undoubtedly illuminating in helping readers to understand the evolution of wealth trends in Russia, but given that offshore wealth is largely out of the reach of the national government, its presence in Russian wealth calculations could also be argued to overestimate its tangible value for the country. In contrast, if the full value of cumulated trade surpluses in Russia's national wealth were considered in estimations, then Russia's national wealth-income ratio would have been at the same level as China's by 2015, at around 700% of national income. The magnitude of change when including and excluding these factors illustrates the macroeconomic significance of this issue.

Finally, China's national wealth-income ratios are higher than in Russia because relative asset prices have increased more in the former than the latter. In particular, Tobin's Q ratios are much closer to one in China than in Russia. This means that the market value of wealth assets in China (that is, their price on the stock market) is much closer to their book value (that is, the value of assets based on the company's balance sheet account; their assets minus liabilities) than in Russia, where these values were consistently very low. The interpretation of this finding may reflect a number of different factors.

On the Chinese side, the key factor influencing the Tobin's Q ratio nearing one is the country's restricted capital markets, which limit the number of Chinese companies listed on the stock exchange. On the Russian side, there are a larger number of factors. One interpretation is that company stakeholder models have various actors other than shareholders—including worker representatives and sometimes regional government, who share corporate decision-making power—which may reduce the market value of equity shares, but not necessarily the social value of companies. A less optimistic interpretation of low Q ratios, which may better fit the Russian case, is that there were ill-defined property rights and low protection of shareholder stakes in companies, not because of the benefit of other well-defined and potentially efficiency-enhancing stakeholders, but simply because the legal system is not working well. In addition, it could also be that this low market valuation reflects the importance of offshore assets and legal outsourcing in the management and control of Russian corporations. That is, Russian corporations are embedded into a complex nexus of contracts and offshore legal entities, of which the system of official shares ruled by the Russian legal system and traded on Moscow stock market is only the visible part.

Understanding the evolution of public wealth in China and Russia

The ex-communist countries of China and Russia have followed the same general patterns of a declining overall share of public property in total wealth as rich countries in recent years, though starting from a much higher level of public wealth. In the ex-communist countries of China and Russia, the share of net public wealth fell from around 70% in 1980 to 35% and 20%, respectively, in

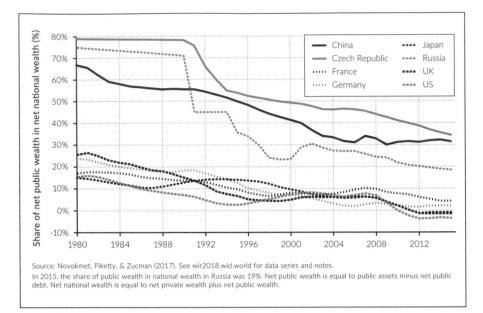

Figure 16.3 The share of public wealth in national wealth in former communist and rich countries, 1980–2015: The decline of public property

2015—a veritable turnaround in their public-private wealth ratios. As depicted by Figure 16.2, the share of net public wealth in net national wealth reversed in both China, from around 70–30% in 1978 to 30–70% in 2015, and in Russia, from 70–30% to 20–80% between 1990 and 2015. These recent figures for the countries' public-private wealth ratios are not incomparable to those observed in the so-called capitalist countries during the mixed-economy period that followed the Second World War (1950–1980). But while these countries have ceased to be communist, in the sense that public ownership has ceased to be the dominant form of property, they still have much more significant public wealth than other capitalist countries. This is due both to low public debt and significant public assets—for instance, Russia's energy sector. (Figure 16.3)

However, there are also strong differences between China's and Russia's experiences. The larger magnitude of the reversal in public-private wealth ratio in Russia, and its occurrence over a shorter time period, serves to underline the greater speed and depth of privatization in Russia relative to China. Indeed, this process is still continuing in China, and the public-private divide could even be stabilized at the current level if the Chinese authorities choose to do so. In contrast, Russia's "shock therapy" approach to privatization was markedly different from that followed in China and other ex-communist countries. This contrast is evident in the period immediately after Russia's transition toward a market economy commenced, from 1990 to 1995, when the fall in the share of net public wealth in

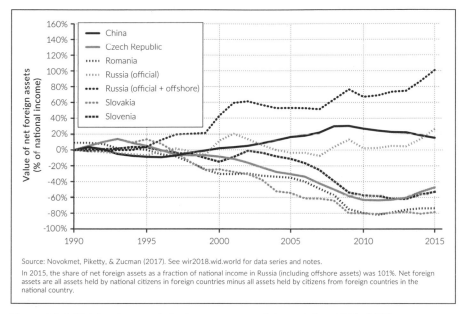

Source: Novokmet, Piketty, & Zucman (2017). See wir2018.wid.world for data series and notes.

In 2015, the share of net foreign assets as a fraction of national income in Russia (including offshore assets) was 101%. Net foreign assets are all assets held by national citizens in foreign countries minus all assets held by citizens from foreign countries in the national country.

Figure 16.4 Net foreign assets in former communist countries, 1990–2015

net national wealth in Russia (70% to 35%) was five times larger than that in China (55% to 50%). Its implications for income inequality and wealth inequality are discussed in more detail in Part II and Part IV, respectively.

In contrast, the importance of foreign assets within China and Russia has been fairly similar since their transitions away from communist models, but have occurred for vastly different reasons. As illustrated by Figure 16.4, both countries have positive net foreign assets, meaning that the assets they own in the rest of the world are more valuable than those owned by foreigners in China and Russia, respectively. In Russia, this has largely been due to the country's economic and natural endowments, given its large, but not necessarily permanent, natural resources, and has allowed the country to accumulate trade surpluses and foreign reserves for the future, as can also be observed in most oil-rich countries in the Middle East and elsewhere.

The accumulation of net foreign assets in China that are similar in magnitude to those of Russia should be viewed as much more striking, however, and indicate significant differences between the two countries. Chinese net foreign assets were accumulated in the absence of any significant natural resource endowment, and with much smaller trade surpluses of less than 3% of national income on average over the 1990–2015 period. In comparison, Russia's trade surpluses averaged 10% of national income for the same period. This reflects more efficient management of trade surpluses and foreign reserves, which are viewed as critical for China's economic and financial sovereignty by its Communist Party, and also the political choice of limiting foreign investors' rights in China.

Differences in political institutions and ideologies seem to have played an even bigger role than purely economic factors in the evolution of wealth-national income ratios in China and Russia, and the share of the public and private sector within national wealth. As has already been stressed, the speed and depth of Russia's privatization strategy was vastly different from the much slower and more gradual transition plan implemented by China, particularly the fire sale of Russian state-owned enterprises through the country's voucher privatization scheme. Furthermore, differences in savings and investment incentives saw a significant proportion of Russian wealth leave the country to be held in offshore assets, while the overwhelming majority of Chinese wealth stayed within the country's boundaries.

17

Capital Accumulation, Private Property, and Rising Inequality in China

Information in this chapter is based on "Capital Accumulation, Private Property and Rising Inequality in China, 1978–2015," by Thomas Piketty, Li Yang, and Gabriel Zucman, 2017. WID.world Working Paper Series (No. 2017/6).

- While Chinese national wealth doubled in recent decades, from 350% to 700% of national income, its composition also changed dramatically. The share of agricultural wealth fell from close to half of total capital in the late-1970s to less than a tenth by the mid-2010s. By contrast, the privatization of the housing sector and the liberalization of capital markets saw the shares of housing and domestic capital dominate the make-up of China's national wealth.
- Perhaps the most spectacular evolution has been in the division of national wealth between public and private wealth. Private wealth rose from around 100% of national income in 1978 to over 450% of national income in 2014, largely due to the privatization of housing stock, reaching a level close to those seen in France, the United States, and the UK.
- The balance of public and private wealth changed from a 70–30 proportional split of public-private assets in 1978 to a 35–65 split by 2015, but public wealth remained important as a share of national income, at around 250%. This level is high when compared to rich countries.
- High Chinese savings rates were an important driver of the rise in wealth accumulation, but according to simulations, they accounted for only 50% to 60% of the rise. The rest can be accounted for by increases in relative asset prices.
- China's wealth accumulation was primarily driven by domestic capital accumulation. Chinese net foreign position, despite

substantial growth since 2000, remains relatively modest compared to Japan or Germany. On the other hand, China remains more suspicious regarding foreign ownership of companies than Europe and North America.

China's transition to a mixed economy led to a surge in national wealth and a radical change in its composition

The Chinese wealth-national income ratio has increased substantially in recent decades. In 1978, national wealth as a percentage of national income was approximately 350%, but by 1993 this figure had reached 500% and grew to over 700% by 2015, as the composition of national wealth changed dramatically. The share of agricultural land used to make up almost half of total capital in 1978, but dropped sharply to less than a tenth of the total in 2015, as illustrated by Figure 17.1. In contrast, housing and other domestic capital wealth (buildings, equipment, machinery, patents, assets used by corporations, public administrations, and households) increased enormously, in volume and in their share of the total: housing wealth increased from around 50% of national income in 1978 to approximately 200% in 2015, while other domestic capital grew to be the largest wealth component, rising from around 100% to over 350% between 1978 and 2015. Net foreign assets have also become a notable addition to China's national wealth since the turn of the twenty-first century, amounting to approximately 25% of national income.

But perhaps the most spectacular evolution since the late 1970s has been the division of national wealth into private and public wealth (Figure 17.2). Private wealth was relatively small in 1978, at around 100% of national income, but grew to represent over 450% of national income in 2014, while public wealth remained roughly stable, between 200% and 250% of national income over the period (first increasing slightly until 1993–1994 and then declining back to its initial level). As a result, the balance of public and private wealth in national wealth has altered enormously, with the 70–30 proportional split of public-private assets in 1978 reversed to a 35–65 split by 2015, as the country transitioned away from a communism-based economic model toward a mixed-form economy.

The extent of national wealth privatization in the Chinese economy differed, however, depending on the type of wealth asset, as can be seen in Figure 17.3. In the housing sector privatization was particularly comprehensive, with the private housing stock rising from roughly 50% to over 95% between 1978 and 2015, while for other forms of domestic capital, the public share has declined but is still

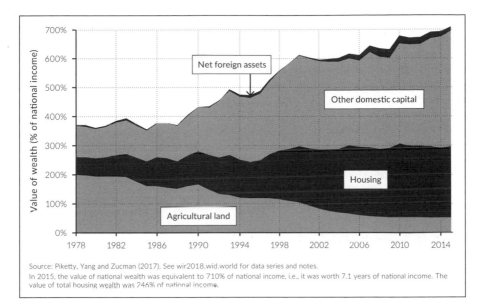

Source: Piketty, Yang and Zucman (2017). See wir2018.wid.world for data series and notes.
In 2015, the value of national wealth was equivalent to 710% of national income, i.e., it was worth 7.1 years of national income. The value of total housing wealth was 246% of national income.

Figure 17.1 The asset composition of national wealth in China, 1978–2015

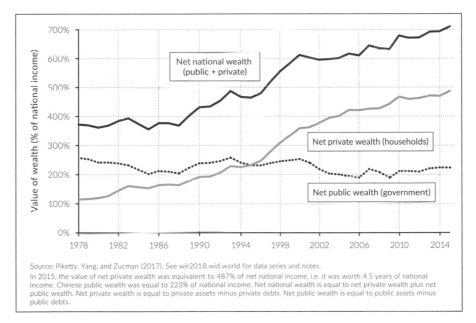

Source: Piketty, Yang, and Zucman (2017). See wir2018.wid.world for data series and notes.
In 2015, the value of net private wealth was equivalent to 487% of net national income, i.e. it was worth 4.5 years of national income. Chinese public wealth was equal to 223% of national income. Net national wealth is equal to net private wealth plus net public wealth. Net private wealth is equal to private assets minus private debts. Net public wealth is equal to public assets minus public debts.

Figure 17.2 The structure of national wealth in China, 1978–2015

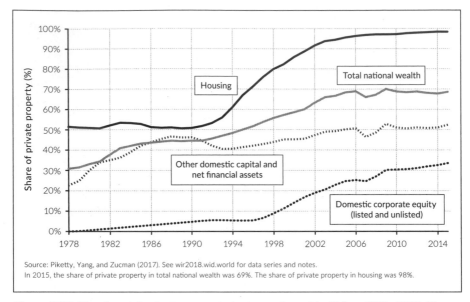

Source: Piketty, Yang, and Zucman (2017). See wir2018.wid.world for data series and notes.
In 2015, the share of private property in total national wealth was 69%. The share of private property in housing was 98%.

Figure 17.3 The share of private property by type of asset in China, 1978–2015: The rise of private property

around 50%. Domestic equities (traded and non-traded), for example, were almost entirely owned by the state (95%) in 1978, but private ownership rose to around 30% by 2015, such that the government continues to own around a 60% share and foreign ownership accounts for the remaining 10%. Interestingly, the fraction of Chinese equities that are publicly owned dropped substantially until 2006, but seems to have stabilized—or even increased somewhat—since 2007.

Public assets remain substantial in China, unlike in most Western countries

The private wealth-national income ratio in China is now in the range of 450–500%, much closer to levels seen in most OECD countries. In the United States and the UK, the ratio is closer to 500% and 550–600%, respectively, but in China, public assets remain substantial unlike in these Western countries where public wealth has become very small, or even negative, with public debt exceeding public assets. Indeed, the share of public property in China today is somewhat larger than, but by no means incomparable to, what it was in the West from the 1950s to the 1980s, and has recently appeared to have strengthened further: since the 2008 financial and economic crisis, the public share in China's mixed economy has seemingly increased and thus domestic capital accumulation has been one of the primary drivers of wealth growth in China.

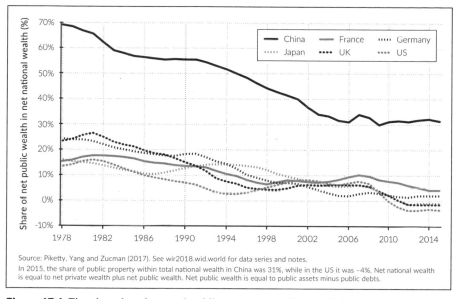

Figure 17.4 The changing shares of public property in China and rich countries, 1978-2015

The size and structure of China's publicly-held wealth assets have large implications for economic development. The size of public property has important consequences for the state's ability to conduct industrial and regional development policies; sometimes more efficiently and sometimes less so. It also has potentially considerable fiscal consequences, as governments with negative net public wealth typically have to pay large interest payments before they can finance public spending and welfare transfers, while those with large positive net public wealth can benefit from substantial capital incomes, enabling them to finance more public spending than would be possible through tax collection.

It is interesting to compare the evolution of the public share in national wealth in China and in a resource-rich country with a large sovereign wealth fund such as Norway. These two countries have essentially switched positions: the public share in Chinese national wealth declined from 70% to 30% between 1978 and 2015, while it rose from 30% to 60% in Norway over the same period (Figure 17.4). A key difference between public wealth in Norway and China is that most of Norway's public wealth is invested abroad. Norway's large positive net public wealth generates capital income that is mostly used to finance further foreign capital accumulation, which in the long run can be used to reduce taxes and to finance more public spending. In that sense, it is a very different form of public property than in China. Norwegian public property has, therefore, largely been accumulated for fiscal and financial purposes, rather than for industrial development and retention of a measure of control over the economy as seen in China. Norway's sovereign fund has, however, also been used at times to promote certain policies, for example, regarding social and environmental objectives.

High savings rates and increases in relative asset prices drove wealth accumulation

High savings and investment rates over the period have been important drivers of Chinese wealth accumulation, but they are insufficient to account for the total increase in the country's wealth—as it has also been the case for several rich countries. The other important element in understanding Chinese wealth accumulation is the rise of relative asset prices, in particular housing and equity prices that grew considerably more than the rise in consumer prices. As per the estimates of Thomas Piketty, Li Yang, and Gabriel Zucman, savings explain 50% to 60% of the rise in the wealth-income ratio since 1978, while the increase in relative asset prices accounts for the remaining 40% to 50%.

Just as in rich countries, the rise in relative asset prices has been the result of a series of factors. First in this series of factors is the high taste preferences and demand for housing assets by Chinese households, which itself may be partly due to limited access to alternative savings and investment vehicles—Chinese citizens could not invest overseas, for example, and capital markets took time to develop—and also to insufficient awareness of expansions in the public pension system. A second important explanation involves changes in the legal system that reinforced private property rights including the lifting of rent controls, increases in the relative power of landlords over tenants, and changes in the relative power of shareholder and workers within enterprises.

Decomposing wealth accumulation by sectors (private and public) and assets (financial and nonfinancial) in China over the period 1996–2015 provides interesting insights. When analyzing private wealth, there are clear differences between the returns on assets: strong, positive capital gains have been made by nonfinancial assets (231%), which centered around residential housing assets (163%), while there were only negligible capital gains for net financial wealth (1%). Conversely, there were strong capital gains for public financial assets (68%) and smaller gains for public nonfinancial wealth (19%). The majority of these large capital gains on public financial assets came from government owned equities, and can be linked to the reform of state-owned enterprises that began in 2003 and the unprecedented wave of initial public offerings of state-owned enterprises that started in 2006. China also made notable capital losses on its net foreign assets, in part due to the appreciation of the yuan after 2004, explaining why despite its large current account surpluses, its net foreign asset position has increased only moderately (from –9% of national income in 2000 to 15% in 2015).

China, like Japan, seems more suspicious vis à vis foreign ownership than Europe or North America

Domestic financial intermediation has also played a key role in the development of wealth in China over the last four decades. The ratio between total domestic financial liabilities—that is, total debt and equity issued by households, the government, and the corporate sector combined—and total domestic capital has risen from 60% in 1978 to 140% in 2015. This is a substantial rise given the limited financial development seen in China in the late 1970s. However, despite this financial development, the level of financial intermediation remains much lower in China than in many Western countries, where financial intermediation ratio rose from between 100 and 140% in 1978 to 200–300% in 2015, as depicted by Figure 17.5.

Foreign ownership of Chinese companies has not played a strong role in the rise of wealth, however. The fraction of domestic financial liabilities owned by the rest of the world reached only 5% in China in 2015, and has not passed 7%

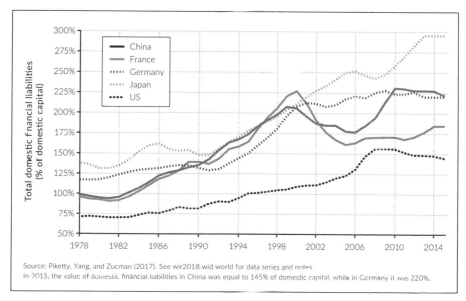

Source: Piketty, Yang, and Zucman (2017). See wir2018.wid.world for data series and notes
In 2015, the value of domestic financial liabilities in China was equal to 145% of domestic capital, while in Germany it was 220%.

Figure 17.5 Domestic financial liabilities in China and rich countries, 1978–2015: The rise of financial intermediation

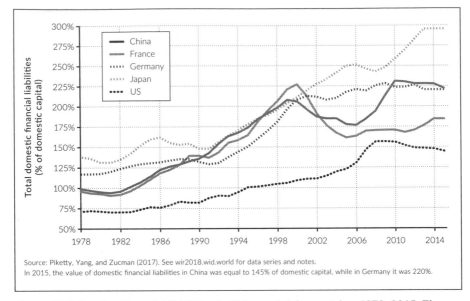

Source: Piketty, Yang, and Zucman (2017). See wir2018.wid.world for data series and notes.
In 2015, the value of domestic financial liabilities in China was equal to 145% of domestic capital, while in Germany it was 220%.

Figure 17.6 Foreign financial liabilities in China and rich countries, 1978–2015: The rise of foreign ownership

across the whole observed period, as seen in Figure 17.6. Japan has the next smallest percentage of foreign ownership at 10% of domestic financial liabilities, followed by 15% in the United States and 25–30% in Germany and France. These differences partly reflect size effects: European countries are smaller, and if ownership were to be consolidated at the European level, the rest of the world would own only about 15% of European wealth (as in the United States). Even so, there does appear to be a tendency that some Asian countries—Japan and even more so China—are less open to foreign ownership than European and North American countries.

18

The Rise of Private Property in Russia

Information in this chapter is based on "From Soviets to Oligarchs: Inequality and Property in Russia 1905–2016," by Filip Novokmet, Thomas Piketty, and Gabriel Zucman, 2017. WID.world Working Paper Series (No. 2017/10).

- Russia's net national wealth-income rose moderately since the country's transition from a communist to a capitalist economic model, increasing from around 400% in 1990 to 450% in 2015. At the same time, there have been significant fluctuations in the country's wealth breakdown, as the shock therapy and voucher privatization strategy transferred enormous wealth at a very fast rate from the public to the private sector. Public wealth amounted to 300% of national income in 1990, but was just 100% in 2015.

- Private housing wealth represented by far the largest component of Russian private wealth in 2015. The gradual rise of housing can be accounted for by real-estate price movements and a privatization of the housing sector that was more gradual than the voucher privatization method used for companies.

- The very low level of official financial assets owned by Russian households—around 70–80% of national income throughout the 1990–2015 period—is particularly striking. This suggests that the privatization of Russian companies did not lead to any significant long-run rise in the value of household financial assets.

- However, discrepancies in Russia's balance of payments allow researchers to estimate that a small number of Russian citizens had offshore wealth assets that amounted to 70% of national income in 2015, doubling the official value of financial assets. This is suspected to be the result of capital flight, made possible through weaknesses in Russia's legal and statistical system.

Russia's transition from public to private property

The evolution of aggregate private and public wealth in Russia has changed dramatically since the fall of the Soviet Union. As the country transitioned from a communist to capitalist model after 1990, public property was transferred to the private sector. Net national wealth amounted to slightly more than 400% of national income in 1990, roughly three-quarters of which was owned by the state and one-quarter by private individuals. But by 2015, these proportions reversed, as illustrated by Figure 18.1. Net private wealth amounted to 350% of national income, while net public wealth represented less than 100%; the overall national wealth to national income ratio had increased by just 12% over 25 years. Furthermore, this dramatic fall in Russia's net public wealth occurred over just a few years, between 1990 and 1995, as the country implemented its so-called shock therapy transition strategies, which included the privatization of state-owned enterprises through vouchers. (More on this will be addressed in Part IV of the report.)

It is noteworthy that aggregate national wealth fell relative to national income in the initial stages of Russia's transition. As can be seen on Figure 18.1, net national wealth decreased between 1990 and 1999, from over 400% of national income to about 300%, such that aggregate national wealth fell even more than national income over this period, which almost halved itself. National wealth rose, then, considerably between 1999 and 2009, reaching about 550% of national

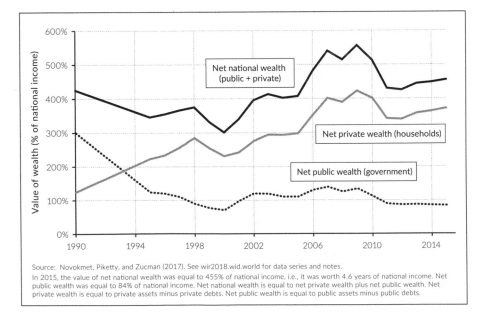

Source: Novokmet, Piketty, and Zucman (2017). See wir2018.wid.world for data series and notes.
In 2015, the value of net national wealth was equal to 455% of national income, i.e., it was worth 4.6 years of national income. Net public wealth was equal to 84% of national income. Net national wealth is equal to net private wealth plus net public wealth. Net private wealth is equal to private assets minus private debts. Net public wealth is equal to public assets minus public debts.

Figure 18.1 The structure of national wealth in Russia, 1990–2015

income. This peak corresponded to a very large rise of Russian stock market prices and housing prices during this decade, but as asset prices then fell in the aftermath of the financial crisis, aggregate national wealth fell back to around 450% of national income in 2015, only just above its value 25 years previously. As a consequence, the major transformation during the 1990–2015 period was the shift from public to private property, rather than any significant and sustained increase in the aggregate value of national wealth.

Private housing has risen to dominate private wealth in Russia

In order to better understand which factors influenced the evolution of national wealth-income ratios in Russia and the composition of the country's wealth, it is critical to look separately at the different asset categories. As seen in Figure 18.2, there was a significant rise in private wealth since 1990. Housing played a critical role here as property prices more than doubled between the year 2000 and the peak of the housing bubble in 2008–2009, increasing the value of housing wealth from less than 50% of national income in 1990 to 250% at its peak, before easing to approximately 200% by 2015. Comparatively, other domestic capital (mostly consisting of unincorporated businesses owned directly by households) and agricultural land (which was also largely privatized during the 1990s)

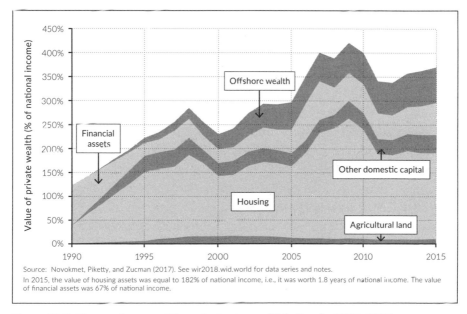

Source: Novokmet, Piketty, and Zucman (2017). See wir2018.wid.world for data series and notes.
In 2015, the value of housing assets was equal to 182% of national income, i.e., it was worth 1.8 years of national income. The value of financial assets was 67% of national income.

Figure 18.2 The asset composition of private wealth in Russia, 1990–2015

increased over time, but these assets played a relatively limited role as compared to the rise of private housing.

In addition to real estate price movements, the gradual rise of private housing wealth between 1990 and 2015 can be accounted for by the more continuous manner in which housing privatization occurred, relative to the voucher privatization method used for companies. Tenants were typically given the right to purchase their housing unit at a relatively low price, but they did not need to exercise this right immediately. Due to various economic, political, and psychological factors, many Russian households waited until the late 1990s and even the 2000s to exercise this right. Indeed, some were concerned about the possible maintenance costs associated with private ownership as under public housing ownership maintenance work was taken care of by public authorities, while others were more concerned about a possible political downturn, particularly following the presidential election of 1996 when Boris Yeltsin won with a relatively small margin against Communist Party leader Gennady Zyuganov.

Official household financial assets are particularly low in Russia, due largely to the voucher method chosen to privatize former state-owned enterprises

What is also particularly striking is the very low level of official financial assets owned by Russian households attained in official Rosbank financial balance sheets and other official sources. Household financial assets have always been less than 70–80% of national income throughout the 1990–2015 period, and they have often been less than 50% of national income; in the late 1990s and early 2000s, they were as little as 20–30% of national income. Thus, it is as if the privatization of Russian companies did not lead to any significant long-run rise in the value of household financial assets, in spite of the fact that it had become possible for individuals to own financial shares in Russian firms. This appears particularly paradoxical.

The initial decline in financial assets was perhaps predictable. Back in 1990, household financial assets—which at the time mostly consisted of saving accounts—amounted to about 70–80% of national income. But as prices were liberalized in the early 1990s, these Soviet-era savings were all but eradicated by hyperinflation. The consumer price index was multiplied by nearly 5000 between 1990 and 1996, with annual inflation rates consistently above 150% and as high as 1 500% in 1992 and 900% in 1993. Following the introduction of the new ruble—worth 1 000 old rubles—in 1998, the inflation rate stabilized at around 20–30% per year on average up to 2006.

What is more surprising is why the new financial assets that were accumulated by Russian households during the 1990s—in particular through voucher privat-ization—did not compensate for this loss in savings. Of course, when vouchers were first introduced in 1992–1993, it was very difficult for Russian households to know what to do with these new financial instruments and how to put a price on them. More generally, it could be argued that in the chaotic monetary and political context of the 1990s, it is not too surprising that the market value of household financial assets remained relatively low until the somewhat more stable mid- to late-1990s. What is more difficult to understand, however, is why such extremely low valuations persisted well after this period. In particular, in spite of the spectacular Russian stock market boom that occurred between 1998 and 2008, it is conspicuous that total financial assets officially owned by Russian households amounted to little more than 70% of national income in 2008—that is, less than the level observed in 1990.

Taking into account offshore wealth doubles Russia's total official financial assets

In the view of Filip Novokmet, Thomas Piketty, and Gabriel Zucman, the main explanation for this paradox is the existence of a small subset of Russian house-holds that own very substantial offshore wealth—that is, nonofficial financial assets in offshore tax havens. According to their benchmark estimates, offshore wealth has gradually increased between 1990 and 2015, representing approxi-mately 75% of national income at the end of the period. As depicted by Figure 18.2, offshore wealth was thus roughly as large as official financial assets owned by Russian households. By definition, offshore assets are difficult to estimate, and the benchmark estimates presented in this section are neither precise nor fully satisfactory, but these orders of magnitude seem to be reasonable, and if anything may be somewhat underestimated given the way in which they are constructed, as explained below.

In order to estimate the rise and magnitude of offshore wealth held by Russian households, it is natural to start by looking at the evolution of Russia's trade balance and its balance of payments. Examining these two balances together, there is a clear contrast between the very large trade surpluses recorded in Russia and the country's relatively modest foreign assets, as illustrated by Figure 18.3.

Russia has had strong trade surpluses each single year since the early 1990s. These trade surpluses—mostly driven by exports in oil and gas—averaged almost 10% of national income between 1993 and 2015, having been at around 5% between 1993 and 1998, and as much as 20% in 1999–2000. Thus, in each of the last 20 years, the Russian economy has exported the equivalent of around 10%

of its annual income in excess of what the country has imported. Given that Russia's initial financial position when beginning its transition was close to zero, with very few foreign assets or foreign debt, these sustained surpluses should have led to a massive accumulation of foreign assets held by Russian citizens in the rest of the world. However, the paradox is that net foreign assets accumulated by Russia are surprisingly small at about 25% of national income in 2015.

Investigating Russia's balance sheet reveals further inconsistent information regarding the ownership of financial assets. Both foreign assets (that is, assets owned by Russian residents in the rest of the world) and foreign liabilities (that is, assets owned by rest-of-the-world residents in Russia) have increased significantly since the fall of the Soviet Union. Both were extremely small in 1990, at around 10% of national income, reflecting low levels of financial integration with the rest of the world and strong capital controls. But by 2015, foreign assets had reached almost 110% of national income, and foreign liabilities were close to 85% of national income, hence a net foreign asset position of about 25% of national income.

How can such a low level of net foreign wealth accumulation be accounted for? An obvious explanation is capital flight: some Russian individuals, and/or some Russian corporations acting on behalf of individuals, and/or some Russian government officials acting on behalf of individuals, were able to appropriate some of Russia's trade surpluses to accumulate offshore wealth—that is, foreign assets that are not properly recorded as such in Russia's official financial statistics. Given the weaknesses of Russia's legal and statistical system, and the widespread use of offshore entities to organize business and financial transactions in Russia over this period, it is maybe not too surprising that such leakages might have occurred.

Discrepancies in Russia's balance of payments can aid estimations of the country's offshore wealth

How large these capital flight leakages are, and the associated accumulation of offshore wealth is, are challenging to measure. Simple calculations of trade surpluses (230%) minus official net foreign assets (30%) over the 1990–2015 period would suggest that cumulated capital flight is on the order of 200% of national income. But this does not include the cumulated capital income flow on these foreign assets, which could have been significant if rates of return on these assets were high. Indeed, it appears that returns on foreign assets were lower than the returns on foreign liabilities over the 1990–2015 period, as illustrated by the small negative net foreign income flows in Figure 18.3. This net capital income outflow hence absorbed approximately a quarter to a third of Russia's annual trade surplus.

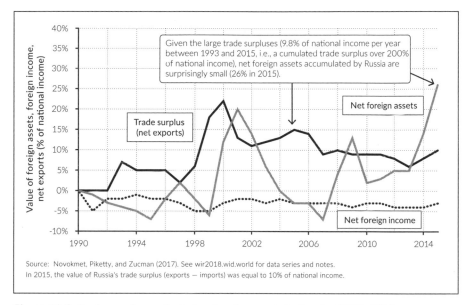

Figure 18.3 Trade surplus and missing foreign assets in Russia, 1990–2015

Furthermore, the capital gains and losses realized on the portfolio of foreign assets and liabilities need to be accounted for. These portfolio effects can be substantial if there are large differences between annual surpluses and the observed evolution of net foreign assets. This is partly what happened in Russia as foreign investors bought Russian assets in the 1990s when stock market prices were extremely low and benefited from the country's booming stock market of the 2000s, providing part of the explanation as to why foreign liabilities rose as much as Figure 18.4 shows. These portfolio effects therefore imply that a substantial part of Russia's trade surpluses was translated into assets held by citizens from elsewhere in the world. But the magnitude of the aforementioned differentials in rates of return and portfolio effects were not large enough to fully explain the missing wealth paradox.

Filip Novokmet, Thomas Piketty, and Gabriel Zucman therefore look to exploit inconsistencies in Russia's balance of payments to estimate the size of offshore wealth—that is, Russia's missing foreign assets. Their relatively conservative estimations indicate that offshore wealth reached approximately 75% of national income by 2015, suggesting that Russians own approximately as much offshore wealth as their official financial asset holdings (about 70–80% of national income in both cases). That is, they own about 50% of their total financial wealth offshore. These results are similar to estimates obtained by Gabriel Zucman's earlier research that used a different methodological approach. Thus they can be viewed as somewhat reassuring. But while these magnitudes are believed to be broadly accurate, these estimations lack absolute precision given the general lack of

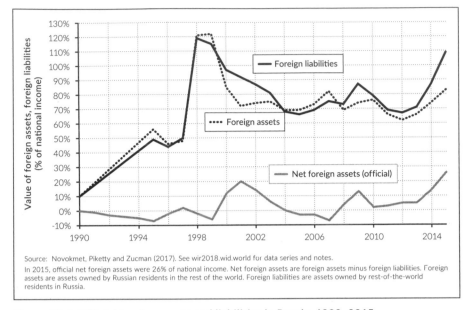

Source: Novokmet, Piketty and Zucman (2017). See wir2018.wid.world for data series and notes.
In 2015, official net foreign assets were 26% of national income. Net foreign assets are foreign assets minus foreign liabilities. Foreign assets are assets owned by Russian residents in the rest of the world. Foreign liabilities are assets owned by rest-of-the-world residents in Russia.

Figure 18.4 Official foreign assets and liabilities in Russia, 1990–2015

international financial transparency—and the difficulties of identifying by whom these missing assets are owned and what form they take potentially pose even greater challenges.

Even more uncertain is the location of the assets held offshore by Russian citizens. Some of this offshore wealth might be invested back in Russian corporations, while it is also discussed that some Russians own significant property assets in cities such as London and in the countryside of nations such as France, and/or have large shares in companies and in sports teams in countries such as Germany, the UK, and the United States. Inspecting the list of Russian billionaires released by *Forbes* illustrates that these individuals collectively own more than $400 billion in assets—that is, the equivalent of about half of the estimated $800 billion in Russian offshore wealth. Comparing the corresponding wealth portfolios published by *Forbes* and other magazines, one could be tempted to conclude that most of the offshore wealth is held in Russian companies, in particular in the energy and financial sectors. On this basis, interpretations of the available data indicate that a large fraction of Russia's official foreign liabilities—over 80% of national income in 2015—is actually held by Russian residents via offshore accounts. But given that the *Forbes* list does not provide any information regarding the fraction of reported billionaire wealth held offshore—likely a very large proportion—it is difficult to provide more conclusive explanations.

PART IV

TRENDS IN GLOBAL WEALTH INEQUALITY

19

Global Wealth Inequality: Trends and Projections

- Data on global wealth inequality are sparser than data on income inequality, so estimates should be interpreted with care. It is not possible to construct at this stage a consistent global wealth distribution. However, available research on key regions—in particular, China, Europe, and the United States—provides valuable insights into global wealth dynamics.
- Evidence points toward a rise in global wealth inequality over the past decades. At the global level—represented by China, Europe, and the United States—the top 1% share of wealth increased from 28% in 1980 to 33% today, while the bottom 75% share hovered around 10%.
- Wealth is substantially more concentrated than income. The top 10% owns more than 70% of the total wealth in China, Europe, and the United States, the bottom 50% owns less than 2%, and the middle 40% ("the global wealth middle class") owns less than 30%.
- If established trends in wealth inequality continue, the top 0.1% alone will own more wealth than the global middle class by 2050.

Global wealth inequality estimates are scarcer than for global income inequality and subject to caution

The available data on wealth inequality are much sparser than for income inequality, especially at the global level. It is therefore more difficult to provide a complete picture of how global wealth inequality has evolved over the past few decades.

We want to be very clear about this: available data sources make it impossible at this stage to properly estimate the level and evolution of the global distribution of wealth. We can to some extent estimate the global distribution of income and its evolution, as we have tried to cautiously show in Part II of this report. The situation is different for wealth. As we have shown in Part III of this report, there are very large areas of the world—particularly in Africa, Latin America, and Asia—where we are not even able to properly measure the aggregate level of national wealth and its decomposition into private and public property, foreign wealth, and natural capital. We first need to make more progress on the measurement of total wealth and its changing structure before we can construct estimates of distribution of private wealth among individuals.

A number of magazines (most notably, *Forbes*) do publish global rankings of billionaires, and some financial institutions (for instance, Credit Suisse) have combined billionaire data with other data sources to estimate global distributions of wealth. Typically these studies find that top wealth holders have been rising at very high speed in recent decades—substantially faster than the size of the world economy—and below we will agree with this general conclusion. However, the methodologies used by *Forbes* and by these institutions often lack transparency; in particular, they do not release their raw data sources and detailed computer codes. It is impossible therefore to reconstruct their statistical results. This is not merely a technical question; methodological choices can indeed have a large impact on the measured evolution of wealth inequality, and transparency of methods and sources is critical if we want to reach some agreement about inequality facts.

In the context of the WID.world project, we choose to proceed in a gradual manner and to release wealth inequality series solely for the countries for which raw sources allow us to do so in a satisfactory manner. Ideally, one needs to combine household wealth surveys together with wealth rankings and administrative fiscal data (coming from both the income tax, using the capitalization method, and the inheritance tax, using the estate multiplier method) to be able to properly estimate the distribution of wealth and to confront sources in a transparent way. At this stage, these conditions are satisfied only for a handful of countries—most notably, the United States, a number of countries in Europe (in particular, France, the UK, and Spain), and to a lesser extent China (where we have access to household wealth surveys and wealth rankings, but where access to fiscal data is extremely limited). We have also produced estimates of wealth inequality for Russia and the Middle East, but they are more fragile, and we do not use them to produce global wealth estimates in this report.

Our global wealth inequality estimates since 1980 therefore combine data from three large regions: the United States, China, and Europe. Europe itself is represented by three countries (France, Spain, and the United Kingdom), which on the basis of other countries for which we have wealth inequality data (in particular, Sweden and Germany) appear to be broadly representative. Starting from 1987, we can also compare our results with the *Forbes* billionaire rankings, which provide a better coverage of countries, though only for a tiny, extremely wealthy part of the population, and with little knowledge of how this information was collected.

Available data show that global wealth inequality is extreme and on the rise

At the global level (represented by China, Europe, and the United States), wealth is substantially more concentrated than income: the top 10% owns more than 70% of the total wealth. The top 1% wealthiest individuals alone own 33% of total wealth in 2017. This figure is up from 28% in 1980. The bottom 50% of the population, on the other hand, owns almost no wealth over the entire period (less than 2%). Focusing on a somewhat larger group, we see that the bottom 75% saw its share oscillate around 10%. Wealth concentration levels would probably be even higher if Latin America, Africa, and the rest of Asia were included in the analysis, as most people in these regions would be in the poorer parts of the distribution. We leave this to future editions of the *World Inequality Report*. (Figure 19.1)

We compare in Table 19.1 the growth rates of the different wealth groups between 1980 and 2017 (all growth rates are expressed in real terms—that is, after deduction of inflation). A number of striking findings emerge. First, one can see that average wealth has grown faster since the 1980s than average income,

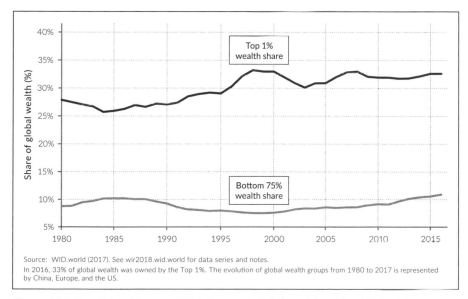

Source: WID.world (2017). See wir2018.wid.world for data series and notes.
In 2016, 33% of global wealth was owned by the Top 1%. The evolution of global wealth groups from 1980 to 2017 is represented by China, Europe, and the US.

Figure 19.1 Top 1% and Bottom 75% shares of global wealth, 1980–2017: China, Europe, and the US

Table 19.1 Global wealth growth and inequality, 1980–2017

	China + Europe + US		World
	1980–2017	1987–2017	1987–2017
Top 1/100 million (*Forbes*)	–	7.8%	6.4%
Top 1/20 million (*Forbes*)	–	7.0%	5.3%
Top 0.01% (WID.world)	5.5%	5.7%	4.7%
Top 0.1% (WID.world)	4.4%	4.5%	3.5%
Top 1% (WID.world)	3.4%	3.5%	2.6%
Average wealth per adult	2.9%	2.8%	1.9%
Average income per adult	1.3%	1.4%	1.3%

Source: WID.world (2017). See wir2018.wid.world for data series and notes.

Between 1987 and 2017, the wealth of the global Top 1% grew by 2.6%. The wealth threshold for an individual to be part of the Top 1% wealthiest in China + Europe + US in 2017 is €1125000, the Top 0.1% threshold is €5209000, the Top 0.01% threshold is €25812000.

reflecting the general tendency of wealth/income ratios to rise in most countries, as documented in Part II of this report. Between 1987 and 2017, per-adult average income has increased at 1.3% per year at the world level, while per-adult wealth has increased at 1.9% per year.

Next, if we now look at the top of world wealth distribution—as measured by the *Forbes* billionaire rankings—we find that the top wealth holders' share has increased a lot faster than average wealth holders: 5.3% since 1987 for the top 1/20 million, and 6.4% for the top 1/100 million (Table 19.1). By definition, this is an evolution that cannot continue forever: if top wealth holders were to grow on a permanent basis at a speed that is three to four times faster than average wealth in the world, then billionaires would ultimately come to own 100% of the world's wealth.

The problem with this billionaire data is twofold: first, as was noted above, it is not entirely clear how it was estimated; next, and most important, it is not clear at all whether this pattern of very fast growth holds only for billionaires, or whether it can be extended to multimillionaires. This is crucial because there are many more individuals who own $5 million, $20 million, or $100 million than there are billionaires, and the former command a potentially much larger fraction of world wealth than the latter.

We unfortunately do not know the full answer to this question, but at least our estimates for the US, Europe, and China distribution of wealth provide some interesting insights. We find that the top 1% average wealth in the US, Europe,

Table 19.2 Share of global wealth growth captured by wealth group, 1980–2017

Wealth group	Share of real growth per capita
Bottom 99%	62.9%
Top 1%	37.1%
Top 0.1%	21.6%
Top 00.1%	12.4%

Source: WID.world (2017). See wir2018.wid.world for data series and notes.

Between 1980 and 2017, the global Top 1% captured 37% of total wealth growth in China, Europe, and the US. The wealth threshold for an individual to be part of the Top 1% wealthiest in China + Europe + US in 2017 is €1 125 000, the Top 0.1% threshold is €5 209 000, the Top 0.01% threshold is €25 812 000.

and China has risen at 3.5% per year between 1987 and 2017 (versus 2.8% for per-adult average wealth and 1.9% for average income). The higher we go in the distribution, the faster the growth: the top 0.1% average wealth has increased by 4.4% per year, and the top 0.01% average wealth has increased by 5.6% per year.

These findings, which were obtained by combining a number of independent data sources (household wealth surveys, income tax data using the income capitalization method, and inheritance tax data using the estate multiplier method, when available), appear to be consistent with the *Forbes* billionaire data. But they also suggest that one needs to go really very high in the distribution of wealth to see growth rates on the order of 5–6% per year. If one considers only the top 1% wealth holders as a whole (that is, all individuals with net wealth higher than about €1.1 million in China, Europe, and the United States in 2016), then the growth rate between 1987 and 2017 has been 3.5% per year. This is faster than average wealth growth (2.8% per year), but the gap is not as huge as for billionaires. This suggests at current speed that rising inequality and the divergence of the wealth distribution will take a couple of decades before it takes really extreme proportions. (See below for a discussion of future prospects.) That being said, the direction in which the distribution is going definitely suggests rising concentration of wealth, and there is no evidence that the financial crisis of 2008 had any impact—other than temporary—on this long-run structural trend.

Our results also show that a large share of the growth of global wealth accrued to the top 1% and even narrower wealth groups. As Table 19.2 shows, the top 1% captured 37% of per capita wealth growth, more than half of which went to the top 0.1%.

All of this implies growing inequality at the top end of the distribution. Note that the bottom of the distribution has also experienced a significant increase of its wealth, driven by rapid growth in China, as shown by Figure 19.2. This pattern

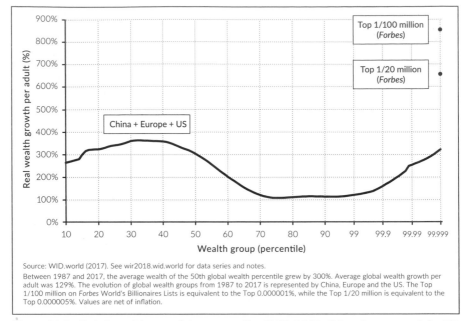

Figure 19.2 Global wealth growth by percentile, 1987–2017: China, Europe, and the US

is reminiscent of the "elephant curve" of global income growth, showing that the global wealth distribution seems to have evolved in ways qualitatively similar to income. The bottom three-quarters of the distribution saw its wealth increase by a sizable amount, though less than the world's billionaires according to *Forbes*. Between those two groups, wealth growth was at its lowest for the middle class in developed countries. The trends in the wealth growth of different groups have been fairly stable over the last three decades, with narrower wealth top groups experiencing higher growth.

Under a business-as-usual scenario, the top 1% wealth share will increase at 1 percentage point every five years

What will happen to the global distribution of wealth if these trends were to continue for the next few decades? Figure 19.3 seeks to answer that question. The top 0.1% wealth owners would progressively catch up with the global wealth middle class, which we define as wealth holders below the top 10% and above the median— that is, 40% of the world population. In 2050, both groups would own the same share of global wealth—that is, 25%. The global wealth middle class comprises 40% of the world population meaning that the top 0.1% wealthiest would be on

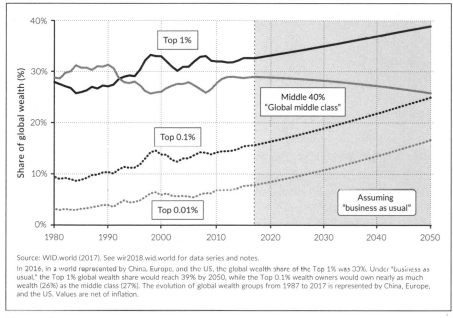

Source: WID.world (2017). See wir2018.wid.world for data series and notes.

In 2016, in a world represented by China, Europe, and the US, the global wealth share of the Top 1% was 33%. Under "business as usual," the Top 1% global wealth share would reach 39% by 2050, while the Top 0.1% wealth owners would own nearly as much wealth (26%) as the middle class (27%). The evolution of global wealth groups from 1987 to 2017 is represented by China, Europe, and the US. Values are net of inflation.

Figure 19.3 Global wealth inequality, 1980-2050: China, Europe, and the US

average four hundred times wealthier than the global middle class. This evolution would take a couple of decades.

The top 1/20 million and 1/100 million of individuals, which comprise about 250 and 50 adults, could respectively own 1.5% and 0.75% of total wealth as soon as 2030, up from 0.5% and 0.25% in the early 1990s. The share of the top 1% would keep on increasing by one percentage point every five years. The shares of the top 0.1% and 0.01% would also grow by one percentage point every five years, meaning that the increase in wealth inequality is in fact driven by these small groups. These groups are much broader than billionaires, but nevertheless quite narrow. (To belong to the top 0.1% or top 0.01% of Europe, the United States, and China in 2016, one needs to own more than €5.2 million or €25.8 million, respectively.)

Global wealth inequality is driven by a large number of forces

As discussed in Part II, global income dynamics are driven by both between- and within-country forces. The rise of private wealth has been faster in large emerging economies than in rich countries, a trend driven by high economic growth and large-scale privatization in transition economies. This tends to reduce global wealth inequality. This effect was more than offset at the top, however, by the rise

> **Box 19.1** Methodological note: How our projections work
>
> We partition the distribution of wealth into several groups:
>
> - the bottom 99%
> - the top 1%, excluding the top 0.1%
> - the top 0.1%, excluding the top 0.01%
> - the top 0.01%, excluding the top 1/20 million
> - the top 1/20 million, excluding the top 1/100 million
> - the top 1/100 million
>
> We calculate the average growth rate of wealth of these groups since 1987 (start of the *Forbes* ranking), and extrapolate the average wealth of each of these groups based on these growth rates. We obtain top wealth shares based on these averages.
>
> Because narrower top groups have experienced higher growth in the past, this method forecasts an increase of wealth inequality. Of course, this trend cannot be extended indefinitely into the future, because with the current parameters it will eventually lead to the top group's owning nearly all of the wealth. However, this problem only arises at very long horizons, so the method is still useful for projections over a few decades.

in wealth inequality within countries. Rising wealth inequality within countries is itself due to a number of factors, including rising income inequality amplified by inequality of savings rates and of rates of return. Other factors, such as the progressivity of taxation, can in turn mitigate or worsen these dynamics. Hence, future global wealth inequality will depend on both catchup growth in emerging economies, and within-country determinants of inequality. We study them at the country level as further described in the next chapters.

We should stress at the onset that there was nothing inevitable about the fact that the very top of the global wealth distribution would rise so much faster than average world wealth beginning in the 1980s. One of the global factors that might have played a role is the larger transfer from public to private wealth that took place in many countries. (See Part II.) To the extent that privatization disproportionately benefited small groups of the population—for example, Russian oligarchs—this can help explain why top wealth holders' shares rose so fast. It is difficult, however, with the data at our disposal to estimate the global impact of this factor. In particular, there are also some cases where privatization has benefited mostly the middle class (for example for housing, as we discuss below for the case of the UK, France, and Spain). Whether this channel is likely to be important for the future (one might be tempted to conclude that large privatization waves are now behind us) is another important and uncertain issue.

Another potentially important global factor behind booming top wealth is the fact that financial deregulation and innovation might have increased the inequality in rates of return that are accessible to different sizes of financial portfolio. Some of the most convincing evidence for this channel comes from the observed real rates of return on university endowments, which varied from

4–5% per year for the smallest endowments to as much as 8–10% per year for largest ones (after deduction of inflation and management costs) in the United States between 1980 and 2010.

Again one might wonder whether this corresponds to a specific financial period or whether this will continue in the future (available data suggest that large endowments were still getting very good returns in recent years). Also the governance of personal family wealth involves many other issues than that of large academic capital endowments, so one cannot directly apply these findings. Unfortunately the data available are insufficient to make similar computations for the highest family wealth.

As we shall see below, however, our country studies do show that differential rates of return—together with differential saving rates—can potentially be an important driving force behind rising wealth concentration. (Box 19.1.)

20

Comparing Trends in Personal Wealth Inequality across the World

- Available data on personal wealth inequality show that it has been on the rise in most countries since the early or late eighties. Increasing income inequality and the large transfers of public to private wealth which occurred over the past forty years drive these dynamics.
- Large rises in top wealth shares have been experienced in China and Russia following their transition from communism toward a capitalist economy, though the different inequality dynamics experienced between these two countries highlights different economic and political transition strategies.
- In the United States, wealth inequality has increased dramatically over the last 30 years and was mostly driven by the rise of the top 0.1% wealth owners. Growing inequality of income and saving rates created a snowballing effect of rising wealth concentration.
- The increase in top wealth shares in France and the UK was more moderate over the past forty years, in part due to the dampening effect of the rising housing wealth of the middle class and lower income inequality relative to the United States. As a result, while wealth concentration has been historically lower in the United States than in Europe, the situation reversed after the 1970s.
- Property prices also played an important tempering role for wealth inequality in Spain as wealth concentration remained roughly unchanged over the observed period with only short-lived fluctuations.
- In the long run, the differential between rates of return to capital and growth rates, as well as the dynamics of savings rate among wealth groups, drives wealth inequality. When rates of returns available to high-wealth portfolios are higher than average economic growth, wealth inequality increases. The same is true when savings inequality is high.

Wealth inequality within countries fell dramatically from the beginning of the twentieth century in some of the world's largest economies, but since the 1980s there have been widespread increases in wealth concentration. The combination of economic, political, and social shocks that led to the long-run decline in wealth inequality experienced throughout Europe and North America from the start of the First World War to the mid-1980s was described in the *Capital in the Twenty-First Century*. These shocks included the Great Depression, the destruction of human and physical capital led by the World Wars, restrictions on capital flows, nationalization of industries and goods provision, and greater government control over the economy. Given the close relationship between wealth and income, the story of the former is similar to that of the latter: collectively, these factors severely impacted the fortunes of the wealthiest and supported the growth of middle class wealth in Europe and the United States.

Unfortunately, relatively little is known about the recent evolution of wealth inequality at a global level. Wealth inequality data discussed in public debates up to now essentially relied on sources which do not allow for a sound analysis of wealth dynamics. It is also difficult to track how wealth inequality statistics are constructed since the methodologies are not always made transparent. This is not merely a technical question: methodological choices can indeed have a large impact on the evolution of measured wealth inequality.

The publicly available information discussed in this report and published on WID.world on the distribution of wealth and cross-border assets is still imperfect. But we see it as a first systematic attempt at generating data on wealth inequality over the globe. It combines in a consistent manner tax data, wealth surveys, and data on cross-border assets. The construction of estimates presented in this report was carried out for China, France, Russia, Spain, the United Kingdom, and the United States which are presented in this chapter and the subsequent ones.

Contrasting transition strategies have generated divergent inequality dynamics in China and Russia

Wealth inequality data for China and Russia are only available from 1995–2015, but even in these last two decades the series confirm huge increases in wealth inequality. Wealth concentration among the top 1% in both countries practically doubled, as their share in China's total wealth rose from just over 15% in 1995 to 30% in 2015, and in Russia's from below 22% to approximately 43%. Interestingly, the share of the top 10% in total wealth in 2015 is much closer between the two countries, at 67% in China and 71% in Russia as illustrated by Figure 20.2,

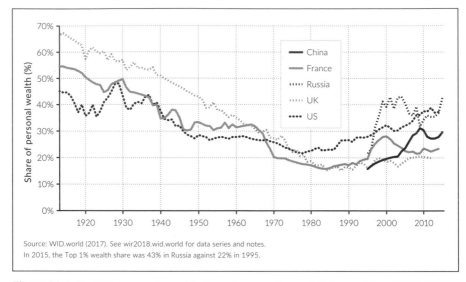

Source: WID.world (2017). See wir2018.wid.world for data series and notes.
In 2015, the Top 1% wealth share was 43% in Russia against 22% in 1995.

Figure 20.1 Top 1% personal wealth share in emerging and rich countries, 1913–2015

indicating that Russia's transition strategy favored its most wealthy citizens more than China's. As seen in Figure 20.1, by 2015 Russia had a higher concentration of wealth than the United States, while China's wealth inequality was roughly in between that of France and the United States.

The variations in inequality increases between the two former communist countries were in part due to differences in their strategies for privatizing housing and state-owned enterprises. In Russia, previously state-owned businesses were transferred to the private sector through a voucher privatization process that can be compared to a fire sale of assets given the extremely fast pace at which it was executed. By contrast, the enormous transfer of public capital into private capital with the sale of state-owned enterprises in China occurred more slowly. Its scale, though, was considerable: close to 100 000 firms with ¥11.4 trillion worth of assets were privatized between 1995 and 2005.

The method by which property wealth was privatized was different, however. Chinese citizens experienced huge reductions in welfare housing allocations and the almost complete privatization of the housing market, and by 2002, 85% of urban housing was privately owned. This property privatization process was very unequal as access to quoted and unquoted housing assets often depended on how wealthy and politically connected the household was, with the wealthiest end of the distribution able to access privatized public wealth more easily through official markets. In contrast, Russians took a more gradual approach to property privatization. Tenants were typically given the right to purchase their housing unit at a relatively low price and did not need to exercise this right

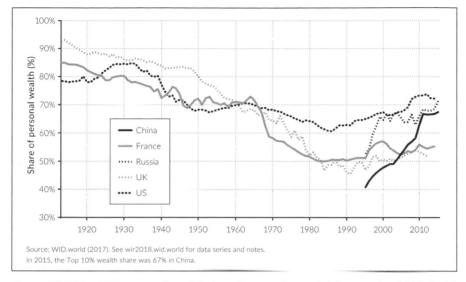

Figure 20.2 Top 10% personal wealth share in emerging and rich countries, 1913–2015

immediately, while uncertainty surrounding the macroeconomic and political environment also meant many Russian households waited until the late 1990s and even the 2000s to exercise this right. Consequently, the property privatization process had a small dampening effect on the rise of wealth inequality. The shares of the middle 40% defined as the top 50% excluding the top 10% fell in both countries across the period. Interestingly, the group's share fell in similar proportions in China and in Russia, from 43% in 1995 to 26% in 2015 in China and from 39% to 25% over the same period in Russia. While the fall was more pronounced in China, it was initially more abrupt in Russia than in China, due to the aftereffects of hyperinflation that followed price liberalization in 1992 and it wiped out savings.

The growing inequality of income and savings rates have caused rapid wealth concentration in the United States

The rise of wealth inequality in the United States was less abrupt, but no less spectacular in historical terms, than the increases experienced in the former communist countries. Wealth inequality in the United States fell considerably from the high levels of the Gilded Age by the 1930s and 1940s, due to drastic policy changes that were part of the New Deal. The development of very progressive income and estate taxation made it much more difficult to accumulate and pass on large fortunes. Financial regulation sharply limited the role of finance and the ability to concentrate wealth as in the Gilded Age model of the financier-indus-trialist. But since the mid-1980s, top wealth shares have risen sharply. The key driver of this rapid increase in wealth concentration has been an upsurge of incomes at the top of the distribution and the stagnation of incomes at the bottom. These dynamics follow the reversal of the policies implemented during the previous period, with financial deregulation and lower top tax rates among others. The differentials between the saving rates of the richest and those of the middle- and lower-class also increased wealth inequality. This had a reinforcing, "snowballing" effect as the purchase of financial assets by the wealthy using the savings from their large incomes has led to a rise in capital income concentration, providing greater incomes for the purchase of more assets and hence larger top wealth shares.

In the United States, the share of wealth owned by the top 1% adults grew from a historic low of below 22% in 1978, to almost 39% in 2014, as depicted in Figure 20.1. This represented a trend reversal from historical patterns as the top 1% wealth share in the United States was almost double that of France and the UK in 2014. These changes enabled the wealthy to purchase more wealth assets with high returns, setting a snowballing effect in motion for those at the top of the distribution, while wealth of the middle class stagnated. Consequently, the wealth share of the middle 40% fell from a historic high of almost 37% of total wealth in 1986, to around 28% in 2014. Pensions and home ownership rates of the middle 40% increased over the preceding period, but after the mid-1980s this trend reversed due to a surge in household debt that included mortgages, student loans, credit card, and other debts. These debts increased from 75% of national income in the mid-1980s to 135% in 2009 and, despite some deleveraging in the wake of the Great Recession, still amounted to close to 110% of national income in 2012; this trend can be seen in the negative share of total wealth owned by the bottom 90% between 2008 and 2013.

The rising housing wealth of the middle-class dampened wealth inequality increases in France and the UK

Between the start of the First World War and the early 1980s, France and the UK experienced dramatic falls in wealth inequality. Large wealth shocks between 1914 and 1945 included the Great Depression, inflation, and the destruction of productive capital and housing during the World Wars, and were followed by policies designed to reduce wealth inequality such as nationalizations, rent control, and tax policies. These factors collectively led to the creation of a patri-monial middle class, which did not exist in Europe before WWI, contrary to the

United States where wealth inequality was relatively lower at the time. Since the mid-1980s wealth inequality has risen in both the UK and France, though to a much lesser extent than in the United States, such that the United States is now more unequal in terms of wealth than Europe. In France and in the UK, strong returns on the financial assets held in proportionately larger quantities by the wealthiest fueled wealth inequality. This factor was, however, moderated by the general rise in house prices that have largely benefited the patrimonial middle class, which owns relatively more housing than top wealth groups.

The beginning of the twentieth century saw the start of dramatic falls in the wealth share of the top 10% and top 1% in both France and the UK, as depicted in Figure 20.1 and Figure 20.2. The share of wealth owned by the top 1% in the UK reached almost 75% in the early 1900s, and represented almost 60% of the total in France. But by the early 1980s, a combination of factors including the destruction of capital during the World Wars and greater state control of economic activity and redistribution thereafter saw the top 1% share fall to 16% in 1985 in both countries and that of the top 10% fell to 47% in the UK and 50% in France, near historic lows (they had previously been as high as 93% and 86%, respectively).

But in the midst of then French President Mitterrand's austerity turn and Prime Minister Margaret Thatcher's premiership, wealth inequality began to rise. Greater wealth concentration was the result of a number of factors including: greater earnings disparities between the top and bottom of the distribution, a fall in tax progressivity, higher returns on financial assets disproportionately owned by the wealthy, and the privatization of large parts of formerly state-run industry.

In France, there were strong short-run fluctuations around 2000, with a substantial rise in top 10% wealth share (up to 57% in 2000) followed by a decline (53% in 2004). This was entirely due to large movements in relative asset prices. Indeed, stock prices were very high in France during the "dot-com bubble" in 2000, as compared to housing prices, which favored the upper class relative to the middle class.

However, despite these fluctuations, the longer-term trend was unchanged. In 2014, the share of total wealth held by the top 10% had increased to 55% in France and the figure was 52% in the UK in 2012, while the shares of the wealthiest 1% reached 23% and 20%, respectively. The rise in wealth inequality in the 2000s was moderate as the rise in general house prices experienced before and over this period improved the value of property wealth—assets held in greater proportion by the middle 40%—thus amplifying the share of the patrimonial middle class.

We should note, however, that high housing prices have ambiguous and contradictory effects on wealth inequality. On the one hand, high housing prices can mitigate rising inequality between the middle and the top, in the sense that property-owning middle classes—who typically own most of their assets in housing—benefit from an increase in the value of their wealth that is stronger than the upper groups—who mostly own financial assets. But on the other hand, high housing prices make it for difficult for the poorer groups to access real estate property to begin with, and this can lead to rising inequality between the poor and the middle. High property prices also create new forms of inequality, for instance between those who bought real estate at the right time and those who did not, or between young wage-earners who can benefit from parental wealth and inter vivos gifts to become home owners and those who remain tenants forever. These are new forms of inequality which have become increasingly important for the generations born in the 1970s–1980s and after, and which were much less important for the earlier cohorts (in particular for those generations born in the 1940s–1950s, who could purchase housing assets at relatively low price with their labor income only).

Property prices also played an important equalizing role for wealth inequality in Spain

The housing market has also played an important role among other European countries. Spain experienced fluctuations in its wealth concentration across the last decades, but inequality has remained broadly stable as a result of housing market evolutions. Asset price movements were key in determining short-run wealth inequality levels. In particular, the country's housing boom saw property prices triple between 1984 and 1990, and triple again between 1996 and 2008, which led to volatility in wealth concentration trends throughout the period between 1984 and 2013. As the wealthiest individuals in Spain bought deeper into the property market through multiple property purchases, the bursting of this bubble in 2008 thus had larger impact on the top 10% and top 1%, neutralizing their previously made gains. A similar story is also evident in the midst of the dot-com boom and bust as the wealth share of the top 1% peaks at around 28% in 2000.

Policies and institutions drive long-run wealth inequality through their impact on returns on capital and savings rates

In the long-run, it is the inequality of savings rates between individuals and the differential between rates of return and growth that determine wealth concentration. Earlier work has shown that wealth inequality within the top wealth groups increases in line with the difference between the rate of return and the rate of growth (r–g). Intuitively, the higher the gap between growth and the rate of return on capital (r > g), the more wealth inequality is amplified as capital is concentrated in the hands of the wealthy. It implies that past wealth is capitalized at a faster pace, and that it is less likely to be overtaken by the general growth of the economy. As was already mentioned above, this effect can be strongly reinforced by the fact that rates of returns tend to increase with the level of wealth: the rates of return available for large financial portfolios usually have little to do with those open to small deposits.

Small changes in savings rates can also have a very large impact on wealth inequality, though it may take several decades and even generations for their impacts to play out. These forces have been evident in France, the UK, and the United States, which all exhibit large differences between the savings rates of the wealthiest individuals and the rest of the distribution. In France, the top 10% of wealth holders generally saved between 20% and 30% of their annual incomes between 1970 and 2012, but this fraction was much smaller and fell notably over the period for the middle 40%, from 15% of annual income in 1970 to less than 5% by 2012, while savings rates among the bottom 50% fell from 8% to approximately 0%. In the United States, the savings rate of the bottom 90% of families fell sharply since the 1970s, while it has remained roughly stable for the top 1%. The annual saving rate of the bottom 90% fell from around 5–10% in the late 1970s and early 1980s to around –5% in the mid-2000s, before bouncing back to about 0% after the Great Recession. These falls in saving rates among the bottom 90% have been largely the consequence of increases in household debt, particularly from mortgages.

Assuming the same inequality of saving rates that was observed in France over the 1984–2014 period—namely, 24.5% for the top 10% and 2.5% for the bottom 90%—will persist, together with the same inequality of rates of return and the same inequality of labor income, the share of total wealth owned by the top 10% in France will gradually increase to the levels that were observed in the nineteenth and early twentieth centuries—that is, approximately 85% of total wealth. If, however, the 1970–1984 trends had persisted after 1984 and continued during the upcoming decades, the top 10% would have owned only slightly more than 45% of total wealth today and this figure would further decrease throughout the twenty-first century.

21

Wealth Inequality in the United States

Information in this chapter is based on the article "Wealth Inequality in the United States Since 1913: Evidence from Capitalized Income Tax Data," by Emmanuel Saez and Gabriel Zucman, 2016. Quarterly Journal of Economics, *131(2), 519–578.*

- Top wealth shares have been risen since the mid-1980s to 2012, with the top 0.1% driving wealth concentration at the top; their wealth share grew threefold from 7% in 1978 to 22% in 2012, a level comparable to that of the early twentieth century.
- United States wealth inequality had previously fallen considerably from the 1930s and 1940s, due to drastic policy changes that were part of the New Deal. These policies included the introduction of progressive income and estate taxation, and greater financial regulation.
- The key driver of this rapid increase in wealth concentration since the 1980s has been an upsurge of top incomes combined with an increase in saving rate inequality across wealth groups. This has had a reinforcing, "snowballing" effect as the accumulation of financial assets by the wealthy has led to a rise in capital income concentrations, allowing for more wealth accumulation at the top.
- The declining wealth share of the bottom 90% of the distribution is the result of plummeting middle-class savings, as their mortgage, consumer credit, and student debt have greatly increased.

Wealth inequality in the United States has risen rapidly and consistently since the mid-1980s

To fix notions of wealth inequality in the United States, it is perhaps best to first consider the distribution of the country's wealth in 2012 that is outlined in Table

Table 21.1 The distribution of household wealth in the US, 2012

Wealth group	Number of families	Wealth threshold ($)	Average wealth ($)	Wealth share
A. Top Wealth groups				
Full Population	160 700 000	–	384 000	100%
Top 10%	16 070 000	740 000	2 871 000	77.2%
Top 1%	1 607 000	4 442 000	15 526 000	41.8%
Top 0.1%	160 700	23 110 000	81 671 000	22.0%
Top 0.01%	16 070	124 525 000	416 205 000	11.2%
B. Intermediate Wealth groups				
Bottom 90%	144 600 000	–	94 000	22.8%
Top 10–1%	14 463 000	740 000	1 470 000	35.4%
Top 1–0.1%	1 446 300	4 442 000	8 178 000	19.8%
Top 0.1–0.01%	144 600	23 110 000	44 537 000	10.8%
Top 0.01%	16 070	124 525 000	416 205 000	11.2%

Source: Saez & Zucman (2016). See wir2018.wid.world for data series and notes.

In 2012, the average wealth of the Top 10% in the US was $2 871 000. All values have been converted to 2016 constant US dollars (accounting for inflation). For comparison, $1 = €0.8 = ¥3.3 at Market Exchange Rates. Numbers may not add up due to rounding.

21.1. The average net wealth per family was over $384 000, but this average masks a large heterogeneity. The bottom 90%—a group of almost 145 million families who possess approximately $94 000 on average—collectively own about as much of the total household wealth (22%) as the 161 000 families who are included in the top 0.1%; their average wealth was approximately $82 million, 845 times larger than the bottom 90%. Wealth is much more concentrated than income in the United States, as the top 0.1% wealth share is about as large as the income share of the top 1%.

Rising wealth inequality since the 1980s is almost entirely due to the top 0.1%

Wealth is becoming significantly more concentrated in the United States, but this trend is not the result of tens of millions of Americans seeing a rise in their fortunes. It is rather the spectacular dynamics of a tiny group of the population owning more than $4.4 million—the entry price of the top 1%.

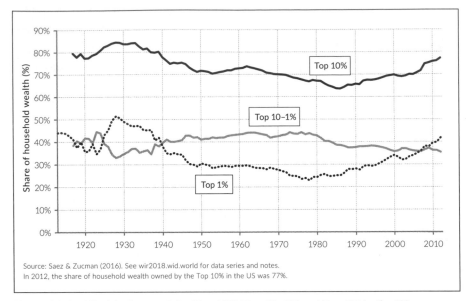

Figure 21.1a Wealth shares of the Top 10%, Top 10–1% and Top 1% in the US, 1913–2012

Top wealth shares have risen sharply since the mid-1980s. Indeed, the share of wealth held by the top 10% in 1985 was approximately 63%, the lowest value it had reached since 1917. But by 2012, the wealth share of the top 10% had reached over 77%, an additional 13 percentage points. More than three-quarters of all wealth in America was owned by just ten percent of its population.

However, since the mid-1980s, the wealth share of families belonging to the top 10% but not to the top 1% has decreased. In fact, the share of total wealth owned by the top 1% increased at a faster pace (up by around 17 percentage points) than the top 10% between 1986 and 2012 (see Figure 21.1a). The rise in the wealth share of the top 1% itself owes almost all of its increase to the growth of the top 0.1% share, which rose from 7% to 22% (15 percentage points). The wealth share of the top 0.1% was thus larger than the share of the top 1–0.1% (that is the top 1% minus the top 0.1%) in 2012, having tripled since 1978. Almost all of the top 1% and top 10% increase over the past four decades has been due to the top 0.1% alone.

The recent rises in wealth concentration contrasts with continual reductions over the previous half-century

The significant increase in the wealth shares of America's wealthiest since the mid-1980s is in direct contrast to the trend that followed the Great Depression.

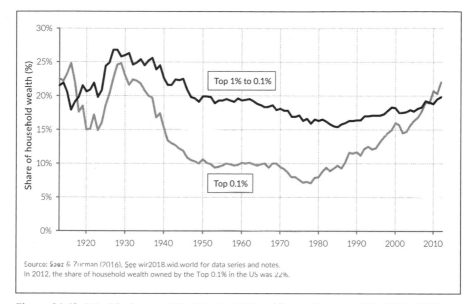

Figure 21.1b Wealth shares of the Top 1–0.1% and Top 0.1% in the US, 1913–2012

The Roaring Twenties saw a huge rise in wealth concentration, as the top 1% accumulated a significantly larger share of total wealth over the decade, rising from 35% in 1923 to almost 52% by 1928, and the top 10% wealth share peaked at 84%. But the impact of the Great Depression, and the New Deal policies implemented under Franklin Roosevelt's presidency, quickly saw this trend reverse.

Wealth inequality fell at a tremendous pace from 1929 until around the end of the Second World War. The loss in the value of financial assets from the collapse of the stock market and the introduction of financial regulation during the New Deal reduced the role of finance and the ability to concentrate wealth relative to the Gilded Age model of the financier-industrialist, while the development of progressive income and estate taxation made it difficult to accumulate and pass on large fortunes. Correspondingly, the share of the top 1% fell from 52% of total wealth to 29% by 1949. Their falling shares were not just accumulated by the top 10–1% either, as illustrated by Figure 21.1b, as the share of total wealth rose from 33% to 42%, leaving the bottom 90% with a 29% share, equal to that of the top 1%.

Following the Second World War, wealth inequality rose moderately, before falling again from the early 1960s onward. The wealth share of the top 10% grew from around 70% to 74% in 1962, before falling in almost every year until the mid-1980s, by which point their share had dipped below 65% of total wealth. As previously described, the Reagan era of deregulation and reduced tax progressivity formed a turning point in wealth inequalities in America. The top personal income tax rate dropped from 50% in 1986 to 28% in 1988, well below the corporate tax rate of 35%.

The rise and fall of middle-class wealth

The second key result of the analysis involves the dynamics of the wealth share of the bottom 90%. Since the bottom half of the distribution always owns close to zero net wealth, that is, when including negative wealth such as credit card and housing debt, the wealth share of the bottom 90% is therefore equal to the share of wealth owned by the middle 40% group, above the bottom 50% but below the top 10%. Within this "middle class," the share of total wealth owned in 2012 was the same as it was 70 years earlier, despite a rise in the value of their pensions and an increase in their home ownership rates.

The share of wealth owned by the middle class began to increase from the early 1930s, and peaked in the mid-1980s. It has subsequently undergone a continuous decline, as illustrated by Figure 21.2. The large rise in the wealth share of the bottom 90%, from 16% in the early 1930s to 35% in the mid-1980s, was driven by the group's accumulation of housing wealth, and to a greater extent by pensions. Pensions were almost nonexistent at the beginning of the twentieth century, but developed in the form of defined benefits plans, and then from the 1980s in the form of defined contribution plans such as Individual Retirement Accounts and the so called 401(k)s (the latter referring to a section of the United States tax code).

The declining share in the wealth share of the bottom 90% that occurred from the mid-1980s was due to a fall in two components of middle-class wealth, namely, the housing component (net of mortgage debt) and the fixed income component (net of non-mortgage debt). This fall was mostly the consequence of an upsurge in debt, as aggregate household debt, including mortgages, student loans, credit cards, and other debts, increased from 75% of national income in the mid-1980s to 135% in 2009. The financial crisis of 2007–2009 and the Great Recession then hit the middle class hard. The share of wealth owned by the bottom 90% collapsed between mid-2007 and mid-2008 because of the crash in housing prices, and the subsequent recovery was uneven: over 2009–2012, real wealth per family declined 0.6% per year for the bottom 90%, while it rose 7.9% per year for the top 0.1%.

Despite a reduction in debt levels in the wake of the Great Recession as the middle class sold a proportion of their assets, their debt still amounted to close to 110% of national income in 2012. This upsurge in the debt of the middle class

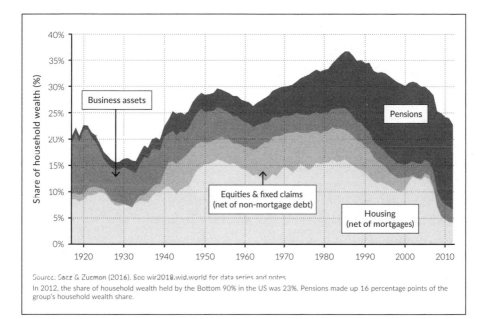

Source: Saez & Zucman (2016). See wir2018.wid.world for data series and notes

In 2012, the share of household wealth held by the Bottom 90% in the US was 23%. Pensions made up 16 percentage points of the group's household wealth share.

Figure 21.2 Composition of the wealth share of the Bottom 90% in the US, 1917-2012

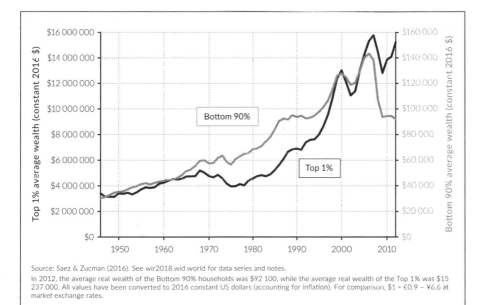

Source: Saez & Zucman (2016). See wir2018.wid.world for data series and notes.

In 2012, the average real wealth of the Bottom 90% households was $92 100, while the average real wealth of the Top 1% was $15 237 000. All values have been converted to 2016 constant US dollars (accounting for inflation). For comparison, $1 = €0.9 - ¥6.6 at market exchange rates.

Figure 21.3 Average wealth of the Bottom 90% and Top 1% in the US, 1946-2012.

has had a dramatic effect on middle-class wealth as approximately 90% of (non-mortgage) debt belongs to the bottom 90% of the wealth distribution, being sufficiently large to more than offset the rise in the value of their pensions. Strikingly, the average real wealth of the bottom 90% of families was no higher in 2012 than in 1986. Real average wealth of the bottom 90% rose considerably during the late 1990s tech-boom and the mid-2000s housing bubble, peaking at $143 000 in 2006, but then collapsed to about $93 800 in 2009 (at constant 2016 $), as depicted in Figure 21.3.

The dynamics of savings rates explains much of the evolution of wealth inequality

Inequalities in income shares and savings rates have been shown to have an impact on wealth dynamics in the long run. There has been a significant difference in the savings rates of the different US wealth groups between 1917 and 2012. The bottom 90% of wealth holders saved approximately 3% of their income on average over the period, while the 10–1% grouping saved about 15% of their income and the top 1%, around 20–25%. The main exception was during the Great Depression (1929–1939), during which the savings rate of the top 1% was substantially negative, because corporations had zero or even negative profits, but still paid out dividends. This period of negative saving at the top greatly contributed to the fall in top wealth shares during the 1930s described above.

Savings rate inequality has also increased in recent decades. The saving rate of bottom 90% families has fallen sharply since the 1970s, while it has remained roughly stable for the top 1%. The annual saving rate of the bottom 90% fell from around 5–10% in the late 1970s and early 1980s to around –5% in the mid-2000s, before bouncing back to about 0% after the Great Recession (from around 2008– 2011). From 1998 to 2008, the bottom 90% dis-saved (spent on credit) each year due to massive increases in debt, in particular mortgages, fueled by an unprecedented rise in housing prices. Concurrently, the top 1% continued to save at a high rate, and so the relative savings rate of the bottom 90% and the top 10–1% collapsed.

While the fall in the savings of the middle class explains much of the decline in the wealth share of the bottom 90%, rising income inequality has nonetheless had several noteworthy impacts on the dynamics of wealth inequality in the United States. First, the fall in the savings rate of the bottom 90% might itself be a consequence of the increase in income inequality and the lackluster growth of middle-class income, further accentuating wealth inequality. Second, simulations indicate that if the bottom 90% had maintained a constant share of national income, as well as saving at 3% per year, then its wealth share would have declined little since the mid-1980s and would be equal to about 33% in 2012 (rather than its actual level of 23%). And finally, rising income inequality at the top has had a significant impact on the wealth shares of the groups at the top of the wealth distribution. For example, the share of income earned by families in the top 1% of the wealth distribution doubled since the late 1970s, to about 16% in recent years. This increase is relatively larger than the increase in the wealth share of the top 1%, suggesting that the main driver of the growth in the wealth share of the top 1% is the upsurge of their income.

22

Wealth Inequality in France

Information in this chapter is based on "Accounting for Wealth Inequality Dynamics: Methods, Estimates and Simulations for France (1800–2014)," by Bertrand Garbinti, Jonathan Goupille-Lebret, and Thomas Piketty, 2016. WID.world Working Paper Series (No. 2016/5).

- Wealth inequality rose moderately in France since the mid-1980s. In 2014, the top 10% owned 55% of total French wealth, up from 50% in 1984, its lowest level ever recorded.
- Wealth inequality has fallen dramatically between 1914 and 1984. In the early 1900s, the wealth share of the top 1% amounted to 55% of total wealth. Large shocks between 1914 and 1945 (depression, inflation, wars) followed by nationalizations, rent control, and tax policies reduced the share of the wealthiest 1% to around 16% by the early 1980s.
- The 1980–1984 period saw the rising prosperity of the middle class as significant increases in the group's absolute wealth levels were experienced. This was in part due to the rise of their saving rates during this high-growth period.
- The rise in housing prices also played a crucial role in moderating the increase in wealth inequality after 1984, as these assets form a large part of the portfolio of the middle class.
- The long-run dynamics of wealth inequality are largely governed by the inequality of savings rates, themselves driven by habit formation, income inequality, and tax and regulatory policies.
- Small variations in savings rates and rates of return can have substantial, long-term impacts on wealth inequality. If the recent trends are prolonged, wealth inequality could return to its 1900 level by the end of the century.

The top 10% richest French own 55% of total wealth, while the middle 40% owns 38%.

If France's total wealth was equally shared among the French adult population in 2014, each adult would own approximately €201 000 in net wealth. However, as Table 22.1 indicates, this was far from the case. The least wealthy half of the adult population have around €25 500 in assets, equal to one-eighth of the national average and which amounted collectively to 6% of the country's total wealth. The average wealth of the middle 40% is almost equal to that of the national average at €193 000, and hence their share of total wealth, at 38%, almost represents what it would have been if French wealth was shared equally. French adults need to own assets totaling over €402 000 to be counted in the top 10%, a group whose average wealth was close to €1.1 million, five-and-a-half times the national average and 43 times the average wealth of the bottom 50%.

Wealth in France is even more highly concentrated among the top 10%. This is immediately obvious when analyzing the wealth share of the top 1%: at 23.4% of total wealth and average net assets of over €4.7 million, their share is almost as large as the wealthiest 10% of the population excluding the top 1%, that is, the 10%–1%. To be among the top 0.1%, French adults must have wealth totaling nearly €7.6 million, with the average for the group closer to €16.5 million. The

Table 22.1 The distribution of personal wealth in France, 2014

Wealth group	Number of families	Wealth threshold (€)	Average wealth (€)	Wealth share
Full Population	51 720 000	–	201 000	100%
Bottom 50%	25 860 000	–	25 500	6.3%
Middle 40%	20 690 000	99 000	193 000	38.4%
Top 10%	5 172 000	402 000	1 097 000	54.5%
Top 1%	517 000	2 024 000	4 703 000	23.4%
Top 0.1%	51 700	7 612 000	16 506 000	8.2%
Top 0.01%	5 170	26 668 000	55 724 000	2.8%
Top 0.001%	517	88 916 000	183 819 000	0.9%

Source: Garbinti, Goupille-Lebret, and Piketty (2017). See wir2018.wid.world for data series and notes.

In 2014, the average wealth of the Top 10% in France was €1 097 000. All values have been converted to 2016 constant euros (accounting for inflation). For comparison, €1 = $1.1 = ¥7.3 at Market Exchange Rates. Numbers may not add up due to rounding.

total wealth of this group of 52 000 adults is thus a third larger than that of the 26 million adults in the bottom 50%. At almost €184 million, the average wealth of the 520 adults in the top 0.001% is 914 times the national average and almost 180 times the average of their peers in the top 10% group.

Wealth inequality has fallen dramatically since the early twentieth century leading to the creation of a patrimonial middle class

Current levels of wealth inequality are far from their early twentieth-century levels. During the nineteenth and early twentieth century, wealth concentration remained stable at an extremely elevated rate. As noted in *Capital in the Twenty-First Century*, while the French Revolution is likely to have reduced wealth concentration in France with the end of fiscal privileges and new taxes on wealth, it is interesting to note that wealth remained highly concentrated in 1800 and throughout the nineteenth century. During the French Third Republic (1870–1940), which brought forward ideals of republican meritocracy, wealth concentration increased rather than decreased. On the eve of the First World War, the share of the top 10% was around 85% of total wealth, while the middle 40% owned a little less than 15% of French wealth, leaving the bottom 50% with almost no wealth. In a sense, there was no "middle class": the middle 40% was almost as propertyless as the bottom 50%. As can be observed in Figure 22.1, the wealth held by the top 10% between 1800 and 1914 was dominated by that of the top 1%, who held almost double the wealth of the top 10–1% at the beginning of the 1900s.

The top 10% wealth share started to fall following the 1914–1945 capital shocks. The First and Second World Wars caused huge losses in the aggregate wealth-income ratio—from around 700% to less than 200%—as significant stocks of total wealth were destroyed. This had a profound impact on wealth inequality in France. The share of total wealth held by the top 1% almost halved between the start of the First and the end of the Second World War, falling from around 55% to 30% to the benefit of the middle class.

The rise of the middle 40% during the 1914–1945 period is not due to the fact that the middle class accumulated a lot of wealth during this period: this simply corresponds to the fact that they lost less wealth—in proportion to their initial wealth level—than the top 10% did. In contrast, during the postwar decades, the rise of the middle class corresponds to a significant rise of their absolute wealth levels partly due to the rise of their savings rates during the high-growth period.

This fall in wealth inequality continued until the early 1980s, and fell to its lowest level recorded in 1983–1984. The share of total wealth held by the top 1%

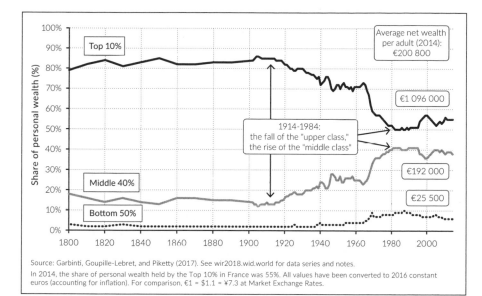

Figure 22.1 Wealth shares in France, 1800–2014

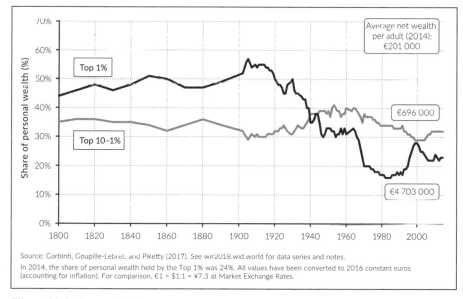

Figure 22.2 Top wealth shares in France, 1800–2014

and the top 10–1% fluctuated during the mid-1940s to mid-1960s, between 30–35% and around 35–40%, respectively, while the middle 40% share of total wealth rose from around 20% to 25%. Top 1% shares dropped from around 33% in 1945 to just over 15% by 1984, while the middle 40% rose from 25% to over 40%. (Figure 22.1 and Figure 22.2)

Wealth has increased moderately since 1984

Wealth inequality increased moderately since the early 1980s. In 1984, French wealth was the least concentrated it had been since data collection began at the beginning of the nineteenth century. But as the 1980s progressed, wealth inequality began to increase notably. The introduction of more laissez-faire economic policies, including the privatizations of large state-owned enterprises and the development of financial markets, that followed then President Mitterrand's austerity turn in 1982–1983 (see Chapter 3 for more detail) saw the wealth share of the top 10% wealthiest French adults increase to around 53% by 1990 and 56% by 1995. This came at the expense of the wealth shares of both the middle class and the lower class, whose shares fell to around 49% and 6%, respectively, by the mid-1990s.

Wealth concentration then rose at a significant rate in the years of the dot-com boom. By 2000, the wealth share of the top 10% passed 60%, leaving the middle 40% with less than 35% and the bottom 50% with around 6%. The year 2000 did, however, appear to be somewhat of a turning point, illustrating the strong short-run fluctuations in wealth concentration experienced over the last three decades. The shares of the middle 40% then began to rise and those of the top 10% fall as stock prices crashed in the wake of the bursting of the dot-com bubble in 2000, and house prices increased at a solid rate. These relative movements in asset prices (discussed in more detail below) left the top 10% with approximately 56% of total wealth in 2005, the middle 40% with around 38%, and the bottom 50% with the remaining 6%. The share of the bottom 50% thus remained unchanged during the first five years of the new millennium, despite the substantial changes for the other half of France's adult population.

The following years leading up to and following the global financial crisis of 2008–2009 had a rather muted impact on wealth inequality in France. The share of total wealth held by the top 10% increased to around 59% in 2010, while those of the middle 40% remained almost unaffected. It was the bottom 50% who suffered instead, seeing their share of total wealth fall to just 5%. The following two years show slight falls in the wealth share of the top 10% and a small increase for the bottom 50%. Again, changes in the shares of the middle 40% were negligible.

Differences in asset portfolios among wealth groups are key in determining wealth inequality dynamics over the recent period

Before we move on to analyzing wealth inequality within asset categories, it is important to recall that the composition and level of aggregate wealth changed

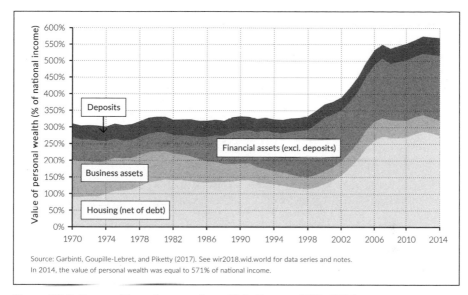

Figure 22.3 Composition of personal wealth in France, 1970–2014

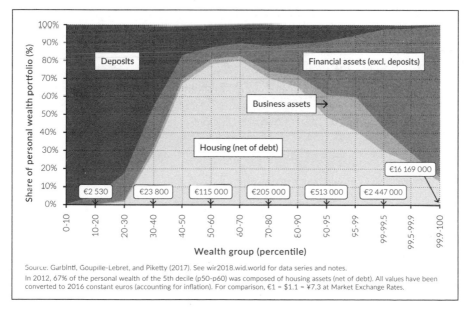

Figure 22.4 Asset composition by wealth group in France, 2012

substantially in France over the 1970–2014 period, as depicted by Figure 22.3. Observing this figure, it is clear to see that the shares of housing assets and financial assets have increased substantially, while the share of business assets has declined markedly, the latter largely due to the fall in self-employment. Financial assets, other than deposits, increased strongly after the privatization

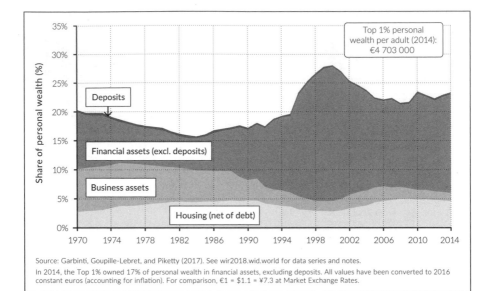

Source: Garbinti, Goupille-Lebret, and Piketty (2017). See wir2018.wid.world for data series and notes.
In 2014, the Top 1% owned 17% of personal wealth in financial assets, excluding deposits. All values have been converted to 2016 constant euros (accounting for inflation). For comparison, €1 = $1.1 = ¥7.3 at Market Exchange Rates.

Figure 22.5a Composition of the wealth share of the Top 1% in France, 1970–2014

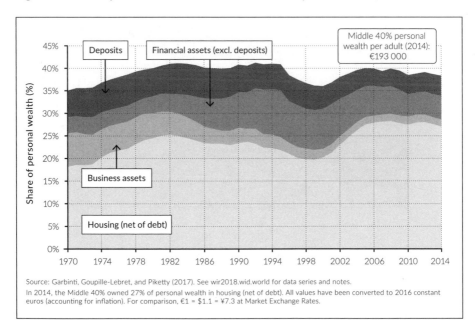

Source: Garbinti, Goupille-Lebret, and Piketty (2017). See wir2018.wid.world for data series and notes.
In 2014, the Middle 40% owned 27% of personal wealth in housing (net of debt). All values have been converted to 2016 constant euros (accounting for inflation). For comparison, €1 = $1.1 = ¥7.3 at Market Exchange Rates.

Figure 22.5b Composition of the wealth share of the Middle 40% in France, 1970–2014

of the late 1980s and the 1990s and reached a high point in 2000 as the stock market boomed in the run-up to the dot-com crash. In contrast, housing prices declined in the early 1990s, but then rose strongly during the 2000s, while stock prices were falling.

These contradictory movements in relative asset prices have an important impact on the evolution of wealth inequality in France, as different wealth groups own very different asset portfolios. As depicted by Figure 22.4, the bottom 30% of the distribution own mostly deposits in 2012, while housing assets are the main form of wealth for the middle of the distribution. However, as one moves towards the top 10% and the top 1% of the distribution, financial assets—other than deposits—gradually become the dominant form of wealth, largely because of their large equity portfolios. These general patterns of asset portfolio construction remain relatively constant throughout the 1970–2014 period, except that business assets played a more important role during the 1970s and early 1980s, particularly among middle-high-wealth holders.

If one now decomposes the evolution of wealth shares going to the bottom 50%, middle 40%, top 10%, and top 1% by asset categories, the impact of asset price movements on inequality is significant. In particular, Figure 22.5 indicates the significant impact the stock market boom of the 2000s and its slide thereafter had on top wealth shares in particular. It also shows the effect of the general increase in housing prices on the wealth shares of the middle 40% during the 2000s, further discussed below.

Rising housing prices moderated wealth concentration since the 1980s

Changes to house prices played a notable role in reducing wealth inequality in France between 1970 and 2014. Similar to trends in a number of other rich nations, house prices in France increased at a faster pace than consumer price inflation (2.4% faster per year) and thus the total return to French adults owning property was significant, growing at an annual rate of over 6% during the observed period. However, this structural increase in house prices has been far from steady, rising particularly strongly between 2000 and 2008, and therefore generated large short-run, rather than long-run, fluctuations in wealth inequality.

The explanation for the short-term fluctuation in wealth concentration experienced as financial asset prices increased up to the beginning of the twenty-first century also follows the same line of reasoning. During the stock market boom, wealth inequality in France increased substantially due to the bias toward financial asset holdings among the wealthiest. However, the reasoning also follows that these increases in asset prices can be discounted as an explanation for the long-run increase in inequality over the period, alongside the changes in house prices.

Once variations in asset prices are corrected for, the data indicate that structural factors have caused a rise in the concentration of wealth between 1970 and 2014. The housing boom of the 2000s did, however, play an important role as a mitigating force to limit the rise of inequality, as the structural increase in the wealth shares of the top 10% and top 1% over the 1984–2014 period would have been substantially larger had housing prices not increased so fast during these years relative to other asset prices.

France is also a clear illustration of the fact that housing prices have an ambiguous and contradictory impact on inequality. They raised the market value of the wealth of the middle class—those who were able to access real estate—and thereby raised the wealth share of the middle 40% relative to the top 10%, whose asset portfolios are more diversified and contain relatively less real estate. But rising housing prices also made it more difficult for people in the lower and working classes (the bottom 50%), and also members of the middle class with no family wealth, to access real estate.

Higher savings rates and returns on assets for the wealthy increased wealth concentration since the 1980s

In the long run, it is the savings rates of groups and the long-run rate of return on the type of wealth (assets) that they hold that determine wealth concentration. In particular, if the savings rates and/or the rates of return of the top wealth groups are higher than the average, this can generate large multiplicative effects, and lead to very high wealth concentrations.

As illustrated by Figure 22.6, there were significant differences in savings rates between wealth groups in France between 1970 and 2012. While the top 10% of wealth holders generally saved between 20% and 30% of their annual incomes over the observed period, this fraction was much smaller and fell notably over the period for the middle 40% and the bottom 50%, from 15% of annual income in 1970 to less than 5% by 2012, and from 8% to approximately 0%, respectively. Similar trends were found in the UK and the United States, reinforcing the assertion that savings rate differentials were the key structural force accounting for rising wealth concentration in many developed economies over this period.

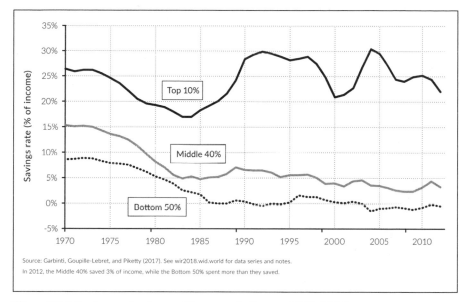

Figure 22.6 Savings rates by wealth groups in France, 1970–2012

Average rates of return on assets also vary significantly between different wealth groups over the 1970–2014 period. The notable inequalities in rates of return between higher and lower wealth groups is due to significant differences in their respective portfolio of assets, as indicated earlier in Figure 22.5. In particular, top wealth groups own more financial assets, particularly equities, which can have much higher rates of return than real estate assets or savings deposited in financial institutions. Indeed, the average annual return on financial assets such as equities, shares, and bonds is over four times greater than the returns on housing assets, though this difference falls to a more modest 50% when including real capital gains.

The elderly hold the keys to French wealth

How did wealth inequality evolve across age groups over the recent period? Looking first at the age-wealth profile, it is evident that the average wealth owned by those aged 20 has consistently been very limited at less than 15% of average adult wealth throughout the series history. Wealth then rises sharply with age, peaking between 55 and 65 years old at 150–170% of average adult wealth depending on which era is examined. Thereafter, wealth slightly declines, but remains at very high levels, around 125–150% of from age 60 to age 80, as illustrated by Figure 22.7.

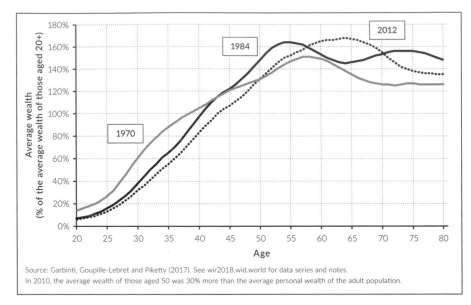

Figure 22.7 Age-wealth profiles in France, 1970–2010

This age-wealth profile slightly evolved over the past forty years, as wealthiest individuals grew older. In 2010, wealth is accumulated notably later in life than in 1995 and 1970, with wealth peaking at age 65, seven to ten years later than in 1970 and 1995. Note also that old-age individuals make very substantial inter vivos gifts in France, so that average wealth at high ages would be even higher without these gifts, particularly at the end of the period. Gifts are made on average about 10 years before death, and the aggregate gift flow has increased from about 20–30% of the aggregate bequest flow in the 1970s to as much as 80% of the aggregate bequest flow in the 2000s–2010s.

Habit formation, income inequality dynamics and tax evolutions are likely to drive the inequality of saving rates

While it is not possible to fully explain why saving rates and rates of return change in the way that they do, it is possible to identify key factors that were at play since the early twentieth century. Between 1914 and 1945, one can imagine that the saving rates of the top wealth groups were severely affected by the capital and fiscal shocks of the 1914–1945 period. In particular, there was no progressive taxation prior to 1914, and in the interwar period, effective tax rates for top income and wealth groups quickly reached very substantial levels, for example 20–40%, and sometimes even more. In the likely scenario that top wealth holders reacted by reducing their consumption levels and living standards less than the increase in tax (which came in addition to a negative shock to their pre-tax capital incomes), then in effect, they had to reduce their saving rate.

After 1945, those at the bottom and in the middle of the wealth distribution saved at higher rates than before, during the high-growth postwar decades due to some form of "habit formation" effect whereby individuals were prudent with their consumption and saved earnings in case of shocks or crises. It is also possible that rising top income shares in recent decades, together with growth slowdown for bottom and middle groups, has contributed to rising inequality in saving rates, and this has been exacerbated by some form of relative consumption effect (see Chapter 6), whereby the bottom 90% is consuming a greater proportion of their income than the top 10% leaving little savings for investment in assets. This is particularly the case for the bottom 50%.

It is clear that changes in the tax system, and in particular in tax progressivity, as seen post–World War II and during the 1960s, can have very large impacts on both the inequality of saving rates between groups and on the inequality of rates of return, and therefore on wealth inequality in the long run. The inequality of rates of return can also be influenced by many other factors, including financial regulation and deregulation seen after the Great Depression and the reduction in capital controls in the mid- to late-1980s, as well as the introduction and end of rent controls.

Wealth concentration could return to Gilded Age level by 2100

The savings rates and rates of return per wealth group can be used to estimate each groups' share of total wealth in the coming decades. Assuming the same inequality of saving rates that were observed over the 1984–2014 period—namely, 24.5% for the top 10% and 2.5% for the bottom 90%—will persist, together with the same inequality of rates of return and the same inequality of labor income, the share of total wealth owned by the top 10% will gradually increase to the levels that were observed in the nineteenth and early twentieth centuries, that is, approximately 85% of total wealth. If, however, the 1970–1984 trends had persisted after 1984 and continued during the upcoming decades, the top 10% would have experienced a decline in their share of total wealth. Using the same average savings rates, the same inequality of rates of return and the same inequality of labor income as during 1970–1984, the top 10% would have owned slightly more than 45% of total wealth today and this figure would further decrease throughout the 21st century. (Figure 22.8)

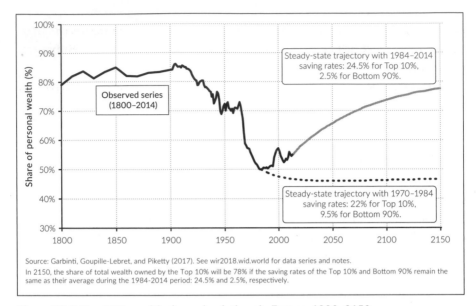

Figure 22.8 Top 10% wealth share simulations in France, 1800–2150

There are two main messages from these relatively simple simulations. First, moderately small evolutions in the inequality of saving rates or rates of return, for example, can have enormous impacts on steady-state wealth inequality. Second, these effects can take decades and even generations before they fully materialize. This delayed-impact can explain why declining wealth concentration continued long after the capital shocks of the 1914–1945 period. Once some structural parameters have changed, it takes many decades to reach a new steady state.

Wealth Inequality in Spain

Information in this chapter is based on "Housing Bubbles, Offshore Assets and Wealth Inequality in Spain (1984–2013)," by Clara Martínez-Toledano, 2017. WID.world Working Paper Series (No. 2017/19).

- The Spanish housing and stock market booms of the last 30 years have seen the country's personal wealth to national income ratio almost double from around 380% in 1984 to 730% in 2007, before falling to just under 650% by 2014.
- With an average wealth of almost €813 000 per adult, the top 10% owned almost 57% of Spain's personal wealth in 2013. The share of the bottom 50% was 7%, with an average wealth of just over €18 900. The relative shares of personal wealth remained virtually unchanged during the last thirty years.
- The ability of the wealthy to adapt and diversify their asset portfolio depending on which assets were experiencing the most growth has enabled them to benefit from the Spanish housing boom and shelter somewhat from the impact of its crash.
- Approximately €146 billion was held by Spanish citizens in offshore wealth in 2012, increasing the concentration of wealth considerably.

Spain has experienced an unprecedented increase in aggregate wealth over the past thirty years, predominantly due to the housing boom the country experienced over the last 30 years. Much has been written about this economic phenomenon, when house prices tripled between 1985 and 1991 and tripled again between 1996 and 2008, and the value of the stock market increased sevenfold before halving, but much less written on its distributional effects. In particular, there has been little research into which groups have benefited from this increase in wealth, how much each of these groups has benefited, how differences in wealth between groups have changed over time, whether the importance of asset categories has altered, and which factors are the source of the aforementioned changes.

Using high-quality, publicly available data, Martínez-Toledano's recent paper seeks to answer these questions. The author combines tax records, national accounts, and wealth surveys, as well as the capitalization method that is used by Saez and Zucman for the United States, to deliver a consistent, unified wealth distribution series for Spain between 1984 and 2013, with detailed breakdowns by age over the period 1999–2013.

The rising value of housing has fueled the growth of Spanish wealth

The Spanish personal wealth to national income ratio almost doubled between 1984 and 2014. As illustrated by Figure 23.1, personal wealth amounted to around 380% in the late eighties and grew to around 470% in the mid-nineties. From 1995 onward, personal wealth started to increase more rapidly, reaching its peak at 728% of national income in 2007, before the global financial crisis. After the bubble burst in 2008, personal wealth dropped notably and continued to decrease thereafter. In 2014, the Personal Wealth to National Income ratio amounted to 646%, a level similar to the Personal Wealth to National Income ratio of years 2004 and 2005, but much higher than the ratios of the eighties and nineties, also as illustrated by Figure 23.1.

Figure 23.1 also shows how the components of total net Spanish wealth have evolved over the 30-year period. The late eighties saw growth in net housing that was more than double the speed of the increase in financial assets, but this trend was reversed during the nineties as financial assets started to be accumulated at a faster pace than property, due mainly to the rise in stock prices that arose from the dot-com bubble. However, after the stock market crash of 2000, housing prices increased at a pace that surpassed even the significant growth of financial assets. The value of housing then reached its peak in 2008, after which the sizable housing bubble that had been built up burst and the fall in housing wealth was larger than that of financial assets.

This period was also characterized by the increasing importance of net housing in the asset portfolios of households. While properties are the most important asset held by the average Spanish household between 1984 and 2014, always representing more than 40% of total household net wealth, the composition of personal wealth has not evolved homogeneously. Indeed, personal wealth has lost importance in periods when financial assets significantly increase, such as the one that preceded the dot-com bubble. The increase in the fraction of property in the total portfolio of households has also been exacerbated by the steady decrease in the fraction of unincorporated business assets, which fell from 23%

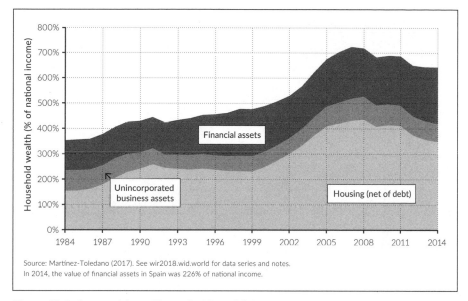

Figure 23.1 Composition of household wealth in Spain, 1984–2014

in 1984 to 11% in 2014, due mainly to the relative reduction in the importance of agriculture within the Spanish economy.

The top 10% has owned more than half of Spain's personal wealth since the mid-1980s

Table 23.1 displays the wealth level, threshold, and shares of personal wealth for Spanish adults in 2013. On average, the net wealth per adult in Spain was approximately €144 000. However, the average wealth within the bottom 50% of the distribution was just 13% of the countrywide average, at €18 900. Cumulatively, the share of personal wealth held by the top 50% was less than 7%. Average wealth within the next 40% of the distribution was slightly over €133 000, giving the group a 37% share of personal wealth, not largely dissimilar to their population share. This left the top 10% holding over 56% of Spanish personal wealth, with an average wealth of approximately €813 000, over five-and-a-half times greater than the national average wealth and 43 times greater than the average wealth of 50% of the Spanish adult population.

The drastic differences in the shares of personal wealth reported in 2013 have remained largely unchanged throughout the preceding 29-year period. As Figure 23.2 shows below, the share of personal wealth held by each group has remained within a band of eight percentage points. The share of personal wealth attributable

Table 23.1 The distribution of household wealth in Spain, 2013

Wealth group	Number of families	Wealth threshold (€)	Average wealth (€)	Wealth share
Full Population	35 083 000	–	144 000	100%
Bottom 50%	17 541 000	–	18 900	6.6%
Middle 40%	14 033 000	43 000	133 000	36.9%
Top 10%	3 508 000	317 000	813 000	56.5%
Top 1%	350 800	1 385 000	3 029 000	21.1%
Top 0.1%	35 080	4 775 000	10 378 000	7.2%

Source: Martínez-Toledano (2017). See wir2018.wid.world for data series and notes.

In 2013, the average wealth of the Top 1% in Spain was €3 029 000. All values have been converted to 2016 constant euros (accounting for inflation). For comparison, €1 = $1.1 = ¥7.3 at Market Exchange Rates. Numbers may not add up due to rounding.

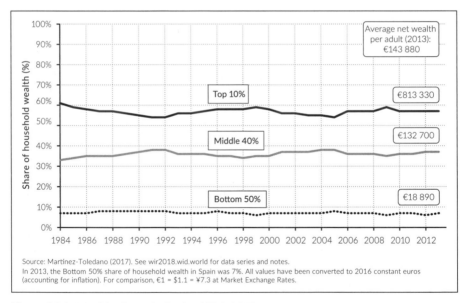

Source: Martínez-Toledano (2017). See wir2018.wid.world for data series and notes.
In 2013, the Bottom 50% share of household wealth in Spain was 7%. All values have been converted to 2016 constant euros (accounting for inflation). For comparison, €1 = $1.1 = ¥7.3 at Market Exchange Rates.

Figure 23.2 Wealth shares in Spain, 1984–2013

to the bottom 50% has always been very small, reaching a peak of 9% in 1992, but fell back to just over 6% in 2013, roughly equal to its level at the start of the period. The personal wealth share of the middle 40% has concentrated between 32% and 39% of total net wealth, remaining over 35% for the majority of the observed period, while the share of the top 10% has fluctuated between 53% and 61%. Notably, the top 10% wealth share dropped from the mid-eighties until the beginning of the 1990s, at the expense of the increased shares of both the middle 40% and the bottom

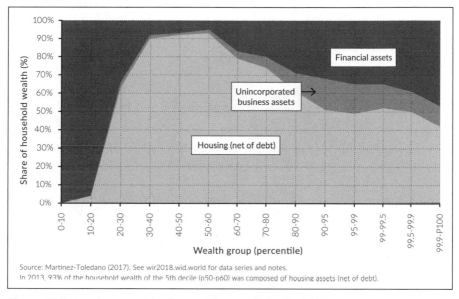

Source: Martinez-Toledano (2017). See wir2018.wid.world for data series and notes.
In 2013, 93% of the household wealth of the 5th decile (p50-p60) was composed of housing assets (net of debt).

Figure 23.3 Asset composition by wealth group in Spain, 2013

50% of the distribution, as house prices rose threefold across Spain. The top 10% wealth share then increased during the nineties, as the stock market grew strongly, before decreasing until the mid-2000s and increasing again until the start of the global financial crisis and burst of the housing bubble in 2008. Since then, the share of the top 10% decreased, before stabilizing at a similar level to that during the mid-nineties.

While the changes in relative assets prices have had a rather limited impact on overall wealth inequality in Spain, there are important differences in the portfolio of assets owned by different wealth groups. As shown by Figure 23.3, in 2013, the bottom 20% of the Spanish wealth distribution mostly owned financial assets, which largely came in the form of savings and current deposits in banks. As one moves toward the center of the wealth distribution, property becomes the most dominant form of wealth (approximately 90% between the 30th and 60th percentiles). Thereafter, the dominance of financial assets within wealth portfolios grows larger as the individuals analyzed become wealthier. However, unlike the bottom 50%, bank deposits form only a minor part of financial assets for the top 10% and the top 1% of the distribution. Instead, the wealthiest Spanish adults own a combination of equities, investment funds, fixed income assets such as bonds, currency, life insurance reserves, and pension funds. The same general pattern of asset composition by wealth group also applies for the period between 1984 and 2012, as can be seen in Figures 23.4 and 23.5. The only notable difference has been the falling importance of unincorporated assets over

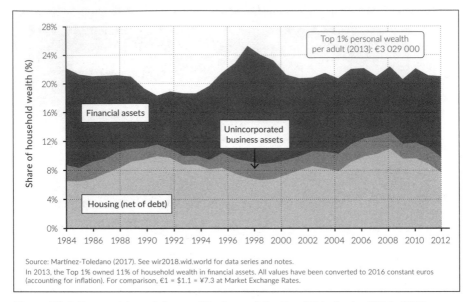

Figure 23.4 Composition of the wealth share of the Top 1% in Spain, 1984–2013

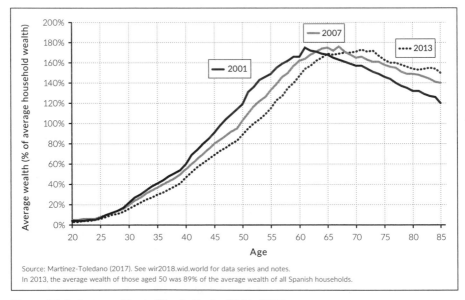

Figure 23.5 Age-wealth profiles in Spain, 2001–2013

the 28-year period, which can mainly be attributed to the reduction in agricultural activity among the self-employed.

By decomposing the evolution of wealth in Spain by asset categories and by wealth group, it is possible to see how asset price movements between 1984 and 2013 affected their respective asset portfolios and shares of personal wealth.

The figures within Figure 23.4 clearly show how the impact of the stock market boom of 2000 and the burst of the housing bubble in 2007 affected portfolios and shares of the top 1%. Reviewing the trend in the financial assets component of the wealth of the top 1%, there is an obvious spike in the value of financial assets and its dominance in their portfolio in 1999, the year preceding the dot-com crisis.

One particularity of the Spanish case relative to other rich nations is the importance of housing assets in the portfolio of households, even at the top of the distribution. This has been the case during the whole of the 29-year period analyzed, but this trend became even more striking in the years up to 2007, when the increase in the value of dwellings was largest. In Spain, the top 10% and top 1% of the wealth distribution own 26% and 8% of total net wealth in housing, respectively, whereas in France these figures are 19% and 5%, respectively.

Increasingly greater sums of wealth are being passed on to the offspring of the wealthy

The detailed micro-files available in Spain from 1999 also allow Martínez-Toledano to analyze how wealth varies between different age groups, and how this has changed over time. As Figure 23.5 shows, average wealth has been consistently very small for those aged 20 during the 14-year period studied, at less than 10% of total wealth. Wealth exhibits a rising trend with age. At age 40, individuals own approximately 50% of average wealth whereas at age 60, they own more than 150% of average wealth. After 60, the average adult wealth declines moderately but never falling below 120%. As average wealth does not decline sharply after age 60 and remains at a level that is notably above average wealth, old-age individuals thus pass away with substantial wealth and transmit this to their offspring.

There are, however, important differences in relative wealth levels across age groups over the 1999–2013 period. Old individuals (+60) are better off and the young (20–39) worse off after the economic crisis, since the average wealth for the old relative to total average wealth is larger in 2013 than in 2001. This is consistent with the large increase in youth unemployment after the burst of the bubble and at the same time the stability in social security pension payments. When decomposing the wealth distribution series by age, it appears that wealth inequality is more pronounced for the young (20–39) than for the old (+60) and middle-old (40–59), for which wealth inequality is almost as large than for the population taken as a whole. A plausible explanation is the importance of bequests that transfer the wealth of the older generations to the younger generation. Higher transfer rates among wealthy families, combined with high youth unemployment rates and consequently a low wealth accumulation through labor income savings by the young (which would moderate wealth inequality), can explain higher inequality levels among the young than among the elderly.

The Spanish property bubble had a neutral effect on wealth inequality

The high level of disaggregation in Martínez-Toledano's wealth distribution series also helps to explain why Spain's housing bubble had a curiously neutral effect on the level of wealth inequality in the country. In Spain, as in many European countries, the increased ownership of property among the bottom 90%, and the significant share that housing represents in their asset portfolios, has contributed to reducing wealth inequality. Figure 23.6 illustrates that wealth concentration for the top 1% is approximately 10 percentage points lower between 1984 and 2013 when housing wealth is included. Moreover, the figure also shows that wealth inequality including and excluding housing followed a similar trend post 2000, confirming that the housing boom and bust had little impact on wealth inequality.

In order to understand this puzzling result, it is important to see how the composition of net housing wealth has changed over time. The fraction of total net housing owned by the top 1% increased considerably between 2005 and 2009, the years in which housing prices skyrocketed, at the expense of the proportion

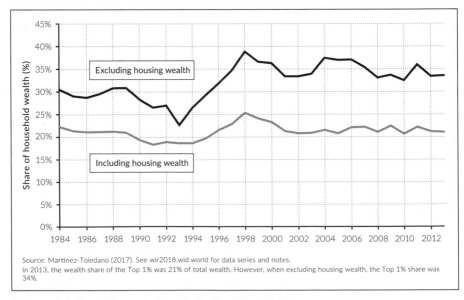

Source: Martínez-Toledano (2017). See wir2018.wid.world for data series and notes.
In 2013, the wealth share of the Top 1% was 21% of total wealth. However, when excluding housing wealth, the Top 1% share was 34%.

Figure 23.6 Top 1% wealth share in Spain, 1984–2013

of homes owned by the middle 40%. This increased concentration of home ownership was principally the result of the increase in the number of secondary properties bought by the top 1%, relative to the middle 40%, and not due to relatively larger increases in the price of properties owned by the wealthiest. The ratio of the house prices of the top 10% (and top 1%) to the value of dwellings of the middle 40% remained constant between 2005 and 2009.

But if housing concentration increased at the top during the bubble and decreased thereafter, why has total wealth concentration remained virtually unchanged? One plausible explanation is that individuals within the top 1% substituted financial assets for property during the period of the housing boom, but then accumulated greater financial assets when house prices began to fall. The fraction of total financial assets held by the top 1% decreased during the boom years. This is consistent with the idea that wealthy individuals can better diversify their portfolios, and have the capabilities to invest more in risky assets, when prices are increasing—and can more easily disinvest when prices fall, to then acquire other assets.

Disparities in savings rates and returns on assets drive long-run wealth inequality

In order to understand the underlying forces driving wealth inequality dynamics in Spain, it is useful to analyze how income, savings rates, and the rate of inequality have evolved between 1999 and 2012.

There are significant differences in the savings rates between wealth groups in Spain and these have changed over time, as illustrated by Figure 23.7a–c. These disparities reflect the high levels of wealth concentration observed in Spain, with an average savings rate of 27% of income for the top 10% over this period, compared to 10% among the middle 40% and just 1% for the bottom 50%.

Analyzing the evolution of savings rates more closely reveals one important point. The housing bubble increased the difference in saving rates between the wealthy and the less-wealthy during the boom years and reduced their stratification during the bust period. Figure 23.7a shows that during the years prior to the property bubble bursting, the savings rate of the top 10% remained high as they accumulated more housing, while the savings rate for the middle 40% and the bottom 50% decreased, as their accumulation of housing assets was facilitated through borrowing. After the property bubble burst, the top 10% sold some of their housing assets and started to accumulate more financial assets to compensate for the decrease in housing prices. Nonetheless, the total savings rate for the top 10% decreased during these years, likely because they needed to consume a

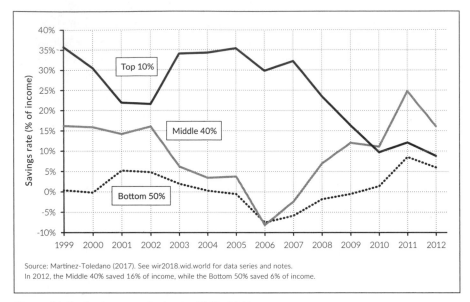

Figure 23.7a Saving rates in Spain, 1999–2012

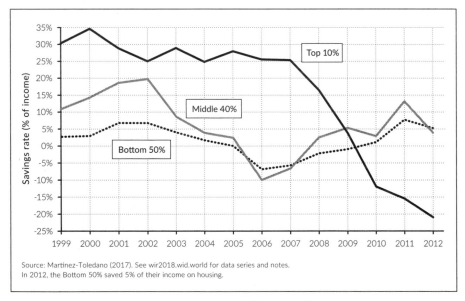

Figure 23.7b Saving rates on net housing in Spain, 1999–2012

larger fraction of their income. The middle 40% instead started to save more in order to repay their housing mortgages, and therefore the difference in saving rates across the two wealth groups was reduced. These two trends thus contributed to neutralizing wealth concentration during Spain's tumultuous period of housing price swings.

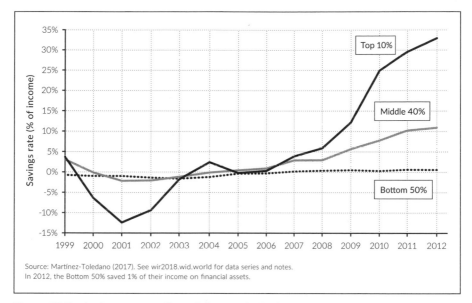

Figure 23.7c Saving rates on financial assets in Spain, 1999–2012

Wealth inequality has also been amplified by the variance in the rates of return on assets owned by different wealth groups in Spain over the 1986–2012 period. This finding is consistent with the large differences in the asset portfolios of Spanish wealth groups documented earlier in the chapter (see Figure 23.1), whereby top wealth groups are more likely to own financial assets such as equity that often have higher rates of return than other assets, including deposits and housing.

Factoring in offshore wealth into the Spanish wealth distribution reveals a higher level of inequality

As is common in many other countries, official financial data in Spain fail to capture a large part of the wealth held by households abroad. Research has shown that Spanish citizens use offshore financial institutions in tax havens for their portfolios of equities, bonds, and mutual fund shares. It is estimated by Zucman that these assets amounted to approximately €80 billion in 2012—the equivalent of 9% of households' net financial wealth in Spain—of which three-quarters goes unrecorded. Thus, by omitting offshore wealth from the Spanish wealth distribution series, both total assets and wealth concentration are substantially underestimated.

Using data series from the Swiss National Bank, offshore wealth taxation forms, and the 2012 tax amnesty, Martínez-Toledano is able to adjust her wealth distribution series for offshore assets. As illustrated by Figure 23.8, the value of

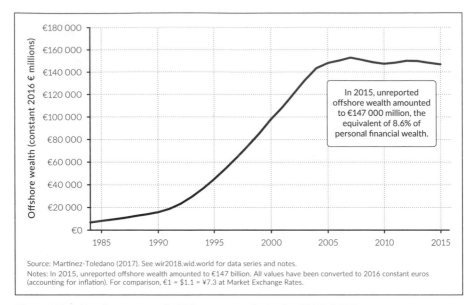

In 2015, unreported offshore wealth amounted to €147 000 million, the equivalent of 8.6% of personal financial wealth.

Source: Martínez-Toledano (2017). See wir2018.wid.world for data series and notes.
Notes: In 2015, unreported offshore wealth amounted to €147 billion. All values have been converted to 2016 constant euros (accounting for inflation). For comparison, €1 = $1.1 = ¥7.3 at Market Exchange Rates.

Figure 23.8 Total unreported offshore assets in Spain, 1984–2015

offshore assets increased rapidly during the eighties, nineties, and at the beginning of the 2000s, before stabilizing after 2007, when Spanish tax authorities became stricter with tax avoidance and evasion schemes. Unreported offshore wealth amounted to almost €150 billion in 2012, representing 8.6% of personal financial wealth. Investment funds represented 50% of total unreported offshore assets in 2012, followed by stocks, 30%, and deposits and life insurance, which made up 18% and 2%, respectively.

The Spanish wealth distribution series is then corrected by assigning the annual estimate of unreported offshore wealth proportionally to the wealthiest 1%. This is consistent with official documentation from the Spanish Tax Agency that states that the majority of foreign assets reported by Spanish residents are held by the top wealth holders and that these assets represented 12% and 31% of the total wealth tax base in 2007 and 2015, respectively. When offshore wealth is included in the wealth distribution, wealth concentration rises considerably, across the period between 1984 and 2013. Including offshore wealth shows that the concentration of wealth was in fact larger during the 2000s than in the eighties, contrary to what it is observed when these offshore assets are not taken into account. The wealth share of the top 1% averages approximately 24% from 2000–2013, notably larger than the 21% estimated when offshore wealth is disregarded. This difference is quite remarkable, particularly given that during this period of time the country experienced a housing boom and both nonfinancial and financial assets held in Spain grew considerably as discussed earlier in this chapter.

Wealth Inequality in the UK

Information in this chapter is based on "Top Wealth Shares in the UK over more than a Century," by Facundo Alvaredo, Anthony Atkinson, and Salvatore Morelli, 2017. WID.world Working Paper Series (No. 2017/2).

- UK wealth inequality has shown a moderate increase since the 1980s, with the share of total wealth owned by the top 1% (almost half a million individuals) rising from 15% in 1984 to 20–22% by 2013.
- The increase in wealth concentration in the last four decades is very much a phenomenon confined to the top 0.5 percent, and, in particular, to the top 0.1 percent (the richest 50 000 Britons), whose share of total wealth doubled from 4.5 to 9% between 1984 and 2013.
- Today's wealth inequality remains, however, notably lower than a century ago. In the wake of the first globalization era in 1914, the share of personal wealth going to the wealthiest 1% of UK individuals was around 70%, but their share began to fall thereafter. This encompassed two World Wars, and much attention has been paid to the loss of capital during the periods 1914 to 1918 and 1939 to 1945. Top shares certainly fell in the UK during the war years, but these only accounted for a part of the large reduction that took place over the period as a whole. The large decline in top wealth shares in the UK in the twentieth century was very much a peacetime phenomenon.
- The substantial rise in owner-occupation during the twentieth century, additionally fostered by the sale of public housing, aided the reduction in wealth inequality to historically low levels in the 1980s, as the wealth share of the top 1% fell to 15%. But in the 1990s there was a change, with the return of private landlords as a result of the "buy to let."

- The concentration of non-housing wealth (financial and business assets) increased substantially between 1995 and 2013. At the same time, the increase in total wealth inequality has been smaller. It appears that housing wealth has moderated a definite tendency for there to be a rise in recent years in top wealth shares in financial wealth. When people talk about rising wealth concentration in the UK, it is probably the latter that they have in mind.

Wealth concentration in the UK underwent enormous transformation during the twentieth century

The evidence in the UK covers an extensive period, starting in the Gilded Age before the First World War. The long-run series since 1895 highlight the enormous transformation that has taken place in the distribution of wealth within the UK over more than a century. Before the First World War, the top 5 percent of wealth holders owned around 90 percent of total personal wealth. There were very few owner-occupiers. A hundred years later, the share was around 40 percent. The top 1 percent used to own two-thirds of total wealth; their share is around one-fifth today, when two-thirds of households own a house.

Figure 24.1 shows the upper tail of the wealth distribution from 1895 to 2013. The changes in top shares can be summarized in terms of three periods. The first

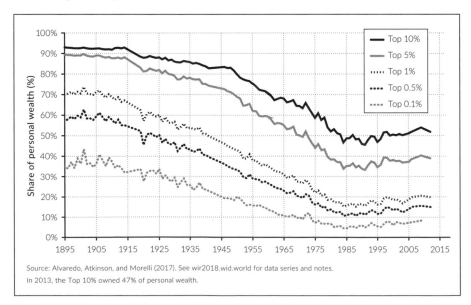

Source: Alvaredo, Atkinson, and Morelli (2017). See wir2018.wid.world for data series and notes.
In 2013, the Top 10% owned 47% of personal wealth.

Figure 24.1 Top wealth shares in the UK, 1895–2013

of these is the twenty-year period leading up to the First World War: in the wake of the first modern globalization, the share of personal wealth going to the wealthiest 1 percent of UK individuals remained relatively stable at around 70 percent. The second period covers more than half of the twentieth century: the share began to fall after 1914 and the decline continued until around 1980. This encompassed two World Wars, and much attention has been paid to the loss of capital during the periods 1914 to 1918 and 1939 to 1945. Although UK top wealth shares certainly fell during the war years, most of the reduction was very much a peace phenomenon. By 1980, the share of the richest 1 percent had decreased to some 17 percent. This is still 17 times their proportionate share, but represents a dramatic reduction. The fall, however, came to an end in the mid 1980s, marking the beginning of the third period. Since the early 1980s the share of the top 1 percent—representing approximately half a million individuals today—has moved in the opposite direction, rising from 15% in 1984 to 20–22% by 2013.

Wealth inequality has increased in the UK since the 1980s, and is by no means insignificant

With the 1980s, the downward trend in top shares came to an abrupt stop and went into reverse. The inequality of wealth has moderately increased over the past four decades. In the early 1980s, when wealth inequality was at historical lows, the top 10% richest owned 46% of total wealth, and the top 1% share was 15%. Since then, the concentration of wealth rose mainly at the very top of the distribution. The top 10% richest individuals in the UK owned more than half of total wealth in 2013. A fifth of total wealth accrued to the top 1% individuals. The lower half of the top 1% (those between the 99th and the 99.5th percentiles) saw a relative stability in their share of total wealth, whereas the upper half saw an increase between 1985 and 2013. Indeed, most of the rise in the share of the top 1% is due to the top 0.5%, and mainly to the top 0.1%—whose share of total wealth doubled from 4.5 to 9% over the period. Consequently, the increase in the concentration of wealth in the last four decades is very much a phenomenon confined to the hands of the top 0.5 percent (the richest 250 000 Britons), and in particular, of the top 0.1 percent (the richest 50 000).

By 2013, the average wealth of British adults was approximately €173 000 (£141 000) in constant 2016 market values, but as can be seen in Figure 24.2, this wealth was far from equally distributed. The average wealth of the bottom 90% of the population was approximately a third of this nationwide average at just €83 200 (£68 000), suggesting that a significant proportion of the bottom 50% of

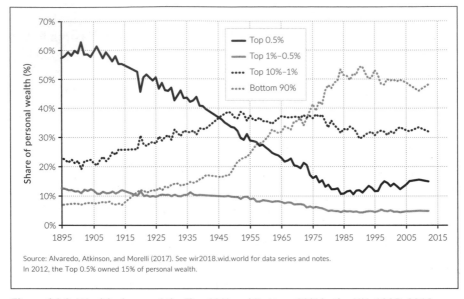

Source: Alvaredo, Atkinson, and Morelli (2017). See wir2018.wid.world for data series and notes.
In 2012, the Top 0.5% owned 15% of personal wealth.

Figure 24.2 Wealth shares of the Top 10% and Bottom 90% in the UK, 1895–2012

the distribution have negligible wealth. The gap with the average wealth of the top 10–5%, 5–1%, top 1–0.5%, and top 0.5% is then huge: their average wealth goes from €393 000 (£321 000) to €723 000 (£591 000), respectively, and further still from €1.48 million (£1.21 million) to €4.54 million (£3.71 million), indicating the exponential trend in wealth holdings the higher up the distribution one examines.

Despite recent rises, the level of wealth concentration is far from its extreme values at the beginning of the twentieth century. The first globalization era (1870–1914) brought with it extremely high shares of total wealth, with the top 10% of the wealth distribution owning almost 95% of total wealth on the eve of World War I. The 0.1% richest individuals then owned at least one-third of total wealth, meaning that they had more than 333 times their proportionate share of total personal wealth. The share of the top 1% was around 70%, and that of the top 5% around 90%.

Inequality within top wealth groups substantially decreased from 1914 to 1980

The past century saw important transformations within top wealth groups, which did not all follow the same trajectory. Figure 24.1 demonstrates the importance of looking within the top 10 percent, and even within the top 1 percent: it is not just the share of the wealthy that has changed but also the shape of the distribu-

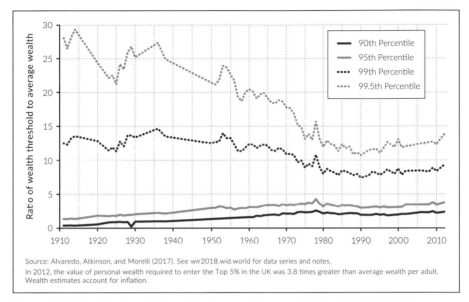

Source: Alvaredo, Atkinson, and Morelli (2017). See wir2018.wid.world for data series and notes.
In 2012, the value of personal wealth required to enter the Top 5% in the UK was 3.8 times greater than average wealth per adult.
Wealth estimates account for inflation.

Figure 24.3 Wealth thresholds of the top wealth groups in the UK, 1910–2012

tion at the top that is, the inequality among the wealthiest. The share in total wealth of those in the top 10 percent, but not in the top 1 percent (that is, the "next 9 percent") saw a rise in their share for the first half of the twentieth century at the expense of the top 1 percent, followed by a period of stability until the end of the 1970s. The lower half of the top 1 percent (those between the 99th and the 99.5th percentiles) saw a relative stability in their share until the 1950s, years when the share of the top 0.5 percent was decreasing dramatically. Since 1980, the share of the lower half of the top 1 percent has been again stable, but at a much lower level, while the upper half has been going up.

The extent of wealth concentration at the top depends on the inequality within the top wealth groups themselves (how unequal are top 1% wealth owners?) but also on the wealth required to become part of the wealthiest groups, the "entry price" (relative to mean wealth). Analyzing the "entry price," the minimum level of wealth required to be part of the top 10% and top 5% (relative to mean wealth) increased from the start of the series up to the end of the 1970s, and then leveled off. However, at the other end of the scale, the entry price to become part of the top 0.1% fell steadily from 1911 to the 1980s, and then began to rise, as depicted by Figure 24.3. The entry price required to become part of the top 1% has halved since 1914. To sum up, the wealth required to enter the top 1 percent in the UK is now some half the level required before the First World War, but it is also the case that wealth became less concentrated within the top 1 percent.

Changes in the composition of property ownership played a key role in reducing wealth inequality before 1980

The role of housing wealth in increasing average total wealth in the UK has been widely discussed. In particular, Tony Atkinson and co-authors identified back in 1989, that "popular wealth," that is, the sum of owner-occupied housing and consumer durables such as automobiles and household appliances, was one of the key determinants of the dynamics of UK top wealth shares up to the end of the 1970s, and moreover, that house price rises had reduced share of the top 1%. However, since then, there have been a number of major changes in the UK housing market.

It is perhaps most illuminating to analyze how tenure changes in the UK have impacted the role of housing wealth in total wealth dynamics, especially how housing policy affected both property prices and the extent of owner occupation. With this framing, the evolution of the housing market in the UK between the end of the First World War and 2011 can be split into three main developments as described below.

First, private landlords were progressively replaced with owner-occupation and social ownership of housing between 1918 and the end of the 1970s. The proportion of owner-occupied properties in England and Wales rose from 23% of households in 1918 to 50% in 1971, and then to 58% by 1981. This coincided with a fall in the share of housing owned by private landlords, from 76% in 1918 to 11% in 1981. Both factors led to a decline in the total wealth share of the top 1%, which contained a disproportionate number of landlords. This shift from a private-rented to owner-occupied housing market did not in itself change the ratio of housing wealth to total personal wealth (different people owned the same house at different points of time), but it was affected by the growth of social housing from 1% of the housing market in 1918 to 31% in 1981.

Second, council houses were widely sold off and housing rose as a percentage of total wealth in the 1980s. The decision to sell public housing by the conservative governments of the 1980s reduced the share of social housing in housing stock to 23%, with owner-occupation going up to 68% and private renting having fallen to 9%. More of the housing stock therefore entered personal wealth, and the ratio of residential housing wealth to total wealth rose by some ten percentage points in the 1980s.

Third, the 1990s saw the return of private landlords. Their share in the housing market doubled from 9% in 1991 to 18% in 2011, as a result of "buy to let" schemes under successive conservative and labor governments. This increased share of private landlords came at the expense of a fall in owner-occupation

(–4 percentage points) and a fall in social housing (–5 percentage points). Furthermore, whereas the selling of council properties may have meant that increases in housing wealth were equalizing in the past, the return of the private landlord is likely to imply that increases in housing wealth may now have a more moderate equalizing effect than in the past.

Housing wealth has moderated the recent tendency for rising wealth concentration

All of this suggests that it is interesting to decompose the assets within the top brackets of the wealth distribution between housing and non-housing assets. Indeed, housing only accounts for a limited fraction of total wealth at the top: since 1970, the share of housing wealth for the top 1 percent has been bounded between 10 and 25 percent of total net worth. It is instructive to look at the distribution of wealth minus residential housing, net of mortgage liabilities. Figure 24.4 shows the top shares of total wealth and of wealth excluding housing for the period since 1971. It appears that, as we should expect, the top shares of the distribution of non-housing wealth are higher: the share of the top 1 percent averages 25 percent over the period 1971 to 1997, compared with 18 percent for the corresponding share for all wealth. Although there is more variability in the shares excluding housing wealth (shares are smoothed to some degree by the

Source: Alvaredo, Atkinson, and Morelli (2017). See wir2018.wid.world for data series and notes.
In 2013, the wealth share of the Top 1% was 20% of total wealth. However, when excluding housing wealth, the Top 1% share was 33%.

Figure 24.4 Top 1% wealth share in the UK, 1971–2012

housing element), overall there is little difference in their evolution over the last quarter of the twentieth century. Up to 2000, we do not get a very different story if one just takes non-housing wealth, with a decided fall in the top shares until the end of the 1970s, and with broad stability until the mid 1990s.

However, in the twenty-first century, there is a distinct difference: the gap between the share of the top 1 percent in wealth excluding housing and the share for all wealth widened. The changes over time are also different, with the concentration of non-housing wealth (financial and business assets) increasing substantially between 1995 and 2013. It appears that housing wealth has moderated a definite tendency for there to be a rise in the concentration of other forms of wealth apart from housing. When people talk about rising wealth concentration in the UK, then it is probably the latter that they have in mind.

PART V

TACKLING ECONOMIC INEQUALITY

25

What Is the Future of Global Income Inequality?

- The future of global income inequality is likely to be shaped by both convergence forces (rapid growth in emerging countries) and divergence forces (rising inequality within countries). No one knows which of these forces will dominate and whether these evolutions are sustainable.

- However, our benchmark projections show that if within-country inequality continues to rise as it has since 1980, then global income inequality will rise steeply, even under fairly optimistic assumptions regarding growth in emerging countries. The global top 1% income share could increase from nearly 20% today to more than 24% in 2050, while the global bottom 50% share would fall from 10% to less than 9%.

- If all countries were to follow the high inequality growth trajectory followed by the United States since 1980, the global top 1% income share would rise even more, to around 28% by 2050. This rise would largely be made at the expense of the global bottom 50%, whose income share would fall to 6%.

- Conversely, if all countries were to follow the relatively low inequality growth trajectory followed by Europe since 1980, the global top 1% income share would decrease to 19% by 2050, while the bottom 50% income share would increase to 13%.

- Differences between high and low inequality growth trajectories within countries have an enormous impact on incomes of the bottom half of the global population. Under the US-style, high inequality growth scenario, the bottom half of the world population earns €4 500 per adult per year in 2050, versus €9 100 in the EU-style, low inequality growth scenario (for a given global average income per adult of €35 500 in 2050 in both scenarios).

The past four decades have been marked by steeply rising income inequality within countries. At the global level, inequality has also risen sharply since 1980, but the situation more or less stabilized beginning in the early 2000s. What will happen in the future? Will growth in emerging countries lead to a sustained reduction in global income inequality? Or will unequal growth within countries drive global income inequality back to its 2000 levels? In this chapter, we discuss different possible global income inequality scenarios between now and 2050.

The projections of global wealth inequality presented in the previous chapter showed that the continuation of current unequal rates of growth among wealth groups would lead to a compression of the global middle-class wealth share and a further rise in wealth inequality. These projections must, however, be interpreted with great care; only China, Europe, and the United States are included in the analysis of the previous chapter given large limitations in wealth inequality data.

Fortunately, more data are available to measure income inequality, and in this chapter we present more elaborate projections of global income inequality. Before discussing the results, it is necessary to stress what can and cannot be reliably projected. As the saying goes, "all models are wrong; some are useful." Our projections are attempts to represent possible states of global inequality in the future, so as to better understand the role played by key determinants. The purpose of our projections is not to predict the future. The number of forces (or variables) that we consider in our analysis is limited. This makes our projections straightforward and simple to understand, but also limits their ability to predict the future. Our projections of global income inequality dynamics are based on the modeling of three forces: within-country income inequality, national level total income growth, and demographics.

One of the key questions we seek to address is the following: will between-country convergence—that is, Asian, African, and Latin American countries catching up with rich countries—dominate in the future and lead to a reduction of global income inequality? Or will forces of divergence (the increase of inequality within countries) take over? Demographic dynamics are also important to take into account. Fast population growth in countries where inequality is rising, for instance, will tend to accentuate global divergence. It is difficult to say which of these forces will dominate a priori. Such an exercise can thus help us understand under what conditions different outcomes might result.

Defining three scenarios to project global income inequality up to 2050

Three scenarios are defined to project the evolution of inequality up to 2050. All our scenarios run up to the halfway mark of the twenty-first century; this has us looking out at a time span similar to the one that has passed since 1980—the starting date of our analyses in the previous chapters. Our first scenario represents an evolution based on "business as usual"—that is, the continuation of the within-country inequality trends observed since 1980. The second and third are variants of the business-as-usual scenario. The second scenario illustrates a high within-country inequality trend, whereas the third scenario represents a low within-country inequality trend. All three scenarios have the same between-country inequality evolutions. This means that a given country has the same average income growth rate in all three scenarios. It also has the same population growth rate in all three scenarios. For estimations of future total income and population growth we turned to the OECD 2060 long-term forecasts. We also relied on the United Nations World Population Prospects.

In the first scenario, all countries follow the inequality trajectory they have followed since the early 1980s. For instance, we know that the bottom 50% income earners in China captured 13% of total Chinese growth over the 1980–2016 period. We thus assume that bottom 50% Chinese earners will capture 13% of Chinese income growth up to 2050. The second scenario assumes that all countries follow the same inequality trajectory as the United States over the 1980–2016 period. Following the above example, we know that bottom 50% US earners captured 3% of total growth since 1980 in the United States. The second scenario then assumes that within all countries, bottom 50% earners will capture 3% of growth over the 2017–2050 period. In the third scenario, all countries follow the same inequality trajectory as the European Union over the 1980–2016 period—where the bottom 50% captured 14% of total growth since 1980.

Under business as usual, global inequality will continue to rise, despite strong growth in low-income countries

Figure 25.1 shows the evolution of the income shares of the global top 1% and the global bottom 50% for the three scenarios. Under the business-as-usual scenario (scenario 1), the income share held by the bottom 50% of the population slightly decreases from approximately 10% today to less than 9% in 2050. At the top of the global income distribution, the top 1% income share rises from less than 21% today to more than 24% of world income. Global inequality thus rises

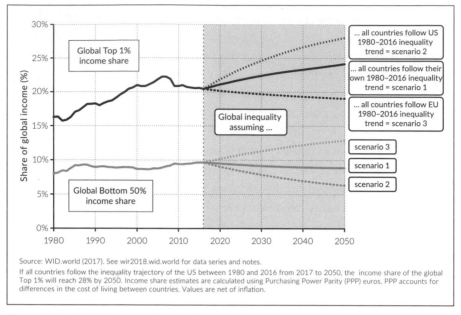

Figure 25.1 Global income share projections of the Bottom 50% and Top 1% , 1980–2050

steeply in this scenario, despite strong growth in emerging countries. In Africa, for instance, we assume that average per-adult income grows at sustained 3% per year throughout the entire period (leading to a total growth of 173% between 2017 and 2050).

These projections show that the progressive catching-up of low-income countries is not sufficient to counter the continuation of worsening of within-country inequality. The results also suggest that the reduction (or stabilization) of global income inequality observed since the financial crisis of 2008, discussed in Chapter 2, could largely be a short-run phenomenon induced by the shocks on top incomes, and the growth slowdown in rich countries (particularly in Europe).

In scenario two, future global income inequalities are amplified as compared to scenario one, as the gap between the global top 1% share and the global bottom 50% share in 2050 widens. In this scenario, the global top 1% would earn close to 28% of global income by 2050, while the bottom 50% would earn close to 6%, less than in 1980, before emerging countries started to catch up with the industrialized world. In this scenario, the increase in the top 1% income share (a positive change of eight percentage points over the 2016–2050 period) is largely, but not entirely, made at the expense of the bottom 50% (a negative change of four percentage points).

Scenario three presents a more equitable global future. It shows that global inequality can be reduced if all countries align on the EU inequality trajectory—or more equitable ones. In this scenario, the bottom 50% income share rises from 10% to approximately 13% in 2050, whereas the top 1% decreases from 21% to 19% of total income. The gap between the shares held by the two groups would, however, remain large (at about six percentage points). This suggests that, although following the European pathway in the future is a much better option than the business-as-usual or the US pathway, even more equitable growth trajectories will be needed for the global bottom 50% share to catch up with the top 1%. Achieving a world in which the top 1% and bottom 50% groups capture the same share of global income would mean getting to a point where the top 1% individuals earn on average fifty times more than those in the bottom half. Whatever the scenarios followed, global inequalities will remain substantial.

Within-country inequality trends are critical for global poverty eradication

What do these different scenarios mean in terms of actual income levels, and particularly for bottom groups? It is informative to focus on the dynamics of income shares held by different groups, and how they converge or diverge over time. But ultimately, it can be argued that what matters for individuals—and in particular those at the bottom of the social ladder—is their absolute income level. We stress again here that our projections do not pretend to predict how the future will be, but rather aim to inform on how it *could* be, under a set of simple assumptions.

Figure 25.2 depicts the evolution of average global income levels and the average income of the bottom half of the global population in the three scenarios described above. The evolution of global average income does not depend on the three scenarios. This is straightforward to understand: in each of the scenarios, countries (and hence the world as a whole) experience the same total income and demographic growth. It is only the matter of how this growth is distributed within countries that changes across scenarios. Let us reiterate that our assumptions are quite optimistic for low-income countries, so it is indeed possible that global average income would actually be slightly lower in the future than in the figures presented. In particular, the global bottom 50% average income would be even lower.

In 2016, the average per-adult annual income of the poorest half of the world population was €3 100, in contrast to the €16 000 global average—a ratio of 5.2 between the overall average and the bottom-half average. In 2050, global average income will be €35 500 according to our projections. In the business-as-usual

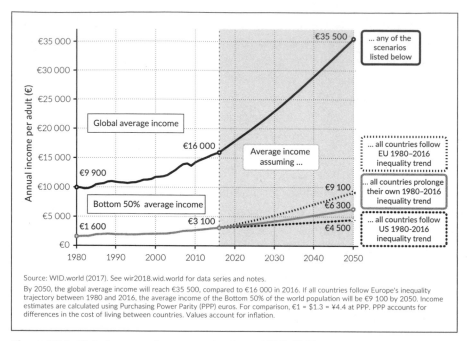

Figure 25.2 Global average income projections, 1980–2050

scenario, the gap between average income and the bottom would widen (from a ratio of 5.2 to a ratio of 5.6) as the bottom half would have an income of €6 300. In the US scenario, the bottom half of the world population earns €4 500 per year and per adult—increasing the global average income to the bottom 50% income ratio of 7.9. Average income of the global bottom half will be €9 100 in the EU scenario, reducing the bottom 50% to average income ratio to 3.9.

The gap between global average income and the average income of the bottom half of the population is particularly high in all scenarios. However, the difference in average income of the bottom 50% between the EU scenario and the US scenario is important, as well. Average income of the global bottom 50% would be more than twice higher in the EU scenario than in the US scenario at €9 100 versus €4 500. This suggests that within-country inequality trajectories matter—and matter substantially—for poverty eradication. In other words, pursuing high-growth strategies in emerging countries is not merely sufficient to lift the global bottom half out of poverty. Reducing inequality within countries is also key.

The scenarios point toward another crucial insight: global inequality is not bound to rise in the future. Our analysis (in Part II) of the different income inequality trajectories followed by countries showed that, if anything, more equitable growth does not mean dampened growth. This result is apparent when time periods are compared (the United States experienced higher growth in the

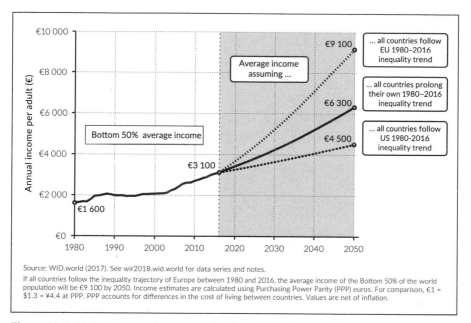

Source: WID.world (2017). See wir2018.wid.world for data series and notes.

If all countries follow the inequality trajectory of Europe between 1980 and 2016, the average income of the Bottom 50% of the world population will be €9 100 by 2050. Income estimates are calculated using Purchasing Power Parity (PPP) euros. For comparison, €1 = $1.3 = ¥4.4 at PPP. PPP accounts for differences in the cost of living between countries. Values are net of inflation.

Figure 25.3 Global average income projections of the Bottom 50%, 1980–2050

1950s–1960s when inequality was at its lowest) or when countries are compared with one another (over the past decades, China grew much faster than India, with a lower level of inequality, and the EU had a more equitable path than the United States but a relatively similar growth rate). This suggests that it is possible to pursue equitable development pathways in a way that does not also limit total growth in the future.

What can governments do to prevent the rise of national and global inequality? The next and final chapters of this report discuss various policy options which need to be democratically debated, on the basis of sound and transparent economic data, if societies are to seriously address the issues raised by rising levels of income and wealth concentration. We do not attempt to resolve any of these policy debates, nor do we claim to have the right answer as to which set of policies will be best suited to a given country given its own economic, political, social, and cultural situation. Recent research, however, points to fundamental economic issues that have not been discussed enough over the past decades. These include the role of progressive taxation and global financial transparency to tackle rising inequality at the top of the distribution, as well as more equal access to education and good paying jobs to put an end to the stagnation of incomes at the bottom. Reassessing the role of public capital to invest in the future should also, in our view, be a key component of these future discussions.

Tackling Rising Inequality at the Top:
The Role of Progressive Taxation

- There has been a rise in global top shares, but different countries have experienced widely different inequality trajectories. Institutional and policy changes implemented since 1980 stand as the most powerful explanations for the different inequality trajectories.
- Income tax progressivity is a proven tool to combat rising income and wealth inequality at the top. Tax progressivity does not only reduce post-tax inequality; it also impacts pre-tax inequality, by discouraging top earners from capturing a higher share of growth via aggressive bargaining for higher pay.
- Tax progressivity was sharply reduced in rich countries from the 1970s to the mid-2000s. During this period, the top marginal income tax rate in rich countries was brought from 70% to 42% on average. Since the global financial crisis of 2008, the downward trend has been halted and reversed in certain countries. Future evolutions remain, however, uncertain.
- Progressive taxation of wealth and inheritances is also a key component of redistribution. In some of the most unequal nations of the world (Brazil, South Africa, India, Russia, and the Middle East), inheritance tax is almost inexistent while the poor often face high tax rates on the basic goods they purchase.
- More generally, tax systems are highly regressive in large emerging countries. Evidence from recent inequality trends (for example, Brazil between 2000 and 2015) suggests that progressive tax reform should be given a higher priority in the future.

The previous chapters of this report confirm that income and wealth inequality largely increased at the top of the distribution. The rise in inequality has been driven by the substantial growth rates enjoyed by the very top groups as compared to the rest of the distribution. A common explanation for this growth is skill-biased technological change. That is, the evolution of technology is said to have increased the relative productivity—and hence the relative pay—of skilled labor relative to unskilled labor, thereby increasing the demand for skilled workers. Globalization could have had a similar impact in developed countries as discussed in Chapter 2.1. As we have already repeatedly stressed, there are many limitations to this purely technological explanation. First, rising income inequality is a broad-ranging phenomenon which also involves capital income and wealth dynamics, and not only the distribution of labor income. The supply of skilled labor is determined by education. That is, the expansion of education leads to a rise in the supply of skills, while globalization and technological may increase the demand for skills. Depending on which process occurs faster, the inequality of labor income will either fall or rise. This idea has been described as the race between education and technology. In other words, different policies can make a large difference.

Another complementary explanation for rising top labor incomes is the "superstar effect." According to this theory, technological change and globalization have made it easier for those who make it to the top to reap a higher share of growth. For instance, recording a song has more or less the same cost today as thirty years ago, but a successful music production can now reach a much broader audience. Because international firms have become larger, managers making it to the top control a much larger business than before, and their pay has increased as a result. Due to the superstar effect, tiny differences in talent—or sometimes in bargaining power and other attributes—can translate into very large income differentials. It should be noted that these global "superstars" are not necessarily more productive or talented than they were thirty years ago. They are perhaps simply luckier to have been born a few decades after their elders.

In any case, the problem behind these two theories—education and superstar—is that they cannot fully account for cross-country divergences in top income trajectories. In a comparison of top remunerations in global firms, it stands out that there are important variations across countries—in particular, between the United States, Europe, and Japan. Germany's largest companies, for instance, are present in all global markets and are not less productive than their US counterparts, though CEO remunerations there are on average half as high as in the United States. As discussed in Chapter 2.3, the rise of labor income inequality was relatively limited in Europe compared to the United States, despite similar technical change and penetration of new technologies over the past forty years in both regions.

For the bottom and middle parts of the distribution, the importance of training and education designed to help individuals adapt to new modes of production cannot be overlooked. Unequal access to education is likely to have played a role in the stagnation of incomes of the bottom half of the distribution in recent decades—in particular, in the United States. These dynamics are discussed in the next chapter. They should, however, be distinguished from rising inequalities at the very top of the income distribution. Changes in policy and institutional contexts better account for the diversity of top income trajectories over the world. In particular, recent research shows that changes in tax progressivity have played an important role in the surge of top incomes over the past decades.

Top marginal tax rates have strong effects on both pre- and post-tax income inequality at the top

Progressive tax rates contribute to the reduction of post-tax income inequality at the top of the distribution via their highest marginal tax rates (that is, tax rates applicable above a certain level of income earned). Indeed, if an individual earns $2 million and if the top marginal tax rate is 50% above one million dollars, this individual will net out only $500 000 on the second million. If the top marginal tax rate is 80% above one million dollars, then the earner will net out only $200 000 on the second million. The reduction of inequality can be further enhanced if the public spending funded by this tax revenue is aimed at fostering equitable growth.

One often-neglected role of top marginal tax rates is their ability to reduce pre-tax income inequality. This can occur via two channels. The most obvious one is that when top marginal income tax rates are high, top earners have less money to save and accumulate wealth, and therefore potentially less income from capital next year. Another way to understand the impact on top income tax rates on income inequality is to focus on rich individuals' bargaining incentives. When top marginal tax rates are low, top earners have high incentives to bargain for compensation increases—for instance, by putting a lot of energy into nominating the right people to the compensation committees who decide on pay packages. Alternatively, high top marginal tax rates tend to discourage such bargaining efforts. Reductions in top tax rates can thus drive upward not only post-tax income inequality but pre-tax inequality, as well.

Higher top tax rates may, however, also discourage work effort and business creation among the most talented. In this scenario, higher top tax rates would lead to less economic activity by the rich and hence less economic growth. In this case, top tax rates are not a desirable policy. In principle, there should be room to discuss these conflicting and legitimate claims on the basis of dispassionate analyses and sound data.

Piketty, Saez, and Stantcheva (2014) have developed a theoretical model and an empirical framework taking into account these different effects. By using a database on CEO compensation and performance in developed countries, they conclude that bargaining elasticities are an important part of the story—in particular, to understand the high rise of US CEOs' pay relative to their counterparts in Japan and Europe (with comparability established by shared corporate sector, firm size, and performance levels). By calibrating the theoretical model, they show top tax rates could rise up to 80% and be welfare-enhancing for everyone apart from the very top of the distribution.

The data at our disposal are still imperfect, and we certainly do not pretend that a mixture of econometric evidence and mathematical formula should replace public deliberation and political decision making on these complex issues. But at the very least, we feel that there is enough evidence to reopen this discussion about sharply progressive taxation at the very top.

It is also important to remember that top tax rates reached more than 90% in the United States and in the UK in the era of the 1940s to the 1970s. Such high tax rates do not appear to have harmed growth. In fact, over the past fifty years, all rich countries have grown more or less at the same rates despite very large tax-policy variations.

Figure 26.1 shows the relationship between changes in top marginal tax rates and in the top 1% pre-tax income share in OECD countries, which occurred

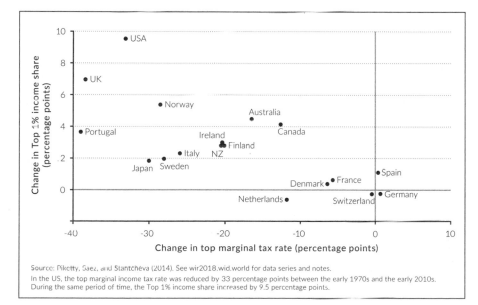

Source: Piketty, Saez, and Stantcheva (2014). See wir2018.wid.world for data series and notes.
In the US, the top marginal income tax rate was reduced by 33 percentage points between the early 1970s and the early 2010s. During the same period of time, the Top 1% income share increased by 9.5 percentage points.

Figure 26.1 Changes in top marginal tax rates and top income shares in rich countries since the 1970s

between the early 1970s and the late 2000s. The correlation is particularly strong: on average, a 2 percentage point drop in the top marginal tax rate is associated with a 1 percentage point increase in the top 1% pre-tax income share. Countries such as Germany, Spain, Denmark, and Switzerland, which did not experience any significant top rate tax cut, did not experience increases in top income shares. Conversely, the United States, UK, and Canada experienced important reductions in top marginal tax rates and saw their top 1% income shares substantially increase. This graph strongly suggests that top tax rates play a key role in moderating pre-tax top incomes. In addition, there was no significant impact on growth, suggesting again that bargaining elasticities are more important than incentive effects.

A window of opportunity for tax progressivity?

Figure 26.2 presents in detail the evolution of top marginal income tax rates in the United States, the UK, Germany, France, and Japan since 1900. In the five countries, there was either no personal income taxation or there was a very modest amount of it at the turn of the twentieth century. Income tax was then introduced, partly to finance the First World War, and top marginal tax rates were brought to very high levels in the 1950s–1970s. (Top tax rates rose up to 94% in the United States, 98% in the UK.) Top rates were then drastically reduced from the 1970s onward (from 70% on average in these countries to 42% on average in the mid-2000s).

How to account for these movements? Up until the 1970s, policymakers and public opinion probably considered—rightly or wrongly—that at the very top of the income ladder, compensation increases reflected mostly greed or other socially wasteful activities rather than productive work effort. This is why the United States and UK were able to set marginal tax rates as high as 80%. More recently, the Reagan/Thatcher revolution succeeded in making such top tax rate levels unthinkable, at least for a while. But after decades of increasing income concentration that has brought about mediocre growth since the 1970s, and a Great Recession triggered by financial sector excesses, a rethinking of the Reagan and Thatcher policies is perhaps under way—at least in some countries.

Top marginal income tax increased in the United States, UK, Germany, France, and Japan over the past ten years. The United Kingdom, for instance, increased its top income tax rate from 40% to 50% in 2010 in part to curb top pay excesses. In the United States, the Occupy Wall Street movement and its famous "We are the 99%" slogan also reflected the view that the top 1% gained too much at the

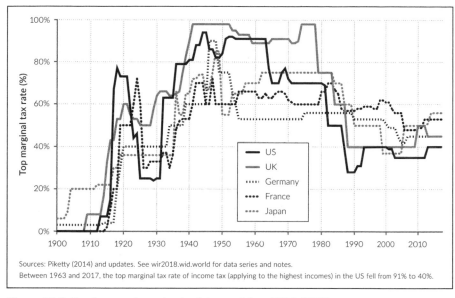

Sources: Piketty (2014) and updates. See wir2018.wid.world for data series and notes.
Between 1963 and 2017, the top marginal tax rate of income tax (applying to the highest incomes) in the US fell from 91% to 40%.

Figure 26.2 Top income tax rates in rich countries, 1900–2017

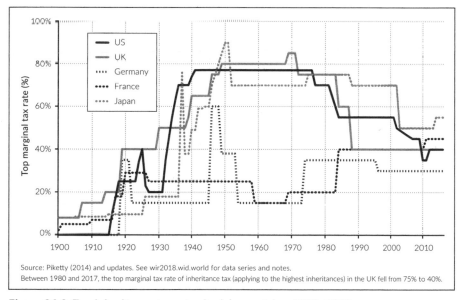

Source: Piketty (2014) and updates. See wir2018.wid.world for data series and notes.
Between 1980 and 2017, the top marginal tax rate of inheritance tax (applying to the highest inheritances) in the UK fell from 75% to 40%.

Figure 26.3 Top inheritance tax rates in rich countries, 1900–2017

expense of the 99%. Whether this marked the beginning of a new tax policy cycle that will counterbalance the steep fall observed since the 1970s remains a question. In the UK, the 2010 increase in top income tax rate was followed by slight reduction down to 45% in 2013. As we are writing these lines, the new US Republican administration and Congress are preparing a major tax overhaul plan. The

French government also projects to reduce tax rates on top incomes and wealth owners.

Top inheritance tax rates were recently increased in France, Japan, and the United States, as shown on Figure 26.3. In Japan and in the United States, this increase halted a progressive reduction in top inheritance tax rates initiated in the 1980s. In France and Germany, top inheritance tax rates have been historically lower than in the United States, UK, and Japan. In earlier chapters of this report we described the two World Wars and various economic and political shocks of the twentieth century. These durably reduced wealth concentration through other means than tax policy. As with the question of income tax progressivity, it is impossible to know whether this increase marks a new era of progressivity. The US tax overhaul plans to abolish the inheritance tax.

Inheritance is exempted from tax while the poor face high consumption taxes in emerging countries

While the past ten years saw some increases in tax progressivity in rich countries, it is worth noting that major emerging economies still do not have any tax on inheritance, despite the extreme levels of inequality observed there. Inheritance is taxed at a particularly small rate in Brazil (at a national average of around 4%, with a maximum federal rate of 8%). In India, China, and Russia, there is no inheritance tax—in contrast to rich countries (Figure 26.4). In India, an 85% tax rate was in place in the 1970s and early 1980s before it was brought to 0% in 1984. One can plausibly argue that India's tax administration—or even Indian society as a whole—was not ready for very high top inheritance tax rates to begin with. But international evidence—in particular, from developed countries—suggests that a fairly progressive income and inheritance tax system can be an important component of a successful development strategy.

In emerging countries, it is also noteworthy that consumption taxes can be particularly high while inheritance tax is inexistent. In Brazil, for instance, the tax rate on electricity is around 30%, and high rates also apply to many other basic goods purchased by the poor. Extreme income and wealth inequality levels are thus sustained and reinforced by a regressive tax system. On a more positive note, the absence of inheritance taxes in emerging countries suggests that there is ample room for progressive tax policies. In a country like Brazil, as shown in Chapter 12, incomes at the bottom rose over the past decades, but this was partly due to the detriment of the middle class, whose share of national income was reduced. This situation is bound to happen when the richest do not contribute

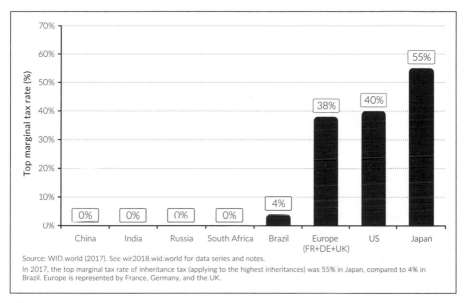

Figure 26.4 Top inheritance tax rates in emerging and rich countries, 2017

fairly to the financing of the welfare state. Indeed, additional fiscal revenues collected through newly introduced progressive inheritance taxes could be used to fund educational or health programs and provide relief for the middle class in Brazil and other emerging countries.

27

Tax Policy in a Global Environment: The Case for a Global Financial Register

- Although the tax system is a crucial tool to tackle inequality, it also faces potential obstacles, among which is tax evasion. The wealth currently held in tax havens is equivalent to more than 10% of global GDP and has increased considerably since the 1970s.
- The rise of tax havens makes it difficult to properly measure and tax wealth and capital income in a globalized world. Reducing financial opacity is critical to improve data on wealth and its distribution; to foster a more informed public debate about redistribution; and to fight tax evasion, money laundering, and the financing of terrorism.
- One key challenge involves recording the ownership of financial assets. While land and real-estate registries have existed for centuries, they miss a large fraction of the wealth held by households today, as wealth increasingly takes the form of financial securities. A global financial register recording the ownership of equities, bonds, and other financial assets would deal a severe blow to financial opacity.
- Little-known financial institutions called central security depositories (CSDs) already gather information about who owns financial assets. These data could be mobilized to create a global financial register. CSDs, however, are private actors in most OECD countries and will not transfer information to authorities in the absence of regulations compelling them to do so.
- Another difficulty lies in the fact that most CSDs do not directly record the names of the ultimate owners of financial securities, but only the names of the intermediaries.
- However, technical solutions have been identified by the CSDs themselves to allow end-investor identification. Moreover, more transparent systems exist in countries like Norway and China, which suggest that end-user transparency is technically and economically feasible at the CSD and at the global level.

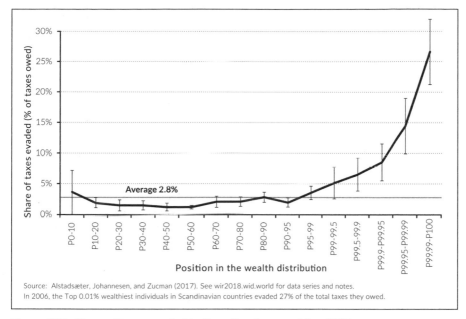

Figure 27.1 Share of taxes evaded in Scandinavian countries, 2006

Multinational corporations and wealthy individuals are increasingly using tax havens to avoid or evade taxes. Fully 63% of all the foreign profits made by US multinationals are booked in a handful of offshore financial centers—Bermuda, Ireland, the Netherlands, Switzerland, Singapore, and Luxembourg—where they face very low tax rates, ranging from 0% to 5%. This represents a tenfold increase since the 1980s.

Assets worth the equivalent of 10% of world GDP are stored in tax havens by wealthy individuals. This figure rises to almost 40% in countries like Greece and Argentina, and to more than 50% in Russia, according to novel research by A. Alstadsæter, N. Johannesen, and G. Zucman. At the global level, tax evasion deprives governments from about €350 billion in tax revenue each year.

Tax evasion also seriously undermines tax progressivity. Figure 27.1 shows the amount of taxes evaded as a share of taxes owed across the wealth distribution, in the case of Scandinavia. These statistics were produced by Alstadsæter, Johannesen, and Zucman (2017), who combine recent, massive data leaks (the "Panama papers" and the Swiss Leaks from HSBC Switzerland) with random audits and administrative records on income and wealth. While most of the population in advanced economies does not evade much tax—because most of its income derives from wages and pensions, which are automatically reported to the tax authorities—leaked data show pervasive tax evasion at the very top. The top 0.01% of the Scandinavian wealth distribution—a group that includes households with more than $45 million in net wealth—evades 25% to 30% of its personal taxes, an order of magnitude

Box 27.1 Toward a Global Financial Register?

This box draws upon Delphine Nougay-
rède, "Towards a Global Financial Register?
Account Segregation in Central Securities
Depositories and the Challenge of Trans-
parent Securities Ownership in Advanced
Economies," a working paper presented at
a Columbia Law School Blue Sky workshop,
April 2017.

**Central Security Depositories as building
blocks for a global financial register**
In the modern financial system, shares and
bonds issued by corporations are represented not by paper certificates but by
electronic account entries. Holding chains
are no longer direct—that is, they do not
connect issuers directly with investors, but
involve many intermediaries often located in
different countries. At the top of the chain,
immediately after the issuers, are the central
securities depositories (CSDs). Their role is
to record the ownership of financial securities and sometimes to handle the settlement
of transactions. The clients of CSDs are
domestic financial institutions in the issuer
country, foreign financial institutions, and
other CSDs. After the CSD participants are
several other layers of financial intermediaries, and at the end of the chain, a final
intermediary, often a bank, holding the
relationship with the investors.

Because so many intermediaries are
involved, the issuers of financial securities
are disconnected from end-investors; public
companies that issue securities no longer
know who their shareholders or bondholders are. CSDs, as a part of the chain of
financial intermediation, both enable and
obscure this relationship. The system was
not intentionally designed for anonymity
but it evolved this way over time because of
the regulatory complexity of cross-border
securities trading. The evolution toward
non-transparency was also facilitated by
the fact that the topic is too technical to be
affected by public opinion.

**Non-transparent accounts prevail in most
Western CSDs**
There are two broad types of accounts in
the CSD world. "Segregated accounts" allow
the holding of securities in distinct accounts opened in the name of the individual end-investors. This model thus allows
transparency. The opposite model is that of
"omnibus accounts" (or in the United States,
"street name registration") where securities
belonging to several investors are pooled
together into one account under the name
of a single account-holder, usually a financial
intermediary, thereby obscuring the identity
of the end-investors.

more than the average evasion rate of about 3%. Because Scandinavian countries
rank among the countries with the highest social trust, lowest corruption, and
strongest respect for the rule of law, that evasion among the wealthy may be even
higher elsewhere.

Several recent policy initiatives have attempted to tackle offshore tax evasion.
Before 2008, tax havens refused to share any information with foreign tax authorities. In 2010, the US Congress enacted the Foreign Account Tax Compliance
Act, which compels foreign banks to disclose accounts held by US taxpayers to
the IRS automatically each year, under the threat of economic sanctions. OECD
countries have obtained similar commitments from most of the world's tax
havens. Apparently, tax havens can be forced to cooperate if threatened with
large enough penalties.

One of the key issues for a global financial register is that non-transparent accounting (that is, "omnibus accounts") prevails in most Western markets. For instance, the US CSD, the Depository Trust Company (DTC), uses omnibus accounts. In its books, the DTC identifies only brokerage firms and other intermediaries, not the ultimate owners of US stocks and bonds. "Omnibus accounts" also prevail in most European countries—in particular, within the Euroclear and Clearstream CSDs. This makes it difficult to construct a global financial register on the basis of the currently existing Western CSDs.

More transparency is possible, however

More transparency within Western CSDs can however be envisioned. The current system creates a number of risks for the financial industry, of which it is very aware. In 2014, Luxembourg's Clearstream Banking agreed to a $152 million settlement with the US Treasury following allegations that it had held $2.8 billion in US securities through an omnibus account for the benefit of the Central Bank of Iran, which was subject to US sanctions. As a result, the securities industry discussed a number of options that could be put in place to allow greater transparency of information on end-investors. This might include discontinuing the use of omnibus accounts, introducing new covering message standards (as is done in the payments industry), or ex-post audit trails, which would enable information on the identity of the ultimate beneficiary of financial transactions to circulate throughout the chain. New technologies such as distributed ledger technology (blockchain) could also foster greater transparency.

Transparent market infrastructures already exist today. In Norway, the CSD lists all individual shareholders in domestic companies, acts as formal corporate registrar, and reports back directly to the tax authorities. In China, the China Securities Depository Clearing Corporation Limited ("Chinaclear") operates a system that is fully transparent for shares issued by Chinese companies and held by domestic Chinese investors. At the end of 2015, it held $8 trillion worth of securities in custody, broadly the range of the CSDs of France, Germany, and the UK, and maintained securities accounts for ninety-nine million end-investors. Some segregation functionalities already exist within some of the larger Western CSDs (like DTC or Euroclear), which could be expanded. Many believe that segregated CSD accounting would support better corporate governance by giving greater voice to small investors. All of this suggests that more could be done within the large Western CSDs to implement greater investor transparency.

However, current enforcement efforts face important obstacles. Many tax havens and offshore financial institutions do not have incentives to provide accurate information, as they do not face large enough sanctions for non- or poor compliance. Second, a large and growing fraction of offshore wealth is held through intertwined shell companies, trusts, and foundations, which disconnect assets from their actual owners. This makes it easy for offshore banks to claim, falsely, that they do not have any European, American, or Asian clients at all— while in fact such persons are the beneficial owners of the assets held through shell companies.

As advocated by Gabriel Zucman in recent work, a global financial register would be a powerful tool for cutting through this opacity. Such a register would allow tax and regulatory agencies to check that taxpayers properly report assets and capital income independently of whatever information offshore financial institutions are willing to provide. It would also allow governments to close corporate tax loopholes by enforcing a fair distribution of tax revenue globally for corporations with increasingly complex overseas operations. A global financial register could also serve as the informational basis for the establishment of a global wealth tax. The establishment of such a register would not, however, mean that ownership of assets would be disclosed to the general public. Such information could remain confidential in the same way that current income tax data are kept confidential.

The establishment of a global financial register could be based on the information already gathered by (mostly private) financial institutions known as central securities depositories (CSD). CSDs are the ultimate bookkeepers of the equities and bonds issued by corporations and governments. They can maintain accounts as end-investor segregated accounts—which is the most transparent model, as it links an individual to an asset. Or they can maintain omnibus accounts—a less transparent model, given that assets held by different investors are lumped into a single account under the name of a financial intermediary, making it difficult to identify end-investors. (Box 27.1)

One key issue with using CSDs as the building brick of a global financial register is that omnibus accounts prevail in most large Western markets. (The Depository Trust Company in the United States and Clearstream in Europe, for instance, operate with omnibus accounts.) However, technical solutions facilitated by developments in information technologies already exist to allow the identification of ultimate asset holders in large Western CSDs. Moreover, in certain countries such as Norway, or large emerging markets such as China and South Africa, CSDs operate through systems which allow the identification of ultimate asset owners. In short, the creation of a global financial register does not face any insuperable technical problems. (Box 27.1)

28

Tackling Inequality at the Bottom:
The Need for More Equal Access
to Education and Good-Paying Jobs

- More equal access to education and good-paying jobs is key to countering the stagnation and sluggish income growth rates of the bottom half of the population. Recent research shows that there can be enormous gaps between the beliefs evinced in public discourses about equal opportunity and the realities of unequal access to education.
- In the United States, for instance, out of one hundred children whose parents are among the bottom 10% income earners, only thirty go to college. The figure reaches ninety when parents are within the top 10% earners.
- On the positive side, research shows that elite colleges in the United States may improve openness to students from poor backgrounds without compromising their outcomes.
- In rich or emerging countries, it might be necessary to set transparent and verifiable objectives—together with changes in the financing and admission systems—in order to equalize access to education.

It is now well known that inequality has risen at the top of income and wealth distributions in recent decades. However, this report also sheds light on the stagnation or sluggish growth rates of the bottom 90%, and especially of the bottom 50% of the distribution. The situation has been particularly extreme in the United States, as shown in Chapter 5. To a lesser extent, bottom income groups have also lagged behind the rest of the population in terms of income growth in European countries as well as in fast-growth emerging countries. To counter such dynamics, progressive income and wealth taxes are not sufficient. More equal access to education and good-paying jobs is key. This chapter explores recent findings on the interaction between educational inequalities and income inequalities.

Novel research allows us to better understand the determinants of educational
inequalities and their interactions with income inequality

To what extent are income and wage inequality the result of a fair, meritocratic
process? How do family resources determine the opportunities of their children?
Publicly available data to assess these questions are still scarce in most countries
around the globe. But recent research has contributed to answering the question.
In particular, using US administrative data on more than fifty million children
and their parents, Raj Chetty, Nathaniel Hendren, Patrick Kline, Emmanuel Saez,
and Nicholas Turner were able to provide remarkable results on intergenerational
mobility.

Intergenerational mobility, broadly speaking, refers to the link between children's economic trajectories and their parents' economic situations. In the United
States, estimations show that mobility levels are low as compared to other countries: fewer than eight American children out of a hundred born in the 20%
poorest families manage to get to the top 20% of earners as adults, as compared
to twelve in Denmark and more than thirteen in Canada. Another powerful way
to illustrate the extent of educational inequality in the United States is to focus
on the percentage of children attending college by income groups. Out of a
hundred children whose parents are within the bottom 10% income earners, only

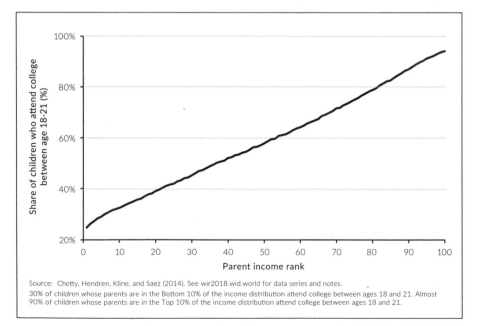

Source: Chetty, Hendren, Kline, and Saez (2014). See wir2018.wid.world for data series and notes.
30% of children whose parents are in the Bottom 10% of the income distribution attend college between ages 18 and 21. Almost
90% of children whose parents are in the Top 10% of the income distribution attend college between ages 18 and 21.

Figure 28.1 College attendance rates and parent income rank in the US for children
born in 1980-1982

thirty go to college. The figure reaches ninety when parents are within the top 10% earners.

The findings displayed by Figure 28.1 show that there is sometimes an enormous gap between official discourses about equal opportunity, meritocracy, and so forth and the reality of unequal access to education. This also suggests that it might be necessary to set transparent and verifiable objectives—together with changes in the financing and admission systems—in order to equalize access to education.

In the United States, intergenerational mobility is also a local issue

In the case of the United States, strong geographical inequalities also interact with educational inequalities. In geographical areas with the highest mobility, a child born in a family from the bottom 20% of the income distribution has a 10% to 12% chance of reaching the top 20% as an adult (that is about as much as in the highly mobile countries of Canada and Denmark). Examples of highly mobile places include the San Francisco Bay area and Salt Lake City in Utah. In areas with low intergenerational mobility, a child born in a family from the bottom 20% of the income distribution has only a 4% to 5% chance of reaching the top 20% as an adult. No advanced economy for which we have data has such low rates of intergenerational mobility. Cities in the US South (such as Atlanta) or the US Rust Belt (such as Indianapolis and Cincinnati) typically have such low mobility rates.

What factors best explain these geographical differences in mobility? Detailed analysis shows that race and segregation play an important role in the United States. In general, intergenerational mobility is lower in areas with larger African-American populations. However, in areas with large African-American populations, both blacks and whites have lower rates of upward income mobility, indicating that social and environmental causes other than race, such as differences in history and institutions, may play a role. Spatial and social segregation is also negatively associated with upward mobility. In particular, longer commuting time decreases opportunities to climb the social ladder, and spatial segregation of the poorest individuals has a stronger negative impact on mobility. This suggests that the isolation of lower-income families and the difficulties they experience in reaching job sites are important drivers of social immobility.

Income inequality at the local level, school quality, social capital, and family structure are also important factors. Higher income inequality among the poorest 99% of individuals is associated with lower mobility. Meanwhile, a larger middle class stimulates upward mobility. Higher public school expenditures per student along with lower class sizes significantly increase social mobility. Higher social capital also favors mobility (for example, areas with high involvement in community organizations). Finally, family structure is also a key determinant; upward mobility is substantially lower in areas where the fraction of children living in single-parent households, or the share of divorced parents, or the share of non-married adults is higher.

What is remarkable is that combining these factors explains very effectively social mobility patterns. Taken together, five factors—commuting time, income inequality among the 99% poorest individuals, high-school dropout rates, social capital, and the fraction of children with single parents—explain 76% of inequalities in upward mobility across local areas in the United States. The vast geographical disparities in mobility in the United States, and the fact that they can be best explained by a combination of social factors at the commuting zone level, show that intergenerational mobility is largely a local issue.

Access to quality higher education is particularly unequal in the United States

The link between school quality and upward mobility that was highlighted above suggests that educational policies, school organization, and access rules can play a key role in promoting intergenerational mobility. Raj Chetty, John Friedman, Emmanuel Saez, Nicholas Turner, and Danny Yagan recently characterized intergenerational mobility in US colleges over a period of nearly fifteen years, from 1999 to 2013. They show the extent of inequality in access to higher education, but also reveal tremendous scope for improvement: if all institutions could be made as efficient as the highest 10% colleges in terms of social mobility, then mobility in the United States would be perfect. Children's outcomes would be unrelated to their parents'.

Intergenerational mobility at the level of a given college may be defined as bringing together two components: the access rate and the success rate. Access rate refers to the openness of that college to students from lower-income groups, and can be measured as the proportion of students in it who come from the poorest 20% families. Success rate refers to that college's ability to help children from poor backgrounds reach higher income groups throughout their life. It might, for instance, be evaluated as the share of students ending up in the top 20% income group, given that they come from families in the bottom 20% of the national income distribution. Putting these together, one might define the mobility rate as the fraction of all students in a given college who come from the poorest 20% families *and* end up in the top 20% group. Theoretically, the mobility rate of a perfectly mobile society would be 4%. The fact that it is currently just 1.7% in the United States as a whole shows that there is room for substantial improvement in providing low-income children with fair opportunities.

It is important to note, nevertheless, that family income differences only weakly predict the income positions of children from the same college. We saw that, at the national level, parental income strongly determined future position in the income distribution. However, within a given college, the relationship between parental income and student income is five times lower. At the national US level, children from the top 20% income groups end up 30 percentiles higher in the distribution than those from the bottom 20%; but among students attending a given elite college, this gap shrinks to close to 7 percentiles on average.

Contribution to mobility varies greatly across US colleges

Access to elite colleges remains highly unequal in the United States. Approximately 3% of children at Harvard University born between 1980 and 1982 come from the bottom 20% poorest families, whereas 70% come from the top 10%. In Ivy-Plus colleges (the most selective colleges in the United States) in general, there are more students coming from the top 1% richest families (14.5%) than from the bottom half (13.5%) of the population.

Such figures contrast sharply with public colleges. At Glendale Community College in Los Angeles, for instance, 32% of students come from the bottom quintile and only 14% from the top quintile. What is interesting is that high-access-rate colleges can also have high success rates (outcomes similar to highly selective colleges), translating into high mobility rates. Colleges helping many low-income students to reach the top of the income distribution tend to be public colleges welcoming a large number of low-income students. The existence of such institutions is particularly meaningful as it indicates that elite colleges may improve openness to students from poor backgrounds without compromising their outcomes.

Trends in mobility are heterogeneous, but show that little progress has been made overall

How did access and success rates evolve in the past decade in the United States? The data allow us to track their evolution between 2000 and 2011. During this period, the fraction of low-income college students increased from 10.6% to 12.8%, and this growth has been concentrated at for-profit institutions and

Box 28.1 Reservation policies in India

In order to tackle extreme social inequalities, India developed a vast system of preferential admission to the universities (as well as in public sector employment) for children from the lowest castes (the SC/ST, or "Scheduled Castes/Scheduled Tribes," the former highly discriminated untouchables, or almost 30% of the population). This nationwide program started in the 1950s. The implementation of reservation policies based on social and cultural segregation, however, faces complex measurement and political challenges. What is the correct way to identify legitimate beneficiaries? How can a dynamic reservation system be designed, which takes into account demographic, cultural, and economic changes?

In India, the so-called reservation policies aroused growing frustration among the children in the intermediate castes (the OBC, or "Other Backward Classes," roughly 40% of the population) caught between the most disadvantaged groups and the highest castes. Since the 1980s, several Indian states extended the policy of preferential admission to these new groups (including the Muslims who were excluded from the original system). Conflicts concerning these arrangements are all the greater because the old boundaries between castes are porous and do not always match the hierarchies in income and wealth. Far from it, in fact. In 2011, the federal government finally resolved to clarify these complex relationships by organizing

a socio-economic census of the castes (the first to be carried out since 1931). The results of this census have been criticized as being unreliable and the central government also agreed on a series of measurement errors.

This reveals the importance of sound and legitimate data production systems to track demographic, economic, and cultural evolutions. In order to bypass current criticisms associated with reservation policies, one option for India could be to gradually transform these preferential admission policies into rules founded on universal social criteria, such as parental income or place of residence, along the lines of the admission mechanisms used for entry to schools or higher education institutions.

To a large extent, it could be argued that a country like India is simply endeavoring to confront the challenge of effective equality with the means available to a state based on the rule of law, in a situation where inequality of status originating in the former society and past discrimination is particularly extreme and threatens to degenerate into violent tensions at any time. However, as we have seen above, rich countries are not exempt from these issues, either—as may sometimes be thought. Indeed, rich and poor countries alike have a great deal to learn from the trials and errors of the Indian reservation system, one of the oldest nationwide affirmative action programs in the world.

two-year colleges. Access rates increased by only 0.65 percentage points among the most selective colleges, even though most Ivy-Plus colleges implemented tuition reductions and other policies to welcome more students from disadvantaged backgrounds. This does not mean that these policies were inefficient. Given the context of rising inequality in the United States, mobility may have worsened without them. All that is visible is that the net combination of these factors left access to elite colleges mostly unchanged.

Differences in mobility rates show that improving poor children's access to high-performing schools could substantially improve the contribution of education to upward mobility. Given that children from low-income families have similar success rates to their peers of a given college, increasing the access to good colleges can hardly be considered as misplacement. Until now, efforts to expand access has mostly focused on elite colleges. Considering changes in admissions criteria may be an important way forward. Improving access and increasing funding to high-mobility-rate colleges may also be critical. These colleges have very good outcomes, admit a large number of low-income students, and operate at relatively low cost compared to elite colleges.

Educational inequalities can also be important in countries with lower levels of income and wealth inequality

European countries experienced a smaller rise of income and wealth inequality than that observed in the United States in recent decades (see Parts II–IV). This certainly does not mean, however, that the issue of education inequality is not relevant in Europe. In particular, France is one of the most unequal OECD countries in terms of educational inequality, as highlighted by the 2015 Programme for International Student Assessment (PISA). While the PISA survey provides information on France's general performance in terms of educational inequalities, still very little is known about the local characteristics explaining the large differences in outcomes between students from low- and high-income backgrounds. Gabrielle Fack, Julien Grenet, and Asma Benhenda have made significant contributions in this respect; their findings based on new data on middle schools and high schools in the Parisian region illustrate a particularly extreme case of educational inequality, but also are encouraging as they reveal how public policies can address these issues.

As their work shows, in 2015, 115 public middle schools and 60 private schools welcomed more than 85 000 students, many of whom came from higher socio-professional groups (49%) and few from disadvantaged backgrounds (16%). Overall, Parisian middle schools appear to be extremely segregated, with the share of students from lower socio-professional groups ranging from 0.3% to 63% in middle schools of the capital. Private schools play a key role in social segregation by concentrating wealthier families: most private schools in Paris included less than 10% of students from low-income groups, and the private school with the highest level of social diversity welcomed only 25%. Therefore, it appears that private schools succeed in crowding out less-advantaged students and contribute directly to the polarization of the French educational system.

Social segregation is closely related to spatial segregation

This polarization is reinforced by territorial segregation. Paris is strongly divided into distinct areas—the north, northeast, east, and south, where median yearly income levels are below €30 000, and the center and west, where they are usually above €40 000. At the same time, access to Parisian middle schools is determined by location in the city. The French system allocates students in restricted geographical areas according to a "school map" *(carte scolaire)*, which implies that a student living at a given address can in principle access only one public middle school. Unsurprisingly, the repartition of students coming from poor and rich backgrounds therefore closely resembles that of parental income: certain middle schools in the relatively modest areas of Paris have more than 50% of students from low-income families, while most schools in the richest areas of the city have less than 10%.

Spatial segregation, however, goes far beyond these geographical areas, and also exists at a very narrow level within Parisian districts *(arrondissements)*. In the Eighteenth District, for instance, the share of students coming from poor backgrounds ranges from 9% to 58%, among high schools that are just a few hundred meters apart from one another. This effect is also reinforced by private schools, as wealthy families have the option to escape the public middle-school system.

Data transparency is a necessary condition to improve public debates on education

Tracking the evolution of educational segregation is fundamental to understanding why France displays such extreme disparities in students from low- versus high-income groups—and it is of crucial importance to evaluate existing policies. Concerning middle schools, segregation has been much higher in Paris than in Versailles or Créteil (both neighboring towns, all managed under different administrative units) since 2002, and has remained relatively stable in the three cities.

However, new evidence from the evolution of segregation in high schools shows a very different picture. In 2007–2008, Paris implemented a new system of student allocation to high schools. Contrary to neighboring towns of Versailles and Créteil, where geographical proximity remained decisive, Paris decided to allocate students to their schools on the basis of their grades, across areas larger

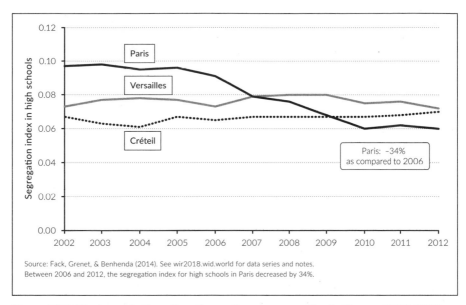

Figure 28.2 The impact of an allocation policy on segregation in France, 2002–2012

than before, to encourage social mixing. Students coming from disadvantaged backgrounds also obtained bonus points and therefore had more flexibility in the choice of their high schools.

Social segregation in public high schools in Paris decreased by one-third between 2002 and 2012 (Figure 28.2), so that Paris has achieved a rate lower than in both Versailles and Créteil since 2010. The analysis of the new high-school allocation system based on students' grades shows that it played an important part in this evolution. Between 2005 and 2012, the share of students with grants based on social criteria, studying in the top 25% Parisian high schools, nearly doubled—from 12% to 21%, while this share remained stable in the neighboring cities, as well as in Parisian middle schools which did not implement the alloca-tion procedure.

This evaluation shows that reducing social segregation is possible. Evaluating and designing new allocation systems are therefore of crucial importance to giving equal opportunities to all children regardless of their socio-economic origin. In this respect, citizens can engage in a transparent, democratic debate informed by reliable information. Indeed, this issue is not limited to rich coun-tries. Emerging countries such as India are also confronted with large educational inequalities. Some have for a long time established reservation systems based on quotas. These are complex and far from perfect, but the study of their strengths and limits can help other countries make progresses (see Box 28.1). Indeed,

Box 28.2 Minimum wage, fair wage, and corporate governance

Educational policies promoting social mobility and equality of opportunity are certainly key to reducing income inequality and widening access to good jobs. They remain, however, limited in their ability to provide decent incomes to all. Policy tools potentially useful for increasing workers' pay include the minimum wage, and more democratic corporate governance.

It is, in this respect, noteworthy to mention that wage inequality and employment precariousness remain of crucial importance, and have been increasing in a range of countries. According to the International Labour Organization, the share of labor in aggregate income has continued its long-run decline in the past five years, and still, 80% of workers are paid less than the average wage of the firm in which they work—a fact that skills-related characteristics fail dramatically to explain. Whether countries record high rates of average income growth or not, if individuals can only expect a declining share of it, equality-of-opportunity policies in education alone will fall short of meeting their demands.

Minimum wages and labor market regulation can be critical to tackling income inequality. **Figure 28.3** illustrates how regulatory policies can be tightly linked to disparities in earnings. While the real minimum wage has been steadily increasing in France since the beginning of the 1970s, in the United

States it was actually higher in 1980 than it is today. Differences in income inequality dynamics between the two countries mirror this pattern, especially at the bottom of the distribution, as Chapters 2.4 and 2.5 showed. Today, minimum wage workers in France earn nearly €10 per hour, almost 50% more than their counterparts in the United States, and this despite an average national income per adult in the United States that is 50% higher than in France. Minimum wages can therefore usefully help in compressing wage disparities, notably differences in earnings between men and women, given that women are overrepresented among the low-paid in both developed and developing countries.

To reduce wage inequality and improve the overall quality of jobs would surely require deep changes in the way the power of different stakeholders is determined and organized. Some Nordic and German-speaking countries have already undergone changes in this direction by promoting "codetermination." For instance, employees' representatives hold half the seats in executive boards of major German firms, which ensures better consideration of workers' interests in companies' strategic choices or decisions over executive or workers' pay. These examples suggest that while being crucial, educational policies cannot suffice on their own to tackle the extreme inequality levels observed in certain countries.

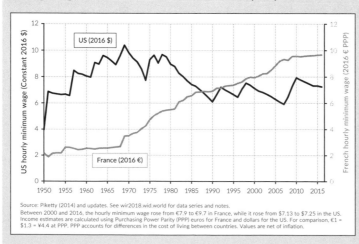

Source: Piketty (2014) and updates. See wir2018.wid.world for data series and notes.
Between 2000 and 2016, the hourly minimum wage rose from €7.9 to €9.7 in France, while it rose from $7.13 to $7.25 in the US. Income estimates are calculated using Purchasing Power Parity (PPP) euros for France and dollars for the US. For comparison, €1 = $1.3 = ¥4.4 at PPP. PPP accounts for differences in the cost of living between countries. Values are net of inflation.

Figure 28.3 Minimum wage in France and the US, 1950–2016

reservation systems cannot be sufficient to ensure equal access to education. If public schools and universities do not have enough resources to pay for good teachers, buildings, and furniture, even the most equalizing allocation system will have little impact on the democratization of quality education. Large public investments in this are essential today, in emerging and rich countries countries alike. In addition, educational policies alone are not sufficient to tackle inequality at the bottom—policies supporting fair wages are also key (Box 28.2).

A Message from the Past:
Let Governments Invest in the Future

- The share of public wealth in national wealth has declined in most countries analyzed in this report. In many rich countries, it is now close to zero (France, Germany, Japan) or even negative (US, UK).
- Such low levels of public wealth make tackling existing and future inequality extremely challenging given that governments do not currently possess the resources necessary for investments in education, healthcare, and environmental protection.
- Selling public assets and/or undergoing prolonged periods of austerity would be barely sufficient, or even insufficient, to repay public debts. Moreover, these policies would leave governments without the means to improve equality of opportunity for their citizens.
- History indicates that there are three different ways — and generally a combination of the three — by which a reduction of large public debts can be achieved: progressive taxes on private capital, debt relief, and inflation. Given the potential difficulties in controlling the incidence and extent of inflation, a combination of the former two policies appears more appropriate.
- Reducing public debt is, however, by no means an easy task. While several options exist and have been used across history, it is challenging to identify the best option(s) for each country. This is a matter for serious public debate, which must be grounded in sound economic, social, and historical data and analyses

The share of public wealth in total national wealth has declined in all the countries analyzed in this report (see Part III). In Russia and China, this decline is the logical consequence of the move away from a communist system. Both countries were, however, successful to maintain relatively high levels of public capital as compared to rich countries. The current situation in rich countries stands out as an anomaly from a historical perspective.

During the postwar economic boom, public assets in European countries were considerable (approximately 100–130% of national income, thanks to their very large public sectors, the result of postwar nationalizations), and significantly higher than public debt (which was typically less than 30% of national income). In total, public capital—net of debt—was largely positive, in the range of 70–100% of national income. As a result, net public wealth made up a significant share of total national wealth between 1950 and 1980, typically around 15–25% or more.

Over the past thirty years, public debt approached 100% of national income in most industrialized economies, with the result that net public capital became almost zero. On the eve of the global financial crisis in 2008, it was already negative in Italy. The latest available data, presented in Part IV, show that net public capital has become negative in the United States, Japan, and the United Kingdom. In France and in Germany, net public capital is just slightly higher than zero.

This situation does not mean that rich countries have become poor: it is their governments which have become poor. As discussed in Part IV, private wealth— net of debt—has risen spectacularly since the 1970s. Private wealth represented 300% of national income back then. Today it has risen to, or exceeded, 600% in most rich countries. This prosperity in private wealth is due to multiple causes: the rise in property prices (agglomeration effects in larger metropolitan areas); the aging of the population and decline in its growth (which automatically increases savings accumulated in the past in relation to current income and contributes to inflating the prices of assets); and the privatization of public assets and rise in debt (which is held in one form or another by private owners, via the banks). Also contributing to this increase were the very high returns obtained by the highest financial assets (which structurally grow faster than the size of the world economy) and the evolution in a legal system globally very favorable to private property owners (both in real estate and in intellectual property).

It is interesting to remark that countries such as China and Russia, despite large shifts in the balance of private and public capital since their transition away from Communism, have succeeded in maintaining relatively high public wealth levels. In China, public wealth is above 200% of national income, and it is close to 100% in Russia. While the ratio has sharply decreased in Russia over the past two decades, it has remained fairly constant in China. In both cases, it is still much higher than in rich countries. Governments in these countries have preserved significant means of action and control over their economies.

Large public property has obviously important consequences for the state's ability to conduct industrial, educational, or regional development policy (some-times efficiently and sometimes less so). In contrast, negative public wealth also has potentially enormous fiscal consequences: governments with negative net public wealth typically have to pay large interest payments before they can finance public spending and welfare transfers, while those with large positive net public wealth can potentially benefit from substantial capital income, and finance more public spending than what they levy in taxes. This situation is particularly problematic in a situation of high income and wealth inequality.

What, then, are the different options for highly indebted governments? One possibility would be to sell all public assets (including all public buildings, schools, universities, hospitals, police stations, and infrastructure). In the United States, Japan, and the UK—and even more true of Italy—this would not be sufficient to repay the totality of public debt. In France and Germany, it would barely be sufficient. In all these cases, moreover, states would then have lost all (or nearly all) means of control over their education and health systems. To put it differently, social states would largely disappear, leaving governments without means to ensure equality of opportunity.

Another option would be to undergo prolonged periods of austerity, via drastic reductions in governments' expenditures. In effect, this also contributes to increasing inequality as governments would slash their redistribution programs to repay debts. In terms of both justice and efficiency, austerity and privatizations stand out as very bad measures.

Fortunately there are also other options. In history, one generally observes three different ways—and generally a combination of the three—to accelerate the reduction of a large public debt: progressive taxes on private capital; debt relief; and inflation.

First, an exceptional tax on private capital can raise substantial revenue to reduce debt. For instance, a flat tax of 15% on private capital in rich countries (about 600% of national income) would yield nearly a year's worth of national income (exactly 90% of national income) and thus allow for immediate reimbursement of all nearly outstanding public debt.

This solution is equivalent to repudiation of the public debt, except for two crucial differences. It is always difficult to predict the ultimate incidence of a debt repudiation (even a partial one). Bondholders are forced to accept what is called a "haircut"—meaning that the value of government bonds held by banks and creditors is reduced by 10–20% or even more. The problem is that it is very difficult to predict which actors ultimately bear the loss and, when applied at a large scale, haircuts can trigger panic among investors and a wave of bankruptcies—and potentially, the meltdown of the financial sector, which few governments are willing to experience. Moreover, an exceptional tax on private capital, contrary to a debt repudiation, can be adjusted to individuals' wealth levels—by

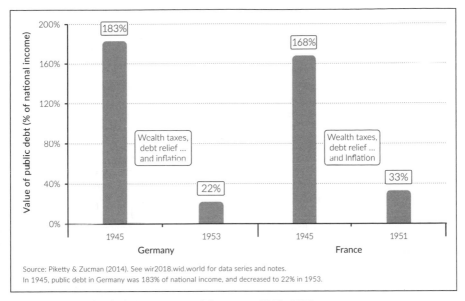

Figure 29.1 Public debt in France and Germany, 1945–1953

using an explicitly progressive rate structure. Given the very large concentration of wealth, this is highly preferable. For instance, the top 1% of the wealth distribution typically owns around 30% of total wealth (that is, the equivalent of 180% of national income if aggregate wealth represents 600% of national income). Instead of using a flat tax of 15% on private capital, one could raise the same revenue by exempting the bottom 99% of the wealth distribution and applying an average effective tax rate of 50% on the top 1% wealth group. Alternatively, one could use an intermediate system. For instance, a progressive tax on capital that levied zero tax on capital up to 1 million euros, a 10% tax between 1 and 5 million euros, and a 25% tax above 5 million euros would raise 20% of national income in Europe—and that would be an important step toward a gradual reduction of public debt.

Interestingly, a special tax on capital was applied in France in 1945 to reduce substantial public debt. This special tax had progressive rates which ranged from 0 to 25%. Most important, special progressive taxes on private wealth were put in place after the Second World War in Germany, and were gradually paid by German private wealth holders between the 1950s and the 1980s.

At that time, exceptional progressive taxes on private wealth were used together with various gradual forms of debt repudiation and debt relief—an obvious second way to accelerate the reduction of a large public debt. In particular, Germany benefited from a near complete reduction of its foreign debt at the London conference in 1953. These were debts that were accumulated by Germany

Box 29.1 The importance of standardized inequality metrics for international comparisons and collective learning

The need for sound economic data to allow civil society, researchers, businesses, and policymakers to debate and develop informed and balanced policy responses to rising economic inequality have been a dominant theme in this report.

In that regard, it is interesting to note that the United Nations agreed in 2015 to seventeen sustainable development goals (SDGs), as part of a global agenda to transform society in rich and poor countries alike. Recognizing that rising income and wealth inequality has become a universal issue, SDG Target 10 commits countries to "reduce inequalities within and among countries." To that end, the SDG framework calls on states to articulate nationally specific implementation strategies and to put in place monitoring and review processes to meet the UN goals.

This development is particularly remarkable since international organizations have until recently paid limited attention to within-country inequality issues, considering the reduction of inequalities to be a sovereign issue for each country, or positing inequalities as a necessary evil towards global improvement of well-being. Concerns about domestic income inequalities were politically confined in the shadow of absolute poverty considerations, until the UN's Sustainable Development Goals replaced its former Millennium Development Goals. In addition, global development goals have so far focused only on poor and emerging countries—leaving rich countries aside. We have seen, however, that both rich and poor countries face rising inequality.

In this context, the unanimous endorsement of SDG Target 10.1 by the UN member states marks an important shift. Target 10.1 aspires to "by 2030, progressively achieve and sustain income growth of the bottom 40 per cent of the population at a rate higher than the national average." This target was subject to harshly contested debates among country representatives. While China argued that within-country inequality reduction was a national prerogative, the United States contended that a stand-alone goal on inequality would better be achieved through economic growth. At some point, the inequality target was even removed from the SDG list. A group of countries led by Denmark, Norway, and Brazil supported its reinsertion, arguing that a specific metric should be used to precisely ensure that growth reduces inequality.[a] If anything, such debates suggest that countries are taking this new indicator seriously.

How do countries fare on SDG Target 10.1? WID.world data is particularly suited to address this question. **Table 5.5.1** compares target achievement of six countries over the following periods of time: 2015–2016, 2000–2016, and 1980–2016. The focus here is on pre-tax income.

In 2016–2015, only one country was able to meet the target: France. In all five other countries, the income growth of the bottom 40% was lower than the national average. These results help underscore the power of this objective: it is transformative in the sense that it cannot be automatically met. Countries will have to act if they want to fulfill their com-

during the reconstruction period of 1945 to 1953. International creditors—largely governments—decided in 1953 to postpone repayment until German unification (with no indexation mechanism), and the debt was eventually entirely canceled.

In the current context, new forms of debt relief might develop in Europe, and to some extent have already started to develop (albeit too slowly, and with multiple hesitations and setbacks). Specifically, public institutions like the European Central Bank (ECB) and the European Stability Mechanism (ESM) could gradually take onto their balance sheets rising fractions of individual countries' public

mitments. The 2000–2016 period provides another crucial insight. During this time span, Brazil, France, and Russia were able to meet the target—with very different average growth trajectories, however. This implies that success has been possible over relatively longer time spans for several countries, and suggests that meeting the target in the future is not only desirable but also feasible—even if results over the 1980–2016 period are less encouraging.

Two points are worth noting
First, as described earlier in this report, inequality also increased at the top. Focusing on the bottom 40% alone can miss important dynamics—in part for the middle class, which may be squeezed between increases in both the bottom 40% share and the top 1% share. In particular, the top 1% can also grow significantly faster, as was the case in most countries for the periods considered. In Brazil from 2000 to 2016, the bottom 40% grew much faster (12%) than the average (1%), but the top 1% grew at 24% in the meantime. To a lesser extent, this also occurred in France over 2015–2016, with the bottom 40% groups and the top 1% growing faster than average. This means that the income share held by individuals richer than the bottom 40% but poorer than the top 1% decreased. This "squeezed middle class" phenomenon obviously poses one of the most important policy challenges for the years to come and deserves very careful scrutiny.

Second, these estimates focus on pre-tax income. Pre-tax income inequality estimates take into account most cash redistribution in rich countries (**see Box 2.4.1**) but do not include personal income and wealth taxes. International comparisons of post-tax income inequality measures are thus also necessary to assess the full impact of fiscal policy. As discussed earlier in this report, more work lies ahead to collect, harmonize, and analyze such information. The United Nations and other international organizations have a responsibility in this regard. WID.world will remain committed to working toward such results, with all its statistical contributors willing to dedicate resources to this task, to enlighten the public democratic debate.

Bearing in mind these remarks, the SDG Target 10.1 on inequality stands out as a very useful tool for stakeholders dedicated to tackling economic inequality. To be sure, an inequality metric based on sound data cannot in itself change policy—but it is a necessary basis for doing so. The SDG framework can also lead to the establishment of a framework for collective learning on inequality reduction policies.[b] As emphasized in this report, there is large scope for learning between rich and poor countries regarding the fiscal, educational, wage, and public investments policies they employ to promote fairer development pathways.

a Chancel, L., Hough, A., Voituriez, T. (2017) "Reducing Inequalities within Countries: Assessing the Potential of the Sustainable Development Goals," 12511. Global Policy.

b Chancel et al., "Reducing Inequalities within Countries."

debts and postpone repayments until certain social, economic, and environmental objectives have been met. This would make it possible to have the advantages of debt repudiation without the financial instability coming from investor panic and bankruptcies.

Finally, the third solution used historically to accelerate the reduction of a large public debt is inflation. Historically, this mechanism played a crucial role in the reduction of most public debts. High levels of inflation were the major mechanisms used in France and Germany to bring their public debts to very low levels after the First World War, and they also played a central role in the aftermath of the Second World War, together with more sophisticated mechanisms like progressive wealth taxes and debt relief. One major problem with inflation as a policy instrument is that it is hard to control. Once it starts, policymakers may have difficulties stopping it. Inflation, moreover, is a much less precise tool than taxation in terms of incidence. In theory, it could act as a tax on those who have idle capital, and provide relief to those who are indebted by reducing the value of their debt. In practice, however, it can have less desirable effects from a fairness point of view. During high-inflation phases, large and well diversified portfolios invested on the stock market can earn a good return while smaller wealth holdings of the middle class and the poor held in savings accounts can be wiped out. A combination of exceptional wealth taxes and debt relief seems like a better option.

Reducing public debt is thus by no means an easy task. Several options exist and have been used across history. We certainly do not pretend that we have identified the best option for each country. This is a matter of serious public debate, which must be grounded in sound economic, social, and historical analysis and comparisons over time and countries. (Box 29.1) In this discussion, there is one crucial element: today, large investments are required to promote more equal access to education or to protect the environment and combat the consequences of climate change. If these challenges go unaddressed they are likely to reinforce tomorrow's levels of economic inequality. Recent history has shown that in exceptional circumstances, exceptional measures were taken by societies through their governments to reinvest in the future.

Conclusion

The *World Inequality Report 2018* draws from data available on the World Wealth and Income Database (WID.world), which combines historical statistical sources in a consistent and fully transparent way to fill a gap in the democratic debate regarding inequality. Our objective in this report has been to present inequality data that are consistent with macroeconomic statistics such as GDP and national income and that can be easily understood and used by the public, to help ground deliberations and decisions in facts. Our data series are fully transparent and reproducible; our computer codes, assumptions, and detailed research papers are available online so that any interested person can access and use them.

Drawing on novel inequality data published on WID.world, Part II showed that since 1980, income inequality has increased rapidly in North America and Asia, has grown moderately in Europe, and has stabilized at extremely high levels in the Middle East, sub-Saharan Africa, and Brazil. The poorest half of the global population has seen its income grow significantly thanks to high growth in Asia (particularly in China and India). Perhaps the most striking finding of this report, however, is that, at the global level, the top 0.1% income group has captured as much of the world's growth since 1980 as the bottom half of the adult population. Conversely, income growth has been sluggish or even nil for the population between the global bottom 50% and top 1%. This includes North American and European lower- and middle-income groups. The diversity of trends observed in the report suggest that global dynamics are shaped by a variety of national institutional and political contexts. There is no inevitability behind the rise of income inequality.

In Part III, we presented recent shifts in public versus private capital ownership. Understanding the dynamics of private and public capital ownership is critical to understanding the dynamics of global inequality, and particularly of wealth inequality. We documented a general rise in the ratio between net private wealth and national income in nearly all countries in recent decades. It is striking to see that this long-run finding has been largely unaffected by the 2008 financial crisis, or by the asset price bubbles experienced by countries including Japan and

Spain. There have also been unusually large increases in the ratios for China and Russia, following their transitions from communist- to capitalist-oriented economies. These shifts were mirrored by the dynamics of public wealth, which has declined in most countries since the 1980s. Net public wealth (public assets minus public debts) has even become negative in recent years in the United States, Japan, and the United Kingdom, and is only slightly positive in Germany and France. This arguably limits government ability to regulate the economy, redistribute income, and mitigate rising inequality.

In Part IV, we discussed how increasing income inequality, and the large transfers of public wealth to private hands which have occurred over the past forty years, have led to a rise in wealth inequality among individuals. At the global level—represented by China, Europe, and the United States—the top 1% share of wealth increased from 28% in 1980 to 33% today, while the bottom 75% share oscillated around 10%. Large rises in top wealth shares have been experienced in China and Russia following their transitions from communism toward capitalist economies, though the different inequality dynamics experienced between these two countries highlight different economic and political transition strategies. In the United States, wealth inequality has increased dramatically over the last thirty years and has mostly been driven by the rise of the top 0.1% wealth owners. Growing inequality of income and saving rates created a snowballing effect of rising wealth concentration. The increase in top wealth shares in France and the UK has been more moderate over the past forty years, in part due to the dampening effect of the rising housing wealth of the middle class and lower income inequality relative to the United States.

In Part V, we presented projections on the future of global income inequality, which is likely to be shaped both by convergence forces (rapid growth in emerging countries) and divergence forces (rising inequality within countries). Our benchmark projections showed that if within-country inequality continues to rise as it has since 1980, then global income inequality will rise steeply, even under fairly optimistic assumptions about growth in emerging countries. The global top 1% income share could increase from nearly 20% today to more than 24% by 2050, in which case the global bottom 50% share could fall from 10% to less than 9%. If all countries were to follow the high inequality growth trajectory followed by the United States since 1980, the global top 1% income share would rise even more. Conversely, if all countries were to follow the relatively low-inequality growth trajectory followed by Europe since 1980, the global top 1% income share would actually decrease by 2050. This finding reinforces one of our main messages: rising income inequality is not inevitable in the future. We also stressed that differences between high and low inequality growth trajectories within countries have enormous impacts on incomes of the bottom half of the global population.

The remainder of Part V was dedicated to a discussion of key policy issues that should be brought back to the center of the political agenda to tackle inequality. We certainly do not claim to have ready-made solutions to rising inequality within all countries. We believe, however, that much more can be done in the four key policy areas we highlight.

We first emphasized that progressive income taxation is a proven tool to combat rising income and wealth inequality at the top. It not only reduces post-tax inequality, it also shrinks pretax inequality by discouraging top earners from capturing higher shares of growth via aggressive bargaining for higher pay. It should be noted that tax progressivity was sharply reduced in rich countries from the 1970s to the mid-2000s. Since the global financial crisis of 2008, however, the downward trend has been halted and reversed in some countries. The future use of progressive taxation remains uncertain and will depend on democratic deliberation.

Second, we argued that although tax systems are crucial mechanisms for tackling inequality, they also face obstacles—among them, tax evasion. The wealth held in tax havens is currently equivalent to more than 10% of global GDP and has increased considerably since the 1970s. The rise of tax havens makes it difficult to properly measure and tax wealth and capital income in a globalized world. Reducing financial opacity is critical to improving data on wealth and its distribution, to fostering a more informed public debate about redistribution, and to fighting tax evasion, money laundering, and the financing of terrorism. One key challenge, however, involves recording the ownership of financial assets. While land and real estate registries have existed for centuries, they miss a large fraction of the wealth held by households today, as wealth increasingly takes the form of financial securities. A global financial register recording the ownership of equities, bonds, and other financial assets would deal a severe blow to financial opacity.

Third, we discussed the importance of achieving more equal access to education and good-paying jobs, if the bottom half of the population is to escape the trap of stagnating or sluggish income growth rates. Recent research shows the enormous gaps that often exist between public discourses about equal opportunity and the practical realities of unequal access to education. In the United States, for instance, out of a hundred children whose parents fall within the bottom 10% of income earners, between twenty and thirty go to college. That figure reaches ninety, however, among children whose parents fall within the top 10% of earners. On the positive side, research shows that elite colleges in the

United States are able to improve openness to students from poor backgrounds without compromising their outcomes. Whether a country is rich or emerging, it might have to set transparent and verifiable objectives—while also making changes in financing and admissions systems—to equalize access to education. Democratic access to education can achieve much, but unless there are also mechanisms to provide people at the bottom of the distribution with access to good-paying jobs, investments in education cannot do enough to tackle inequality. Better representation of workers in corporate governance bodies and boosts in minimum wages are important tools to achieve this.

Finally, we stressed the need for governments to invest more in the future, both to address current income and wealth inequality levels and to prevent further increases. This is particularly difficult given that governments have become poor and heavily indebted in rich countries over the past decades. Reducing public debt is by no means an easy task, but several options exist for accomplishing it (including taxation, debt relief, and inflation), all of which have been used across history. Finding the proper combination of solutions will require serious public debate, which must be grounded in sound economic, social, and historical analysis.

To conclude, we must repeat that current knowledge of global income and wealth inequality remains limited and unsatisfactory. Much more data collection work lies ahead of us to expand the geographical coverage of our inequality data, as well as to provide more systematic representations of pre- and post-tax income and wealth inequality. WID.world, the World Inequality Lab, and their partner institutions are committed to pursuing these efforts in the coming years.

The WID.world database is currently being expanded to increase its coverage of emerging countries in Asia (in particular, Malaysia and Indonesia), Africa (for instance, in South Africa), and Latin America (Chile and Mexico, among others).

We are also currently working toward better integration of natural capital in national wealth estimates, as the importance of environmental degradation as a dimension of inequality continues to grow.

More gender inequality data are also being integrated to WID.world and we are developing estimates of inequality at the regional (subnational) level, with the aim of further reducing the gap between individuals' perceptions of inequality and what economic statistics are able to measure. Indeed, WID.world is just one step in a long, cumulative research process.

We welcome efforts made by other institutions and researchers to take part in this collective endeavor. And we very much hope that, together with all interested actors and citizens, we will continue making progress toward financial transparency and economic democracy in the years to come.

Appendix

- In order to improve the ease of reading of the *World Inequality Report*, we have not included all technical details in the main body of the text.
- However, interested readers are warmly invited to visit the report's dedicated website (wir2018.wid.world) for methodological details on how estimations were constructed. In our efforts to be as transparent as possible, the website hosts all the methodological documents, country technical papers, raw data sources, and computer codes used for the production of the series presented in the *World Inequality Report*.
- In particular, for detailed technical notes on each of the graphs presented in the report, users should refer to the document: "World Inequality Report 2018 Technical Notes" (WID.world Technical Notes 2017/7). This document at times redirects readers toward other working papers or scientific articles where more exhaustive information can be ascertained.
- The online publication of these documents is essential in our view to increase the level of transparency and reproducibility of global inequality data. We would encourage as many people as possible to view the site, make their own estimations, and discover ways in which our data can be improved and what alternative assumptions would be made in order to do so.
- Below is a limited selection of Appendix graphs that we refer to earlier in the *World Inequality Report*. Figures A.1 to A.3 show alternative methods to represent our main results on global income inequality dynamics. Figure A.4 focuses on income inequality dynamics in India and China and provides an example of the types of additional graphs which can be obtained on wir2018.wid.world.

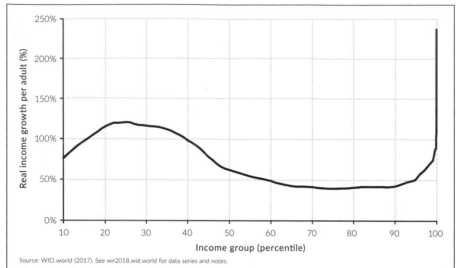

Source: WID.world (2017). See wir2018.wid.world for data series and notes.

This graph is scaled by population size, meaning that the distance between different points on the x-axis is proportional to the size of the population of the corresponding income group. The income group p0p1 (lowest percentile), for instance, occupies 1% of the size of the x-axis. On the horizontal axis, the world population is divided into a hundred groups of equal population size and sorted in ascending order from left to right, according to each group's income level. The Top 1% group is divided into ten groups, the richest of these groups is also divided into ten groups, and the very top group is again divided into ten groups of equal population size.
The vertical axis shows the total income growth of an average individual in each group between 1980 and 2016. For percentile group p99p99.1 (the poorest 10% among the richest 1% of global earners), growth was 74% between 1980 and 2016. The Top 1% of income earners captured 27% of total growth over this period. Income estimates account for differences in the cost of living between countries. Values are net of inflation.

Figure A.1 Total income growth by percentile across all world regions, 1980–2016: Scaled by population

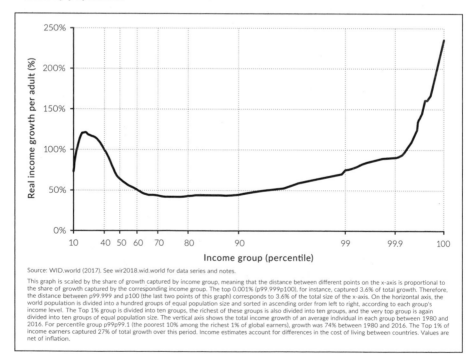

Source: WID.world (2017). See wir2018.wid.world for data series and notes.

This graph is scaled by the share of growth captured by income group, meaning that the distance between different points on the x-axis is proportional to the share of growth captured by the corresponding income group. The top 0.001% (p99.999p100), for instance, captured 3.6% of total growth. Therefore, the distance between p99.999 and p100 (the last two points of this graph) corresponds to 3.6% of the total size of the x-axis. On the horizontal axis, the world population is divided into a hundred groups of equal population size and sorted in ascending order from left to right, according to each group's income level. The Top 1% group is divided into ten groups, the richest of these groups is also divided into ten groups, and the very top group is again divided into ten groups of equal population size. The vertical axis shows the total income growth of an average individual in each group between 1980 and 2016. For percentile group p99p99.1 (the poorest 10% among the richest 1% of global earners), growth was 74% between 1980 and 2016. The Top 1% of income earners captured 27% of total growth over this period. Income estimates account for differences in the cost of living between countries. Values are net of inflation.

Figure A.2 Total income growth by percentile across all world regions, 1980–2016: Scaled by share of growth captured

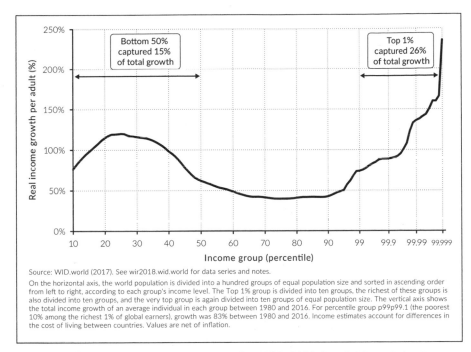

Source: WID.world (2017). See wir2018.wid.world for data series and notes.

On the horizontal axis, the world population is divided into a hundred groups of equal population size and sorted in ascending order from left to right, according to each group's income level. The Top 1% group is divided into ten groups, the richest of these groups is also divided into ten groups, and the very top group is again divided into ten groups of equal population size. The vertical axis shows the total income growth of an average individual in each group between 1980 and 2016. For percentile group p99p99.1 (the poorest 10% among the richest 1% of global earners), growth was 83% between 1980 and 2016. Income estimates account for differences in the cost of living between countries. Values are net of inflation.

Figure A.3 Total Income growth by percentile, 1980–2016: Brazil, China, India, Europe, the Middle-East, Russia, and US-Canada

In this representation of global income inequality dynamics discussed in Chapter 2, we scale the horizontal axis by population size, meaning that the distance between different points on the x-axis is proportional to the size of the population of the corresponding income group. (See Box 2.1.)

In this representation of global income inequality dynamics discussed in Chapter 2, we scale the horizontal axis by the share of growth captured by income group, meaning that the distance between different points on the x-axis is proportional to the share of growth captured by the corresponding income group. (See Box 2.1.)

In this representation of global income inequality dynamics discussed in Chapter 2, we adopt a combination of the scaling methods used in Figure A.1 and Figure A.2 so as to better visualize global inequality dynamics throughout the entire distribution. (See Box 2.1.)

This graph shows the evolution of top 1% and bottom 50% income shares in India and China. It is an example of the additional graphs which can be produced online on wid.world and which are discussed in the various methodological documents referred to in the report.

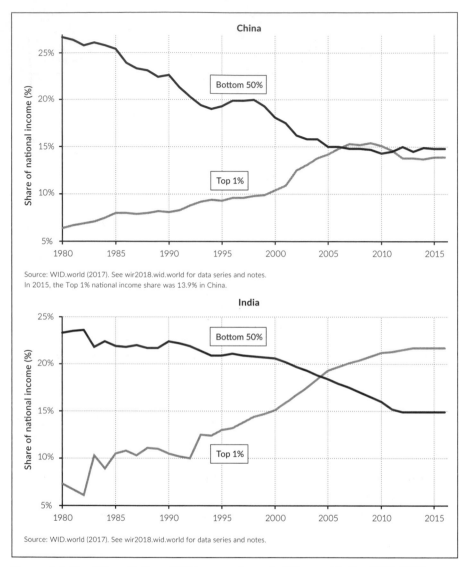

Source: WID.world (2017). See wir2018.wid.world for data series and notes.
In 2015, the Top 1% national income share was 13.9% in China.

Source: WID.world (2017). See wir2018.wid.world for data series and notes.

Figure A.4 Top 1% vs. Bottom 50% income shares in China and India, 1980–2015

Notes

PART I

1 T. Piketty, L. Yang, and G. Zucman, "Capital Accumulation, Private Property and Rising Inequality in China, 1978–2015," NBER Working Paper no. 2338, National Bureau of Economic Research, June 2017, http://www.nber.org/papers/w23368.pdf.

2 L. Chancel and T. Piketty, "Indian Income Inequality, 1922–2014: From British Raj to Billionaire Raj? WID.world Working Paper no. 2017/11, July 2017. http://wid.world/document/chancelpiketty-2017widworld/.

3 See, in particular, T. Piketty, *Les hauts revenus en France au XXème siècle* (Paris: Bernard Grasset, 2001); T. Piketty and E. Saez, "Income Inequality in the United States, 1913–1998," *Quarterly Journal of Economics* 118, no. 1 (2003): 1–39; A. B. Atkinson and T. Piketty, *Top Incomes over the 20th Century: A Contrast between Continental European and English-Speaking Countries* (Oxford: Oxford University Press, 2007); A. B. Atkinson and T. Piketty, eds., *Top Incomes: A Global Perspective* (Oxford: Oxford University Press, 2010); A. B. Atkinson, T. Piketty, and E. Saez, "Top Incomes in the Long Run of History," *Journal of Economic Literature* 49, no. 1 (2011): 3–71.

4 S. Kuznets, *Shares of Upper Income Groups in Income and Savings* (New York: National Bureau of Economic Research, 1953).

5 F. Alvaredo, A. B. Atkinson, L. Chancel, T. Piketty, E. Saez, and G. Zucman, "Distributional National Accounts (DINA) Guidelines: Concepts and Methods Used in the World Wealth and Income Database," WID.world Working Paper no. 2016/2, December 2016, http://wid.world/document/dinaguidelines-v1/.

6 J. E. Stiglitz, A. Sen, and J. P. Fitoussi, "Report by the Commission on the Measurement of Economic Performance and Social Progress," Paris, http://ec.europa.eu/eurostat/documents/118025/118123/Fitoussi+Commission+report.

7 See T. Blanchet and L. Chancel, "National Accounts Series Methodology," WID.world Working Paper no. 2016/1, September 2016, http://wid.world/document/1676/; and G. Zucman, "The Missing Wealth of Nations: Are Europe and the U.S. Net Debtors or Net Creditors?" *Quarterly Journal of Economics* 128, no. 3 (2013): 1321–1364.

8 We multiplied each income group's average fiscal income by National Income/Total Fiscal Income.

9 A. B. Atkinson and A. J. Harrison, *Distribution of Personal Wealth in Britain* (Cambridge: Cambridge University Press, 1978).

10 See Zucman, "The Missing Wealth of Nations"; G. Zucman, "Taxing across Borders: Tracking Personal Wealth and Corporate Profits," *Journal of Economic Perspectives* 28, no. 4 (2014): 121–148; and A. Alstadsæter, N. Johannesen, and G. Zucman, "Who Owns the Wealth in Tax Havens? Macro Evidence and Implications for Global Inequality," NBER Working Paper no. 23805, National Bureau of Economic Research, September 2017, http://www.nber.org/papers/w23805.pdf.

11 S. Anand, and P. Segal, "The Global Distribution of Income," *Handbook of Income Distribution* 2, part A (2015): 937–979.

12 L. Chancel and T. Piketty, "Carbon and inequality: from Kyoto to Paris," CEPR Policy Portal Vox, December 1, 2015, http://voxeu.org/article/carbon-and-inequality-kyoto-paris; L. Chancel and T.

Piketty, "Trends in the Global Inequality of Carbon Emissions (1998–2013) and Prospects for an Equitable Adaptation Fund," Paris School of Economics, November 3, 2015, http://piketty.pse.ens.fr/files/ChancelPiketty2015.pdf.

PART II

1 See, for instance, C. Lakner and B. Milanovic, "Global Income Distribution: From the Fall of the Berlin Wall to the Great Recession," *World Bank Economic Review* 30, no. 2 (2016): 203–232; as well as P. Liberati, "The World Distribution of Income and Its Inequality, 1970–2009," *Review of Income and Wealth* 61, no. 2 (2015): 248–273; and I. Ortiz and M. Cummins, "Global Inequality: Beyond the Bottom Billion: A Rapid Review of Income Distribution in 141 Countries," UNICEF Social and Economic Policy Working Paper, UNICEF, April 2011, https://www.unicef.org/socialpolicy/files/Global_Inequality.pdf. For existing global wealth reports, see the "Global Wealth Report 2016," Credit Suisse Research Institute, Credit Suisse AG, Zurich, November 2016, http://publications.credit-suisse.com/tasks/render/file/index.cfm?fileid=AD783798-ED07-E8C2-4405996B5B02A32E.

2 Lakner and Milanovic, "Global Income Distribution: From the Fall of the Berlin Wall to the Great Recession."

3 J. E. Stiglitz, A. Sen, and J. P. Fitoussi, "Report by the Commission on the Measurement of Economic Performance and Social Progress," Paris, http://ec.europa.eu/eurostat/documents/118025/118123/Fitoussi+Commission+report.

4 Measured at Market Exchange Rate. At Purchasing Power Parity, the corresponding value is $790.

5 G. Zucman, "The Missing Wealth of Nations: Are Europe and the U.S. Net Debtors or Net Creditors?" *Quarterly Journal of Economics* 128, no. 3 (2013): 1321–1364.

6 Our figures for the European Union include all countries on the European continent, apart from Russia and Ukraine.

7 T. Piketty, *Capital in the Twenty-First Century* (Cambridge MA: Belknap Press of Harvard University Press, 2014).

8 Not represented on the graph for the sake of clarity. Readers should refer to WID.world/world to view all graphs.

9 L. Czajka, "Income Inequality in Côte d'Ivoire: 1985–2014," WID.world Working Paper no. 2017/8, July 2017, http://wid.world/document/income-inequality-cote-divoire-1985–2014-wid-world-working-paper-201708/.

10 Very top incomes, however, grew more in post-tax terms than in pre-tax terms between 1946 and 1980 (194%), because the tax system was more progressive at the very top in 1946.

11 The growth in Medicare and Medicaid transfers reflects an increase in the generosity of the benefits, but also the rise in the price of health services provided by Medicare and Medicaid—possibly above what people would be willing to pay on a private market. See, for example, A. Finkelstein, N. Hendren, and E. F. P. Luttmer, "The Value of Medicaid: Interpreting Results from the Oregon Health Care Experiment," NBER Working Paper no. 21308, National Bureau of Economic Research, June 2015, http://www.nber.org/papers/w21308.pdf—and perhaps an increase in the economic surplus of health providers in the medical and pharmaceutical sector.

12 In turn, most of the growth of the post-tax income of the elderly Americans in the *bottom 50%* has been due to the rise of health benefits. Without Medicare and Medicaid (which cover nursing home costs for poor elderly Americans), average post-tax income for the bottom 50% seniors would have stagnated at $21 000 since the early 2000s, and would have increased only modestly since the early 1980s when it was around $15 500.

13 Piketty, *Capital in the Twenty-First Century.*

14 See E. Saez, "Taxing the Rich More: Preliminary Evidence from the 2013 Tax Increase," *Tax Policy and the Economy* 31, no. 1 (2017): 71–120.

15 The US Congressional Budget Office also finds an increase by about 4–5 points in the federal tax rate of the top 1% from 2011 to 2013. US Congressional Budget Office, "The Distribution of Household Income and Federal Taxes, 2013," US CBO Report, June 2016, Congress of the United States, Washington DC, https://www.cbo.gov/sites/default/files/114th-congress-2015–2016/reports/51361-householdincomefedtaxes.pdf.

16 In keeping with the national accounts conventions, the nonrefundable portion of tax credits and tax deductions are treated as negative taxes, while the refundable portion of tax credits are seen as transfers. Subsequently, nobody can have negative income taxes.

17 This general periodization is relatively well known and has been studied elsewhere. See, in particular, T. Piketty, "Income Inequality in France, 1901–1998," *Journal of Political Economy* 111, no. 5 (2003): 1004–1042; and Piketty, *Capital in the Twenty-First Century.*

18 See Piketty, "Income Inequality in France, 1901–1998," and Piketty, *Capital in the Twenty-First Century.*

19 See Piketty, *Capital in the Twenty-First Century,* ch. 9 in particular.

20 T. Piketty, E. Saez, and S. Stantcheva, "Optimal Taxation of Top Labor Incomes: A Tale of Three Elasticities," *American Economic Journal: Economic Policy* 6, no. 1 (2014): 230–271.

21 A. Bozio, R. Dauvergne, B. Fabre, J. Goupille, and O. Meslin. "Fiscalité et redistribution en France, 1997–2012," Rapport IPP, 2012. See, in particular, p. 28 for tax rates on primary incomes (before pensions and unemployment insurance) and p. 30 for tax rates on secondary incomes (including pensions and unemployment insurance). In the former case, tax rates at the top are lower than for any other income group. In the latter case, tax rates are lower for the bottom 50% than for the richest, but the middle class has a higher total tax rate than the top 0.1%.

22 T. Ferguson and H.-J. Voth, "Betting on Hitler: The Value of Political Connections in Nazi Germany," *Quarterly Journal of Economics* 123, no. 1 (2008): 101–137.

23 T. Piketty, L. Yang, and G. Zucman, "Capital Accumulation, Private Property and Rising Inequality in China, 1978–2015," NBER Working Paper no. 23368, National Bureau of Economic Research, June 2017, http://www.nber.org/papers/w23368.pdf.

24 Comparing the paper's inequality series to the official survey-based estimates highlights that although the trends are similar in both calculation methods, the data used in Piketty, Yang, and Zucman, "Capital Accumulation," show both a much larger level and rise in inequality over the period. Most of the difference between these estimates comes from the use of high-income tax data.

25 In particular, the lack of national data on high-income taxpayers since 2011 forces the authors to apply the 2006–2010 average correction factors to years 2011–2015 (in effect, making it impossible to detect a possible rebound of inequality since 2011).

26 See R. Kanbur, Y. Wang, and X. Zhang, "The Great Chinese Inequality Turnaround," ECINEQ WP 2017-433, Society for the Study of Economic Inequality (ECINEQ), April 2017, http://www.ecineq .org/milano/WP/ECINEQ2017-433.pdf; and R. Garnaut, L. Song, C. Fang, and L. Johnston, "Domestic Transformation in the Global Context," in *China's Domestic Transformation in a Global Context,* ed. L. Song, R. Garnaut, C. Fang, and L. Johnston, 1–16 (Acton, Australia: Australian National University Press, 2015).

27 As a result, the middle 40% income share is now similar in China to urban China: the top 10% income share is higher in China than in urban China, while the bottom 50% income share is lower, leaving the share of the middle 40% at about 43–44% in both cases in recent years.

28 The Western European average referred to is the simple arithmetic average of per-adult income in Germany, France, and Britain. Note that using the Western European average income as a reference point is clearly an oversimplification and does not do justice to the complexity of country-specific trajectories. For example, Germany, France, and Britain have quasi-identical average incomes in 2016, but Britain lagged behind Germany and France in 1980 (only slightly above Russian level), and was well ahead in 1870–1914.

29 The best indicator of the mediocre Soviet economic and social performance in the postwar decades is perhaps the stagnation of life expectancy. See, for example, E. Todd, *The Final Fall: An Essay on the Decomposition of the Soviet Sphere,* trans. J. Waggoner (New York: Karz, 1979).

30 See, for example, B. Milanovic, *Income, Inequality, and Poverty during the Transition from Planned to Market Economy* (Washington, DC: World Bank, 1998).

31 See J. Nellis, "Time to Rethink Privatization in Transition Economies?" *Finance and Development* 36, no. 2 (1999): 16–19.

32 In 1995, the government of Boris Yeltsin adopted a "loans-for-shares" scheme, whereby some of the largest state industrial assets were leased through auctions for money lent by commercial banks to the government. The auctions were thought by many to have been rigged and lacked competition, being largely controlled by favored insiders with political connections or used for the benefit of the

commercial banks themselves. Since neither the loans nor the leased enterprises were returned in time, this effectively became a form of selling, or privatizing, state assets at very low prices. See I. W. Lieberman and D. J. Kopf, eds., *Privatization in Transition Economies: The Ongoing Story* (Amsterdam: Elsevier JAI, 2008).

33 See J. Flemming and J. Micklewright, "Income Distribution, Economic Systems and Transition," in *Handbook of Income Distribution,* ed. A. B. Atkinson and F. Bourguignon, 843–918 (Amsterdam: Elsevier, 2000).

34 See also B. Milanovic and L. Ersado, "Reform and Inequality during the Transition: An Analysis using Panel Household Survey Data, 1990–2005," UNU-WIDER Working Paper no. 2010/62, United Nations University World Institute for Development Economics Research, Helsinki, May 2010, https://www.wider.unu.edu/sites/default/files/wp2010-62.pdf.

35 All figures are presented in 2016 Euros using Purchasing Power Parity (PPP) conversions. In 2016, €1 = ₽74.5 (rubles) at the Market Exchange Rate or ₽28.3 using PPP conversions.

36 European Bank for Reconstruction and Development (EBRD), *Transition for All: Equal Opportunities in an Unequal World,* Transition Report 2016–2017, October 2016, available for download at http://www.ebrd.com/transition-report.

37 The corrected inequality series combines survey data with income tax data and wealth data, while the EBRD growth incidence curve relies solely on self-reported survey data. For a more detailed discussion, see F. Novokmet, T. Piketty, and G. Zucman, "From Soviets to Oligarchs: Inequality and Property in Russia 1905–2016," WID.world Working Paper no. 2017/09, July 2017, http://wid.world/wp-content/uploads/2017/08/NPZ2017WIDworld.pdf.

38 See Part I.

39 S. L. Richman, "War Communism to NEP: The Road to Serfdom," *Journal of Libertarian Studies* 5, no. 1 (1981): 89–97.

40 This figure from 1905 relies not on actual income tax data, since the tax was never implemented in tsarist Russia, but on income tax projections that were made by the imperial tax administration at the time the regime was considering implementing such a tax. Similar estimates were made during the same period in France, but their implementation revealed that the tax administration was significantly underestimating top income levels. See T. Piketty, *Les hauts revenus en France au XXème siècle* (Paris: Bernard Grasset, 2001).

41 See A. Banerjee and T. Piketty, "Top Indian Incomes, 1922–2000," *World Bank Economic Review* 19, no. 1 (2005): 1–20.

42 Economic policies also sought to rationalize the public sector; its branches now had to pursue the objectives of profitability and efficiency. Trade was opened, an exchange rate floating regime was implemented, and banking as well as capital market were also liberalized.

43 I. Anand and A. Thampi, "Recent Trends in Wealth Inequality in India," *Economic and Political Weekly* 51, no. 50 (December 2016).

44 United Nations Development Programme (UNDP), "Towards the Developmental State in the Arab Region," Arab Development Challenges Report 2011, UNDP Regional Centre for Arab States, Cairo, 2011, available for download at http://www.undp.org/content/undp/en/home/librarypage/hdr/arab-development-challenges-report-2011.html.

45 E. Ianchovina, L. Mottaghi, and S. Devarajan,"Inequality, Uprisings, and Conflict in the Arab World," World Bank Middle East and North Africa (MENA) Region Economic Monitor, World Bank, Washington, DC, October 2015, http://documents.worldbank.org/curated/en/303441467992017147/pdf/99989-REVISED-Box393220B-OUO-9-MEM-Fall-2015-FINAL-Oct-13-2015.pdf.

46 J. Kinninmont, "Future Trends in the Gulf," Chatham House Report, The Royal Institute for International Affairs, London, February 2015, https://www.chathamhouse.org/sites/files/chathamhouse/field/field_document/20150218FutureTrendsGCCKinninmont.pdf.

47 Human Rights Watch, "South Asia: Protect Migrant Workers to Gulf Countries," Human Rights Watch news, December 18, 2013.

48 Ibid.; and A. Kapiszewski, "Arab versus Asian Migrant Workers in the GCC Countries," United Nations Expert Group Meeting on International Migration and Development in the Arab Region, United Nations Secretariat, Beirut, May 15–17, 2006, http://citeseerx.ist.psu.edu/viewdoc/download?doi=10.1.1.403.7975&rep=rep1&type=pdf

49 Kinninmont, "Future Trends in the Gulf."

50 R. Barros, R., M. De Carvalho, S. Franco, and R. Mendonça, "Markets, the State and the Dynamics of Inequality in Brazil," in *Declining Inequality in Latin America: A Decade of Progress?* ed. L. F. López-Calva and N. Lustig (New York: UNDP, and Washington, DC: Brookings Institution Press, 2010).

51 See B. Keeley, *Income Inequality: The Gap between Rich and Poor*, OECD Insights (Paris: OECD Publishing, 2015).

52 M. Medeiros, P. H. G. F. Souza, and F. A. de Castro, "The Stability of Income Inequality in Brazil, 2006–2012: An Estimate Using Income Tax Data and Household Surveys," *Ciência y Saúde Coletiva* 20, no. 4 (2015): 971–986.

53 J. Lewis, *Industrialisation and Trade Union Organization in South Africa, 1924–55: The Rise and Fall of the South African Trades and Labour Council* (Cambridge: Cambridge University Press, 1984).

54 C. H. Feinstein, *An Economic History of South Africa: Conquest, Discrimination, and Development* (Cambridge: Cambridge University Press, 2005).

55 M. Leibbrandt, I. Woolard, A. Finn, and J. Argen, "Trends in South African Income Distribution and Poverty since the Fall of Apartheid," OECD Social, Employment and Migration Working Papers, no. 101, OECD Publishing, Paris, May 28, 2010

56 World Bank, Southern Africa Department, "South African Agriculture: Structure, Performance and Options for the Future," Informal Discussion Papers on Aspects of the Economy of South Africa, no. 6, World Bank, Washington, DC, February 1994, http://documents.worldbank.org/curated/en/309521468777031091/pdf/multi-page.pdf.

57 M. Aliber and R. Mokoena, "The Land Question in Contemporary South Africa," in *State of the Nation: South Africa 2003–2004*, ed. J. Daniel, R. Southall, and A. Habib, 330–346 (Cape Town, HSRC Press, 2003).

PART III

1 T. Piketty and G. Zucman, "Capital Is Back: Wealth-Income Ratios in Rich Countries 1700–2010," *Quarterly Journal of Economics* 129, no. 3 (2014): 1255–1310.

2 T. Piketty, *Capital in the Twenty-First Century* (Cambridge, MA: Belknap Press of Harvard University Press, 2014).

3 A. Atkinson, *Inequality: What Can Be Done?* (Cambridge, MA: Harvard University Press, 2015).

4 T. van den Bremer, F. van der Ploeg, and S. Wills, "The Elephant in the Ground: Managing Oil and Sovereign Wealth," *European Economic Review* 82 (2016): 113–131.

5 See Piketty and Zucman, "Capital Is Back," for a complete analysis and decomposition of volume and price effects. See also Piketty, *Capital in the Twenty-First Century*, part 2. Here we summarize only the main conclusions and emphasize the more recent evolutions.

6 See Piketty and Zucman, "Capital Is Back."

7 See Piketty and Zucman, "Capital Is Back," in particular Figures VII and VIII.

8 See Piketty and Zucman, "Capital Is Back."

9 J. Tobin and W. C. Brainard, "Asset Markets and the Cost of Capital," in *Economic Progress, Private Values and Public Policy*, ed. B. Balassa and R. Nelson, 235–262 (Amsterdam: Elsevier North Holland, 1977).

10 In Germany, book-value national wealth was substantially above market-value national wealth (about 5 years of national income instead of 4 years) between 1970 and 2010. The opposite occurred in the UK over this period

11 Annette Alstadsæter, Niels Johannesen, and Gabriel Zucman find that the equivalent of 10% of world GDP is held in tax havens globally, but this average masks a great deal of heterogeneity—from a few percent of GDP in Scandinavia, to about 15% in Continental Europe, to about 60% in Gulf countries and some Latin American economies. See A. Alstadsæter, N. Johannesen, and G. Zucman, "Who Owns the Wealth in Tax Havens? Macro Evidence and Implications for Global Inequality," NBER Working Paper no. 23805, National Bureau of Economic Research, September 2017, http://www.nber.org/papers/w23805.pdf..

12 See Piketty and Zucman, "Capital Is Back," Table VII.

13 See Piketty and Zucman, "Capital Is Back," Table VIII.

14 See T. Piketty, "On the Long-Run Evolution of Inheritance: France 1820–2050," *Quarterly Journal of*

Economics 126, no. 3 (2011): 1071–1131; and T. Piketty and E. Saez, "A Theory of Optimal Inheritance Taxation," *Econometrica* 81, no. 5 (2013):1851–1886.

15 See G. Zucman, "Taxing across Borders: Tracking Personal Wealth and Corporate Profits," *Journal of Economic Perspectives* 28, no. 4 (2014): 121–148; and Alstadsæter, Johannesen, and Zucman, "Who Owns the Wealth in Tax Havens?"

16 See T. Piketty, L. Yang, and G. Zucman, "Capital Accumulation, Private Property and Rising Inequality in China, 1978–2015," NBER Working Paper no. 23368, National Bureau of Economic Research, June 2017, http://www.nber.org/papers/w23368.pdf, for a detailed volume-price decompositions of China's wealth accumulation.

17 Piketty, Yang, and Zucman, in "Capital Accumulation," estimate Tobin's Q of these Chinese companies that are not listed on the stock exchange to be 1. Given that these not-listed companies represent approximately 80% of all Chinese companies, this has a tendency to move the average Tobin's Q toward 1.

18 See D. Nougayrède, "Outsourcing Law in Post-Soviet Russia," *Journal of Eurasian Law* 6, no. 3 (2013): 383–448; D. Nougayrède, "Yukos, Investment Round-Tripping and the Evolving Public/Private Paradigms," *American Review of International Arbitration* 26, no. 3 (2015): 337–364; and D. Nougayrède, "The Use of Offshore Companies in Emerging Market Economies: A Case Study," *Columbia Journal of European Law* 23, no. 2 (2017): 401–440.

19 One key argument behind the shock therapy doctrine was that rapid privatization would prevent any possible return to public property and communism. See, for example, M. Bojko, A. Shleifer, and R. W. Vishny, *Privatizing Russia* (Cambridge, MA: MIT Press, 1995).

20 Note, however, a fall in aggregate national wealth right after the fall of communism, not presented here to simplify the interpretation over the 1990 to 2015 period.

21 See, for example, the work by legal experts, such as Nougayrède, "Outsourcing Law in Post-Soviet Russia"; Nougayrède, "Yukos, Investment Round-Tripping"; and Nougayrède, "The Use of Offshore Companies."

22 See G. Zucman, "The Missing Wealth of Nations: Are Europe and the US Net Debtors or Net Creditors?" *Quarterly Journal of Economics* 128, no. 3 (2013): 1321–1364; G. Zucman, "Taxing across Borders: Tracking Personal Wealth and Corporate Profits," *Journal of Economic Perspectives* 28, no. 4 (2014): 121–148; and G. Zucman, *The Hidden Wealth of Nations: The Scourge of Tax Havens*, trans. T. L. Fagan (Chicago: University of Chicago Press, 2015).

PART IV

1 In comparison, the top 10% of the global income distribution typically receives between 50% and 60% of total income (depending on whether one uses Purchasing Power Parity or Market Exchange Rates). See Part II.

2 See T. Piketty, *Capital in the Twenty-First Century* (Cambridge, MA: Belknap Press of Harvard University Press, 2014), ch. 12, table 12.2.

3 Piketty, *Capital in the Twenty-First Century.*

4 Y. Guo, J. Gan, and C. Xu, "A Nationwide Survey of Privatized Firms in China," *Seoul Journal of Economics* 21, no. 2 (2008): 311–331.

5 T. Piketty, "On the Long-Run Evolution of Inheritance: France 1820–2050," *Quarterly Journal of Economics* 126, no. 3 (2011): 1071–1131.

6 For more detail, see B. Garbinti, J. Goupille-Lebret, and T. Piketty, "Accounting for Wealth Inequality Dynamics: Methods, Estimates, and Simulations for France (1800–2014)," WID.world Working Paper no. 2016/5, December 2016, http://wid.world/document/b-garbinti-j-goupille-and-t-piketty-wealth-concentration-in-france-1800-2014-methods-estimates-and-simulations-2016/.

7 See Piketty, *Capital in the Twenty-First Century*; and T. Piketty and E. Saez, "Inequality in the Long Run," *Science* 344, no. 6186 (2014): 838–-843.

8 Piketty, *Capital in the Twenty-First Century.*

9 See A. Mian and A. Sufi, *House of Debt: How They (and You) Caused the Great Recession and How We Can Prevent It from Happening Again* (Chicago: University of Chicago Press, 2014).

10 M. Bertrand and A. Morse, "Trickle-Down Consumption," NBER Working Paper no. 18883, Na-

tional Bureau of Economic Research, March 2013, http://www.nber.org/papers/w18883.pdf.

11 Piketty, *Capital in the Twenty-First Century.*

12 For more detail, see Garbinti, Goupille-Lebret, and Piketty, "Accounting for Wealth Inequality Dynamics."

13 Garbinti, Goupille-Lebret, and Piketty, "Accounting for Wealth Inequality Dynamics," Table 2.

14 Piketty, "On the Long-Run Evolution of Inheritance."

15 T. Piketty, *Les hauts revenus en France au XXème siècle* (Paris: Bernard Grasset, 2001); and Piketty, *Capital in the Twenty-First Century.*

16 C. D. Carrol, J. Overland, and D. N. Weil, "Saving and Growth with Habit Formation," *American Economic Review* 90, no. 3 (2000): 341–355.

17 O. Rullan and A. A. Artigues, "Estrategias para Combatir el Encarecimiento de la Vivienda en España. ¿Construir Más o Intervenir en el Parque Existente?" *Revista Electrónica de Geografía y Ciencias Sociales* 11, no. 245 (28), Universidad de Barcelona, August 1, 2007, http://www.ub.edu/geocrit/sn/sn-24528.htm.

18 C. Martínez-Toledano, "Housing Bubbles, Offshore Assets and Wealth Inequality in Spain (1984–2013)," WID.world Working Paper no. 2017/19.

19 The capitalization method entails applying a capitalization factor to the capital income distribution in order to arrive at the wealth distribution.

20 E. Saez and G. Zucman, "Wealth Inequality in the United States since 1913: Evidence from Capitalized Income Tax Data," *Quarterly Journal of Economics* 131, no. 2 (2016): 519–578.

21 Garbinti, Goupille-Lebret, and Piketty, "Accounting for Wealth Inequality Dynamics."

22 S. Scarpetta, A. Sonnet, and T. Manfredi, "Rising Youth Unemployment during the Crisis: How to Prevent Negative Long-Term Consequences on a Generation?" OECD Social, Employment and Migration Working Papers, no. 106, OECD Publishing, Paris, April 14, 2010, http://www.oecd-ilibrary.org/docserver/download/5kmh79zb2mmv-en.pdf?expires=1510199048&id=id&accname=guest&checksum=729E512C84DEDEA22B73D109937D5AD0.

23 See C. Martínez-Toledano, "Housing Bubbles, Offshore Assets and Wealth Inequality in Spain (1984–2013)," WID.world Working Paper no. 2017/19, Figure A21.

24 See G. Zucman, "The Missing Wealth of Nations: Are Europe and the U.S. Net Debtors or Net Creditors?" *Quarterly Journal of Economics* 128, no. 3 (2013): 1321–1364; and G. Zucman, *The Hidden Wealth of Nations: The Scourge of Tax Havens,* trans. T. L. Fagan (Chicago: University of Chicago Press, 2015).

25 Martínez-Toledano, "Housing Bubbles, Offshore Assets and Wealth Inequality in Spain (1984–2013)," Figure A26.

26 The study focuses on the shares of total personal wealth, that is, the value of the assets owned by individuals, net of their debts. Assets include financial assets, such as cash, bank accounts or bonds or company shares; and real assets, such as houses and farmland; consumer durables; and household business assets. The total wealth considered in the paper differs in important respects from total national wealth, as measured in the national accounts balance sheets. Contrary to personal wealth, total national wealth includes the wealth of nonprofit institutions serving households. Estimation methods also differ between the two concepts.

27 See A. B. Atkinson, J. P. F. Gordon, and A. Harrison, "Trends in the Shares of Top Wealth-Holders in Britain, 1923–1981," *Oxford Bulletin of Economics and Statistics* 51, no. 3 (1989): 315–332.

28 See Office for National Statistics, "A Century of Home Ownership and Renting in England and Wales," Release, 2011 Census Analysis, ONS, London, April 19, 2013, http://webarchive.nationalarchives.gov.uk/20160107120359/http://www.ons.gov.uk/ons/rel/census/2011-census-analysis/a-century-of-home-ownership-and-renting-in-england-and-wales/short-story-on-housing.html.

PART V

1 OECD (2017), GDP long-term forecast. doi: 10.1787/d927bc18-en. Note that the rates we use are voluntarily more optimistic than the rates assumed by the OECD to compute their total global income in 2050 for Africa, Latin America, and Asia. Assuming higher growth rates tends to reduce

global inequality. Ours should be seen as a conservative approach to the rise of global inequality in the coming decades.

2 UNDESA (2017) UN Population Prospects. https://esa.un.org/unpd/wpp/. Note that we use the medium variant of the UN prospects.

3 These projections may be done at the level of regions rather than of countries, when there are not sufficiently detailed data over the 1980–2016 period.

4 Goldin, C. D., and Katz, L. F. (2009). *The Race between Education and Technology*. Harvard University Press.

5 "The Economics of Superstars," *American Economic Review*, 71 (5): 845–858, 1981.

6 Gabaix, X., and Landier, A. (2008). "Why Has CEO Pay Increased So Much?" *Quarterly Journal of Economics*, 123(1), 49–100. https://doi.org/10.1162/qjec.2008.123.1.49.

7 Bloomberg (2017). Global CEO Pay Index. Bloomberg database.

8 Piketty, T., Saez, E., and Stantcheva, S. (2014). Optimal Taxation of Top Labor Incomes: A Tale of Three Elasticities. *American Economic Journal: Economic Policy*.

9 Piketty, T., Saez, E., and Stantcheva, S. (2014). Ibid.

10 See also Piketty, T. (2014). *Capital in the Twenty-First Century*. Harvard University Press.

11 A. Alstadsæter N. Johannesen, and G. Zucman (2017). "Who Owns the Wealth in Tax Havens? Macro Evidence and Implications for Global Inequality," NBER Working Paper No. 23805.

12 Zucman, G. (2015). *The Hidden Wealth of Nations: The Scourge of Tax Havens*. University of Chicago Press and updates.

13 Zucman, Gabriel (2014). "Taxing across Borders: Tracking Personal Wealth and Corporate Profits." *The Journal of Economic Perspectives*, 28(4), 121–148.

14 Chetty, R., Hendren, N., Kline, P., Saez, E., and Turner, N. (2014). "Is the United States Still a Land of Opportunity? Recent Trends in Intergenerational Mobility." *The American Economic Review*, 104(5), 141–147. And Chetty, R., Hendren, N., Kline, P., and Saez, E. (2014). "Where is the Land of Opportunity? The Geography of Intergenerational Mobility in the United States." *The Quarterly Journal of Economics*, 129(4), 1553–1623.

15 The raw correlation between upward mobility and the Gini coefficient in commuting zones is −0.58. The top 1% income share, however, is only weakly correlated with mobility (−0.19), so that upward mobility correlates more with inequality when measured by the Gini coefficient computed on the bottom 99% of the income distribution.

16 The size of the middle class is measured by the fraction of parents in a community zone who have family incomes between the twenty-fifth and seventy-fifth percentiles in the national income distribution.

17 The authors use a social capital index developed by Rupasingha and Goetz (2008) which factors in voter turnout rates, fraction of people returning census forms, and various measures of participation in community organizations.

18 Chetty, R., Friedman, J. N., Saez, E., Turner, N., and Yagan, D. (2017). *Mobility Report Cards: The Role of Colleges in Intergenerational Mobility* (No. w23618). National Bureau of Economic Research.

19 Indeed, perfect mobility would mean that there was no link between a family's income group and its child's income group. Thus, children coming from the poorest 20% families would be evenly distributed across the five quintiles, so that 4% of them (20% divided by 5) would join the top 20%.

20 Fack, G., Grenet, J., and Benhenda, A. (2014). L'impact des procédures de sectorisation et d'affectation sur la mixité sociale et scolaire dans les lycées d'Île-de-France. *Rapport de l'Institut des Politiques Publiques*, (3).

21 See, for example, A. Ritschl, "Does Germany Owe Greece a Debt? The European Debt Crisis in Historical Perspective," LSE, 2012.

22 See Chancel, L. and Piketty, T. (2015). "Carbon and Inequality: From Kyoto to Paris. Trends in the Global Inequality of Carbon Emissions (1998–2013)" and "Prospects for an Equitable Adaptation Fund." Paris School of Economics.